The First Book of

Quattro Pro®

Revised Edition

Patrick Burns

SAMS

A Division of Macmillan Computer Publishing

11711 North College, Carmel, Indiana 46032 USA

For Ken Baca, entrepreneur, mentor, and friend.

SECOND EDITION
SECOND PRINTING—1991

International Standard Book Number: 0-672-27367-5
Library of Congress Catalog Card Number: 91-61288

Product Manager: *Marie Butler-Knight*
Acquisitions Editor: *Stephen R. Poland*
Manuscript Editors: *Ronda Carter Henry*
Cover Art: *Held & Diedrich Design*
Production:*Brad Chinn, Martin Coleman, Joelynn Gifford, Sandy Grieshop, Bob LaRoche, Sarah Leatherman, Howard Peirce, Cindy Phipps, Tad Ringo, Suzanne Tully, Johnna VanHoose, Lisa Wilson*
Indexer: *Jill D. Bomaster*
Technical Editor: *Stephen R. Poland*

Printed in the United States of America

Contents

Introduction, ix

1 *A First Look at Quattro Pro, 1*

In This Chapter, 1
What Is a Spreadsheet?, 2
Quattro Means "Four", 3
Quattro Pro Learning Strategies, 7
What You've Learned, 8

2 *Getting Started, 9*

In This Chapter, 9
Learning About the Quattro Pro Screen, 11
Using Your Keyboard, 13
Moving Around a Spreadsheet, 16
Using a Mouse, 17
Using Quattro Pro Menus and Commands, 19
Cancelling a Menu or Command, 22
Saving Your Work, 22
Ending a Quattro Pro Work Session, 24
Getting Answers to Questions, 27
What You've Learned, 29

3 Building a Spreadsheet Application, 31

In This Chapter, 31
Learning Spreadsheet Terminology, 32
Two Types of Spreadsheet Data, 32
Entering Labels, 33
Entering Values, 37
File Management Basics, 48
Learning Cell Management Basics, 51
Viewing Your Spreadsheet Data, 58
What You've Learned, 61

4 Working with Blocks of Cell Data, 63

In This Chapter, 63
What Is a Cell Block?, 64
Cell Block Basics, 65
POINT Mode Basics, 70
Applying Cell Block and POINT Mode Basics, 72
Creating Names for Cell Blocks, 76
What You've Learned, 82

5 Printing Spreadsheets, 83

In This Chapter, 83
An Overview of Printing, 83
Preparing for Basic Printing, 84
Selecting the Print Destination , 90
Setting Layout Options, 96
Changing A Printout's Display Format, 106
What You've Learned, 108

6 Understanding Formulas and @function Commands, 109

In This Chapter, 109
What Makes a Quattro Pro Formula?, 110
Understanding How Quattro Pro Calculates, 114

What Is an @function Command?, 117
Copying @function Commands, 119
Troubleshooting Spreadsheet Formulas, 123
An Overview of Quattro Pro's @function Commands, 127
Solving Formulas in Reverse, 136
What You've Learned, 138

7 Improving Your Spreadsheet Style, 141

In This Chapter, 141
Changing Global Format Settings, 142
The /Style Menu Commands, 143
Formatting the Display of Cell Data, 148
Protecting Spreadsheet Cells, 153
Working with Columns, 154
Drawing Lines and Shading Cells, 160
Experimenting with Different Fonts, 166
Style Enhancement Extras, 171
What You've Learned, 173

8 Designing Graphs, 175

In This Chapter, 175
What Is a Graph?, 176
What You Need To Display a Graph, 178
The Eleven Types of Graphs, 179
Creating a Fast Graph, 187
The Basic "From-the-Ground-Up" Graph, 190
Enhancing the Appearance of the Basic Graph, 192
Annotating a Graph, 200
Managing Your Quattro Pro Graphs, 204
Printing a Quattro Pro Graph, 209
What You've Learned, 211

9 Writing Macros To Automate Spreadsheet Tasks, 213

In This Chapter, 213
What Is a Macro?, 213
How To Create a Basic Macro, 217
Recording a Macro Program, 224
Managing Your Macros, 229
Using the Macro Debugger, 232
Using Quattro Pro's Macro Command Language, 234
What You've Learned, 236

10 Managing and Linking Spreadsheet Files, 237

In This Chapter, 237
What Is a File?, 237
The File Menu Commands, 241
Using the File Manager, 248
Linking Spreadsheets with Formulas, 253
Spreadsheet File Management Extras, 258
What You've Learned, 260

11 Managing Databases, 263

In This Chapter, 263
What Is a Database?, 263
Designing a Database, 266
Adding Data and Controlling Data Entry, 268
Sorting a Database, 273
Searching Through a Database, 279
Deleting Records From a Database, 285
Other Query Operations, 288
What You've Learned, 288

A Installing Quattro Pro, 289

Getting Started With Installation, 289
What You Need to Run Quattro Pro, 290
Installing the Program, 290
Upgrading to Version 3.0 from a Previous Version of Quattro Pro, 303
Adding Screen Fonts after Quattro Pro is Installed, 304

B Setting Program Options, 307

In This Appendix, 307
What Are Your Options?, 307
Learning About Hardware Options, 309
Learning About Color Options, 312
Learning About International Options, 314
Zooming Your WYSIWYG Display, 316
Learning About Display Mode Options, 317
Learning About Startup Options, 318
Learning About Mouse Palette Options, 319
Learning About Other Options, 320
Updating Option Settings, 321
Reviewing the Status of Quattro Pro's Current Default Settings, 322
Learning About Global Options, 322
What You've Learned, 323

Index, 325

Introduction

Borland International first released the Quattro electronic spreadsheet program in 1987. Quattro instantly established itself as a more affordable (but equally powerful) alternative to using Lotus 1-2-3 or Microsoft Excel. Since that time Quattro has undergone three major transformations.

In September 1989, Borland released Quattro Professional (Pro) Version 1.0. Quattro Pro Version 1.0 integrates four elements (spreadsheet, graph, macro, and database) into a graphical environment ideal for producing "published-quality" reports. Today, Quattro Pro is the most powerful spreadsheet program available for IBM PCs and XTs and their compatibles.

In October 1990, Borland released the first major program upgrade of Version 1.0, appropriately called Quattro Pro Version 2.0. Improvements in this version include 3-D graphs, a command that lets you solve formulas "backwards," and direct linking to Paradox, Borland's best-selling database program.

And now in April 1991, Borland has released Quattro Pro 3.0, the first version to incorporate advanced WYSIWYG (What-you-see-is-what-you-get) graphics technology. This new graphical interface allows you to produce presentation-quality spreadsheets and graphs on-screen. These spreadsheets show the true printed look of a report, including fonts, drawn lines, and shaded cells. A significant benefit of WYSIWYG viewing is that when you fine-tune spreadsheet presentation features, you are assured an accurate reflection of a printout. This eliminates the need for "trial-by-error" spreadsheet publishing. Other improvements in Version 3.0 include improveed printer management, adjustable row heights, and the ability to add sound and special effects to graph slide shows.

Spreadsheet users from all walks of life continue to hail Quattro Pro as their spreadsheet program of choice for four important reasons:

- Quattro Pro offers the familiar "keystroke feel" of 1-2-3.
- Quattro Pro offers spreadsheet publishing, graph design, and printout previewing capabilities found only in Excel.
- These features and many more are accessible in one program as long as you own an IBM XT with 640K of random-access memory (RAM).
- Quattro Pro offers advanced WYSIWYG graphics so that you can produce quality spreadsheets on-screen.

Who This Book Is For

The First Book of Quattro Pro furnishes the beginning spreadsheet user with all of the basics necessary to get up and running with Quattro Pro. You may have some experience with personal computers, other spreadsheet programs, or software in general. Even so, this book provides comprehensive and explicit steps throughout—steps that show you the easiest, most effective ways of using Quattro Pro.

The first part of this book teaches you how to install the program, how to begin and end a work session, how to move around the screen display, how to execute menu commands, and how to build a basic spreadsheet.

Next, this book demonstrates how to enhance the look of a basic spreadsheet, how to work with blocks of data, how to use Quattro Pro's @function commands, and how to print a spreadsheet.

Finally, this book illustrates how to design and "publish" a graph, how to write basic macros to automate spreadsheet tasks, how to build a database, and how to set Quattro Pro options.

Features of the Book

The First Book of Quattro Pro contains several features designed to help you quickly learn Quattro Pro. The three categories of features are icons, boxed tips and cautions, and typeface conventions.

Icons

This book uses two special icons. These icons highlight important topics, instructions, and procedures.

The Quick Steps icon points out text that describes the exact sequence of steps needed to perform many common spreadsheet tasks.

The mouse icon precedes instructions for using a mouse to execute commands.

Tips and Cautions

Boxed tips offer clues about the inner workings of Quattro Pro, while boxed cautions describe operations that may affect a spreadsheet or permanently erase data. These visual aids will be useful as quick references when you return to this book in the future.

Tip: Helpful tips and shortcuts are included in tip boxes throughout this book.

Caution: Boxed warnings remind you to proceed carefully!

Typeface Conventions

In this book, new terms appear in *italic* when first introduced. Screen messages and dialog box prompts appear in `computer typeface`. Data that you type appears in `color computer typeface.`

The following Quattro Pro words always appear in uppercase:

- Menu and command keystrokes, such as /FSR.
- Range names, such as (REVENUES).
- @Function commands, such as (@SUM).
- Mode and status indicators, like (POINT) and (READY).
- Cell references, such as (A1..D10).

The following conventions apply to macro programs:

- Macro names are formed with a backslash (\) followed by a lowercase, single-character name, such as \m. This naming convention also means that you can execute this macro program by pressing Alt-a.
- Quattro Pro menu keystrokes that appear within a macro program, such as /fsr, are displayed in lowercase.
- Range names that appear within a macro program, such as /ecREVENUES, are displayed in uppercase.
- The tilde (~) character symbolizes the action of pressing the Enter key in a macro.

About Assumptions and Screen Shots

This book assumes that you have installed the Quattro Pro menu tree. Therefore, each menu command and action step called for in this book refers only to commands found on the Quattro Pro menu tree.

Instructions about executing Quattro Pro menu commands appear in their keystroke form, such as

Step 1. Press /FSR.

In some cases you will also see the mouse icon and instructions about how to perform a task using the mouse.

This book's screen shots reflect Quattro Pro's appearance when displayed in WYSIWYG mode on an ATI VGA display system. All screen shots were produced using Collage Plus by Inner Media Corporation.

Acknowledgments

I wish to thank Tony Stauffer for sharing his unique perspectives, and for pitching in his when time was at a premium.

Trademarks

All terms mentioned in this book that are known to be trademarks or service marks are listed on the next page. In addition, terms suspected of being trademarks or service marks have been appropriately capitalized. SAMS cannot attest to the accuracy of this information. Use of a term in this book should not be regarded as affecting the validity of any trademark or service mark.

1-2-3 is a registered trademark of Lotus Development Corporation.

Bitstream is a registered trademark of Bitstream, Inc.

DESQview is a trademark of QuarterDeck Office Systems.

Excel and Word are products of the Microsoft Corporation. Microsoft is a registered trademark of the Microsoft Corporation.

Hercules monochrome card is a registered trademark of Hercules Computer Technology.

HotShot Graphics is a registered trademark of Symsoft Corporation.

IBM, IBM PC, and IBM PC XT are registered trademarks of International Business Machines Corporation.

LaserJet is a trademark of Hewlett-Packard Co.

Logitech Mouse is a product of Logitech, Inc.

MS-DOS is a registered trademark of Microsoft Corporation.

Panasonic is a registered trademark of Technics.

Paradox, Quattro, and Turbo C are registered trademarks of Borland International, Inc.

Rolodex is a registered trademark of Rolodex Corporation.

WordPerfect is a registered trademark of WordPerfect Corporation.

XTreePro is a trademark of Executive Systems, Inc.

Collage Plus is a trademark of Inner Media, Inc.

All other product and service names are trademarks and service marks of their respective owners.

Chapter 1

A First Look at Quattro Pro

In This Chapter

1

- *What is a spreadsheet?*
- *A look at a spreadsheet application*
- *Displaying a graph*
- *Using a spreadsheet as a database*
- *Automating tasks with macro programs*
- *Strategies for learning Quattro Pro*

If you've ever balanced a checkbook, checked inventory, or created a financial statement, you know the problems that arise when you try to perform the tasks manually. You have to key in the figures and perform the calculations at the same time, checking and cross-checking to make sure you don't make a mistake. Make a mistake, and you have to do it all again, calculating and recalculating until the figures balance.

With Quattro Pro's electronic spreadsheet, such tasks are no longer so tiresome. You create a customized spreadsheet that tells the program what you want to do with the numbers, then you simply enter the numbers. Quattro Pro does the rest, calculating the figures and presenting the results. If you key in the wrong number, simply change that number and Quattro Pro recalculates the result in a matter of seconds.

What Is a Spreadsheet?

A spreadsheet is a grid consisting of vertical *columns* and horizontal *rows*. The columns and rows intersect to form boxes, called *cells*, each capable of holding a piece of information or data, such as a customer's name or a sales figure. Each cell has an address, designated by a column letter and a row number. For example, the first cell (in the upper left corner of Figure 1.1) is A1.

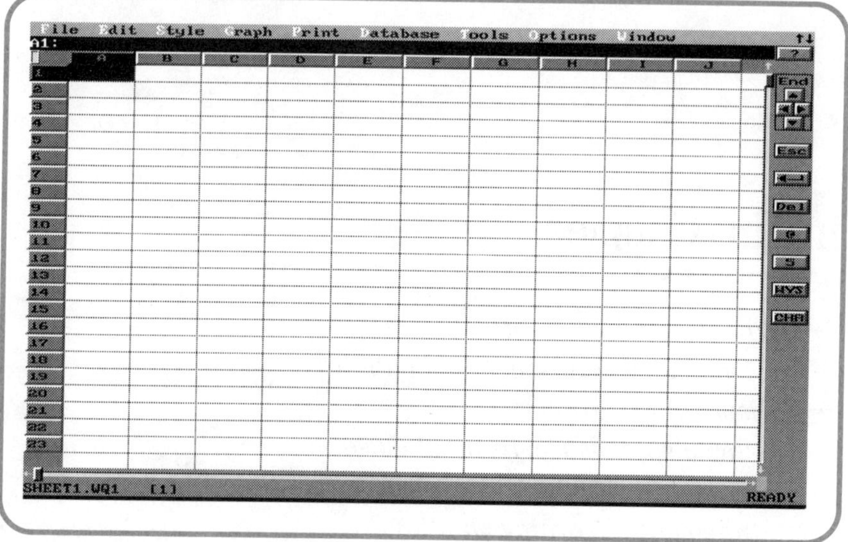

***Figure 1.1** An example of a new, blank Quattro Pro spreadsheet.*

In addition to being capable of holding raw data, cells also can contain formulas that use cell addresses as variables. For example, say you want to determine the total amount you owe for your personal bills: rent (A1), electricity (A2), food (A3), water (A4), gas (A5), and car payment (A6). You can type the following formula into cell A7: A1+A2+A3+A4+A5+A6. Then, type the amount you owe for each bill in its designated cell. Quattro Pro calculates the result and inserts it directly into cell A7. If your rent goes down, simply retrieve the spreadsheet and change the value in cell A1. Quattro Pro recalculates the result.

When you set up a spreadsheet in this way, you create a *spreadsheet application*; you are applying the basic structure of the spreadsheet to a particular task—in this case, bill management. You can save these applications and reuse them or modify them to perform other tasks.

But Quattro Pro is more than just an expensive calculator with memory. With Quattro Pro you can turn a spreadsheet into a financial statement, design attractive graphs, build and manage lists of data, and write miniprograms that automate repetitive tasks. In a nutshell, Quattro Pro combines the essence of the manual-entry accounting system with the number-crunching power of today's personal computers.

Quattro Means "Four"

The word Quattro means "four" in Italian, so it's no coincidence that there are four distinct parts to Quattro Pro: the spreadsheet builder, the graph designer, the database manager, and the macro programmer. Let's take a look at examples of each part, and see how all four relate to one another.

Building a Spreadsheet Application

You can build spreadsheet applications to meet a wide variety of needs. In business you can create financial statement spreadsheets, budget spreadsheets, and ratio analysis spreadsheets. In science, you can use spreadsheets to record the results of an experiment, and then perform statistical analyses using those results. You can even build spreadsheets that balance your checkbook, store names and phone numbers from your address book, and accurately evaluate two investment opportunities.

Spreadsheet applications should be easy to use. Remember, a colleague or friend may need to use applications that you've created. To build spreadsheet applications that are both useful and easy-to-use, keep their design as "true to life" as possible. For example, if you want to create a checkbook management application, design the spreadsheet so that it resembles your checkbook. Figure 1.2 shows a sample application called the Checkbook Manager.

The highlighted rectangle shown in cell F8 is called the *cell selector*. You use the cell selector to move around a spreadsheet, to enter data into cells, and to highlight blocks of cells to operate on. The arrow to the right of the cell selector is the *mouse pointer*.

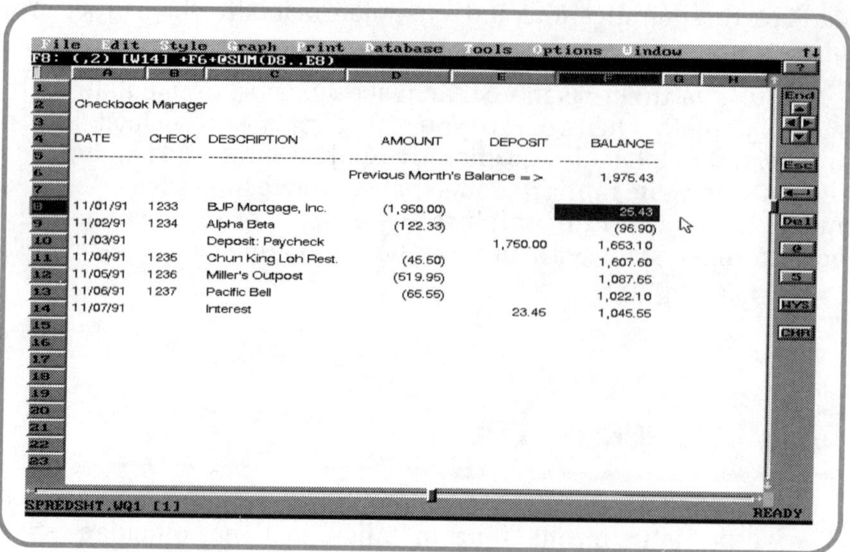

Figure 1.2 A sample Quattro Pro spreadsheet.

This example shows four types of data that you can enter into a spreadsheet. These are labels (see row 4), dates (see column A), numbers (see column B), and formulas (see column F). The formulas in column F add deposits and subtract checks from the ongoing checkbook balance. As you can see, this application looks very much like a standard checkbook.

Designing a Graph

With Quattro Pro, it's a snap to design graphs using data from your spreadsheet applications. There are many ways to use Quattro Pro graphs. You can create a basic graph and review it on-screen, or design a more polished, complex graph and print it out on a laser printer. If you wish, you can even create a special graph file that can be converted into a 35mm slide for use in a formal presentation.

Quattro Pro graphs are "smart." Each time you change spreadsheet data that is used by the graph, Quattro Pro automatically redraws the graph, showing the new data. The line graph shown in Figure 1.3 was created using data from the BALANCE column shown in Figure 1.2.

Other spreadsheet programs require you to create a spreadsheet application before you create a graph. Quattro Pro allows you to create graphs that do not rely upon spreadsheet data. These text graphs are useful for creating flowcharts, organizational charts, and Quattro Pro slide shows.

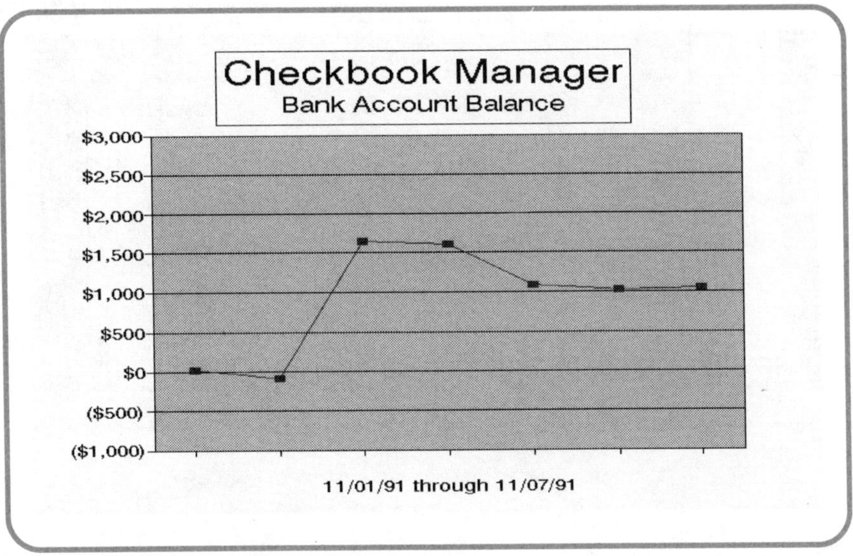

Figure 1.3 A sample Quattro Pro graph.

Managing a Database

A *database* is an electronic filing cabinet. When you need to arrange spreadsheet data in an organized, logical fashion, you use a database. Quattro Pro has excellent database management capabilities. To use Quattro Pro as a database manager, you enter your data into a spreadsheet as follows: each row stores a single record and each column stores a single field. Once you create a database, you can sort records, extract portions of the database, produce a report of unique records, and much more.

The database records shown in Figure 1.4 originated in the Checkbook Manager application. Notice that the structure of this database differs slightly from the spreadsheet application shown in Figure 1.2. This database does not use all of the data from the spreadsheet application, only the data that is important for the task at hand.

You can produce several types of reports with this database. For example, you can sort the records by CHECK# to see if duplicate check numbers exist. Or, to see which payees receive the largest checks, sort the database by AMOUNT. The database shown in Figure 1.4 is sorted by CHECK#.

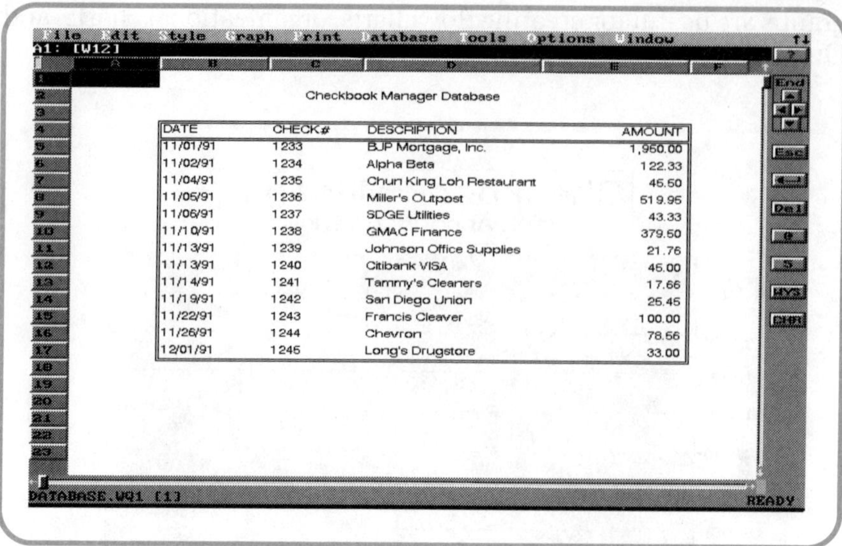

DATE	CHECK#	DESCRIPTION	AMOUNT
11/01/91	1233	BJP Mortgage, Inc.	1,950.00
11/02/91	1234	Alpha Beta	122.33
11/04/91	1235	Chun King Loh Restaurant	45.50
11/05/91	1236	Miller's Outpost	519.95
11/06/91	1237	SDGE Utilities	43.33
11/10/91	1238	GMAC Finance	379.50
11/13/91	1239	Johnson Office Supplies	21.76
11/13/91	1240	Citibank VISA	45.00
11/14/91	1241	Tammy's Cleaners	17.66
11/19/91	1242	San Diego Union	25.45
11/22/91	1243	Francis Cleaver	100.00
11/26/91	1244	Chevron	78.56
12/01/91	1245	Long's Drugstore	33.00

Figure 1.4 A sample Quattro Pro database.

Writing a Macro Program

As your spreadsheet application library grows, you'll find yourself using certain Quattro Pro menu commands over and over. For example, each time you create a new spreadsheet, you probably format it, enter data into it, and then save and print it. A Quattro Pro macro program (or macro, for short) can perform all of these operations for you.

To create a macro, you "write" instructions into cells on a Quattro Pro spreadsheet. Once you create a macro program, you assign an Alt-letter name to it, like Alt-D. To run the macro, just press Alt-D and sit back and watch as Quattro Pro duplicates each of the menu commands that you tell it to execute in the cell instructions.

Figure 1.5 shows a sample macro program. This macro is used to enter column labels onto row 4 of the Checkbook Database (see Figure 1.4).

The \d appearing in cell B8 is the macro name. To execute this macro, you press Alt-D. The descriptions in column D explain the task that each cell instruction performs. Don't worry if the data in this macro seems completely foreign to you. When you have a little more background in writing macros, creating this macro will seem as easy as opening a new spreadsheet.

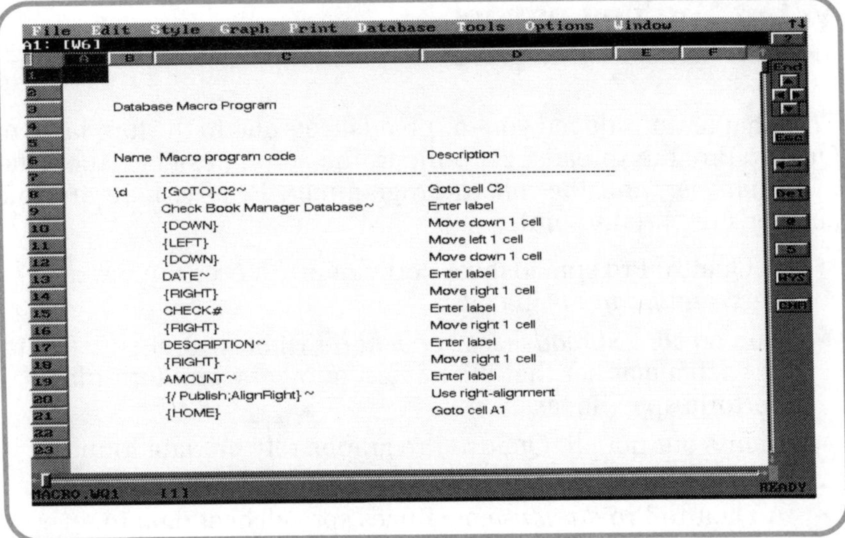

Figure 1.5 A sample Quattro Pro macro program.

Quattro Pro Learning Strategies

If you are a beginning spreadsheet user, you should concentrate on Chapters 1 through 6. These chapters cover the 50% of Quattro Pro's features that you'll use 90% of the time.

Of course the further you read, the more you learn about Quattro Pro. If you are familiar with other spreadsheets, then you may find it more interesting to start with Chapters 7, 8, and 9. These chapters cover topics such as spreadsheet enhancement, designing graphs, and creating macros to automate spreadsheet tasks.

Chapters 10 and 11 discuss spreadsheet linking and databases. Appendix A coaches you through the process of installing Quattro Pro and Appendix B describes how to set program options.

What You've Learned

This chapter introduced you to spreadsheets and to the four faces of Quattro Pro: the spreadsheet builder, the graph designer, the database manager, and the macro programmer. Briefly, here are this chapter's important points:

- A Quattro Pro spreadsheet permanently stores *names, numbers,* and *formulas* in cells.
- You create a *spreadsheet application* when you organize data in such a manner that the names, numbers, and formulas perform specific tasks.
- Many, but not all, Quattro Pro graphs rely on data found in your spreadsheet applications.
- A Quattro Pro *database* organizes spreadsheet data in a very specific way. You can reorder a database to create several types of reports, or when you wish to perform statistical analyses on a set of data.
- A Quattro Pro macro program automates many Quattro Pro operations that you otherwise must perform by hand.

Chapter 2

Getting Started

In This Chapter

- *Starting and ending a work session*
- *Saving a spreadsheet file*
- *Using the keyboard and the mouse to move around a spreadsheet*
- *Using pull-down menus*
- *Executing commands*
- *Getting on-line help*

Starting a Quattro Pro Work Session

The Installation Utility copied a file named Q.EXE into the \QPRO directory during installation. To start Quattro Pro, you must change to the drive and directory that contains this file and type `q` at the DOS prompt. You can change the way Q.EXE loads Quattro Pro by typing a *switch* after the start-up command. For example, to load Quattro Pro in black-and-white mode on a color monitor, you would type `q /ib` (for Black and White) or `q /im` (for Monochrome). See Appendix B for complete coverage of Quattro Pro's start-up parameters.

Starting a Quattro Pro Work Session

1. Turn the computer on or quit whatever program you're working in.	The familiar DOS command prompt appears. This prompt looks like `C>` or `C:\WP51>`.
2. Type the letter of the drive that contains the Quattro Pro program files, and press Enter.	The DOS command prompt changes to show the selected drive. For example, if you entered d, the prompt looks like `D>` or `D:\WS>`.
3. Type `cd\qpro` and press Enter to change to the \QPRO directory.	The DOS command prompt changes to display the \QPRO directory. For example, `C:\QPRO>` or `D:\QPRO>` appears on-screen.
4. Type `q` followed by any start-up parameters you wish to use, and press Enter.	DOS loads Quattro Pro and displays a blank spreadsheet (SHEET1.WQ1) as shown in Figure 2.1. □

If you have a mouse connected to your computer, Quattro Pro displays a mouse pointer on-screen. If the mouse pointer is a rectangle, you are in text display mode. If you see an arrow (as in Figure 2.2), you are in graphics display mode. See Appendix B for complete coverage of Quattro Pro's display modes.

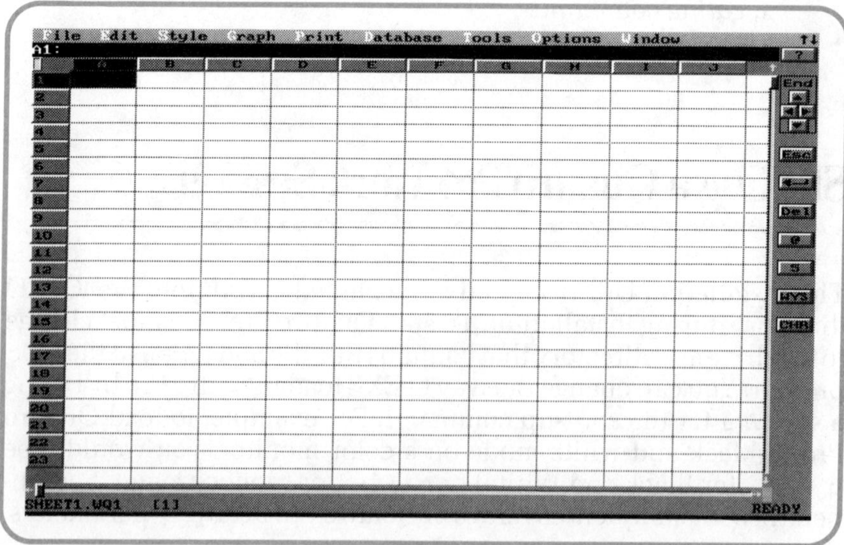

Figure 2.1 Quattro Pro loads a new, blank worksheet named SHEET1.WQ1 each time you start a work session.

Learning About the Quattro Pro Screen

As shown in Figure 2.2, the Quattro Pro screen has five major sections: the menu bar, the mouse palette, the input line, the spreadsheet area, and the status line.

The Pull-Down Menu Bar

The *pull-down menu bar* is located at the top of the screen. You'll immediately recognize this area because it contains the names of the nine Quattro Pro menus. When you select a menu name, you pull down a menu that contains a list of additional commands. You can then select a command to accomplish a task, such as saving a file, editing the contents of a cell, displaying a graph, and printing a spreadsheet.

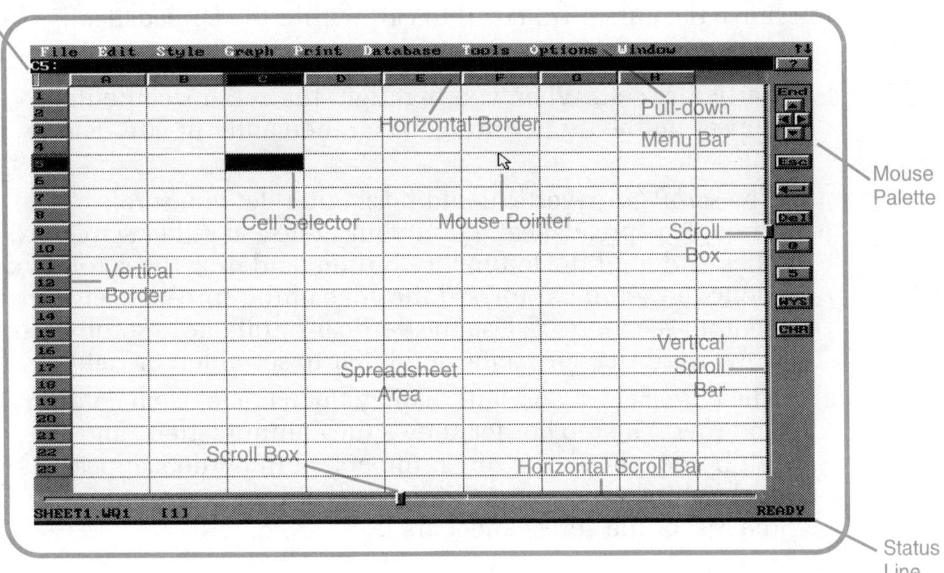

Figure 2.2 The Quattro Pro screen.

The Input Line

Just below the pull-down menu bar is the *input line*. Whenever you highlight a cell in the spreadsheet, the contents of that cell appear on the input line. You can then type information that you want to enter in the cell or edit the information that's already in the cell. As you type, the information appears on the input line. When you press Enter, the data you typed is inserted in the cell. The input line tells you a cell's address and displays the cell's contents. When appropriate, it also displays the cell's numeric format, its protection status, its column width, and its font.

The Spreadsheet Area

The *spreadsheet area* is the largest part of the Quattro Pro screen. It shows an entire section of the spreadsheet, although some of the spreadsheet may be off the screen. The spreadsheet area contains several additional elements that let you view the rest of the spreadsheet and move the cursor from cell to cell within the spreadsheet:

The *cell selector* is a rectangle that you use to highlight a particular cell. When you highlight the cell, its contents appear on the input line. You can then enter or edit data in the cell.

The *scroll bars* (vertical and horizontal) let you scroll through a spreadsheet. Point your mouse at either *scroll box*, click and hold the left mouse button, and drag the scroll box along the scroll bar toward the edge of the spreadsheet you want to see more of. Use the vertical scroll bar to scroll up or down, and the horizontal scroll bar to scroll left or right.

The *borders* (top and left) display the name of each column and row. The top border shows the column letters, and the left border shows the row numbers. Both borders appear highlighted or in reverse video so that they stand out from the rest of the spreadsheet area.

The Status Line

The *status line* is below the horizontal scroll bar. It displays information about the current work session, such as the current spreadsheet's filename and whether you are pulling down a menu (MENU mode) or editing data (EDIT mode). The right-hand portion of the status line displays the status of keyboard keys. For example, the word CAP indicates that the Caps Lock key is on.

The Mouse Palette

The *mouse palette* is the long rectangular box on the right side of the screen. The mouse palette buttons let you access many of the keyboard functions. For example, you can use the arrow keys to move the cursor, click on the question mark to display a help window, click on the Enter key to enter information, click on the CHR button to switch to text display mode, and more. See the section titled "Using the Mouse Palette" for a description of each button.

Using Your Keyboard

Before you begin to build your own spreadsheet applications, you should familiarize yourself with certain keys on your keyboard. Take a look at the three keyboards displayed in Figure 2.3. Note that each keyboard has three sections in common: an alphanumeric keypad, a numeric keypad, and a function keypad.

Using the Alphanumeric Keypad

The *alphanumeric keypad* is located roughly in the center of each keyboard. With the exception of a few keys, the keys on the alphanumeric keypad are just like those found on a typewriter.

The following three keys have special significance when used in Quattro Pro:

Key	**Function**
Alt	Press Alt plus a single letter to start a macro or to quickly execute a particular menu operation.
Ctrl	Press Ctrl plus a single letter to quickly pull down menus and execute commands.
/	Press / once to enter MENU mode. This activates the pull-down menu bar.

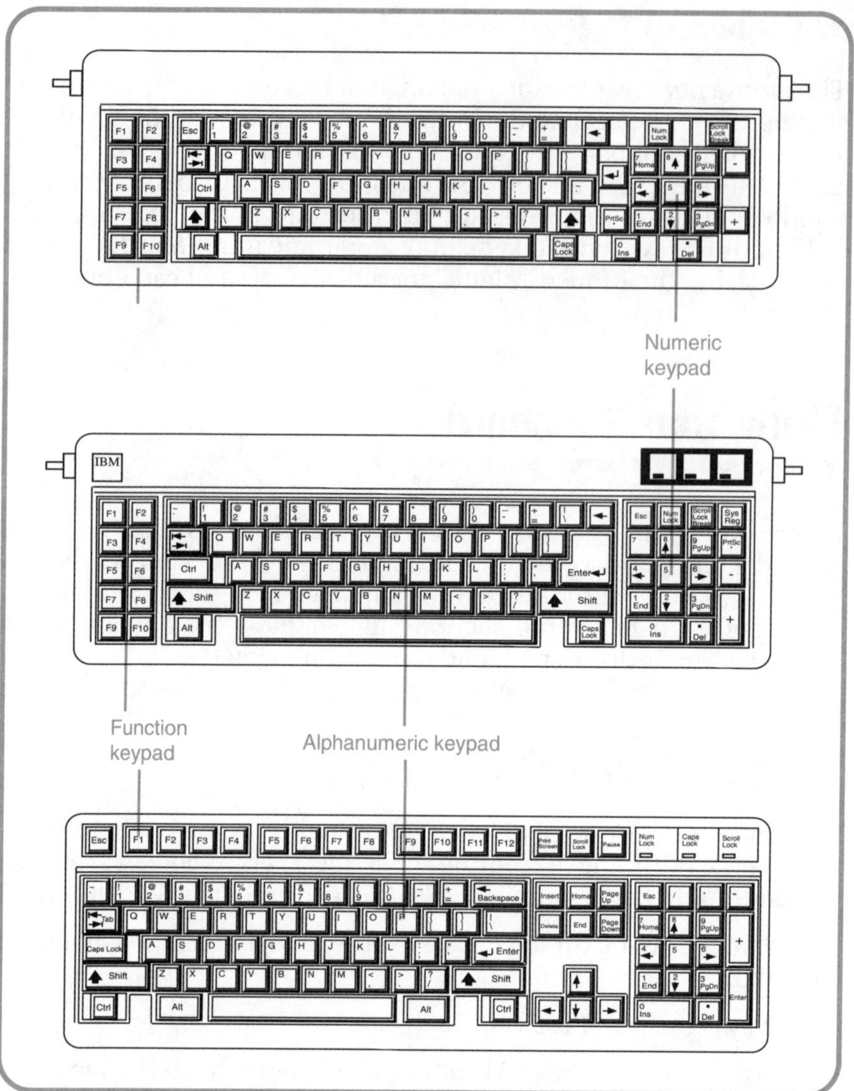

Figure 2.3 The IBM PC Keyboard
The IBM AT Keyboard
The IBM AT Extended Keyboard

Using the Numeric Keypad

The *numeric keypad* has two functions. When the Num Lock key is disabled, you can use the arrow keys to move the cell selector around a spreadsheet. When it is enabled, you can use the numeric keys to enter numbers into a cell. If you have an extended keyboard (a keyboard that has a separate cursor keypad), enable the Num Lock key so that you can use the cursor keypad to move the cell selector and the numeric keypad to enter data.

Using the Function Keys

Certain Quattro Pro spreadsheet operations are performed using the 10 *function keys* located at the top or left side of your keyboard. (Although your keyboard may have 12 function keys, Quattro Pro makes use of only 10.) For example, to move the cell selector to another location on the spreadsheet, press F5, the GoTo key. Other spreadsheet operations are performed by pressing Ctrl, Shift, or Alt before pressing a function key. For example, to undo the last spreadsheet operation, (when this feature is enabled) press Alt-F5, the Undo key.

Familiarize yourself with the function key assignments shown in Table 2.1. They make it easy for you to organize and present data stored on a spreadsheet at the touch of a key. Don't worry if they make little sense to you at this point. You'll soon learn how important they are to every Quattro Pro work session.

Table 2.1 Quattro Pro function key assignments.

Press	To
F1	Display a context-sensitive help window.
F2	Enter EDIT mode so that you can edit the contents of a cell.
Alt-F3	Display a list of Quattro Pro's @function commands.
F4	Toggle a cell address' reference format.
F5	Move the cell selector to a different cell address.
Alt-F5	Reverse the effects of a Quattro Pro operation.
F9	Recalculate the formulas on a spreadsheet.
F10	Display a graph of selected spreadsheet data.

Moving Around a Spreadsheet

Now it's time to learn how to navigate around a spreadsheet. This is important because the Quattro Pro spreadsheet is much larger than the area shown on-screen. Depending on the type of display system you're using, you probably see only 10 columns (A through J) and 23 rows (1 through 23) on-screen at once. However, a Quattro Pro spreadsheet has a total of 256 columns and 8,192 rows. What you see on-screen is only a small fraction of the entire available area!

Moving from Cell to Cell

Use the cursor movement keys (the arrow keys) to move around the spreadsheet one cell at a time. Say your cell selector is in cell D5. Press → once. Now you're in cell E5. Press ↓ twice to move to cell E7. Press ← once to move to cell D7. To move back to cell D5 press the ↑ key twice.

Leaping Around a Spreadsheet

As your spreadsheet applications grow in size and complexity, you'll need to work with larger areas of the spreadsheet. For example, if you're putting together a quarterly stockholder report, you may have to deal with hundreds of columns and thousands of rows. Moving the cursor cell by cell is hardly the way to go!

There are several ways to take big steps around a spreadsheet. When you do not know the exact address of the cell you wish to move to, consider using the Ctrl and End keys in combination with the cursor movement keys, as described in Table 2.2.

Table 2.2 Keys used to move the cell selector around a spreadsheet.

Press	To
Ctrl-←	Move the cell selector one screen to the left.
Ctrl-→	Move the cell selector one screen to the right.
End-←	Move the cell selector left, until Quattro Pro finds the first nonblank cell.

Press	To
End-→	Move the cell selector right, until Quattro Pro finds the first nonblank cell.
End-↑	Move the cell selector up, until Quattro Pro finds the first nonblank cell.
End-↓	Move the cell selector down, until Quattro Pro finds the first nonblank cell.

Tip: There's a better way to relocate the cell selector when you know exactly which cell you want to activate. Press F5, the GoTo key. Quattro Pro asks you to type a cell address. Type the letter and number of the cell you want to go to and press Enter. The cell selector immediately moves to the specified cell.

Using a Mouse

Quattro Pro works with both a keyboard and a mouse, but to take full advantage of Quattro Pro's capabilities, you really should use a mouse. With a single click of your mouse, you can activate and select a menu; activate and select a menu command; and mimic the action of the Esc key, the Enter key, and the Del key. You can use the mouse to invoke Quattro Pro help windows, select a single cell or a block of cells, scroll the active spreadsheet vertically or horizontally, resize the active spreadsheet, and much more.

If you don't own a mouse, then consider buying one—prices range from $75 to $125. Quattro Pro supports the Microsoft mouse, the Logitech mouse, and their compatibles. When you connect a mouse to your PC, the *mouse pointer* (an arrow) appears the next time you load the program into your PC.

Basic Mouse Movement

There are several brands of mice available in the market today. The Microsoft Bus and Serial Mouse and the Logitech Mouse are among the most popular. Some mice have two keys, while others have three or more. In order to accommodate as many as possible, Quattro Pro uses only the left and right mouse buttons.

The following is a description of the six terms used throughout this book to describe the basic mouse movement techniques. Familiarize yourself with the techniques and terminology before proceeding:

Click	Press and release a mouse button once.
Double-click	Press and release a mouse button two times in quick succession.
Hold Down	Press and hold down a mouse button.
Drag	Hold down a mouse button and move the mouse in the direction you want the pointer to move.
Point	Place the mouse pointer (the arrow or rectangle) at a specific location onscreen.
Release	Release a mouse button that you've been holding down.

Using The Mouse Palette

As shown in Figure 2.4, the mouse palette contains 12 buttons, each having a special purpose:

Click on the *help button* to display a help window that pertains to the operation at hand. You can also press F1 to display a help window.

Click on one of the four *direction arrows* to take big steps around your spreadsheet. When you click the down arrow, for example, Quattro Pro moves the cell selector down the current column until it locates a cell that contains data.

Click on the *Esc button* to cancel menu and command choices. This button mimics pressing Esc on your keyboard.

Click on the *Enter button* to accept menu and command choices and to enter the data you typed on the input line into a cell. This button mimics pressing Enter on your keyboard.

Click on the *Del button* to remove data from the active cell. This button mimics pressing the Del key on your keyboard.

Click on the *@ button* to display a list of Quattro Pro's @functions. This button is equivalent to pressing Alt-F3 on your keyboard.

The buttons labeled 5, WYS, and CHR are *macro buttons*. You assign specific tasks to these buttons. By default, button 5 executes the {BEEP} macro which causes your computer to beep once. The specific tasks performed by the remaining two macro buttons are described below.

Click on the *WYS button* to switch to WYSIWYG display mode. This button is equivalent to selecting /**O**ptions **D**isplay Mode and choosing the **B:** WYSIWYG option.

Click on the *CHR button* to switch to text display mode. This button is equivalent to selecting /**O**ptions **D**isplay Mode and choosing the **A:** 80x25 option.

The zoom button and resize box are two additional "mouse-action" buttons. These buttons appear above and below the mouse palette, respectively, and are available only when Quattro Pro is *not* in WYSIWYG display mode. In WYSIWYG display mode, the actions performed by these two buttons are instead available as menu commands (covered later in this book).

Click on the *zoom button* to shrink or enlarge the active spreadsheet windows. If other windows are open behind the active window, you can shrink the active window to view the other window. When you enlarge a window, it fills the entire screen.

Drag the *resize box* to change the size of a spreadsheet window, and to reposition a spreadsheet window.

Using Quattro Pro Menus and Commands

Quattro Pro has nine pull-down menus, listed in the pull-down menu bar at the top of the screen. Figure 2.5 shows the pull-down menu bar with the Edit menu pulled down. In every menu name and in every command listed on the pull-down menus, one letter appears bold (red on a color monitor or brighter on a monochrome monitor). This bold letter tells you what letter you must press to pull down the menu or select the command.

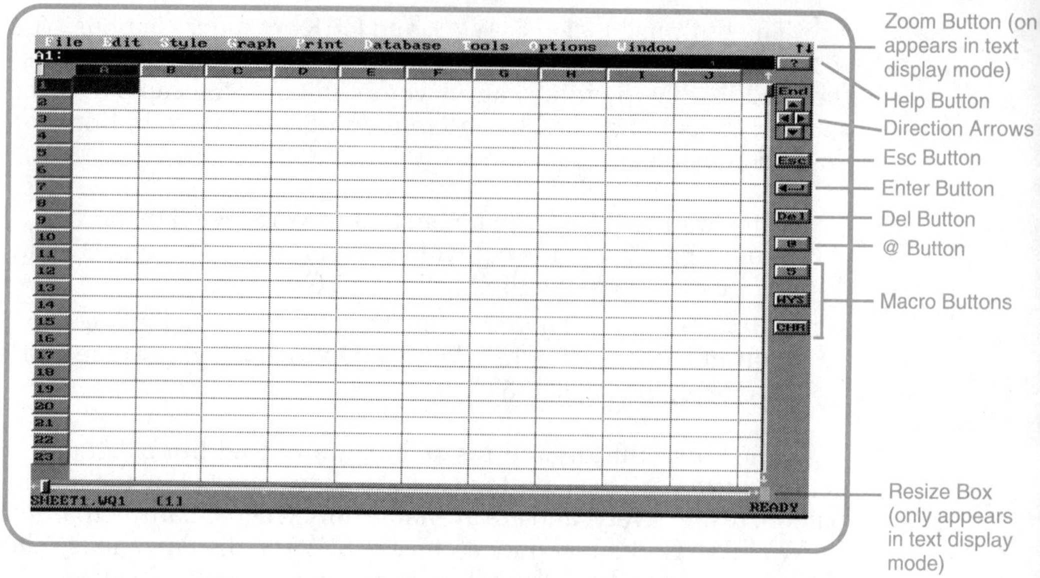

Zoom Button (only appears in text display mode)
Help Button
Direction Arrows
Esc Button
Enter Button
Del Button
@ Button
Macro Buttons
Resize Box (only appears in text display mode)

Figure 2.4 The mouse palette buttons do specific tasks when you click on them with the mouse.

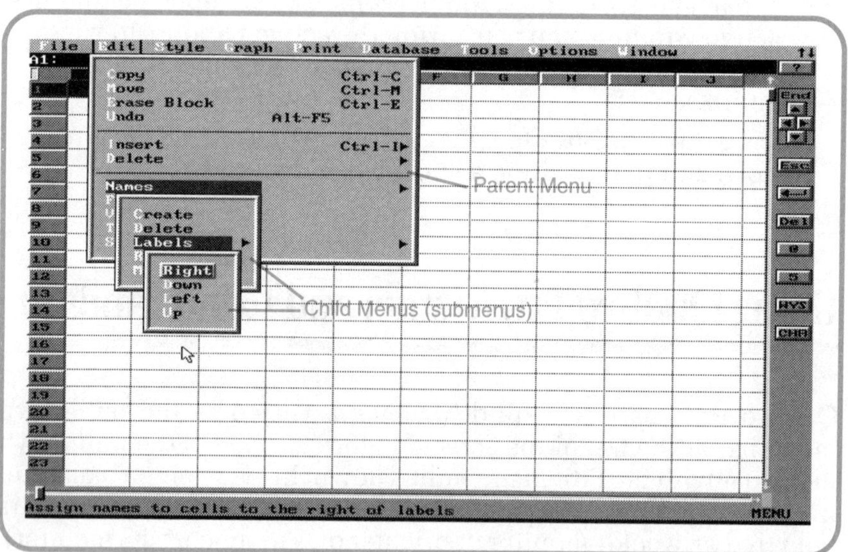

Figure 2.5 Special features on each menu tell you more about the menu commands and how to select them.

Next to some of the more frequently used commands are shortcut-key combinations, such as Ctrl-C for the Copy command or Alt-F5 for Undo. These shortcut keys let you bypass the pull-down menus. For example, instead of pulling down the Edit menu and selecting Copy, you can hold down the Ctrl key and press C.

You'll notice that a few of the commands listed, such as Insert and Delete, have arrows off to the right. These arrows indicate that if you select the command, you'll open a *submenu*, also called a *child menu*, that lists additional, more specific options. Figure 2.5 illustrates what happens if you choose Names from the Edit menu and then select Labels from the Names menu.

Once you've opened the menu of your choice, you will probably want to select a command from the menu. There are several ways to execute a command. You can execute a command with a mouse, with the keyboard, or with both in concert. Perform the Quick Steps that follow to pull down a menu and execute a command:

Executing a Command from a Pull-Down Menu

Step	Result
1. Press the forward slash (/) key once.	By default, Quattro Pro highlights the File menu name.
2. Press the → key until you highlight the menu name and press Enter, or press the boldfaced letter appearing in the menu name.	Quattro Pro pulls down the menu and displays a list of that menu's commands.
3. Press ↑ or ↓ until you highlight the command you wish to execute and press Enter, or press the boldfaced letter in the command name.	Quattro Pro executes the command or opens a submenu, listing additional commands.
4. If a submenu appears, select another command as in step 3.	Continue working your way through the submenus until you execute a command. □

To pull down a menu with a mouse, use the mouse pointer to point to the name of the menu you want to pull down, and click the left mouse button once. Point to the command you wish to execute, and click the left mouse button again. If a submenu appears, continue to click the left mouse button on the command of your choice until Quattro Pro executes a command.

Cancelling a Menu or Command

If you pull down the wrong menu or execute the wrong command, you need to know how to cancel a choice. There are three direct ways to cancel menu and command choices. The first way is to choose the Quit command that appears as the last command on many of the pull-down menus. This option closes the menu that's currently open.

The second way to cancel a choice is to press the Esc key. This option backs you out of the current menu and returns you to the previous one. For example, to remove the last submenu displayed in Figure 2.5, press Esc once. To remove the remaining submenu, press Esc again. To remove the Edit menu, press Esc again.

To immediately remove all menus from the screen, press Ctrl-Break. When you do that, Quattro Pro removes each menu one at a time until only a blank spreadsheet remains.

To cancel a choice with a mouse, place the mouse pointer on the Esc button on the mouse palette (the long, vertical bar at the right side of the screen) and click the left button once.

> **Tip:** If you click the mouse pointer on a parent menu's **Q**uit command when several submenus are displayed, Quattro Pro removes all of the menus from the screen. This is just like pressing Ctrl-Break on a keyboard.

Saving Your Work

Whenever you create or edit a spreadsheet, the spreadsheet you created and the changes you've entered are stored only temporarily in your computer's RAM, an electronic storage area. If you quit the program, turn off your computer, or experience a power outage, the spreadsheet you just created and the changes you've entered are gone. In order to protect your work, you must save the spreadsheet and your changes to disk, your computer's permanent storage facility.

Saving a Spreadsheet to a File for the First Time

1. Press / and then F to pull down the **F**ile menu. — The **File** menu appears, offering a list of commands.
2. Press S to execute the **S**ave command. — Quattro Pro displays the filename prompt box pictured in Figure 2.6.
3. Type a new filename and press Enter. — Quattro Pro writes all of the spreadsheet data in a file on your hard disk, using the name that you specify.

A filename cannot exceed eight characters. Quattro Pro adds a .WQ1 extension to the filename. □

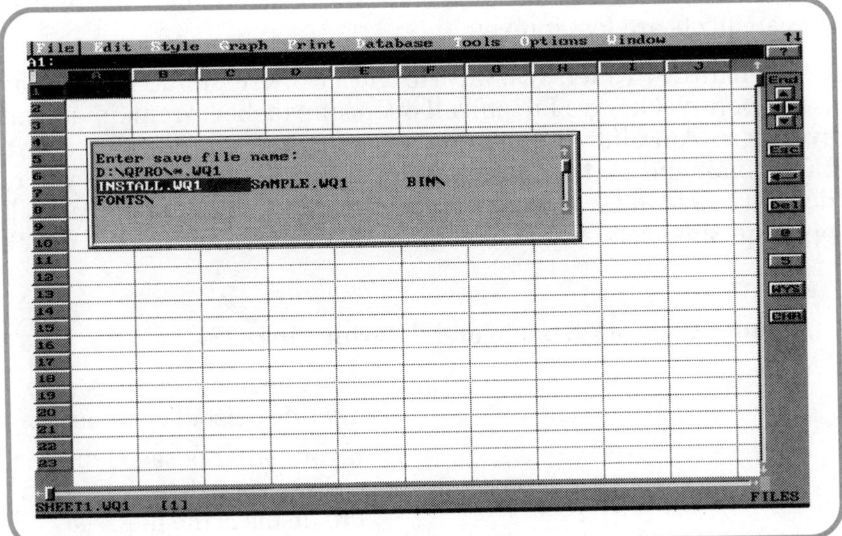

Figure 2.6 The filename prompt box asks you to highlight a filename.

The next time you select the **S**ave command to resave the file, Quattro Pro displays a prompt asking if you wish to **C**ancel, **R**eplace, or **B**ackup the existing file. Press C to cancel the operation, R to save all changes to the same filename, or B to create a backup of the original spreadsheet file.

> **Tip:** To save a spreadsheet to a file on a floppy diskette, add the drive name and a colon before the filename. For example if you type the filename b:\data, Quattro Pro saves the current spreadsheet in a file named DATA.WQ1 on a diskette in drive B. Be sure to place a diskette in drive B before you use this method.

Ending a Quattro Pro Work Session

When you are finished working in Quattro Pro, you must exit the program and return to DOS. Always be sure to save your work before exiting the program. Once you return to DOS, Quattro Pro is no longer in your computer's RAM. This means that all unsaved spreadsheets are lost forever.

Quattro Pro offers two ways to end a work session. The first way is temporary; Quattro Pro and all open spreadsheets remain in your system's RAM after you exit the program. You can then execute a DOS command without having to restart Quattro Pro when you're done. The second way is permanent; it removes Quattro Pro and all open spreadsheets from your system's RAM and returns you to DOS.

Q Ending a Work Session and Returning to DOS

1. Press / and then F to pull down the **F**ile menu.
   The **F**ile menu appears, offering a list of commands.
2. Press X to execute the E**x**it command.
   If you have not saved the current spreadsheet, Quattro Pro displays the message shown in Figure 2.7. If you've saved the spreadsheet or if you haven't entered changes to the spreadsheet, Quattro Pro returns you to DOS.
3. If you see the message shown in Figure 2.7, press S to execute the **S**ave & Exit command.
   Quattro Pro saves the current spreadsheet to disk, removes the program from RAM, and displays the familiar DOS command prompt. □

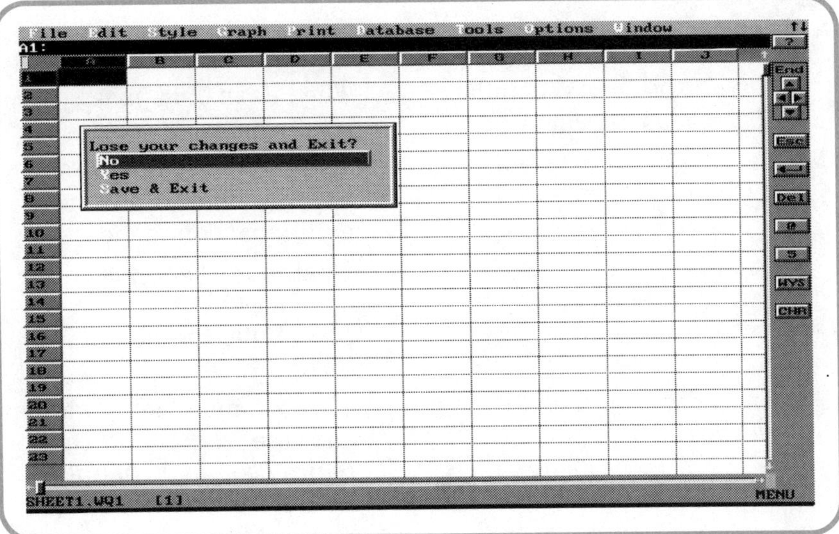

Figure 2.7 Quattro Pro asks if you wish to lose changes before you exit the program.

> **Caution:** If you press Y in answer to Quattro Pro's warning message, Quattro Pro permanently discards all changes made to the current spreadsheet since the last time you saved it.

The DOS Shell gives you quick access to DOS commands without having to exit Quattro Pro completely. Once you choose the DOS Shell command, Quattro Pro prompts you to type a DOS command (for a partial DOS Shell) or press Enter for the full DOS Shell. If you type a DOS command, Quattro Pro executes the command and then immediately returns you to the active spreadsheet. If you press Enter, Quattro Pro returns you to the DOS command level where you may execute as many DOS commands as you desire.

If you are accustomed to using commands such as DIR or DEL, then you will appreciate the timesaving nature of the DOS Shell. Quattro Pro does not prompt you to save your current spreadsheet prior to exiting to the DOS Shell. Even so, it's a good idea for you to do so in the event you experience a power failure while in DOS.

Temporarily Returning to DOS

1. Press / and then F to pull down the **F**ile menu. — The **F**ile menu appears, offering a list of commands.
2. Press U to open up the Utilities submenu. — The Utilities submenu appears, offering a list of additional commands.
3. Press D to execute the **D**OS Shell command. — Quattro Pro prompts you to enter a DOS command, or press Enter for the full DOS Shell.
4. Press Enter for the full DOS Shell. — This command temporarily ends the work session and returns you to the familiar DOS command prompt (see Figure 2.8). □

While in DOS, execute commands exactly as if you had permanently ended the work session. To return to Quattro Pro, type `exit` and press Enter. Quattro Pro returns you to the exact location on the spreadsheet from where you departed.

```
Type Exit to return to Quattro

Microsoft(R) MS-DOS(R)  Version 3.30
             (C)Copyright Microsoft Corp 1981-1987


D:\QPRO>dir
```

Figure 2.8 Executing the DIR command from Quattro Pro's DOS Shell.

Getting Answers to Questions

Whenever you have a question during a work session, press F1 or click on the question mark key in the mouse palette to view Quattro Pro's help window. This help window offers both general and specific information about menus, commands, and Quattro Pro procedures.

Getting General Help

When you press F1 from the current spreadsheet, Quattro Pro displays the help window shown in Figure 2.9, offering a list of topics for which you can get additional help. Boldfaced names appearing in a help window are called *keywords*. These keywords lead to other, more specific, help windows. To select more specific help topics, move the cursor to the keyword that represents the topic and press Enter. If you use a mouse, simply point at the keyword and click once.

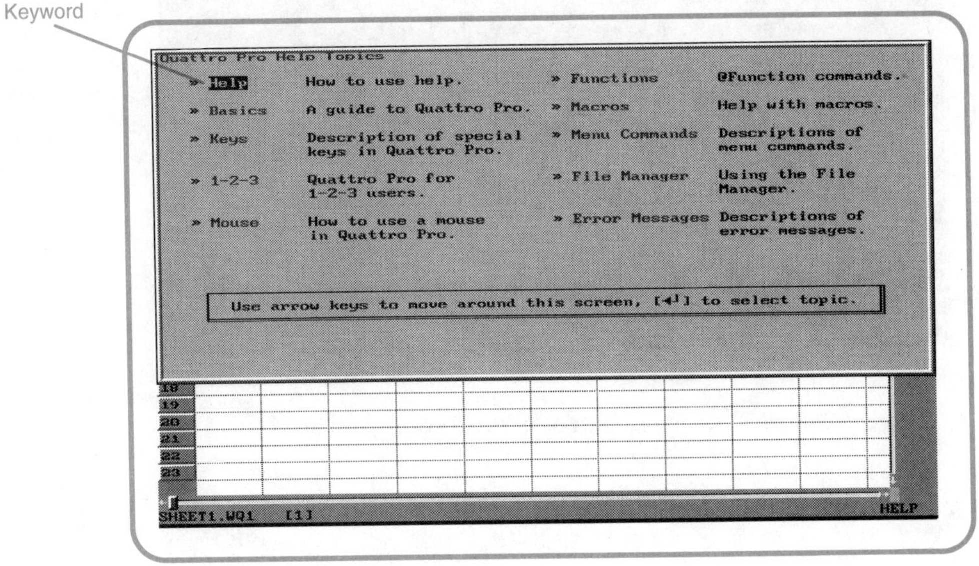

Figure 2.9 Viewing the main help window.

Getting Specific Help

To get context-sensitive help, press F1 while on a submenu. For example, suppose you've pulled down the Edit menu and executed the Insert command. Press F1 to display a help window that specifically relates to the Insert command. This help window is shown in Figure 2.10. In certain cases, the help windows display boldfaced keywords that lead to even more specific help windows. To exit a help window and return to the current spreadsheet, press Esc, or click the mouse pointer anywhere on the spreadsheet area shown underneath the help window.

Tip: When Quattro Pro displays an error message, press F1 to learn more about the error and how to correct it.

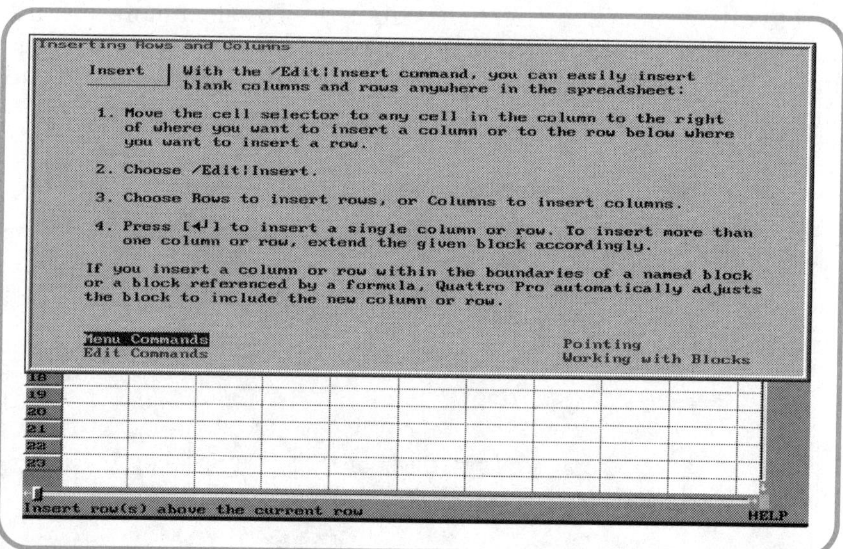

Figure 2.10 Getting context-sensitive help.

What You've Learned

This chapter introduced everything you need to know to get started with Quattro Pro. Before moving on to Chapter 3, let's take a brief look at the important topics we covered here:

- Installing Quattro Pro is a two-part process: copying the program files and defining your computer equipment.
- When you pull down a parent menu, Quattro Pro displays a list of that menu's commands, along with some shortcut keys for the more commonly used commands.
- When you execute a command on a parent menu, Quattro Pro often displays a submenu, which lists additional commands.
- You can use a mouse to quickly pull down a menu and execute a command.
- Whenever you create or edit a spreadsheet, you should save the spreadsheet to disk to protect it from getting lost in the event of a power outage. You must also save your work before ending a Quattro Pro work session.
- There are two ways to leave Quattro Pro and return to the operating system. You can either exit the program permanently after saving your spreadsheet file with the /**F**ile E**x**it command. Or you can use the /**F**ile **U**tilities DOS Shell command to return to DOS temporarily to enter a DOS command.
- You can get both general and context-sensitive help during a work session, by pressing F1 or clicking the question mark key on the mouse palette.

Chapter 3

Building a Spreadsheet Application

In This Chapter

- ▶ *Entering labels, numbers, dates, and basic formulas*
- ▶ *Understanding the basics of spreadsheet file management*
- ▶ *Copying and moving cell data*
- ▶ *Erasing and editing cell data*
- ▶ *Inserting and deleting columns and rows*
- ▶ *Exploring options for spreadsheet viewing*

In Quattro Pro, most activity takes place in the spreadsheet. As you learned in Chapter 1, the spreadsheet application is the basic ingredient with which you create graphs, databases, and macro programs. This chapter teaches you skills for constructing applications that serve a variety of reporting functions. These application-building techniques are more easily learned by following along, so load Quattro Pro into your computer now (using the procedure described in Appendix A), and let's begin your first work session.

Learning Spreadsheet Terminology

In Quattro Pro, the term *spreadsheet* describes the physical area of the program into which you enter data. When you type data into a spreadsheet the program stores it in a *cell*—the basic unit of a spreadsheet. A cell is the intersection of a *row* and a *column*. The Quattro Pro screen shows row numbers down the left side, from 1 to 8,192. Alphabetical column letters appear across the top of the spreadsheet area, from A through IV. In Quattro Pro there are 2,097,152 individual cells (8,192 rows times 256 columns)!

You assign a *filename* to a spreadsheet once you finish creating or modifying it. Quattro Pro permanently stores a spreadsheet in a *file* on a floppy or hard disk drive, using the filename plus the .WQ1 extension to label the file. Each spreadsheet must have a unique filename, so Quattro Pro can distinguish between them. When you wish to work with a saved application, retrieve the file to load the spreadsheet back into Quattro Pro (the specific steps appear later in this chapter).

A *window* is an area on-screen where you view a single spreadsheet. Quattro Pro allows you to open and work with up to 32 windows at a time. Multiple window viewing—displaying several spreadsheets at the same time—makes it easier to create spreadsheet linking formulas (a topic covered in Chapter 10).

Two Types of Spreadsheet Data

Quattro Pro can store two types of data in a cell: labels and values. A *label* is any nonnumerical entry that contains letters. A *value* can be a number, a formula, or a date and time. Quattro Pro knows whether an entry is a label or a value the moment you type the first character. When you enter a label into a cell, Quattro Pro displays the LABEL mode indicator on the status line in the lower right corner of the screen. When you enter a value into a cell, Quattro Pro displays the VALUE mode indicator.

Entering data into a cell is simple—even if you've never worked with a spreadsheet program before. Use the following steps as a guideline for entering data into a spreadsheet cell.

1. Select a cell using the cursor movement keys, or click on a cell with the mouse.
2. Begin typing using the keyboard keys.
3. Press the Enter key, and Quattro Pro stores the data in the current cell. To immediately move to another cell after entering data, press one of the cursor movement keys instead of pressing Enter.

As you type data into a spreadsheet, keep an eye on the status line for the LABEL and VALUE indicators to see if Quattro Pro correctly interprets your entry. This is particularly important when you enter formulas into cells. Because formulas calculate answers using spreadsheet data, incorrectly entered formulas calculate incorrect answers.

Entering Labels

The term *label* is another way of saying text. In Quattro Pro, a label is more than just text. Labels describe the contents of a spreadsheet, much like a cereal box label describes its contents. The label *Year,* for example, could describe a cell that contains a year like *1991*. The label *Names* could describe a column of cells that contains names like *Johnson*, *Franklin*, and *Jones*. The labels that you enter into a spreadsheet must begin with a letter (*A* to *Z* or *a* to *z*), a blank space, or a label prefix (' " ^ and |). Examples of valid and invalid labels follow.

'Payroll Register (Valid)

^September 23, 1991 (Valid)

3rd and long (Invalid—starts with a number)

+Sales (Invalid—starts with the plus symbol)

"3rd and long (Valid)

'+Sales (Valid)

The following Quick Steps demonstrate how to enter a label into a spreadsheet cell.

Entering a Label into a Quattro Pro Spreadsheet

1. Move the cell selector to the cell into which you want to enter the label.

   The mode indicator displays `READY`.

2. Type the label. Press Space Bar to insert spaces between words.

   Quattro Pro displays the text on the input line as you type it. The mode indicator displays `LABEL` (see Figure 3.1).

3. After you finish typing the label, press Enter to store the label in the cell.

   If you enter an invalid label, Quattro Pro beeps. Press Esc, retype a valid label, and press Enter. Quattro Pro moves the label from the input line into the cell. The mode indicator displays `READY` again. □

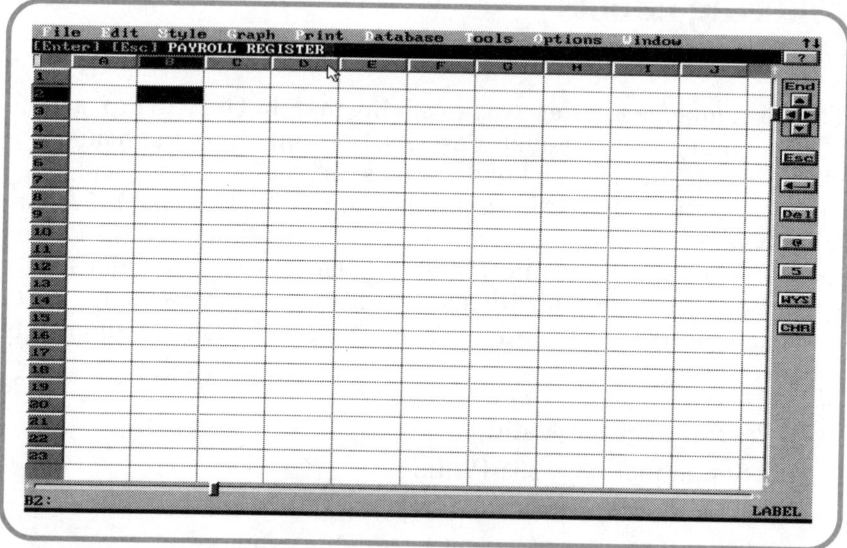

Figure 3.1 Quattro Pro displays a label entry on the input line before transferring it into a cell.

Move the cell selector to cell B2, type `PAYROLL REGISTER`, and then press Enter, so your screen looks like the one in Figure 3.2. Notice that the label in cell B2 overflows into cell C2. Quattro Pro overflows labels that are longer than the width of the column where you enter the label. You can widen column B so it can hold at least 16 characters—the number of characters in the label in cell B2. Or you can type data into cell C2, so that Quattro Pro only displays part of the label in B2. Quattro Pro never places data from one cell over data in the cell to the right.

For instance, if you did type data into cell C2, the portion of cell B2's label that you would see is highlighted by the cell selector, as shown in Figure 3.2 (PAYROLL). The rest of the label "disappears" from view because the data in cell C2 obscures it. To see that the full cell entry is really still there, just look at the input line.

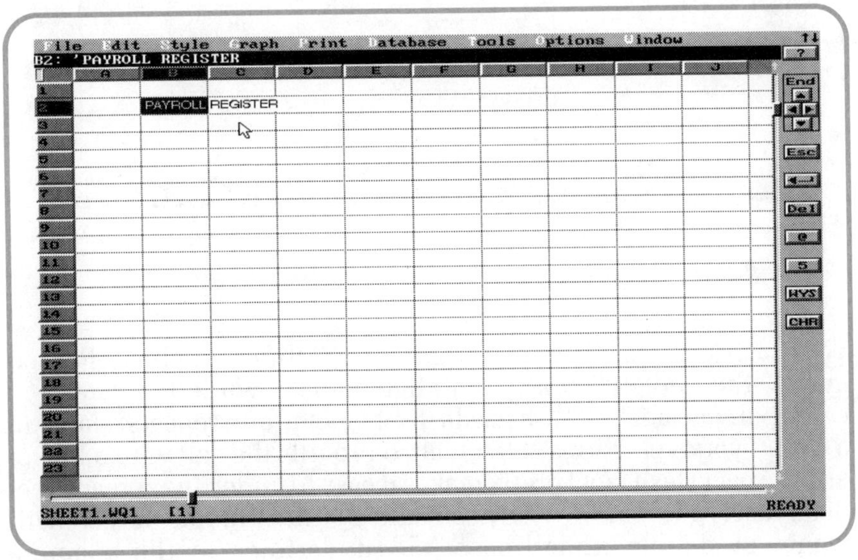

Figure 3.2 A label entered into a cell.

You can enter data into a cell and move directly to another cell using one of the cursor movement keys. For instance, to enter five more labels into your sample spreadsheet, move to cell B3, type November, 1991, and press ↓ twice. Type TITLE, press →; type EMPLOYEE, press →; type DEPT, press →, type SALARY, press →; type BONUS, press →; type TOTAL, and press Enter. Your spreadsheet now looks like the one pictured in Figure 3.3.

By default, Quattro Pro attaches the apostrophe (') label prefix to the beginning of each label entry that you make. This prefix *right-aligns* the label in a cell. You can't see a label prefix by looking at the label in the spreadsheet cell, but you can see prefixes by looking on the input line. Look at the input line in Figure 3.3 to see that Quattro Pro stores the label in cell G5 as 'TOTAL.

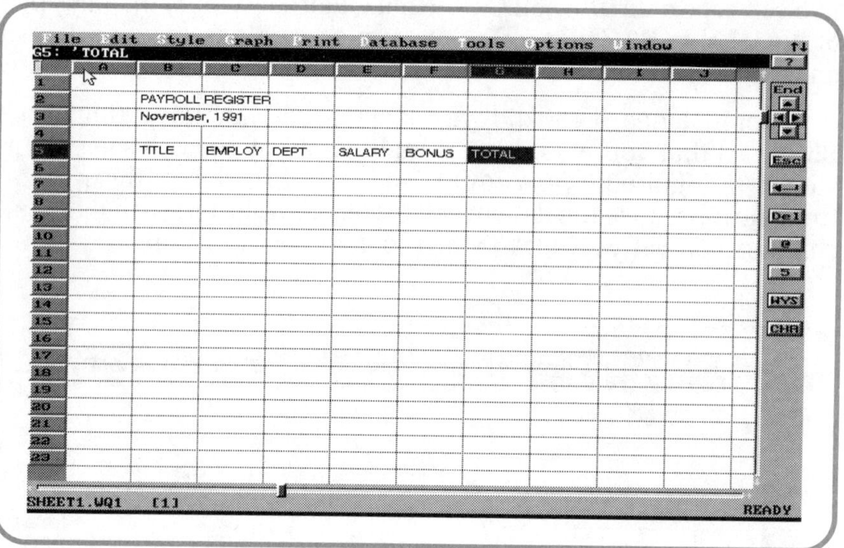

Figure 3.3 Adding more labels to the sample spreadsheet.

Each label prefix symbol produces a different effect. For example, the quote (") prefix left-aligns labels, while the carat (^) center-aligns labels. The backslash (\) label prefix repeats a label in a cell. If you type \R in a cell, Quattro Pro fills the cell with a line of Rs. The backslash label prefix makes it easy to underline spreadsheet data. Just type \- or \= in any cell, and Quattro Pro fills the cell with single or double underlines. Add underlines to the example spreadsheet to give the application a more structured look by typing \- in cells B6 through G6. Figure 3.4 shows the payroll register spreadsheet with labels, values, and underlines.

In Figure 3.4, notice that you can't see the complete entry for many of the labels in columns B and C. This is because Quattro Pro prevents them from overlapping the data appearing in the column immediately to the right. In their entirety, the labels appearing in columns B and C are as follows:

CEO — Chaney, L.
Assistant — Karloff, B.
Chairman — Price, V.
PR Director — Lorrey, P.
Sales — Eastwood, C.
Sales — Palance, J.

Data Entry	Jackson, M.
Warehouse	Simpson, B.
Accounting	Cat, F.T.

When you create your copy of the example spreadsheet, be sure to enter these labels as they appear above. In Chapter 7, you'll learn how to expand the width of a column to reveal the labels in their entirety. (If you're dying to try it now, use the /**S**tyle **C**olumn Width command.)

PAYROLL REGISTER
November, 1991

TITLE	EMPLOY	DEPT	SALARY	BONUS	TOTAL
CEO	Chaney,	4	2500	0	
Assistant	Karloff, B.	4	9000	0	
Chairman	Price, V.	4	13000	0	
PR Direct	Lorrey, P.	4	2000	0	
Sales	Eastwoo	2	15000	350	
Sales	Palance,	2	3000	350	
Data Entr	Jackson,	3	22000	50	
Warehou	Simpson,	1	18000	0	
Accounti	Cat, F.T.	1	1500	250	

Figure 3.4 Adding single underlines to enhance the display of spreadsheet labels.

Entering Values

Values in Quattro Pro include numbers, formulas, or date and time entries. A *number* is any single digit or series of digits. A *formula* is an entry that performs a calculation on two or more numbers. A *date* and *time* entry is a number converted to a date when properly formatted. Unlike a label, which must begin with one of the four label prefixes, a value must begin with a number (*0* through *9*), a decimal point (.), a plus sign (+), a minus sign (–), the left parenthesis

((), or the dollar symbol ($). Quattro Pro does not accept numbers that contain blank spaces or commas. Following are some valid and invalid value entries.

10 (Valid)

98.1 (Valid)

10023.1254 (Valid)

–3 (Valid)

+29 (Valid)

.981 (Valid)

98.1% (Valid)

.98.1 (Invalid—one too many decimal points)

10,023.1254 (Invalid—contains a comma)

10 023.1254 (Invalid—contains a space)

> **Tip:** When you type a percentage (%) sign at the end of a number, Quattro Pro converts the number to a decimal value. Quattro Pro stores the number 25%, for instance, as the decimal value 0.25.

Quattro Pro has two methods for dealing with entries that contain a mixture of letters and numbers. Look again at Figure 3.4. Quattro Pro treats the entry `November, 1991` in cell B3 as a label (even though it contains numbers), because the first character is a letter. If you try to enter the label as `1991, November`, however, the program beeps and displays an error message because typing `1` enters VALUE mode. Quattro Pro will not accept blanks, commas, or letters as part of regular number entries. If you wish the label to read `1991, November`, type a label prefix before typing the *1* in 1991 (as in `^1991, November`).

Although entering numbers into a cell really is as simple as it seems, keep the following guidelines in mind:

1. Don't use parentheses to signify that a number is negative, as in the entry *(100)*. Instead, precede a negative number with a minus sign, as in the entry *–100*.
2. Don't enter commas as part of a number entry. (In Chapter 7 you'll learn how to use the /**S**tyle **N**umeric Format command to do that.)
3. Don't make the mistake of using the lowercase *L* for the number one *(1)*, or the uppercase *O* for the number zero *(0)*.

When you enter a value that is longer than the width of the active cell's column, Quattro Pro does not overlap the entry into an adjacent blank cell. Instead, it tries to convert the number to scientific notation form (for example, the number entry *987654321* displays as `9.9E+08`). If Quattro Pro can't convert the value entry to scientific notation, then it fills the cell with asterisks (********). You'll learn how to modify a cell's display format in Chapter 7. For now, use the following Quick Steps as a guide for entering a number into a Quattro Pro spreadsheet.

Q Entering a Number into a Quattro Pro Spreadsheet

1. Place the cell selector in the cell where you want to enter the number.	The status line displays the `READY` mode indicator.
2. Type the number.	Quattro Pro displays the number on the input line as you type and displays the `VALUE` mode indicator in the status line.
3. Press Enter, or one of the Arrow keys, to store the number in the cell.	Quattro Pro transfers the number from the input line to the cell. The status line displays `READY` again. If you pressed an Arrow key, the cell in that direction now is active. □

Figure 3.4 shows several different names and values entered into the example payroll register spreadsheet we've been building. Type this data into your sample spreadsheet before you move on to the next section.

Entering Basic Formulas

Formulas are the "brains" of every spreadsheet application. Without its ability to work with numbers and formulas, Quattro Pro would be a fancy word processor. By permanently storing numbers, and manipulating these numbers via formulas, you can create Quattro Pro spreadsheet applications to fulfill all of your reporting and analysis needs.

It's simple to build basic formulas that add, subtract, multiply, and divide numbers on a spreadsheet. Building formulas with Quattro Pro involves three steps, as follows:

1. Select a spreadsheet cell into which you will type the formula.
2. Create the formula and type it on the input line.
3. Press Enter to transfer the formula into the cell. Quattro Pro evaluates the formula and displays a result (the answer).

A Quattro Pro formula can contain up to 254 characters. Formulas must begin with a plus (+) or minus (–) sign so Quattro Pro immediately recognizes it as a formula. A formula also can begin with @ to signify an @function command (these formulas are covered in Chapter 6). Formula *operands* (the values upon which Quattro Pro performs its calculations) can begin with a number (*0* through *9*) or one of the five value symbols: + – . ($.

You can create Quattro Pro formulas to handle a wide variety of tasks. Quattro Pro knows exactly what to do with your spreadsheet data by examining the mathematical operators in the formula. For instance, the plus operator (+) tells Quattro Pro to add. You use the minus symbol (–) to subtract two numbers, much like you do in a handwritten subtraction problem. To multiply or divide numbers, use the times (*) symbol and the divide (/) symbol.

Quattro Pro recognizes two types of operands: *numeric-only* and *cell-referencing*. A formula with numeric-only operands performs a calculation exclusively with numbers, as in the formula *198*100+2*. A formula with cell-referencing operands performs a calculation using both numbers and cell addresses (or cell addresses only), as in *+B10*100+D5*. If the values 198 and 2 were stored in cells B10 and D5, Quattro Pro would multiply 198 by 100, and then add 2 to perform the formula calculation.

Let's continue building our sample payroll register spreadsheet. Use the following Quick Steps to build formulas to sum the numbers stored in the SALARY and BONUS columns on each row and display the answer in the TOTAL column of the same row.

Entering a Formula into a Spreadsheet Cell

1. Place the cell selector in cell G7. — The status line displays the READY mode indicator.
2. Type the formula +E7+F7. — The status line displays the VALUE indicator and shows the formula on the input line.

3. Press Enter once (or press ↓ to move to the next formula cell). If you entered an invalid formula, Quattro Pro beeps. Press Esc, retype a valid formula and press Enter.

Quattro Pro displays the formula result in cell G7. The mode indicator changes to `READY`. If you used Enter rather than an Arrow key to accept your cell formula, you can see the formula in the input line, as shown in Figure 3.5. □

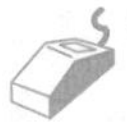

Using your mouse, you can enter formulas into cells using the "point-and-click" method. For example, in the previous Quick Step you also could have done the following:

1. Point and click on cell G7.
2. Press + on the keyboard.
3. Point and click on cell E7.
4. Press + on the keyboard.
5. Point and click on cell F7.
6. Click the Enter button on the mouse palette.

While this method for entering formulas may seem a bit involved for such a small formula, it is invaluable for building formulas that use three or more cell addresses.

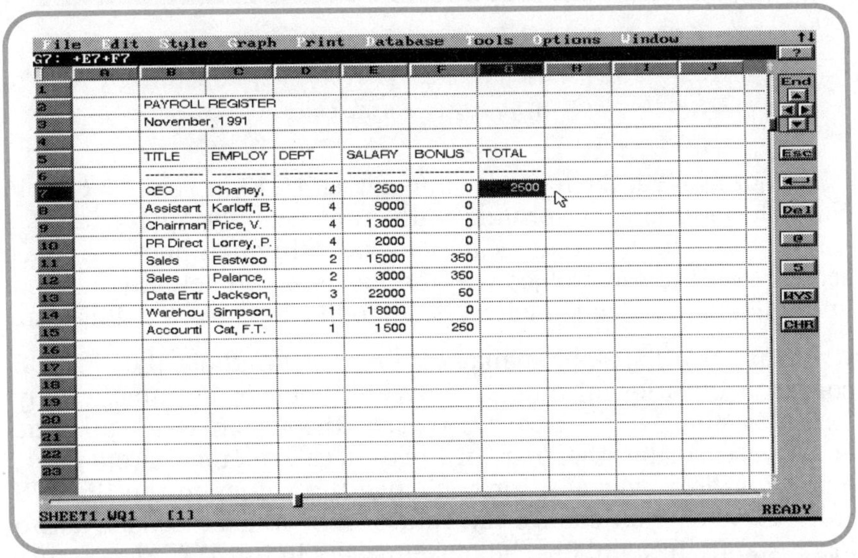
G7: +E7+F7
PAYROLL REGISTER
November, 1991
TITLE EMPLOY DEPT SALARY BONUS TOTAL
CEO Chaney, 4 2500 0 2500
Assistant Karloff, B. 4 9000 0
Chairman Price, V. 4 13000 0
PR Direct Lorrey, P. 4 2000 0
Sales Eastwoo 2 15000 350
Sales Palance, 2 3000 350
Data Entr Jackson, 3 22000 50
Warehou Simpson, 1 18000 0
Accounti Cat, F.T. 1 1500 250
SHEET1.WQ1 [1]
READY

Figure 3.5 Quattro Pro adds the values stored in two cells, and displays the result in a third cell.

The formula +E7+F7 adds the value stored in cell E7 to the one stored in F7. This formula displays the total payroll expense (2500) for the first employee (Chaney) on the list. Using the procedure outlined by the preceding Quick Steps, enter formulas into cells G8 through G15 to calculate total payroll expenses for the remaining employees. Be sure to change the cell address references used in each formula so that each formula reflects the particular row that you're on. The final formula on the payroll register spreadsheet, stored in cell G15, appears in the input line of Figure 3.6.

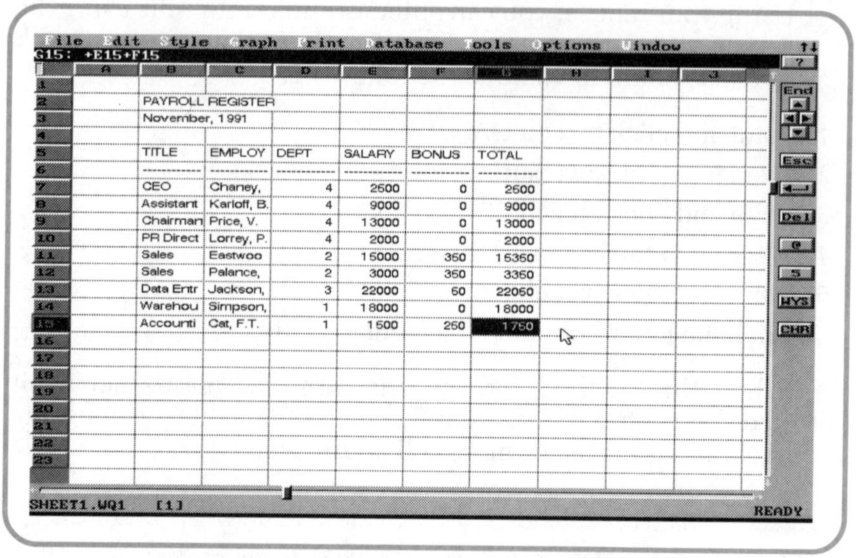

G15: +E15+F15

	A	B	C	D	E	F	G
2		PAYROLL REGISTER					
3		November, 1991					
5		TITLE	EMPLOY	DEPT	SALARY	BONUS	TOTAL
7		CEO	Chaney,	4	2500	0	2500
8		Assistant	Karloff, B.	4	9000	0	9000
9		Chairman	Price, V.	4	13000	0	13000
10		PR Direct	Lorrey, P.	4	2000	0	2000
11		Sales	Eastwoo	2	15000	350	15350
12		Sales	Palance,	2	3000	350	3350
13		Data Entr	Jackson,	3	22000	50	22050
14		Warehou	Simpson,	1	18000	0	18000
15		Accounti	Cat, F.T.	1	1500	250	1750

SHEET1.WQ1 [1] READY

Figure 3.6 The formula in cell G15 looks just like the one in cell G7—only the row number is different.

Look again at the formula shown in cell G15 in Figure 3.6. You could have entered a formula with numeric-only operands, like +1500+250, to derive the same answer. Although both formulas accomplish the same objective, the formula you actually entered into cell G15 offers you much more flexibility. Let's see why this is so.

Suppose that your manager tells you to adjust the BONUS column values for all nine employees. If you used numeric-only formulas, then you'd have to recreate the formulas for all nine employees. On the other hand, if you used cell-referencing operands (and you did!), you need only change the values in the BONUS column. When you change the values in referenced cells, Quattro Pro instantly recalculates the new answers in the TOTAL column. Making changes to the values in column E or F does not affect the formulas stored in column G. The cell addresses in the column G formulas remain exactly as you entered them. Test this now. For example, change the value in the BONUS column for employee Cat to 500. Quattro Pro immediately displays a new answer in column G, as shown in Figure 3.7. (Change it back to 250 before you continue.)

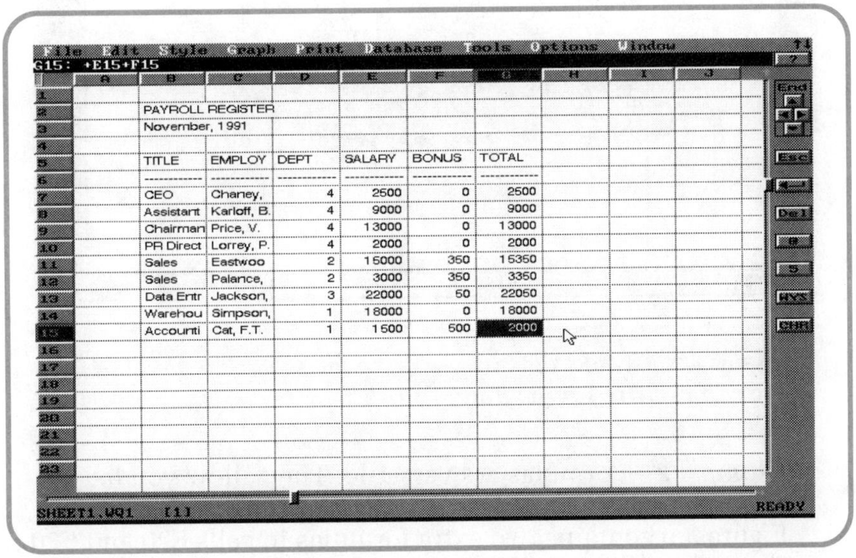

File Edit Style Graph Print Database Tools Options Window

G15: +E15+F15

TITLE	EMPLOY	DEPT	SALARY	BONUS	TOTAL
CEO	Chaney,	4	2500	0	2500
Assistant	Karloff, B.	4	9000	0	9000
Chairman	Price, V.	4	13000	0	13000
PR Direct	Lorrey, P.	4	2000	0	2000
Sales	Eastwoo	2	15000	350	15350
Sales	Palance,	2	3000	350	3350
Data Entr	Jackson,	3	22000	50	22050
Warehou	Simpson,	1	18000	0	18000
Accounti	Cat, F.T.	1	1500	500	2000

PAYROLL REGISTER
November, 1991

SHEET1.WQ1 [1] READY

Figure 3.7 Quattro Pro updates formulas with cell-referencing operands as soon as you change the values to which they refer.

The payroll register spreadsheet offers you a glimpse into the powerful nature of Quattro Pro formulas. You may have guessed that the formula is a critical component of any spreadsheet application. In fact, it's likely that you've already thought of some uses for formulas in your own applications. Write your ideas down, so that you can remember them later and use them in your own spreadsheets.

For now, consider the following three ways of modifying the payroll register spreadsheet. Each example illustrates an important spreadsheet-building principle.

> *Example 1*—A spreadsheet must be complete to be useful. Create formulas to total the values that appear in the SALARY, BONUS, and TOTAL columns. Store these formulas in cells E17, F17, and G17. Figure 3.8 shows the final version of the payroll register spreadsheet. Look at the formula used in cell G17, which sums all of the values in the TOTAL column, to see how to create your formulas.

File Edit Style Graph Print Database Tools Options Window

G17: (,0) +G7+G8+G9+G10+G11+G12+G13+G14+G15

	B	C	D	E	F	G
2	PAYROLL REGISTER					
3	November, 1991					
5	TITLE	EMPLOY	DEPT	SALARY	BONUS	TOTAL
6	----------	----------	----------	----------	----------	----------
7	CEO	Chaney,	4	2,500	0	2,500
8	Assistant	Karloff, B.	4	9,000	0	9,000
9	Chairman	Price, V.	4	13,000	0	13,000
10	PR Direct	Lorrey, P.	4	2,000	0	2,000
11	Sales	Eastwoo	2	15,000	350	15,350
12	Sales	Palance,	2	3,000	350	3,350
13	Data Entr	Jackson,	3	22,000	50	22,050
14	Warehou	Simpson,	1	18,000	0	18,000
15	Accounti	Cat, F.T.	1	1,500	250	1,750
16				----------	----------	----------
17				86,000	1,000	87,000
18				=====	=====	=====

SHEET1.WQ1 [1] READY

Figure 3.8 It takes just three more formulas to complete the payroll register application.

Example 2—Formulas are versatile. They allow you to analyze your spreadsheet data in many different ways. Figure 3.9 contains two extra formulas in cells E20 and F20. These formulas calculate total salary and total bonus as a percentage of total payroll.

File Edit Style Graph Print Database Tools Options Window

F20: (P2) +F17/G17

	B	C	D	E	F	G
2	PAYROLL REGISTER					
3	November, 1991					
5	TITLE	EMPLOY	DEPT	SALARY	BONUS	TOTAL
6	----------	----------	----------	----------	----------	----------
7	CEO	Chaney,	4	2,500	0	2,500
8	Assistant	Karloff, B.	4	9,000	0	9,000
9	Chairman	Price, V.	4	13,000	0	13,000
10	PR Direct	Lorrey, P.	4	2,000	0	2,000
11	Sales	Eastwoo	2	15,000	350	15,350
12	Sales	Palance,	2	3,000	350	3,350
13	Data Entr	Jackson,	3	22,000	50	22,050
14	Warehou	Simpson,	1	18,000	0	18,000
15	Accounti	Cat, F.T.	1	1,500	250	1,750
16				----------	----------	----------
17				86,000	1,000	87,000
18				=====	=====	=====
20				98.85%	1.15%	

SHEET1.WQ1 [1] READY

Figure 3.9 Looking at the payroll register data in a different light.

Example 3—Spreadsheets often can be converted for use in other applications. The payroll register spreadsheet, for instance, could be changed into a checking account register. Figure 3.10 shows how this can be done by changing the report title in cell B2, and the labels on row 5 to reflect this new application. This approach to spreadsheet-building saves you valuable time. Note that on this spreadsheet, check issue entries appear as negative values (a deduction from the running balance in column G), while deposit entries are positive values.

File Edit Style Graph Print Database Tools Options Window

G17: (G) [W12] +G16+(E17+F17)

CHECKING ACCOUNT REGISTER

November, 1991

CHECK#	PAYEE	TYPE	CHECK	DEPOSIT	BALANCE
	Deposit	1	0	25000	22500
1007	Chaney	2	-2500	0	20000
1008	Karloff	2	-9000	0	11000
1009	Price	2	-13000	0	-2000
1010	Lorrey	2	-2000	0	-4000
1011	Eastwood	2	15350	0	11350
	Deposit	1	0	35000	46350
1012	Palance	2	-3350	0	43000
1013	Jackson	2	-22050	0	20950
1014	Simpson		-18000	0	2950
1015	Cat		-1750	0	1200

SHEET2.WQ1 [1] READY

Figure 3.10 Converting the payroll register spreadsheet into a checking account register spreadsheet.

Improving Spreadsheet Style: A Preview

Did you notice in Figure 3.8 that the data in column D is aligned differently from the version on your screen? Did you notice that the numbers in cells E7 through G17 contain commas to separate the thousands place in each number? The spreadsheet in Figure 3.8 illustrates how you can improve the appearance of a basic spreadsheet.

In this section we preview some of the stylistic tools that Quattro Pro places at your disposal. Use the following sets of steps to enhance your version of the sample spreadsheet. Don't worry if you don't fully grasp the material covered in this preview. In the next few chapters you'll learn all about using cell blocks and enhancing spreadsheet style.

Start by aligning the data in column D. This helps clarify that the numbers 1, 2, 3, and 4 refer to departments. Do the following:

1. Place the cell selector in cell D5 and reenter the label as `^DEPT` (the carat prefix label center-aligns the label in cell D5.)
2. Place the cell selector in cell D7.
3. Press Ctrl-A, the shortcut keystroke for the /**S**tyle **A**lignment command, to display the **A**lignment menu.
4. Press C to execute the **C**enter option. Quattro Pro prompts you for the block to align.
5. Type `D7..D15` and press Enter. Quattro Pro immediately center-aligns the values in that cell block.

Now let's format the values in cells E7 through G17 so that they display commas in the right places. This makes it easier to see the exact value in every cell. Do the following:

1. Place the cell selector in cell E7.
2. Press Ctrl-F, the shortcut keystroke for the /**S**tyle **N**umeric Format command, to display the **N**umeric Format menu.
3. Press the comma (,) key once to select the comma format. Quattro Pro prompts you to type the number of decimal places you wish to display in the number.
4. Type 0 and press Enter for zero decimal places. (You don't need them because there are no cents attached to these dollar figures.) Quattro Pro prompts you to for the block to format.
5. Type `E7..G17` and press Enter. Quattro Pro immediately formats all of the values in the cell block. Note that formatting the repeating labels in cells E16 through G16 has no effect on their display.

Your copy of the example spreadsheet now should look exactly like the one shown in Figure 3.8.

Entering Dates and Times

Quattro Pro uses *date serial* and *time serial* numbers to represent moments in time. A date serial number is based on the number of days that have elapsed since December 31, 1899. For instance, the date serial number for December 31, 1900 is *366*, and the date serial number for December 31, 1991 is *33603*. Time serial numbers are fractional parts of a date serial number.

You can perform mathematical operations on date and time serial numbers, just like you do on other values. This makes them ideal ingredients for applications that rely on time-sensitive data. Spreadsheets that calculate invoice discount dates, delivery times, or accounts receivable and accounts payable due dates are good examples of time-sensitive applications.

> **Tip:** You can change the display format for a date or time entry using the /**S**tyle **N**umeric Format **D**ate command, covered in Chapter 7.

The easiest way to enter a date or time is to use the *DATE mode shortcut key*. The Quattro Pro shortcut key for entering a date is Ctrl-D. To learn how to use this shortcut, you can try the following Quick Steps on an empty cell of your spreadsheet.

Entering a Date into a Spreadsheet

1. Place the cell selector in the cell where you wish to show the date.	The status line displays the READY mode indicator.
2. Press Ctrl-D.	The status line displays the DATE mode indicator.
3. Type the date on the input line in the form *DD/MM/YY*.	Quattro Pro displays the date on the input line as you type.
4. Press Enter to store the date serial number in the active cell.	Quattro Pro displays the date serial number in the input line. The date, in the DD/MM/YY format, appears in the spreadsheet cell. The mode indicator changes to READY (see Figure 3.11). □

Figure 3.11 illustrates the difference between the stored and displayed format of a date serial number entry (look at cell E4, then observe the entry on the input line). The data on the input line means that 33,269 days have elapsed since December 31, 1899.

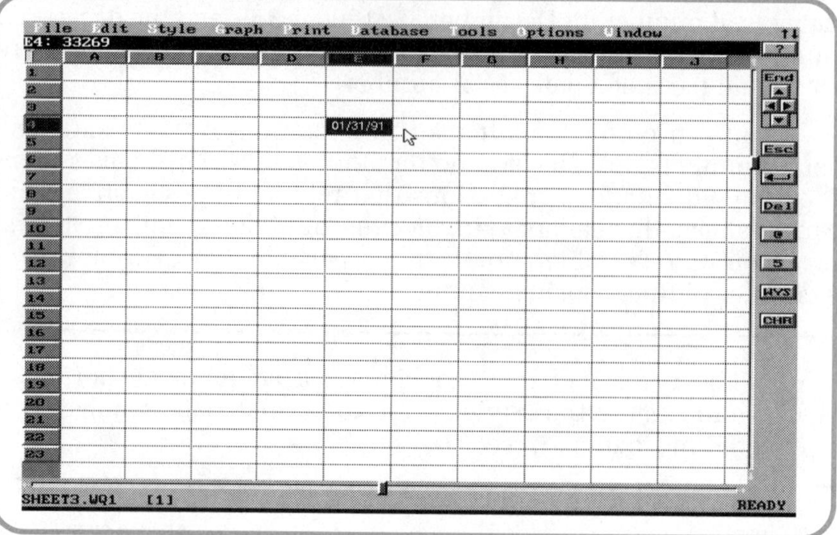

Figure 3.11 Entering a date serial number into an empty spreadsheet.

File Management Basics

We're now finished with the payroll register spreadsheet example. Once you build a spreadsheet application, you need to create a permanent record of the work that you've done. To do this, you first must become familiar with the basics of spreadsheet file management. In Quattro Pro, the /**F**ile menu contains commands for managing your spreadsheet files. Press /F now and review the commands on this menu.

> ***N**ew* loads a blank spreadsheet into a new Quattro Pro window. The second window loads atop the original window and can be recognized by the [2] on the status line at the bottom of the spreadsheet.
>
> ***O**pen* loads a saved spreadsheet back into Quattro Pro. If another spreadsheet is open, the loaded spreadsheet opens in its own window.
>
> ***R**etrieve* loads a saved spreadsheet back into Quattro Pro. If another spreadsheet is open, Quattro Pro closes the active spreadsheet before loading the saved spreadsheet.
>
> ***S**ave* creates a spreadsheet file with a name you specify.
>
> *Save **A**s* prompts you for a filename and then saves the current spreadsheet using that name.

Save All saves all open spreadsheets, beginning with the spreadsheet in the active window. When appropriate, Quattro Pro prompts you to supply a filename for the active spreadsheet.

***C**lose* removes the spreadsheet in the current window revealing other open spreadsheets (if any).

*Close **A**ll* closes all spreadsheets in all open windows.

***E**rase* removes the spreadsheet from the current window and displays a new, blank spreadsheet.

***D**irectory* specifies the default path name of the directory into which Quattro Pro saves files. Quattro Pro also scans the default directory when you wish to open or retrieve a saved file.

The **S**ave command is fundamental to all of the activity that you do in Quattro Pro, because if you don't save a spreadsheet you lose the data permanently. Use the following Quick Steps to save the payroll register spreadsheet. You'll need to retrieve this application later in Chapter 4 when you learn how to work with cell blocks.

Saving a Spreadsheet

1. Press /FS to select the /**F**ile **S**ave command.

   Quattro Pro displays the filename prompt box the first time you save a spreadsheet. (If you later resave it, Quattro Pro displays a prompt asking if you wish to replace the file. Press C to **C**ancel the operation or R to **R**eplace the old spreadsheet with the new version.) The prompt box automatically displays the drive letter and directory path name that appear next to the /**F**ile **D**irectory command. If the directory contains any filenames ending in .WQ1, Quattro Pro displays a list of files below the prompt. To type a different drive or directory, press the Backspace key to erase the default names. Then, retype a new drive letter and/or path name.

2. Type PAYROLL.

   Quattro Pro displays the filename on the prompt box input line as you type it (see Figure 3.12).

3. Press Enter (or click it with your mouse).

   Quattro Pro writes the data into a file named PAYROLL.WQ1 on your hard disk drive. The filename appears on the status line at the bottom of the spreadsheet. □

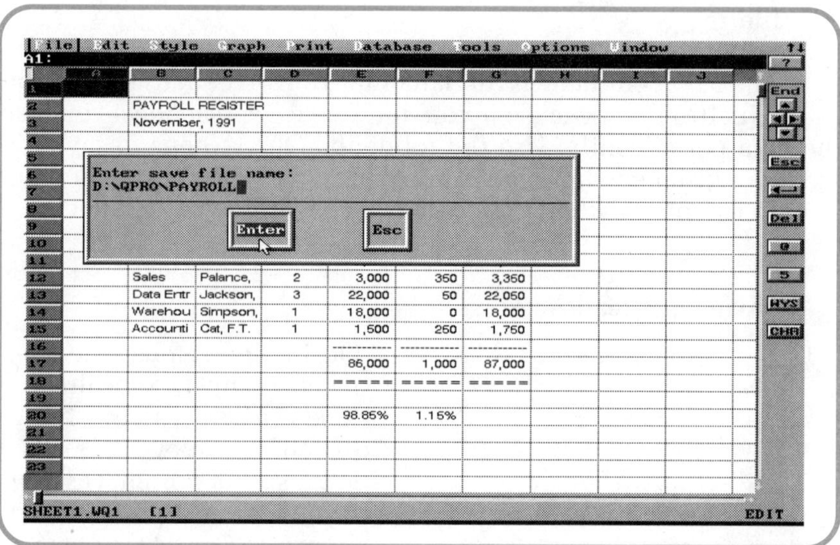

Figure 3.12 Saving the payroll register in a spreadsheet file named PAYROLL.WQ1.

Quattro Pro automatically adds the .WQ1 filename extension to your spreadsheet files. When you save a file, you only need to supply a name that is eight characters or less in length.

See Chapter 10 for further information about managing Quattro Pro spreadsheet files and windows.

Learning Cell Management Basics

The commands on the /**E**dit menu make it much easier to build spreadsheet applications. Press /E now to pull down the /**E**dit menu. In the next several sections you'll learn how to use the first six commands on this menu: **C**opy, **M**ove, **E**rase Block, **U**ndo, **I**nsert, and **D**elete.

Copying and Moving the Contents of a Cell

The **C**opy and **M**ove commands let you build applications in the most efficient manner possible. Think back to the example where the payroll register spreadsheet was converted into a checking account register. This feat was accomplished by editing a few labels and adding new formulas. It'd be great if you could build all of your applications this way, but that's just not possible. When data requires a special and unique presentation, you'll have to create the spreadsheet application from the ground up.

Look at the partially completed income statement spreadsheet in Figure 3.13 (this report was built around the date serial number example from Figure 3.11). For the most part, all income statements resemble the one shown in this figure. Note how this spreadsheet report has a unique layout, one that can not easily be converted, say, from our payroll register spreadsheet.

Now enter this application into a Quattro Pro spreadsheet so that you can follow along with the next few examples. If necessary, refer back to previous Quick Steps that show how to enter labels, numbers, formulas, and dates. The formulas in cells E14 and F14 add the data in cells E9 through E12. The formulas in cells E16 and F16 subtract the values stored in cells E14 and F14 from those stored in E6 and F6 (that is, the formulas are +E6–E14 and +F6–F14).

Now let's learn how to use the **C**opy command to complete this spreadsheet. Use the following Quick Steps to copy data on a spreadsheet.

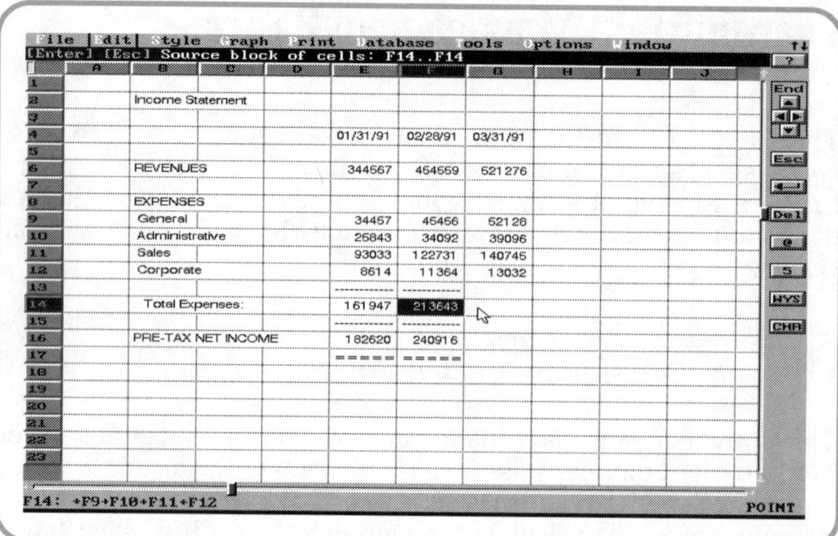

Figure 3.13 Creating a basic financial reporting application.

Copying Data from One Cell to Another

1. Place the cell selector in cell F14.

   The READY mode indicator shows on the status line. The contents of the active cell display on the input line.

2. Press /EC to select the /Edit Copy command.

   Quattro Pro prompts you to enter the source block of cells (see Figure 3.14).

3. Press Enter once to accept the active cell as the source cell.

   Quattro Pro prompts you to enter the destination block of cells.

4. Enter cell G14.

5. Press Enter to complete the copy operation.

   Quattro Pro copies the data from the source cell to the destination cell.

> ▶ **Tip:** When you execute a command that prompts you to enter data on the input line (as in the Copy operation shown in Figure 3.14), Quattro Pro displays the contents of the active cell on the status line at the bottom of the spreadsheet. This way, you can always be sure that you are performing the operation on the correct cell.

Look at your screen and notice that the copied value displayed in cell G14 is different than the one displayed in cell F14. What gives, you ask? Well, when you copy a formula, Quattro Pro adjusts the cell addresses in the copied formula so that they refer to the data in column G. To see this place your cell selector in cell G14 and review its contents on the input line at the top of the screen—it should display the formula +G9+G10+G11+G12.

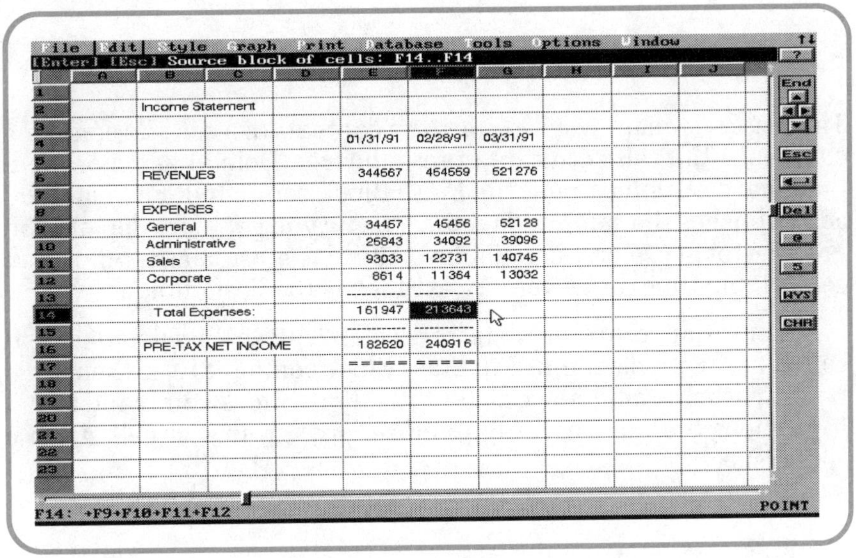

Figure 3.14 Copying data from one cell to another on the same spreadsheet.

The important thing to remember here is that you can copy formulas just as easily as you copy labels, values, and date and time serial numbers. In fact, when you do copy a label, value or date serial number, Quattro Pro creates an exact duplicate of the source cell data and places it in the destination cell. Now can you see how valuable the **C**opy command can be for building spreadsheets? Use the same procedure to copy the data in cells F13, F15, F16, and F17 into cells G13, G15, G16, and G17.

Moving spreadsheet data is very much like copying it—with one important difference. When you use the /**E**dit **M**ove command, Quattro Pro physically moves the data elsewhere—it does not create a copy of it. For example, after moving data from cell B1 to B5, cell B1 is blank and cell B5 contains the data that originally was stored in cell B1. Try this command out on the income statement now to see how it works. Be sure to move all of the data back to its original location before proceeding.

Erasing the Contents of a Cell

There are two main ways to erase the contents of a cell. To erase one cell, make the cell active and press the Del (Delete) key. For more than one cell, you can use the **E**rase Block command. Each method accomplishes the same end result, so how you get there depends on your personal preference. When you need to erase a large number of cells at one time, however, **E**rase Block is the best choice.

For instance, to erase data from cell B2, place the selector in that cell, type /EE to select the /**E**dit **E**rase Block command and then press Enter. The main advantage of using the **E**rase Block command is that it provides the quickest way to erase large groups of cells from a spreadsheet.

Inserting and Deleting Rows and Columns

Like the **C**opy and **M**ove commands, the /**E**dit **I**nsert command is a time-saving resource for building spreadsheets. Using this command, you can insert blank rows and columns anywhere on a spreadsheet. Imagine that you need to add an extra expense category to the income statement spreadsheet. Instead of retyping the entire application, insert a row at the location where you wish to enter the new expense category.

For instance, Figure 3.15 illustrates where to place the cell selector if you want to insert a blank row between the Administrative and Sales expense categories. Now select /**E**dit **I**nsert. Quattro Pro displays a menu with two choices: **R**ows and **C**olumns. Press Enter twice (or click on the `Rows` option with your mouse, and then the Enter icon) to insert a row.

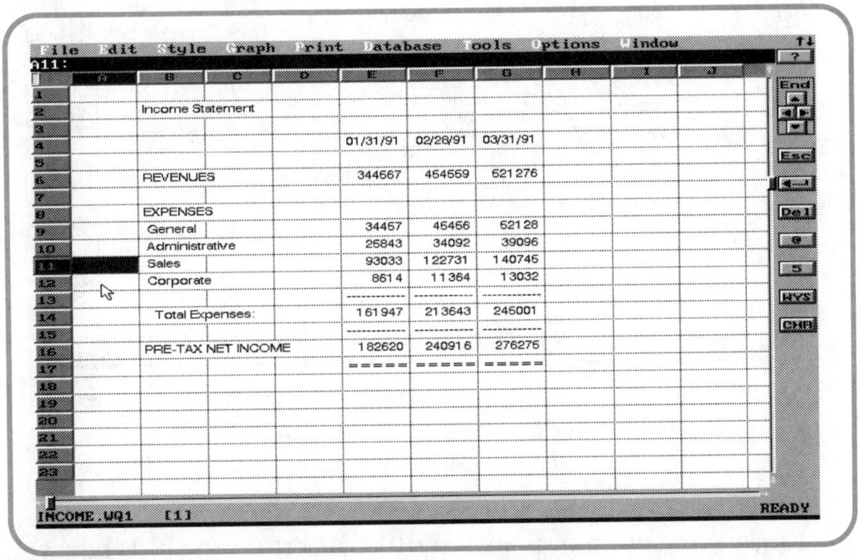

Figure 3.15 Inserting a row on the income statement spreadsheet.

Now enter the label `Warehouse` in cell B11, and the values `46517`, `61365`, and `70372` into cells E11, F11, and G11 respectively. There's one additional thing that you must do to complete the spreadsheet. Place your cell selector in cell G15. Notice that the formula in this cell (+G9+G10+G12+G13) does not reference row 11 anymore. That's because when you inserted a blank row, old row 11 became new row 12 and old row 12 became new row 13, so Quattro Pro changed the cell address in the formula to reflect this. Quattro Pro automatically adjusts your formulas when you insert rows and columns.

When you add new data on an inserted row (such as on row 11) you must also add the new cell address to your formula. For example, you must edit the formulas in cells E15, F15, and G15 so that they contain references to the Warehouse expense data on row 12.

There are two ways to edit formulas. One, you can retype new formulas into those cells or, two, you can edit the formula so it reflects the new cell address. You'll learn how to edit spreadsheet cell data in the upcoming section so look ahead now if you wish, otherwise, just retype the formulas in all three cells. When you're finished, your screen should look like the one shown in Figure 3.16.

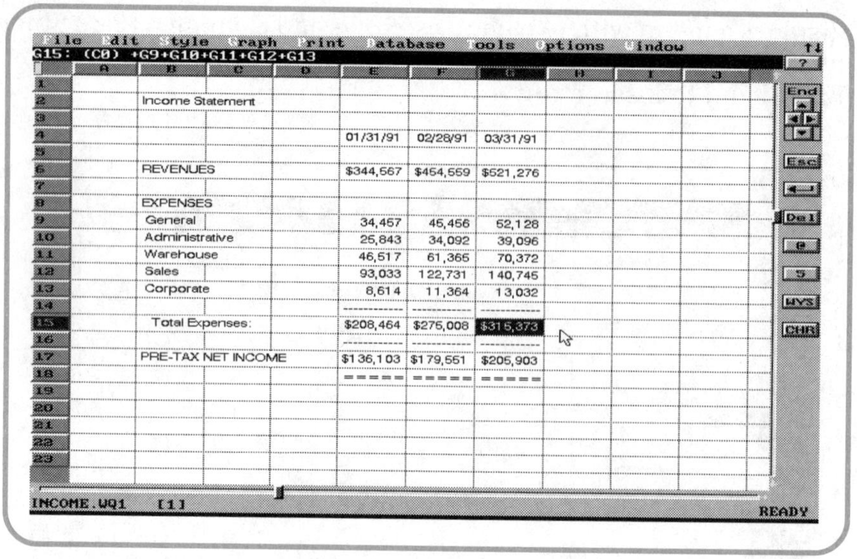

Figure 3.16 Sometimes you must edit formulas when you insert or delete rows and columns.

Inserting columns is exactly like inserting rows. When you insert a column, all of the data on the spreadsheet is pushed one column to the right of the column in which the cell selector is located.

The /**E**dit **D**elete command removes columns and rows from a spreadsheet at the location of the cell selector. For instance, to delete row 1 (even though it's blank on our income statement spreadsheet), place the cell selector anywhere on row 1 and select the /**E**dit **D**elete **R**ows command. Quattro Pro removes the blank row, which causes the entire spreadsheet to shift up one row. When you delete a column all of the data to the right of the cell selector shifts left one column.

> **Caution:** Be extremely careful when you delete spreadsheet rows and columns. If you delete a row or column that contains a formula, that formula and its result are lost. If you delete a value whose cell address is used in a formula, Quattro Pro can no longer reference that value (although the cell address remains in the formula) so it displays ERR as the formula result. Chapter 6 discusses how to deal with ERR formula results.

If you accidentally delete a row or column that you need, press Alt-F5, the Undo key, and Quattro Pro will reinstate the row or column. When you first install Quattro Pro, the Undo key is disabled. To enable it, press /OOUE to select the /**O**ptions **O**ther **U**ndo **E**nable command. To save this setting for future work sessions, select the /**O**ptions **U**pdate command.

Look back at Figure 3.16. You probably noticed that the values in this spreadsheet have been formatted to display commas and dollar signs. Before saving this spreadsheet, use the /**S**tyle **N**umeric Format command and format your version of the sample spreadsheet. (Hint: rows 6, 15, and 17 are formatted with the Currency option, and rows 9 through 13 are formatted using the , (comma) option.)

The income statement spreadsheet is now finished, so use the /**F**ile **S**ave command and assign the name INCOME.WQ1 (remember, Quattro Pro automatically adds the .WQ1 extension to the file name). You'll see this spreadsheet again in later chapters.

Editing Cell Data

Editing cell data is an important and necessary part of building a spreadsheet application. You can edit data as you type it on the input line, and after you type it into a spreadsheet cell. To edit data stored in a cell, press F2, the Edit key. This action places Quattro Pro in EDIT mode and displays the contents of the active cell on the input line at the top of the screen. While in EDIT mode, you may use any of the following keys to edit data on the input line:

Backspace deletes from right to left, one character at a time. Press *Ctrl-Backspace* to erase everything on the input line.

Ctrl- deletes everything to the right of the cursor on the input line.

Del deletes the character that the cursor is on.

End moves the cursor to the last character on the input line.

Enter transfers data from the input line into the active cell. Press Enter to exit EDIT mode and reenter READY mode.

Esc erases everything on the input line the first time that you press it. Press Esc again to cancel EDIT mode and return to READY mode.

F2, the Edit key, enters EDIT mode and displays the contents of the active cell on the input line.

Home relocates the cursor to the first character on the input line.

Press the *Insert* key to toggle between insert and overwrite modes. In OVERWRITE mode, you can type over existing data on the input line; Quattro Pro displays OVR on the status line. In INSERT mode, Quattro Pro pushes all existing text to the right of the edit cursor as you type.

Pg Dn and *Pg Up* enter data into the active cell, exit EDIT mode, reenter READY mode, and then move the cursor one full screen in the appropriate direction.

Shift-Tab and *Ctrl-←* move the cursor five characters to left on the input line.

Tab and *Ctrl-→* move the cursor five characters to the right on the input line.

Arrow keys enter data into the active cell, exit EDIT mode, reenter READY mode, and then move the cursor one cell in the selected direction.

Editing cell data with a mouse is simple. Click the mouse pointer on the cell you wish to edit, then click once on the input line. Quattro Pro displays the cell data on the input line.

When you finish editing the data in a cell, press Enter or click the Enter box on the input line with your mouse to record the changes. Quattro Pro has a built-in protection mechanism that lets you recall the most recent changes made to a cell, or reverse the most recent menu command execution. When you need to undo an operation, press Alt-F5, the Undo Key.

Viewing Your Spreadsheet Data

Once you've entered data into a spreadsheet and edited it to your satisfaction, it's time to view the data. The /**W**indow and /**O**ptions menus contain several commands that let you control how Quattro Pro displays your spreadsheets. Using these commands, you can split a spreadsheet into two vertical panes or two horizontal panes, show all open spreadsheets on-screen simultaneously, or change the Quattro Pro display mode. The last section in this chapter teaches you different methods for viewing your spreadsheet data.

The Basic Spreadsheet Window

Quattro Pro's screen display default setting is one full-screen window. As you've seen in previous figures in this chapter, one window is big enough to display a small spreadsheet that has ten columns and 23 rows. (The number or rows and columns you can see varies depending upon your graphics display system.) Except for the simplest applications, though, you'll want to use the rest of the spreadsheet, which exists to the right of and below what you can see in one full-screen window.

Horizontal and Vertical Split-Screen Viewing

As your spreadsheets grow in size, you'll find it useful to use the /**W**indow **O**ptions **H**orizontal (or **V**ertical) commands to split a window into two vertical or two horizontal panes. These commands allow you to simultaneously work with noncontiguous parts of the same spreadsheet. To split a window, place the cell selector in the location where you wish to split and choose either command. To "unsplit" a window, choose the /**W**indow **O**ptions **C**lear command.

As a rule you should split applications that contain more rows than columns horizontally (see Figure 3.17), and split applications that contain more columns than rows vertically (see Figure 3.18).

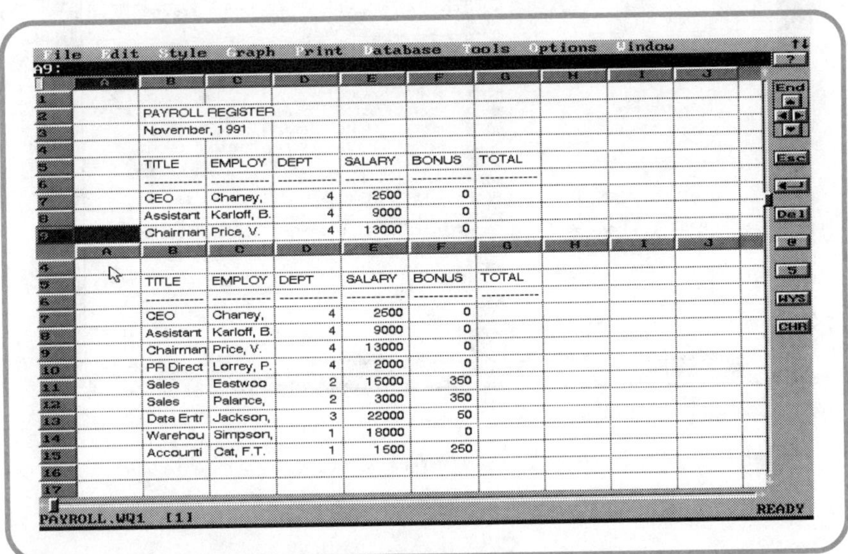

Figure 3.17 Splitting a window into two horizontal panes.

When you split windows in this manner, you can arrange each window pane simultaneously, because cell selector movement on one pane will not affect the other. Place your cell selector in the top pane shown in Figure 3.17 and press Pg Dn. Notice that both panes scroll down one screen. If you don't want actions in one pane to affect both panes, you must unsynchronize the window panes using the Unsync/**W**indow **O**ptions **U**nsync command.

> **Tip:** Press F6, the Pane key, to move back and forth between window panes. With a mouse, just point anywhere inside a pane and click once to activate that pane.

Changing the Screen Display Mode

Another way to change the basic on-screen look of your spreadsheets is to select a new display mode. To do this, select the /**O**ptions **D**isplay Mode command (see Figure 3.19).

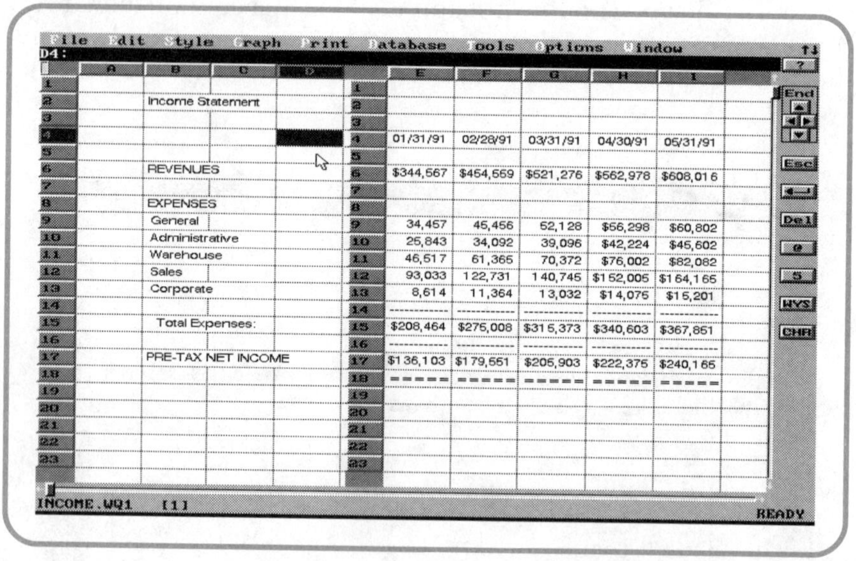

Figure 3.18 Splitting a window into two vertical panes.

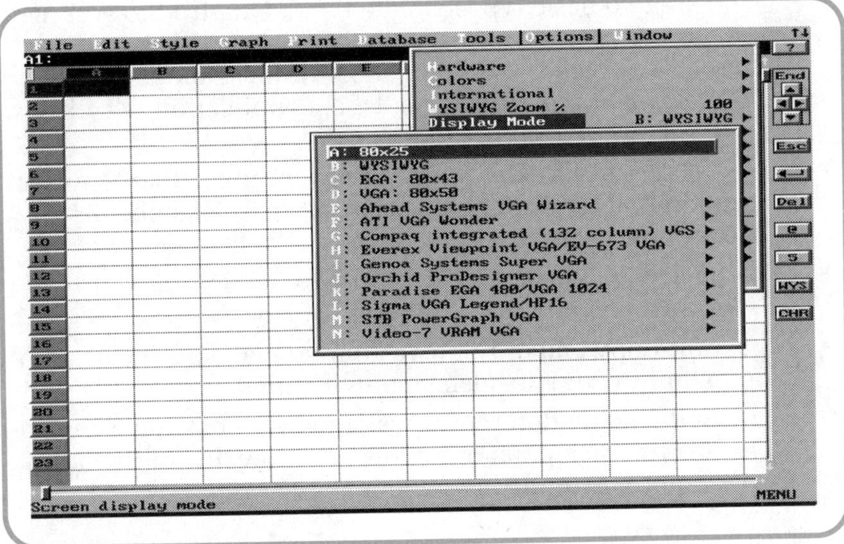

Figure 3.19 Selecting a new display mode.

Highlight the display mode you wish to use and press Enter. Quattro Pro immediately resets your screen display mode. In some cases, the display modes shown in Figure 3.19 will not work on your screen. For instance, the **F**: ATI VGA Wonder mode only works if you have an ATI-compatible graphics card. If you don't have this card, you may have difficulty reading your screen display. If this happens, press Enter twice to reselect the **D**isplay Mode command, then select the **A**: 80x25 display mode (this setting works for all display systems).

> **Tip:** Remember, you can also click the WYS and CHR buttons on the mouse palette to toggle between the WYSIWYG and 80x25 text display modes.

What You've Learned

This chapter has covered most of the basics that you need to know when you're ready to enter, edit, view, and save data on a Quattro Pro spreadsheet. In short, you now should be familiar with the following:

- There are two basic types of data that a Quattro Pro spreadsheet can store in its cells: values and labels. *Labels* are letters, while *values* are numbers, formulas, and dates and times. When you build a spreadsheet application, it's likely that you'll use both types of data.
- Quattro Pro stores dates and times as numbers that represent the amount of days that have passed since December 31, 1899.
- You have a wide variety of keystroke selections at your disposal when you are editing a spreadsheet.
- The /**E**dit **C**opy and /**E**dit **M**ove commands make it easier for you to build your spreadsheet applications.
- Among the many different ways of viewing data on a spreadsheet, the most popular are in one window, in split window panes, and in extended text mode.

Chapter 4

Working with Blocks of Cell Data

In This Chapter

- *Learning basics about cell blocks*
- *Learning POINT mode basics*
- *Executing menu commands on blocks of cells*
- *Copying, moving, and erasing cell blocks*
- *Creating cell block names to use in formulas*

Using *cell blocks* greatly simplifies spreadsheet application-building. Cell blocks are powerful tools because they let you streamline Quattro Pro operations that otherwise would require many steps. When you work with cell blocks, you are working with many spreadsheet cells at one time.

This chapter teaches you how to execute commands on cell blocks, work in POINT mode, and assign names to cell blocks. Cell blocks and cell block names make copying, moving, and erasing large groups of spreadsheet data a breeze.

What Is a Cell Block?

A *cell block* is a contiguous group of cells. As the word "contiguous" implies, the cell block is solid—there can be no gaps inside a Quattro Pro cell block. You already know that a cell address describes the intersection of a column and a row. For example, the address of the cell in the upper left corner of a Quattro Pro spreadsheet is A1. The address of a cell block is expressed in terms of *coordinates*. In Quattro Pro, *cell block coordinates* consist of two cell addresses separated by two periods. Cell block coordinates G7..G10 describe all of the cells between cell address G7 and cell address G10.

In larger cell blocks (more than one row and column) the two coordinates refer to the cell in the upper left corner of the block, and the cell in the lower right corner of the block. Cell block D1..F10 includes cells D1 through D10, E1 through E10, and F1 through F10.

Figure 4.1 shows examples of several valid Quattro Pro cell blocks. (For illustration purposes, Figure 4.1 shows several cell blocks. Quattro Pro only permits you to highlight one cell block at a time.)

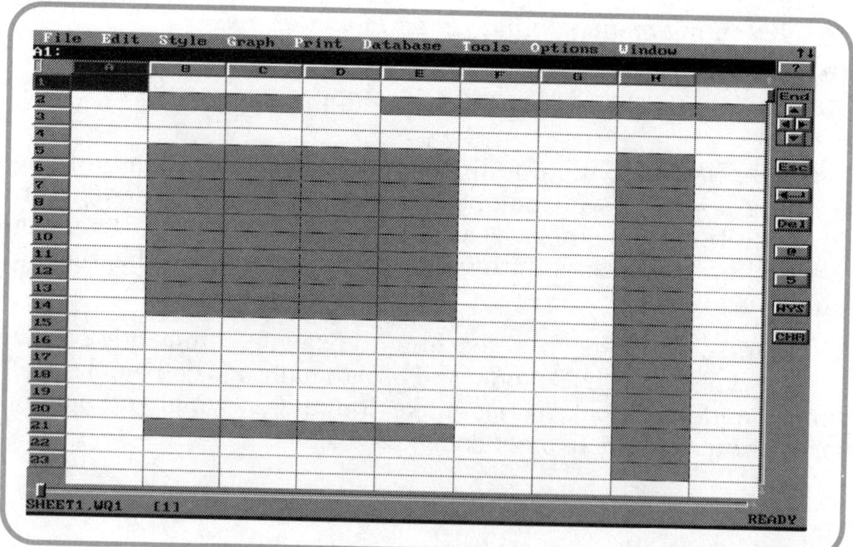

Figure 4.1 Valid cell blocks come in many shapes and sizes.

Cell Block Basics

Cell blocks consist of cells on a single spreadsheet. You can also associate cell blocks from two or more spreadsheets using special linking formulas (Chapter 10 discusses linking formulas). However, the real power of cell blocks comes into play when you use menu commands. You can simplify most Quattro Pro tasks that affect many individual cells by organizing the cells into cell blocks. Take the /**E**dit **C**opy command, for example. To copy data stored in 10 adjacent cells, you could perform 10 individual /**E**dit **C**opy operations. But doesn't it sound more efficient to reproduce all 10 cells at once by copying a cell block that contains all 10 cells?

As Figure 4.1 illustrates, Quattro Pro cell blocks come in many shapes and sizes. The shapes and sizes of the cell blocks you create depend entirely on how you need to work with your spreadsheet data. For example, Figure 4.2 shows the payroll register spreadsheet (PAYROLL.WQ1) from Chapter 3.

> **Note:** The spreadsheet in Figure 4.2 looks slightly different from the one on-screen. The reason is that the column widths have been altered so that you can clearly read the employees' names and titles.

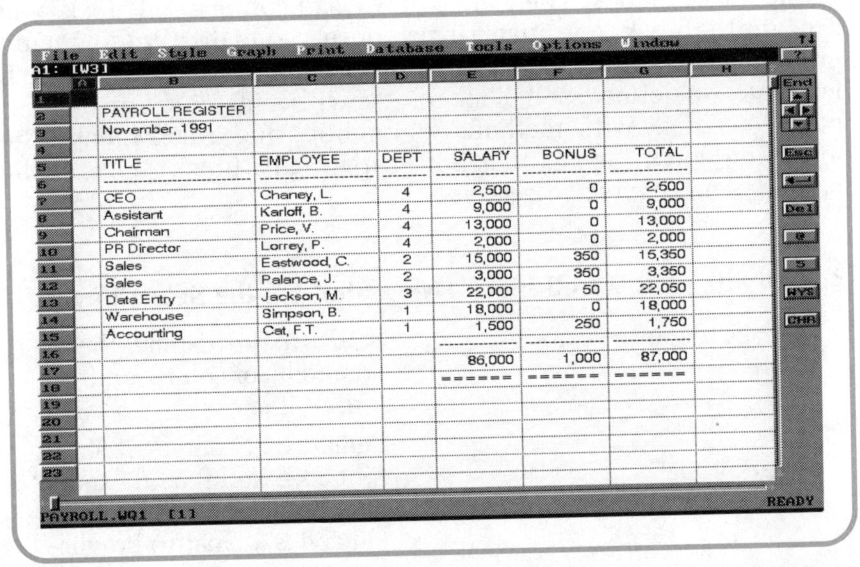
File Edit Style Graph Print Database Tools Options Window
A1: [W3]
PAYROLL REGISTER
November, 1991
TITLE EMPLOYEE DEPT SALARY BONUS TOTAL
CEO Chaney, L. 4 2,500 0 2,500
Assistant Karloff, B. 4 9,000 0 9,000
Chairman Price, V. 4 13,000 0 13,000
PR Director Lorrey, P. 4 2,000 0 2,000
Sales Eastwood, C. 2 15,000 350 15,350
Sales Palance, J. 2 3,000 350 3,350
Data Entry Jackson, M. 3 22,000 50 22,050
Warehouse Simpson, B. 1 18,000 0 18,000
Accounting Cat, F.T. 1 1,500 250 1,750
86,000 1,000 87,000
PAYROLL.WQ1 [1]
READY

Figure 4.2 The payroll register application revisited.

In this application, employee titles appear in column B, names, department numbers, and payroll register values appear in columns C through G. Suppose that you wish to copy a list of the employee names (stored in cells C7 through C15) elsewhere on the spreadsheet. In this case, you'd work with a cell block that is tall and narrow, because the original cell block spans several rows and only a single column. On the other hand, if you want to copy payroll register data for the first three employees (in cells B7 through G9), you'd work with a cell block that is short and wide (a few rows and many columns).

You'll find that there are many ways to use cell blocks in your work sessions. For instance, suppose you want to add the values in cells G7 through G10 of the payroll spreadsheet. You can either create a formula like *+G7+G8+G9+G10*, or create a formula that uses cell blocks. Quattro Pro's built-in formulas (called *@function commands*) do just that. To add the values in cell block G7..G10, you could create a formula that looks like *@SUM(G7..G10)*. See Chapter 6 for more information about Quattro Pro's @functions.

As you read through the material in this chapter, practice the Quick Steps on your payroll register spreadsheet file.

Highlighting a Cell Block

You now know what cell blocks are and how they can be useful. Before Quattro Pro can use a cell block in a spreadsheet operation, you must define the cell block. There are two ways to define a cell block. You can type the block coordinates in response to a Quattro Pro command prompt, or you can *highlight* the cell block. Later in this chapter, you'll learn how to define a cell block for use with a menu command. For now, let's stick with methods for highlighting a cell block. The following Quick Steps explain how to highlight a block of cells on the payroll register spreadsheet.

Q Highlighting a Cell Block Using Shift-F7, the Select Key

1. Place the cell selector in cell B7.	Quattro Pro displays the contents of cell B7 on the input line.
2. Hold down the Shift key and press F7.	Quattro Pro enters EXT (block extend) mode and anchors the block beginning at cell B7. Quattro Pro displays EXT on the status line.

3. Press the → key five times.

Quattro Pro extends the highlighted cell block to include cells C7 through G7.

4. Press the ↓ key eight times.

Quattro Pro extends the highlighted cell block to include cells B8 through G15 (see Figure 4.3). □

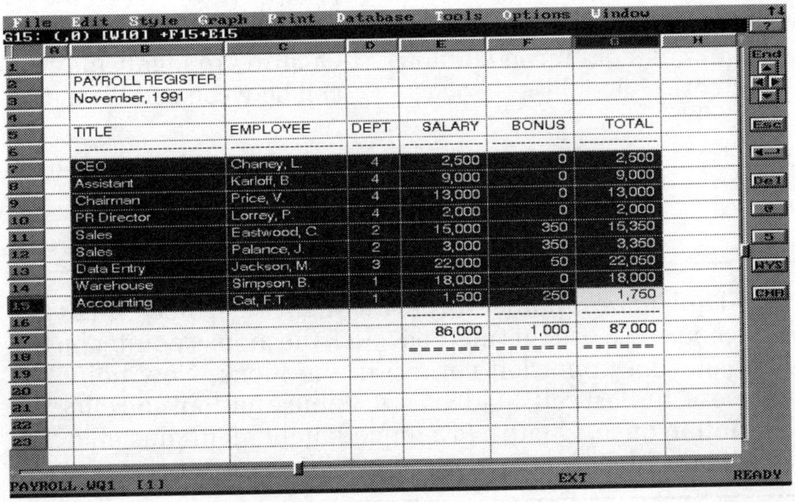

Figure 4.3 Highlighting cell block B7..G15 on the payroll register spreadsheet.

Once you highlight a cell block, you can work with it as a single unit, just as you work with a single cell. For instance, if you press Del, Quattro Pro erases all of the data in the highlighted cell block. (Do this now if you are following along with your copy of the payroll register spreadsheet. Then press Alt-F5 to undo the operation.) When you highlight a cell block prior to executing certain menu commands, Quattro Pro uses the cell block as the source block. If you perform the preceding Quick Steps and then select /**E**dit **C**opy, Quattro Pro assumes that you wish to copy cell block B7..G15. To complete this copy operation, you could type in the destination block and press Enter.

Go ahead and turn off block extend mode by pressing Shift-F7 once more. When you do this, Quattro Pro removes the EXT mode indicator from the status line. Cell block B7..G15 remains highlighted in case you decide to perform some other cell block operation.

It's quite easy to highlight a cell block using the mouse. Run through the following Quick Steps to learn how to use the mouse to highlight cell block B7..G15.

Highlighting a Cell Block with the Mouse

1. Place the mouse pointer on cell B7 and click the left button once.

   Quattro Pro moves the cell selector to cell B7 and displays its contents on the input line.

2. Click and hold the left button, and drag the mouse pointer to cell G15.

   Quattro Pro highlights each cell between cell B7 and G15.

3. Release the left mouse button.

   Cells in B7..G15 are defined as a cell block. □

> **Tip:** There's another way to highlight a cell block with your mouse. To use this method, click the mouse pointer on the first cell (the upper left corner) in the block. Now point the mouse on the last cell, hold the right mouse button, and click the left button once. Quattro Pro immediately highlights all of the cells in the block between the two cells.

Saving Keystrokes with the End Key

By now, you may be asking yourself, "Isn't there a faster way to highlight a large block of cells when you don't own a mouse?" Yes, there is. You can use the End key on the numeric keypad and the Arrow (cursor movement) keys to quickly highlight a cell block. But before we examine this process, let's review how to use the End key to control the movement of the cell selector on a Quattro Pro spreadsheet. All Quattro Pro users can find this technique useful, mouse or no mouse.

When you press the End key, Quattro Pro displays END on the status line at the bottom of your spreadsheet. While in END mode, press an Arrow key to quickly move the cell selector to the next non-empty cell in the arrow direction. The Quick Steps below illustrate how to use the End key to quickly move around the payroll register spreadsheet pictured in Figure 4.3.

Moving Around a Spreadsheet Using the End Key

1. Place the cell selector in cell B5. — Quattro Pro displays the contents of cell B5 on the input line.
2. Press End-↓ once. — Quattro Pro enters END mode and moves the cell selector to cell B15.
3. Press End-→ once. — Quattro Pro enters END mode and moves the cell selector to cell G15.
4. Press End-↑ twice. — Quattro Pro enters END mode, moves the cell selector to cell G5, and then to cell G1.
5. Press End-← once. — Quattro Pro enters END mode and moves the cell selector to cell A1. □

Pressing End-→ with the cell selector in an empty row moves the cell selector to the last cell on that row. (Press End-← now if you are following along with your copy of the payroll register spreadsheet, and Quattro Pro moves the cell selector to cell IV1.) Pressing End-↓ while the cell selector is in an empty column moves the cell selector to the last cell in that column. (Again, do this if you're following along, and Quattro Pro moves the cell selector to cell IV8192.)

Pressing Home from anywhere on the spreadsheet moves the cell selector to cell A1. Cell A1 is also known as the *home position* on a spreadsheet. Pressing End-Home from anywhere on the spreadsheet moves the cell selector to the last cell on the spreadsheet that contains data (for example, cell G18 in Figure 4.3).

You now know how to highlight a cell block by pressing Shift-F7 and how to move around a spreadsheet using the End key. When you use these techniques together, you can quickly highlight any portion of a spreadsheet that contains data. Think about the steps that you'd have to take to highlight cell block B5..G18 in preparation for a **C**opy operation. Starting with the cell selector in cell B5, you would use the following procedure:

1. Press Shift-F7 to enter EXT mode.
2. Press the → key five times to highlight B5..G5.
3. Press the ↓ key 13 times to highlight B5..G18.

In all, it takes 20 individual keystrokes to complete those steps. Now simplify this procedure using the End key. Starting with the cell selector in cell B5, you would complete the following steps:

1. Press Shift-F7 to enter EXT mode.
2. Press End-→ once to highlight B5..G7.
3. Press End-↓ once to highlight B5..G18.

The second method of defining a cell block requires only six keystrokes—a savings of 14 keystrokes! Now that may not sound like a big deal, but as you build larger spreadsheet applications, you'll come to appreciate every opportunity to save keystrokes. In fact, it's not unrealistic to project that you'll save yourself hundreds of keystrokes per work session by using End plus the Arrow keys. In the long run, your time is better spent analyzing your spreadsheet applications—not building them.

POINT Mode Basics

Every mouse owner is intimately familiar with the concept of *pointing*. You use a mouse to point to spreadsheet data that you wish to work with. All of the methods described so far in this chapter use pointing techniques to accomplish Quattro Pro tasks. For example, highlighting a cell block (with or without a mouse) is one way to point. Moving around a spreadsheet with the End key is another pointing technique.

In Quattro Pro, the term "pointing" takes on a special meaning when discussed in the context of a POINT mode operation. In a POINT mode operation, you use the cell selector to help you build formulas, execute menu commands, and more. Let's see how this works.

Move to a blank cell on a spreadsheet and type the + symbol. Quattro Pro enters VALUE mode. Now press the ↑ key once. Two things happen. First, the status line displays the POINT mode indicator. Second, Quattro Pro writes the cell address of the current cell next to the plus symbol on the input line. Now type a second + symbol and press the → once. This time, Quattro Pro does several things. First, the moment that you type the + symbol, Quattro Pro re-enters VALUE mode and returns the cell selector to the formula cell. Second, when you press the →, Quattro Pro re-enters POINT mode and displays the cell address of the current cell next to the second plus symbol on the input line. Press Enter to record the formula.

That's one way to build a formula in POINT mode. Let's look at another. Suppose that you wish to create a formula that totals the values in cell block G7..G15, and you want to enter this formula into cell G17 on the payroll register spreadsheet. The following Quick Steps show you how to enter the formula using POINT mode.

Building a Formula While in POINT Mode

1. Place the cell selector in cell G17. — Quattro Pro displays the contents of cell G17 on the input line.
2. Type @SUM(— The formula appears on the input line as you type, and the status line displays VALUE.
3. Press ↑ 10 times to move the cell selector to cell G7 (or press End-↑ and then ↓ twice). — The mode indicator changes to POINT. The formula on the input line now displays G7 next to the open parenthesis (see Figure 4.4).
4. Press the period key (.) to anchor cell G7 as the first coordinate in the formula. — Two periods and a second G7 cell address appear after the first cell address.
5. Press ↓ eight times to move the cell selector to cell G15 (or press End-↓ and then ↑ three times). — Quattro Pro highlights the cell block, and displays G15 as the second coordinate on input line (see Figure 4.5).
6. Type a) to complete the formula. — The cell selector jumps back to cell G17, the formula cell.
7. Press Enter to store the formula in cell G17. — Quattro Pro displays a formula result in cell G17. □

Sometimes while building a formula, you'll type a period (.) to anchor a cell coordinate—but it's not the cell you want. Just press Esc to remove the current cell address from the formula. Then move the cell selector to the correct cell and press the period key again.

Building a formula by pointing is much easier with a mouse. After typing @SUM(on the input line, place the mouse pointer on cell G7. Click and hold the left mouse button while dragging the mouse pointer to cell G15. Release the mouse button, and Quattro Pro stores the correct cell block coordinates next to the formula. Type the closing parenthesis and press Enter to store the formula in cell G17.

Applying Cell Block and POINT Mode Basics

In Chapter 3 you learned how to execute Quattro Pro commands on individual spreadsheet cells. Easy, right? Now it's time to apply your new knowledge of cell blocks, the End key, and POINT mode operations. You can use all of these pointing methods with any Quattro Pro command that operates on cell blocks, such as /**E**dit **C**opy, /**E**dit **M**ove, and /**E**dit **E**rase Block. You'll produce the same results, only a *lot* faster!

Copying a Cell Block

You use the /**E**dit **C**opy command to copy a cell block on a Quattro Pro spreadsheet. Remember the rules and cautions offered about this command in Chapter 3. Specifically, avoid overwriting existing data by selecting an empty area on the spreadsheet to copy to. The following Quick Steps describe the procedure for copying a block of cells.

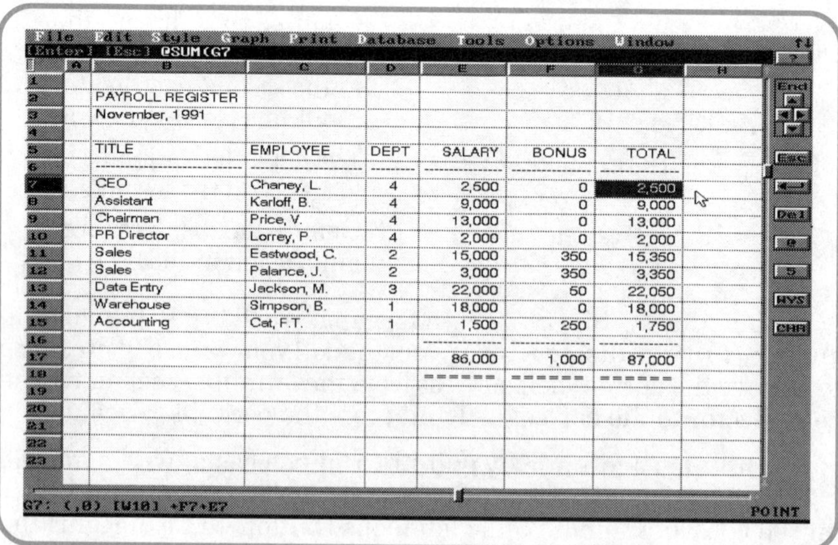

	A	B	C	D	E	F	G	H
1								
2		PAYROLL REGISTER						
3		November, 1991						
4								
5		TITLE	EMPLOYEE	DEPT	SALARY	BONUS	TOTAL	
6								
7		CEO	Chaney, L.	4	2,500	0	2,500	
8		Assistant	Karloff, B.	4	9,000	0	9,000	
9		Chairman	Price, V.	4	13,000	0	13,000	
10		PR Director	Lorrey, P.	4	2,000	0	2,000	
11		Sales	Eastwood, C.	2	15,000	350	15,350	
12		Sales	Palance, J.	2	3,000	350	3,350	
13		Data Entry	Jackson, M.	3	22,000	50	22,050	
14		Warehouse	Simpson, B.	1	18,000	0	18,000	
15		Accounting	Cat, F.T.	1	1,500	250	1,750	
16								
17					86,000	1,000	87,000	
18					======	======	======	

Figure 4.4 Entering an @function while in POINT mode.

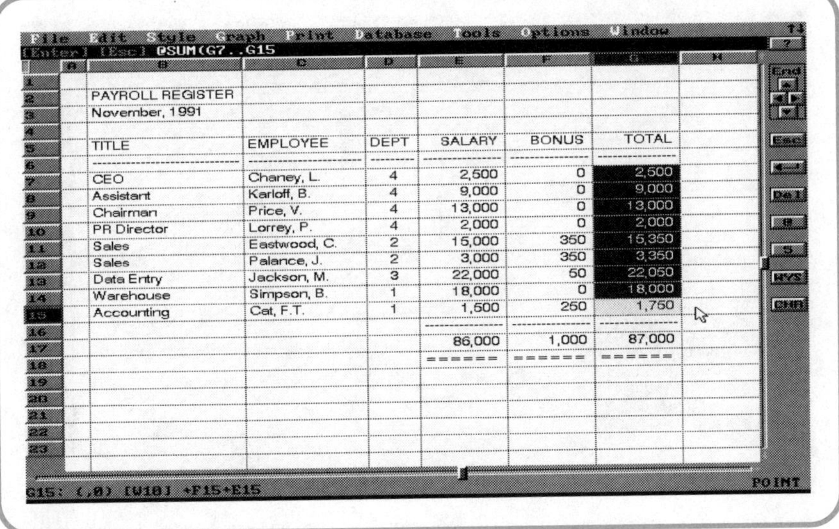

Figure 4.5 Writing the second cell block coordinate in a formula.

Q Copying a Cell Block

1. Highlight the block you want to copy with the keyboard or mouse. (I'll use B5..B15 on PAYROLL.WQ1.)

   Quattro Pro displays the contents of last cell in the block on the input line.

2. Press /EC to select the /Edit Copy command (or press Ctrl-C).

   Quattro Pro prompts you for the destination cell block. `POINT` appears on the status line.

3. Press ↓ twice to move to the cell B17, the first cell in the destination cell block.

   Quattro Pro displays the cell address on the input line.

4. Press . (period) to anchor the first cell.

   Quattro Pro writes two periods and B17 next to the first B17.

5. Press ↓ ten times to highlight block B17..B27.

   This step highlights the destination cell block (see Figure 4.6).

6. Press Enter to complete the copy operation.

   Quattro Pro copies the source lock to the destination block. □

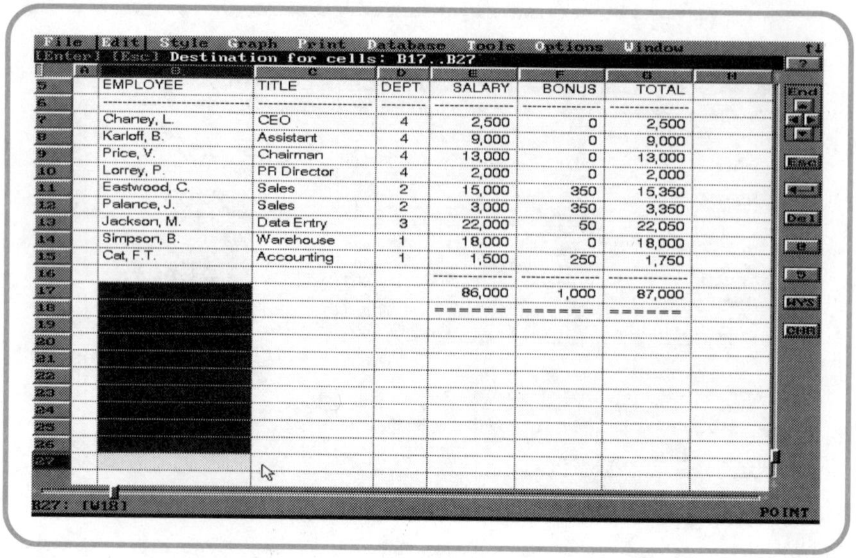

Figure 4.6 Highlighting the entire destination cell block in a copy operation.

> **Tip:** You don't have to highlight the entire destination cell block if it has the same shape as the source cell block. Instead, just supply the first coordinate in the destination block and press Enter. Quattro Pro creates a destination block that is exactly the same size as the source block, beginning at the location of the single destination coordinate.

Moving a Cell Block

After designing a spreadsheet application, you may decide that certain blocks of data would look better or make more sense in a different location on the worksheet. Suppose that you'd rather show the employee names column after the titles column on the payroll register spreadsheet. You've already created a copy of the employee names block, so all that's left to do is to relocate the titles block. (Relocating means either copying again or moving the cell block.) Let's move it. In fact, you can even overwrite cell block B5..B15 with cell block C5..C15 since you already have a copy of the employee names below. To conclude this exercise, you'll move the copied block back up to the area vacated by the titles block. Got all that? Good. Use the Quick Steps that follow to accomplish these objectives.

Overwriting an Existing Cell Block with /Edit Move

1. Highlight cell block C5..C15. — The input line displays the contents of cell C15.
2. Press /EM to select the /**E**dit **M**ove command (or press Ctrl-M). — Quattro Pro prompts you for the destination block and displays `POINT` on the status line.
3. Type `B5` (or point to B5) as the destination block. — The input line displays `B5`.
4. Press Enter to move the block. — Cell block C5..C15 overwrites cell block B5..B15, leaving a blank area in its original location (see Figure 4.7). The cursor moves back to the last cell in the vacated block. □

File Edit Style Graph Print Database Tools Options Window

C15: [W14]

	A	B	C	D	E	F	G	H
1								
2		PAYROLL REGISTER						
3		November, 1991						
4								
5		TITLE		DEPT	SALARY	BONUS	TOTAL	
6		------------------------		--------	------------	------------	------------	
7		CEO		4	2,500	0	2,500	
8		Assistant		4	9,000	0	9,000	
9		Chairman		4	13,000	0	13,000	
10		PR Director		4	2,000	0	2,000	
11		Sales		2	15,000	350	15,350	
12		Sales		2	3,000	350	3,350	
13		Data Entry		3	22,000	50	22,050	
14		Warehouse		1	18,000	0	18,000	
15		Accounting		1	1,500	250	1,750	
16					------------	------------	------------	
17		EMPLOYEE			86,000	1,000	87,000	
18		------------------------			======	======	======	
19		Chaney, L.						
20		Karloff, B.						
21		Price, V.						
22		Lorrey, P.						
23		Eastwood, C.						
		Palance, J.						

PAYROLL.WQ1 [1] READY

Figure 4.7 Reviewing the effect of overwriting one cell block with another.

All that remains is to move cell block B17..B27 into the cell block vacated by the previous move operation. Again, use the /**E**dit **M**ove command—if you use /**E**dit **C**opy, there will be an extra block left over on your spreadsheet. Once you've moved the cell block, your screen should look like the one shown in Figure 4.8.

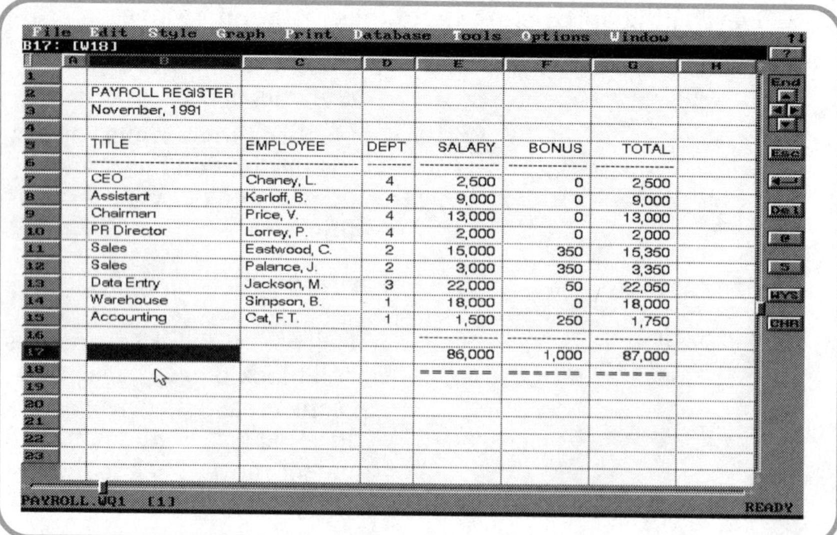

Figure 4.8 Moving the copied cell block into the space vacated by the previous move operation.

Erasing the Contents of a Cell Block

Erasing a cell block is the easiest cell block operation of all, because there's no need to specify a destination cell block. Once you erase a cell block, it's gone. To erase a block of cells, highlight the source cell block and select the /**E**dit **E**rase Block command or press Ctrl-E, the Ctrl-key shortcut for this command. Quattro Pro simply wipes the cell block clean of all labels and values.

> **Tip:** The quickest way to erase a block of cells is to highlight them and press the Del key. The highlighted cells instantly disappear!

Creating Names for Cell Blocks

Earlier in this chapter, you learned how to refer to a cell block using its cell coordinates. Using the /**E**dit **N**ames command, you can create names of up to 15 characters in length and assign them to any single spreadsheet cell or cell block. In Quattro Pro, block names simplify many operations. You can use a block name in place of coordinates whenever Quattro Pro prompts you for a cell address, a source block, or a destination block.

Block names are more efficient than cell block coordinates because it's much easier to remember a name like TOTAL than it is to remember coordinates like G7..G15. With block names, you can simplify a formula like @SUM(G7..G15) into @SUM(TOTAL). Or you can copy a block of labels named EMPLOYEE elsewhere on the spreadsheet. When you assign names to a cell block, create a name that describes the data in that block. On the payroll register spreadsheet, for example, you might assign the name DEPT to the cell block that contains the department numbers. Or you might assign the name BONUS to the cell block that contains the bonus values.

In short, whenever possible, create names using existing column and row titles. That way, you'll always remember what the name refers to. Abbreviate long names like DEPARTMENT to DEPT so that you won't have to retype long names into formulas and at command prompts—extra typing defeats the purpose of using names at all.

The following Quick Steps show how to create the name TOTAL for cell block G7..G15 on the payroll register spreadsheet. Once you complete this exercise, repeat the procedure and create names for cell blocks E7..E15 (SALARY) and F7..F15 (BONUS).

Q Creating a Name for a Cell Block

1. Highlight cell block G7..G15. — Quattro Pro displays the contents of G15 on the input line.
2. Press /ENC to select the /**E**dit **N**ames **C**reate command. — The **C**reate submenu appears on-screen.
3. Type TOTAL and press Enter. — Quattro Pro assigns the name TOTAL to cell block G7..G15 (see Figure 4.9). □

This approach to creating block names has an interesting side effect. Place the cell selector in cell G17. Notice that the word TOTAL appears in place of the cell block coordinates that you entered when creating the formula in that cell. Here's what happened. When you create a name for a block, Quattro Pro automatically replaces the cell block coordinates with the new block name in a spreadsheet formula. Press F2 and look at the contents of cell G17 on the input line. Quattro Pro now displays the original cell block coordinates. Press Enter to replace the formula in cell G17, and you'll see the name TOTAL reappear in the formula on the input line.

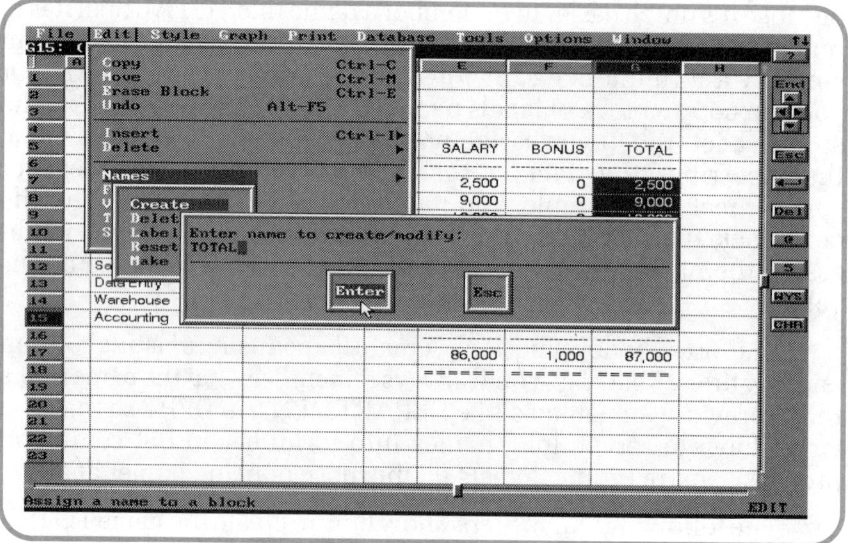

Figure 4.9 Assigning a name to a cell block.

You can enter data onto a spreadsheet and create block names for each data grouping. Then, as you build the formulas into the spreadsheet, type the block names in with the formulas.

> **Tip:** You can use the GoTo key to move the cell selector to the first cell in any named block. For example, to move to the first cell in TOTAL, press F5, type `TOTAL`, and press Enter. Quattro Pro moves the cell selector to cell G7.

Making a Block Name Table

Once you familiarize yourself with block names, you'll find yourself using them more and more. Choosing the /**E**dit **N**ames **M**ake Table command constructs a table of names and corresponding cell block assignments to help you manage your spreadsheet names. A block name table contains two columns of information. The first column contains each block name, and the second column contains the coordinates of the named block.

It's easy to reference a block name table when you need to verify the location of data, modify formulas, or delete rows and columns. Block name tables also help ensure that you don't accidentally create the same name for two different blocks. If you do this, Quattro Pro overwrites the original coordinates with new ones.

The following Quick Steps show how to make a table of block names on a spreadsheet.

Making a Table of Block Names

1. Locate an unused area of the spreadsheet (such as B19..C21 on the payroll spreadsheet).	You need two columns, one for the block name, another for its coordinates. You need as many rows as there are names.
2. Press /ENM to select the /Edit Names Make Table command.	Quattro Pro prompts you to enter a destination block for the names table.
3. Type the address of the first cell in the target block, and press Enter.	Quattro Pro copies the table into your spreadsheet (see Figure 4.10). □

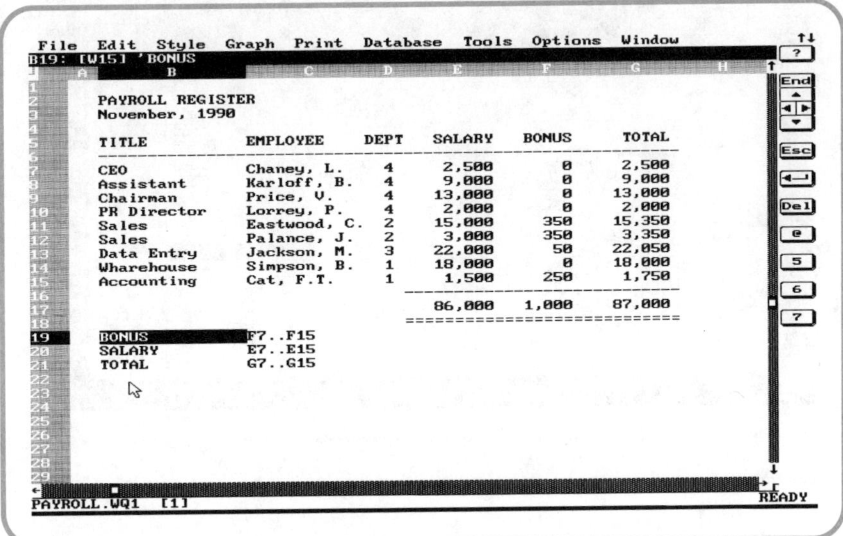

Figure 4.10 A block names table reveals the location of each assigned name on the current spreadsheet.

Quattro Pro does not automatically update a block name table when you modify a name or its cell block coordinates. You must create a new table to update a name. Specifically, be sure to make a new table whenever you add or delete names, or add or delete columns and rows.

Using the Choices Key To See Block Names

The Choices key (F3) displays a list of current block name assignments for you as you build or edit a spreadsheet formula. The Choices key is particularly useful when you're not sure about the exact spelling of a block name that you wish to include in a formula. To use the Choices key, place the edit cursor next to an open parenthesis, (, on the input line and press F3. Quattro Pro shows the list box pictured in Figure 4.11. Press the + key on the numeric keypad to reveal the cell block coordinates and the – key to remove them. When the Choices list is on-screen, press F3 once more to fill the entire screen with the list.

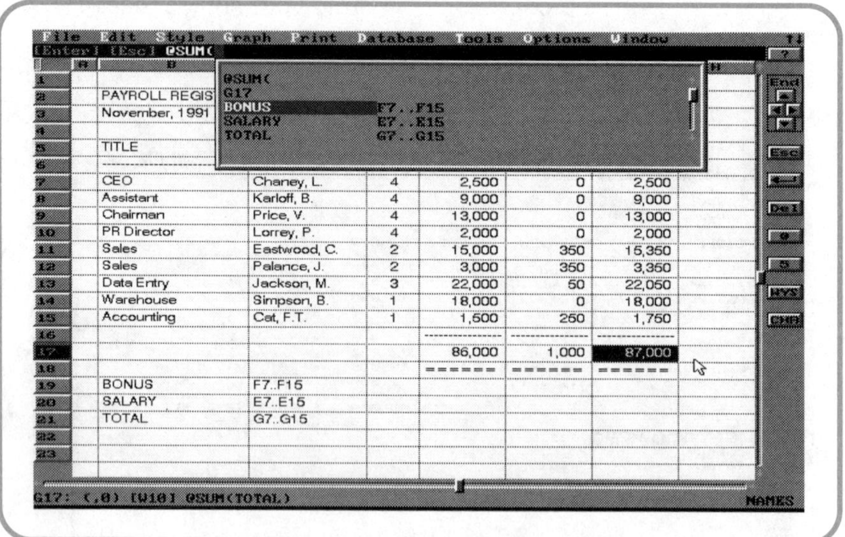

Figure 4.11 Viewing a block name table by pressing F3, the Choices key.

Deleting Cell Block Names

When you modify or update a spreadsheet, you may need to delete a stored block name. To do this, choose the /Edit **N**ames **D**elete command. Highlight the name you want to delete, or type the name at the prompt.

Deleting a block name has no effect on the cell block coordinates—it only removes the name connected to the coordinates. Likewise, deleting a cell block from a spreadsheet has no effect on the block name. When you delete a cell block, the block name remains on the block name table and will display on the Choices list. When you delete a block name, Quattro Pro redisplays the cell block coordinates in all formulas that use that name.

If you start naming cell blocks using one naming strategy, and then decide to use a different strategy, use the /Edit **N**ames **R**eset command. This command deletes all block name assignments for the current spreadsheet. Quattro Pro displays the prompt shown in Figure 4.12, asking if you wish to delete all named blocks. Press Y to do so, or press N to cancel the operation.

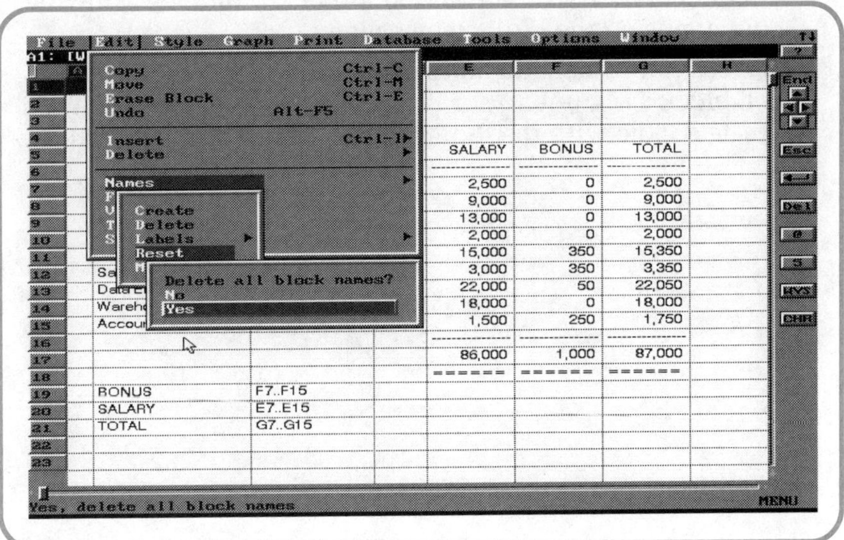

Figure 4.12 Deleting all of the block names from a spreadsheet.

What You've Learned

This chapter introduced you to a powerful and easy-to-use spreadsheet tool: the cell block. Now you are familiar with the following cell block basics.

- *Pointing* is a spreadsheet technique that is integral to using Quattro Pro. POINT mode operations help you specify cells you wish to use in formulas and command executions.
- You easily can modify a spreadsheet by *copying, moving*, and *erasing* cell blocks.
- Many Quattro Pro commands work more efficiently with blocks of cells than on single cells.
- Pressing Alt-F5, the Undo key, reverses the effects of copying, moving, and erasing cell blocks. Remember, to use the Undo feature you must first select /**O**ptions **O**ther **U**ndo **E**nable to turn it on.
- You create names for cell blocks to make them easier to remember, and easier to work with in formulas and command operations. Create and modify *block names* using the commands on the /**E**dit **N**ames menu.
- A *block name table* displays a list of block names and their cell block assignments for the current spreadsheet. You can create a table with the /**E**dit **N**ames **M**ake Table command.

Chapter 5

Printing Spreadsheets

In This Chapter

- ► *An overview of printing*
- ► *Defining the printer make, model, and mode*
- ► *Selecting different print destinations*
- ► *Using layout options to manage printouts*
- ► *Printing to fit*

This chapter introduces you to several methods for printing with Quattro Pro. After reading this chapter, you'll be able to preview a printout on-screen, produce printed copies of your spreadsheets and create special printer-ready (.PRN) files. Plus, you'll learn how to use layout options to enhance your printouts and control how Quattro Pro works with your printer.

An Overview of Printing

Printing is the process of transforming a spreadsheet or graph from a file on a disk into a tangible document that you can share with friends, colleagues, and business associates. Every software program has its own set of commands and procedures that you must follow to create a printout. In Quattro Pro, you use the /**P**rint menu commands to produce printouts that are organized, suitably formatted, and legible to the reader.

Before we review the /**P**rint menu commands, let's look at a more crude method of creating printouts—printing a screen dump. When you print a *screen dump*, your computer sends an unformatted snapshot of the entire screen display (including the column and row borders) to your printer. You do not need to execute a Quattro Pro command to print a screen dump. You can do it using only two (or possibly one) keys on your keyboard.

Printing a screen dump is easy: just display what you want to print on-screen, turn on your printer, and press Shift-PrtScr. If you own an extended keyboard, press the Print Screen key by itself. Try this procedure once so you can see the type of output produced. A screen dump printout shows the data from the spreadsheet area, Quattro Pro's row numbers and column letters, the menu names, and the name of the spreadsheet at the bottom. You may also see some gobbledygook along the top and right edges of the printout—ignore it.

> **Tip:** Quattro Pro must be in text display mode to print a screen dump. To select this mode, choose /**O**ptions **D**isplay Mode **A**: 80x25. Or click once on the mouse palette's CHR button.

In certain cases, you can use screen dumps to make building spreadsheets a bit easier. Think about a large application that uses a lot of formulas. Instead of having to scroll back and forth to see which data to include in a formula, you can print several screen dumps of the data. As you build the formulas, you can refer to the printouts to find specific cell addresses.

Remember, though, that screen dumps are only a shortcut for the full printing process. Once you've built a spreadsheet and are ready to share its information with others, use the commands on the /**P**rint menu to control Quattro Pro's printing options.

Preparing for Basic Printing

When you installed Quattro Pro, you defined your printer model, and selected a print mode and print resolution setting. Quattro Pro uses these *default printer settings* when it produces a basic printout. A basic printout doesn't contain *custom format settings* like headers, footers, or compressed print (all covered later in this chapter). As long as you supplied Quattro Pro with valid settings for your printer, you'll have no problems producing basic printouts. If you do encounter printing problems, you may need to configure Quattro Pro to work with your printer.

Configuring Quattro Pro To Work with Your Printer

Before you try to print a spreadsheet, verify that Quattro Pro correctly stored your printer settings. This information is available on the /**O**ptions **H**ardware **P**rinters **1**st Printer submenu. When you select this command, Quattro Pro displays the screen pictured in Figure 5.1.

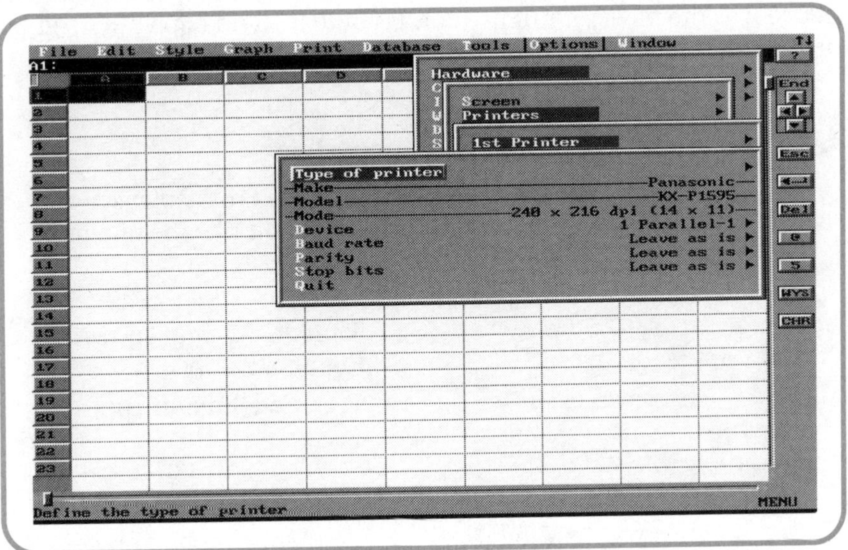

Figure 5.1 The 1st Printer submenu shows the settings for the printer you selected during program installation.

Figure 5.1 shows that the default printer is a Panasonic KX-P1595, set to print 240 x 216 dots per inch (dpi) on 14-by-11-inch paper, and connected at the first parallel port. (Your screen lists the settings for your printer instead of those for the Panasonic KX-P1595.) The *default printer* is the one that Quattro Pro normally prints to. The command below the default printer settings are for use only with a serial printer—normally, you can leave these settings alone. If you buy a second printer, or want to change any of the settings for the first printer, you'll need to select the **T**ype of Printer command from this submenu.

Adding a Second Printer

Many personal computer buyers choose a dot-matrix printer as their first printer. Before long, it becomes apparent that for printing certain types of work (such as reports, proposals, and graphs), a laser printer is a better choice. Whenever you wish to use a new printer with Quattro Pro—whether it's a laser, daisywheel, or new dot-matrix printer—you'll need to create new default printer settings using the **T**ype of Printer command.

Use the following Quick Steps to add a second printer to your system (for example, a Hewlett-Packard LaserJet III), and then configure it as the new default printer. If you'd rather keep your original printer as the default printer, then skip steps 7 and 8.

Adding a Second Printer to Your System

Step	Result
1. Press /OHP2 to select the /**O**ptions **H**ardware **P**rinters **2**nd Printer command.	Quattro Pro displays a submenu like the one in Figure 5.1, but with a blank settings area.
2. Press T to select the **T**ype of Printer command.	The Make menu shown in Figure 5.2 appears.
3. Highlight a printer make and press Enter (for this example, highlight the HP Printers option).	The Model menu appears.
4. Highlight a printer model and press Enter (highlight the LaserJet III option).	The Mode menu appears.
5. Highlight a printer mode and press Enter (highlight the 300 x 300 dpi (8.5 x 11) option).	Quattro Pro writes the make, model, and mode data onto the 2nd Printer submenu (see Figure 5.3).
6. Type Q to **Q**uit the **2**nd Printer submenu.	The submenu disappears, revealing the **P**rinters submenu.

7. Press D to execute the **D**efault Printer command.

   Quattro Pro displays a submenu listing two options: **1**st Printer and **2**nd Printer.

8. Press 2 to select the **2**nd Printer option.

   The new printer becomes the default printer that Quattro Pro writes to when you print.

9. Press Q to **Q**uit the **H**ardware submenu.

   You return to the /**O**ptions menu.

10. Press U to select the **U**pdate command.

    Quattro Pro stores the new default printer settings for the second printer.

11. Press Q to **Q**uit the /**O**ptions menu.

    You return to the active spreadsheet. □

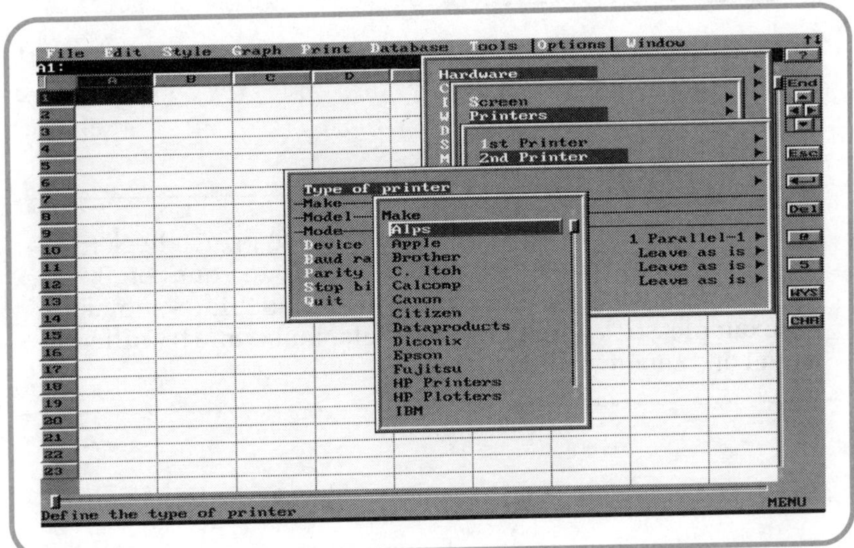

Figure 5.2 Selecting a printer manufacturer from the Make menu.

Before you continue, check to be sure that your new printer works with Quattro Pro and your computer. Try printing a small section of a spreadsheet (the next section describes how) to determine if there's a good connection between the computer and printer.

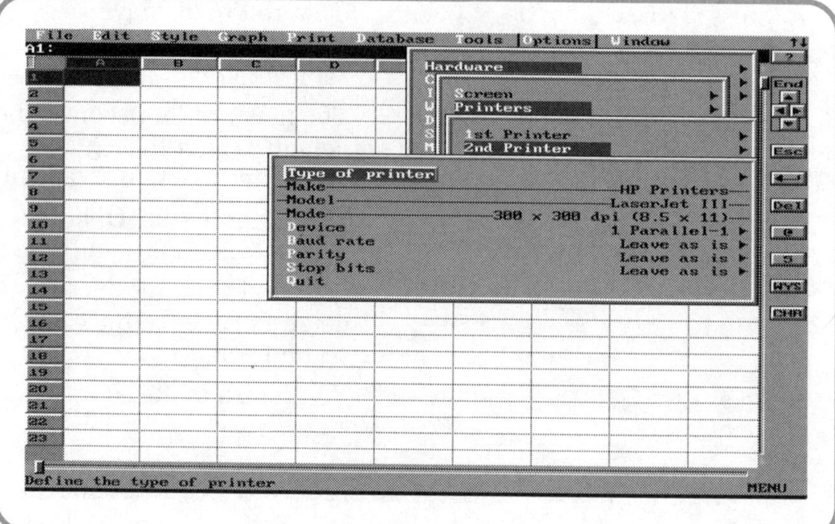

Figure 5.3 Quattro Pro updates the 2nd Printer submenu once you finish creating the printer settings.

> **Tip:** If you can't get your new printer to print, check to be sure that the cable is connected firmly to your computer. If it is, experiment with the settings on the **2**nd Printer submenu. For example, stick with the same printer make, and try different model and mode settings.

Basic Spreadsheet Printing

Quattro Pro's printing process is easy to understand. It takes only four steps to produce a basic printout.

1. Select an area of a spreadsheet to print—this is called the print block.
2. Tell Quattro Pro the cell block coordinates of the print block.
3. Align the paper in your printer to prepare it for a printout.
4. Print the spreadsheet block.

For example, suppose that you want to print the INCOME.WQ1 spreadsheet that you built in Chapter 3 (you can do this if you saved the spreadsheet.) Select /**F**ile **R**etrieve and load the spreadsheet into Quattro Pro (see Figure 5.4).

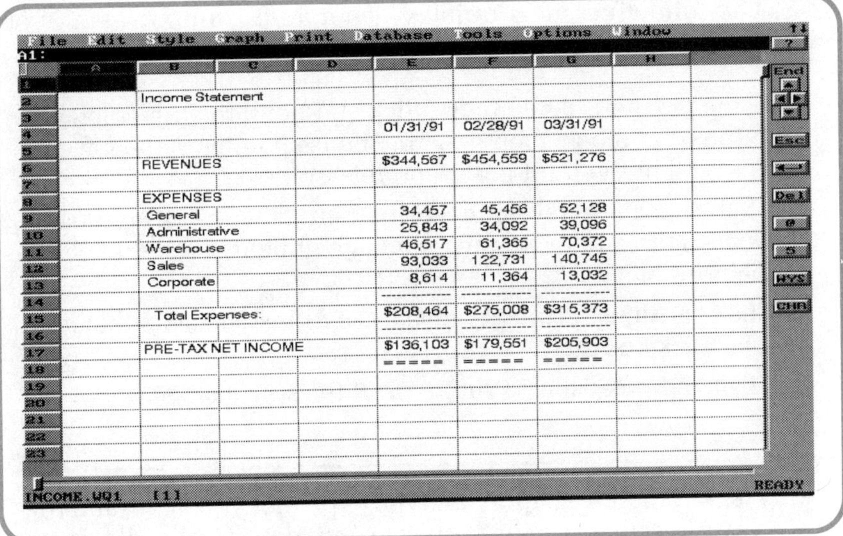

File Edit Style Graph Print Database Tools Options Window
A1:
Income Statement
01/31/91 02/28/91 03/31/91
REVENUES $344,567 $454,559 $521,276
EXPENSES
General 34,457 45,456 52,128
Administrative 25,843 34,092 39,096
Warehouse 46,517 61,365 70,372
Sales 93,033 122,731 140,745
Corporate 8,614 11,364 13,032
Total Expenses: $208,464 $275,008 $315,373
PRE-TAX NET INCOME $136,103 $179,551 $205,903
INCOME.WQ1 [1]
READY

Figure 5.4 Loading the INCOME.WQ1 spreadsheet into Quattro Pro for printing.

Look at Figure 5.4 and visualize the cell block coordinates that include the data you wish to print. Cell block A1..G18 is the most obvious candidate for print block. The following Quick Steps illustrate the printing procedure.

Printing a Spreadsheet Using Quattro Pro's Default Settings

1. Press /PB to select the /**P**rint **B**lock command. — Quattro Pro asks for the block of spreadsheet cells you want to print.
2. Type in a valid cell block address and press Enter. (I selected A1..G18 on the income statement spreadsheet.) — Quattro Pro stores the block selection on the /**P**rint menu next to the **B**lock command.
3. Manually align the paper in your printer. Press AA to execute the **A**djust Printer and **A**lign commands. — These commands tell Quattro Pro that your paper is positioned in the printer and ready to receive data.
4. Press S to select the **S**preadsheet Print command. — Quattro Pro sends the spreadsheet block to the printer.
5. Press Q to **Q**uit the /**P**rint menu. — Quattro Pro returns you to the main screen.

The following steps quickly generate a printout using your mouse:

1. Using the mouse, highlight (click and hold) the upper left cell in the print block, then drag the mouse pointer to the lower right cell in the print block and release.
2. Click on **P**rint to reveal the /**P**rint menu, then click on **B**lock. Quattro Pro automatically uses the highlighted range of cells as the print block.
3. Click on **A**djust Printer to reveal the **A**djust Printer submenu, then click on **A**lign.
4. Click on **S**preadsheet Print to print the spreadsheet.

> **Tip:** Depending upon the type of printer you have, and the print destination that you selected, you may have to issue an extra command to complete this printing exercise. For instance, when the print destination is **P**rinter, HP LaserJet owners must select the /**P**rint **A**djust Printer **F**orm Feed command to eject the printed page from the printer. When the print destination is **G**raphics Printer, Quattro Pro automatically ejects the page.

This printing method uses all of Quattro Pro's default printer settings, and assumes that you want a draft-quality printout that is no more than 80 characters wide (see Figure 5.5). If you need more flexibility in creating the final product, or if you want to print to a different destination, you'll need to learn how to use the /**P**rint **D**estination and /**P**rint **L**ayout commands.

Selecting the Print Destination

Quattro Pro allows you to print to a variety of destinations. To view a list of the choices, select /**P**rint **D**estination. As you can see in Figure 5.6, there are two draft mode and three final quality printing destinations.

Income Statement			
	01/31/91	02/28/91	03/31/91
REVENUES	$344,567	$454,559	$521,276
EXPENSES			
General	34,457	45,456	52,128
Administrative	25,843	34,092	39,096
Warehouse	46,517	61,365	70,372
Sales	93,033	122,731	140,745
Corporate	8,614	11,364	13,032
	----------	----------	----------
Total Expenses:	$208,464	$275,008	$315,373
	----------	----------	----------
PRE-TAX NET INCOME	$136,103	$179,551	$205,903
	=====	=====	=====

Figure 5.5 The income statement spreadsheet, printed using Quattro Pro's default printer settings.

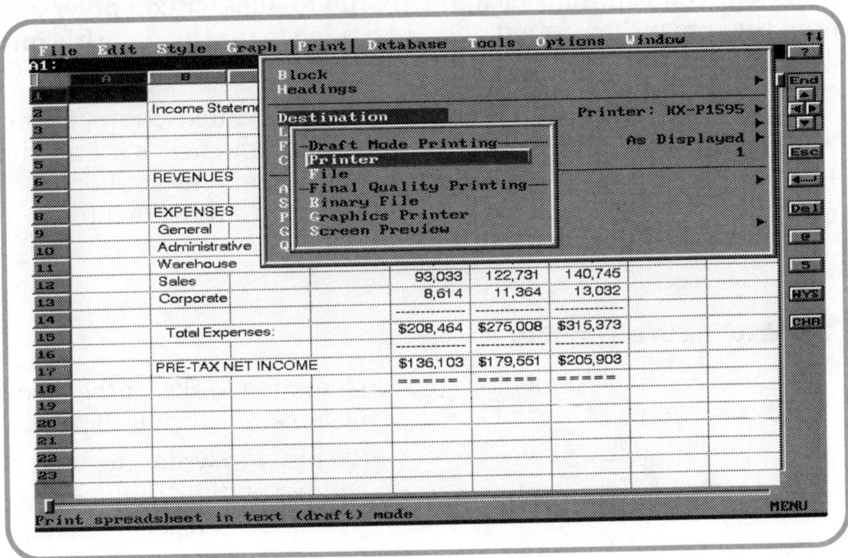

Figure 5.6 The Destination submenu allows you to select different destinations for your printouts.

Printing to a Text Printer

Choose the **P**rinter destination for most printouts. This destination, Quattro Pro's default, routes a text-quality printout to the Default Printer specified on the /**O**ptions **H**ardware **P**rinters submenu. (The previous Quick Step used **P**rinter as the destination.) The name of the Default Printer appears on the /**P**rint menu next to the **D**estination command (see Figure 5.6).

Printing to a Text File

The **F**ile choice on the **D**estination submenu allows you to transmit spreadsheet data to a .PRN print file. Files with the .PRN file name extension are *printer-ready*—you can print these files from DOS using the COPY command.

.PRN files have many uses. You can import a .PRN file as an ASCII text file into documents created in word processing programs like WordPerfect or Microsoft Word. This technique enables you to include spreadsheet data in the body of a word processing document. Or, you can transfer the .PRN file to another computer and print the spreadsheet report without having to first load the file into Quattro Pro.

Suppose that your CPA wants a laser-printed copy of your income statement for your annual report, and he needs it quickly. You could send a .PRN file to him via modem, and he could print it on his printer. To print a spreadsheet report to a .PRN text file, use the following Quick Steps.

Q Printing to a Text File

1. Press /PB to select the /**P**rint **B**lock command.

   Quattro Pro asks for the block of spreadsheet cells to print.

2. Type in a valid cell block and press Enter. (Again, I selected A1..G18.)

   Quattro Pro writes the block address on the /**P**rint menu next to the **B**lock command.

3. Press B to execute the **B**lock command and verify the print block that you selected. Then press Enter to finish the **B**lockcommand.

   Quattro Pro highlights the print block, as shown in Figure 5.7.

4. Press DF to select the **D**estination and **F**ile commands.

   Quattro Pro prompts you to enter a print file name.

5. Type in a file name and press Enter (or click Enter with your mouse).	Quattro Pro returns you to the /**P**rint menu.
6. Press AA to execute the **A**djust Printer and **A**lign commands.	Those commands tell Quattro Pro that the print file is ready to receive data.
7. Press S to select the **S**preadsheet Print command.	Quattro Pro sends the spreadsheet block to the print file. Quattro Pro returns you to the /**P**rint menu.
8. Press Q to **Q**uit the /**P**rint menu.	Quattro Pro closes the print file and adds the .PRN extension to the file name. ☐

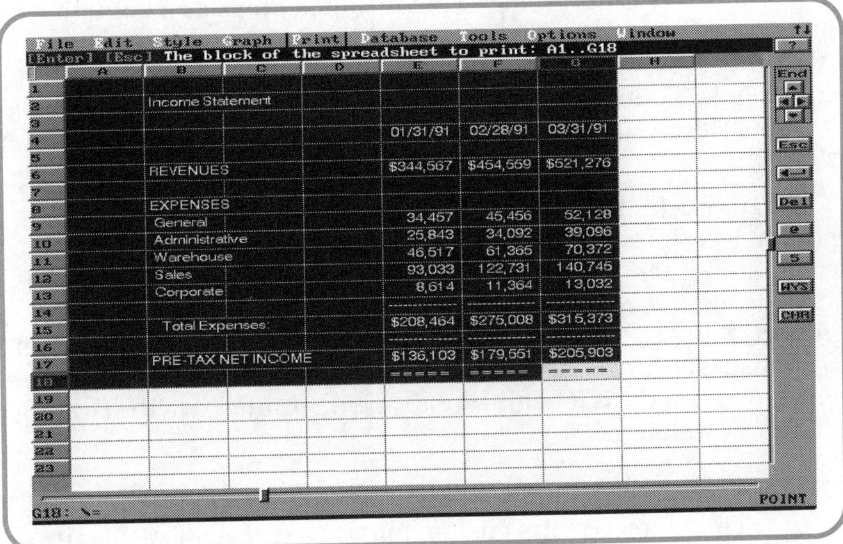

File Edit Style Graph Print Database Tools Options Window
[Enter] [Esc] The block of the spreadsheet to print: A1..G18
Income Statement
01/31/91 02/28/91 03/31/91
REVENUES $344,567 $454,559 $521,276
EXPENSES
General 34,457 45,456 52,128
Administrative 25,843 34,092 39,096
Warehouse 46,517 61,365 70,372
Sales 93,033 122,731 140,745
Corporate 8,614 11,364 13,032
Total Expenses: $208,464 $275,008 $315,373
PRE-TAX NET INCOME $136,103 $179,551 $205,903
G18: \=
POINT

Figure 5.7 Quattro Pro highlights cell block A1..G18 on the sample income statement spreadsheet.

> **Note:** To print a .PRN file from the DOS command prompt, type *COPY [filename].PRN PRN* and press Enter. The [filename] is the name of the file created with the /**P**rint **D**estination **F**ile command. DOS immediately sends the file to your printer for printing.

Printing to the Screen

Usually, it's hard to visualize how the final version of a printed spreadsheet will look on paper. With Quattro Pro's Screen Preview tool, however, you can preview a spreadsheet on-screen before you print it.

When you preview a printout on-screen, Quattro Pro displays a presentation-quality version of the spreadsheet. This means that if the spreadsheet contains stylistic enhancements such as customized fonts, drawn lines, or shaded cells, they'll appear on-screen (Chapter 7 discusses the Quattro Pro style enhancement commands). Even if you didn't add any of these items to your spreadsheet, Quattro Pro displays a screen preview version of the spreadsheet in the default screen display font (Bitstream Dutch 10-point).

You also can use the preceding Quick Steps as a guideline for producing "hard copy," presentation-quality spreadsheet printouts. In step 4, press DG to select the **D**estination and **G**raphics Printer commands. This step routes a final-quality version of a spreadsheet to your printer, and because the destination is a printer, you can skip step 5.

Printing to the screen is just like printing to a text or graphics printer—except you do not need to issue the /**P**rint **A**djust Printer **A**lign command. First, select the /**P**rint **B**lock command and define the spreadsheet area you want to print. Next, select the /**P**rint **D**estination **S**creen Preview command. Finally, select the /**P**rint **S**preadsheet print command. Quattro Pro displays your spreadsheet on-screen exactly as it would appear if you printed it to the **G**raphics Printer destination.

> **Tip:** When you use custom fonts in a spreadsheet, Quattro Pro may pause to build screen fonts before printing the spreadsheet to the screen. If you installed the entire screen font library during program installation, this probably won't happen. Once a screen font is built, Quattro Pro never has to build it again.

The **S**creen Preview tool is a print destination as well as a unique environment. While in the Screen Preview mode, Quattro Pro displays a list of command options at the top of your spreadsheet. To display a full-screen view of the spreadsheet, click the Zoom option [+] option once with your mouse. Then click the Guide option (see Figure 5.8).

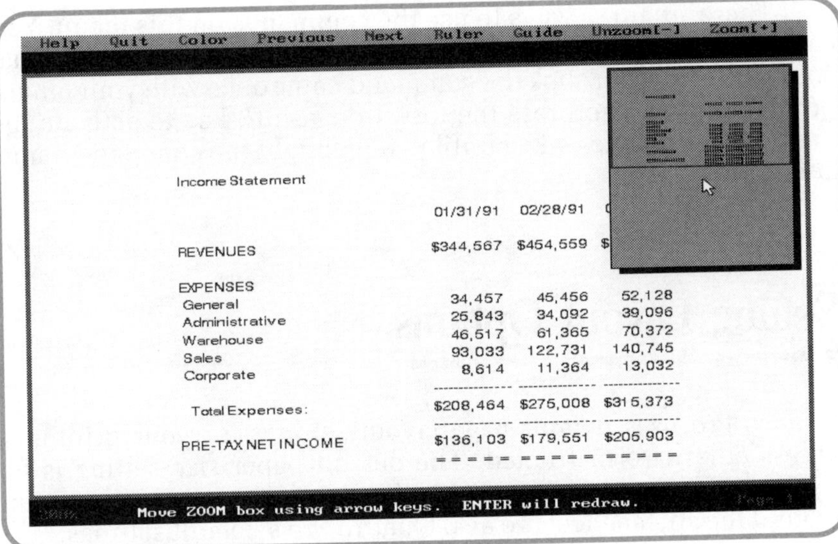

Help Quit Color Previous Next Ruler Guide Unzoom[-] Zoom[+]
Income Statement
01/31/91 02/28/91
REVENUES $344,567 $454,559
EXPENSES
General 34,457 45,456 52,128
Administrative 25,843 34,092 39,096
Warehouse 46,517 61,365 70,372
Sales 93,033 122,731 140,745
Corporate 8,614 11,364 13,032
Total Expenses: $208,464 $275,008 $315,373
PRE-TAX NET INCOME $136,103 $179,551 $205,903
Move ZOOM box using arrow keys. ENTER will redraw.

Figure 5.8 Quattro Pro prints the selected block in the Screen Preview environment.

The ***Help*** command displays a window that describes how to use the Screen Preview tool and its commands.

The ***Quit*** command cancels the **S**preadsheet Print operation and returns you to the active spreadsheet.

The ***Color*** command toggles between black-and-white and color screen displays.

The ***Previous*** command displays the previous page of the printout when there are multiple pages.

The ***Next*** command displays the next page of the printout when there are multiple pages.

The ***Ruler*** command displays a one-inch grid atop the spreadsheet on-screen.

The ***Guide*** command displays a miniature page that shows a small section of the spreadsheet in the upper right corner of the screen. (This command only works after you have zoomed the screen.) Press any of the Arrow keys to show different areas of the spreadsheet in the Guide box, then press Enter or click with your mouse to display that portion of the spreadsheet full-size on-screen.

The ***Unzoom [-]*** command displays a full page view of the spreadsheet. The ***Zoom [+]*** command magnifies the view of the spreadsheet by 100%, 200%, or 400%.

There are three ways to use the commands on this menu. You can press the boldfaced letter in the command name to select that command. You can click the command name once with your mouse pointer. Or you can press the forward slash (/) key to activate the menu bar, press the → key until you highlight the command name, and press Enter.

Setting Layout Options

Quattro Pro uses default page layout settings for your printouts, unless otherwise instructed. The default paper size setting is for 8 1/2-by-11-inch paper. Portrait (vertical) page orientation and margins around the spreadsheet are also Quattro Pro's default settings.

When you wish to modify the default settings, use the commands on the /**P**rint **L**ayout submenu. The Layout commands append report headers and footers; print a report without page breaks; let you change the default margins, page length, dimensions, and print orientation; and send special setup strings to your printer.

Changes made on the **L**ayout submenu apply only to the current spreadsheet. So, when you print another spreadsheet, Quattro Pro uses the default layout settings unless you tell it otherwise. If you find that you use certain layout settings often, you can store the settings and apply them to all new printouts. To save the current **L**ayout settings as the new defaults, select the /**P**rint **L**ayout **U**pdate command. To reinstate the previous set of default settings, select the /**P**rint **L**ayout **R**eset command.

Adding Headers and Footers

Headers and *footers* are lines of text that you add to the top and bottom of each page in a printout. Headers and footers tell a reader more about the data appearing in a spreadsheet report. On the income statement spreadsheet, for instance, you may want to add a header to clarify that all of the dollar values shown represent thousands. (That is, the $8,614 value in cell C12 really stands for 8,614 thousands, or $8,614,000.) You can enhance report headers by including special symbols as part of the header text. For instance, add the # symbol to display a page number, the @ symbol to display the current date, and the ¦symbol to control the alignment of header text. Use the following Quick Steps to add a header (or footer) to your spreadsheet printout.

Adding a Header to a Spreadsheet

1. Press /PLH to select the /**P**rint **L**ayout **H**eader command.

   The **H**eader submenu appears.

2. Type in the header text and add special symbols as desired. (Figure 5.9 shows center-aligned header text being entered into the income statement spreadsheet.)

   The header text prompt box displays the text, as shown in Figure 5.9.

3. Press Enter, or click Enter once with a mouse.

   Quattro Pro stores the header information on the **L**ayout menu next to the **H**eader command. □

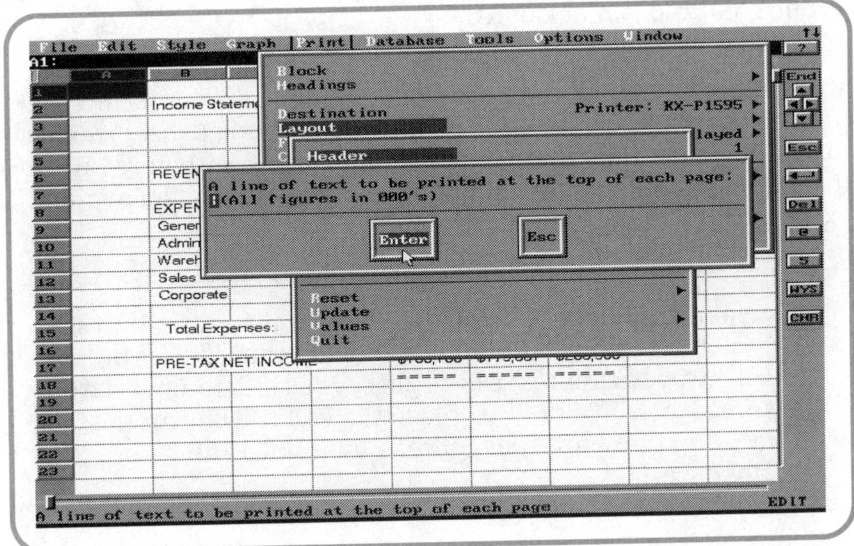

Figure 5.9 Adding a header to your spreadsheet report.

Add a single ¦symbol to your header text to center it on the printout; add two ¦¦ symbols to right-justify the header text. If you don't add special symbols, Quattro Pro left-justifies headers and footers. It's easy to remove or modify headers and footers. Just reselect the appropriate command and backspace over (or change) the text entry. When you press Enter, Quattro Pro stores a "blank" as the entry.

Inserting Page Breaks

Normally, Quattro Pro decides where to divide pages in a multiple page printout. It determines page breaks by comparing the size of the selected print block to the page length and margin settings. Quattro Pro automatically inserts *soft page breaks* to tell your printer when to move to a new page in the printout. You can tell Quattro Pro where to break pages using the /**S**tyle **I**nsert Break command (discussed in Chapter 7). This command inserts a *hard page break* that overrides a soft page break.

When your print destination is a .PRN file, you may wish to suppress automatic placement of soft page breaks. That way, you can use the file in another program without worrying about conflicting page formats. To suppress a soft page break, select /**P**rint **L**ayout **B**reak Pages **N**o. This command tells Quattro Pro to print the spreadsheet as one continuous block of data.

Controlling page breaks comes in handy when you want to print a graph and a spreadsheet on a page together (Chapter 8 covers printing graphs). Normally, after printing the spreadsheet you have to roll the paper back and realign it in your printer before printing the graph. A properly placed hard page break helps you avoid this extra work.

> **Note:** The /**P**rint **L**ayout **B**reak Pages command suppresses soft page breaks only—it does not affect hard page breaks. The only way to suppress a hard page break is to remove it from the spreadsheet. To do this, place the cell selector in the cell containing the hard page break symbol, and press the Del key once.

Scaling A Printout of a Spreadsheet

Quattro Pro allows you to scale the printed size of spreadsheet text without requiring you to first adjust font point sizes (covered in Chapter 7). The /**P**rint **L**ayout **P**ercent Scaling command is a spreadsheet printout scaling tool. By default, Quattro Pro scales all printouts by a factor of 100%. This setting produces the normal-sized printouts you are accustomed to seeing. To shrink the size of text on a printout, select a scaling factor in a range from 1 to 99 percent. To magnify the size of text, choose a scaling factor in a range from 101 to 1000 percent. Figure 5.10 shows the percent scaling setting that enlarges your printed output to 2.5 times its original size.

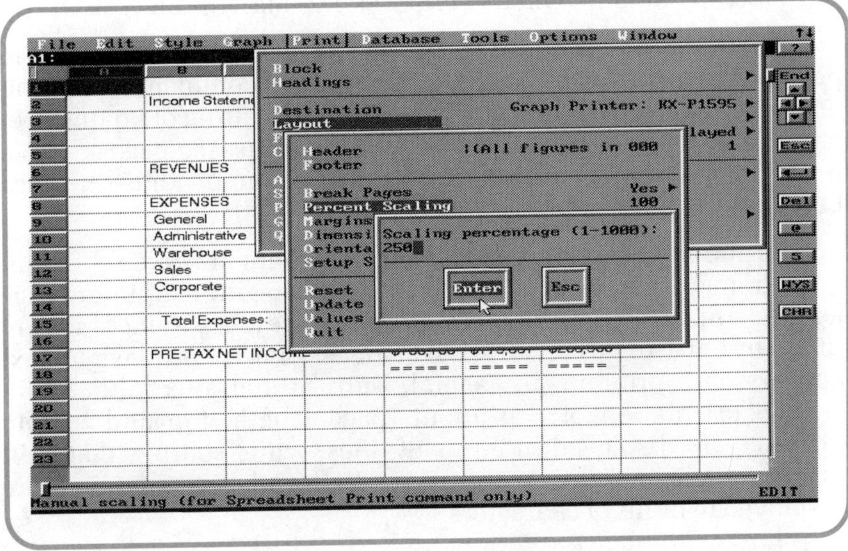

Figure 5.10 Scaling your spreadsheet printout by 250%.

The **P**ercent Scaling command is operative only when the print destination is a graphics printer. Be sure to select /**P**rint **D**estination **G**raphics Printer before you attempt to print a scaled spreadsheet. Also, Quattro Pro ignores the scaling percentage setting when you generate a printout using the /**P**rint **P**rint to Fit command (covered later in this chapter). Be sure to use the **S**preadsheet Print command if you wish to print a scaled spreadsheet.

The Screen Preview tool is very useful for previewing the look of a scaled spreadsheet prior to printing it. While in the Screen Preview environment, you can verify that you selected an appropriate scaling percentage setting.

> **Tip:** Scaling percentages greater than 200% enlarge the size of a printout so much that Quattro Pro must print the spreadsheet on two or more sheets of paper. If this is not your intent, try experimenting with different scaling percentage settings until you find the right one.

Changing the Margins and Page Length Settings

The commands on the /**P**rint **L**ayout **M**argins submenu enable you to choose the exact spacing between the printed text and each edge of the paper. By default, Quattro Pro uses 1/2" margins all around.

Quattro Pro also allows you to choose how many lines of text to print per page, up to 100, with the **P**age Length command. Most dot-matrix and daisywheel printers use a default setting of 66 lines per page. Laser printers generally work best with lines per page set to 60. If your pages don't break where you want them to, adjust the **P**age Length setting until they do.

In the next section you'll learn that there are three different measurement systems available to you for managing margin and page length settings. It's important to be aware of the measurement system in use by Quattro Pro because the layout settings control where text appears on a printout. In general, settings that affect the top-to-bottom orientation of a printout (page length, top and bottom margins) are displayed in terms of lines, while settings that shift printouts left or right on the paper (left and right margins) are displayed in terms of characters.

By default, all **L**ayout submenu settings conform to the "lines and characters" measurement system. If you wish, you can change the measurement system to inches or to centimeters.

The Quick Steps below demonstrate how to change the page length and left margin settings for a spreadsheet.

Changing the Top Margin and Page Length

1. Press /PLM to select the /**P**rint **L**ayout **M**argins command. — The **M**argins submenu displays the default printer settings.
2. Press P to select the **P**age Length command. — A prompt box asking you to type a new page length appears.
3. Type a number. (Figure 5.11 shows **P**age Length for the sample income statement spreadsheet being set to 60). — The number appears in the number prompt box (see Figure 5.11).
4. Press Enter, or click Enter with a mouse. — The number appears on the submenu next to the **P**age Length command.

5. Press L to select the **L**eft option.
   A prompt box appears asking you to type a new left margin.
6. Type a number. (I'll set the sample income statement spreadsheet left margin to 6.)
   The number appears in the number prompt box.
7. Press Enter once, or click Enter with a mouse.
   The number appears on the submenu next to the Left command, as shown in Figure 5.12.
8. Press Q twice to return to the /**P**rint menu. Print the spreadsheet with the new settings.
   Quattro Pro displays the /**P**rint menu, and you can select more commands. □

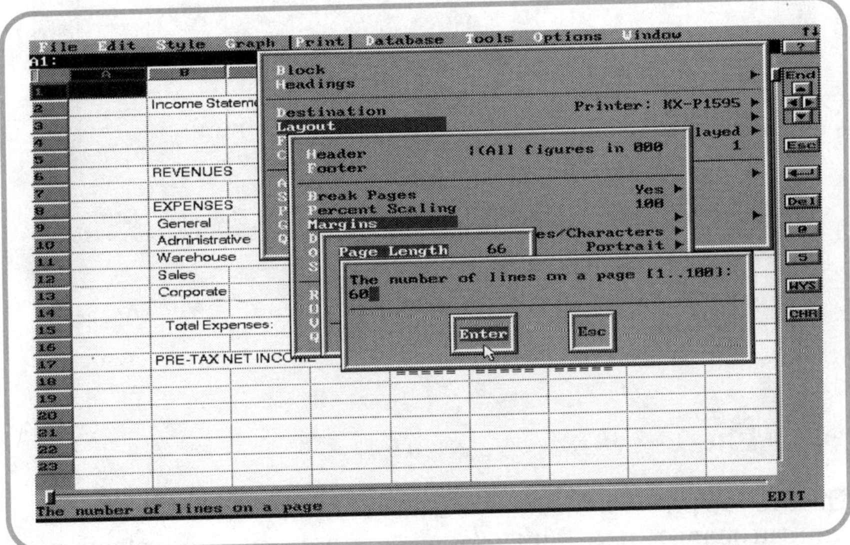

Figure 5.11 Changing a spreadsheet's page length setting.

Changing the Page Dimensions

By default, Quattro Pro uses the size of a character as the standard of measurement for the page length and margin settings. There are 10 characters to an inch horizontally and six per inch vertically. If you prefer, you can specify margin and page lengths in inches or centimeters rather than characters. You can choose either measurement system by selecting /**P**rint **L**ayout **D**imensions.

For example, if you choose **I**nches all of the page layout settings appearing next to the **L**ayout submenu commands are shown in terms of inches or fractions of inches. The top and bottom margins might be .5 inch, the page length setting would probably be 8.5 inches, and so on.

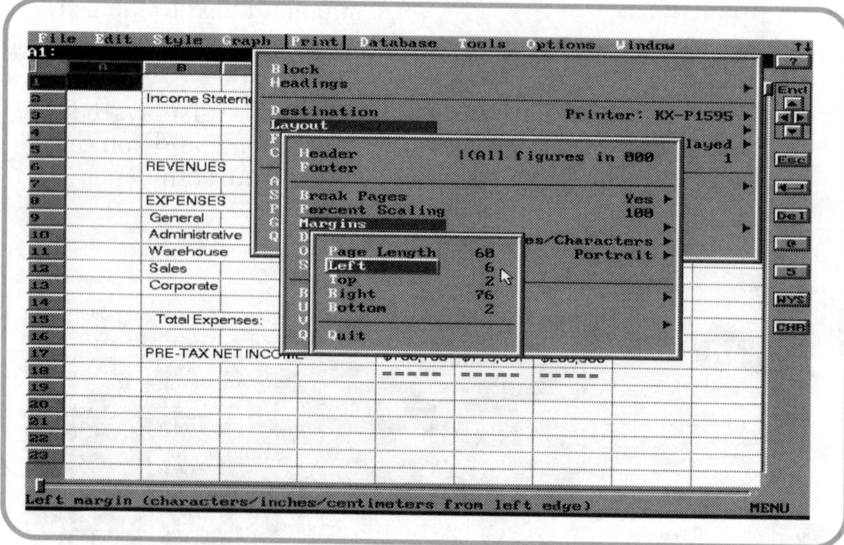

Figure 5.12 Quattro Pro stores new printer settings to the right of commands on the Margins submenu.

Adjusting the Print Orientation

Quattro Pro prints spreadsheets using *portrait* (vertical) orientation. You can change this default to *landscape* (horizontal) by selecting the **O**rientation option on the **L**ayout submenu. When you print using landscape orientation, Quattro Pro rotates the spreadsheet data 90 degrees (you don't see this on-screen) before printing. Landscape printing is useful for times when the spreadsheet print block is more than 80 characters wide. You may already have noticed that it's easy to create "wide" spreadsheets when you need 10 or 20 columns to show your data. For example, a spreadsheet displaying a 24-month cash flow statement would be in a wide format.

Quattro Pro can only print a spreadsheet in landscape orientation when the /**P**rint **D**estination command is set to **G**raphics Printer. For example, if /**P**rint **D**estination is set to **P**rinter, Quattro Pro produces the printout in portrait format.

A third orientation option allows you to print sideways across several sheets of continuous feed paper. The **B**anner option creates an effect similar to landscape printing—minus the usual page breaks. That is, instead of ejecting the first page before printing on the second page, Quattro Pro prints a continuous stream of text. Banner style printing requires continuous feed paper, so laser printer owners can not use this orientation style.

With the exception of the right margin setting, Quattro Pro recognizes and applies all header and margin settings in banner printing. Quattro Pro ignores the right margin setting because a banner's right margin is determined solely by the size of your print block. Quattro Pro prints sideways from left to right until the entire print block is printed.

> **Tip:** When you save a spreadsheet, Quattro Pro automatically saves the **O**rientation setting. That way, if you later wish to print the spreadsheet, you can be sure that your original orientation setting is intact.

Using Printer Setup Strings

All printers use special codes to create nonstandard printing effects such as underlining, compressed print, and letter-quality printing. These special printer codes are called *setup strings*. On many printers, you can select various printing modes directly from a printer control panel. Even when an option that you wish to use is not available on your printer control panel, you can issue the special code to the printer via the /**P**rint menu.

Refer to your printer manual for a list of the setup strings that your printer uses. For instance, many dot-matrix printers use the \015 code to print in compressed mode. In compressed mode, Quattro Pro prints 17 characters per inch. The \018 code returns a printer to standard mode, or 10 characters per inch for Quattro Pro. Figure 5.13 shows how to enter a setup string when you select the /**P**rint **L**ayout **S**etup String command.

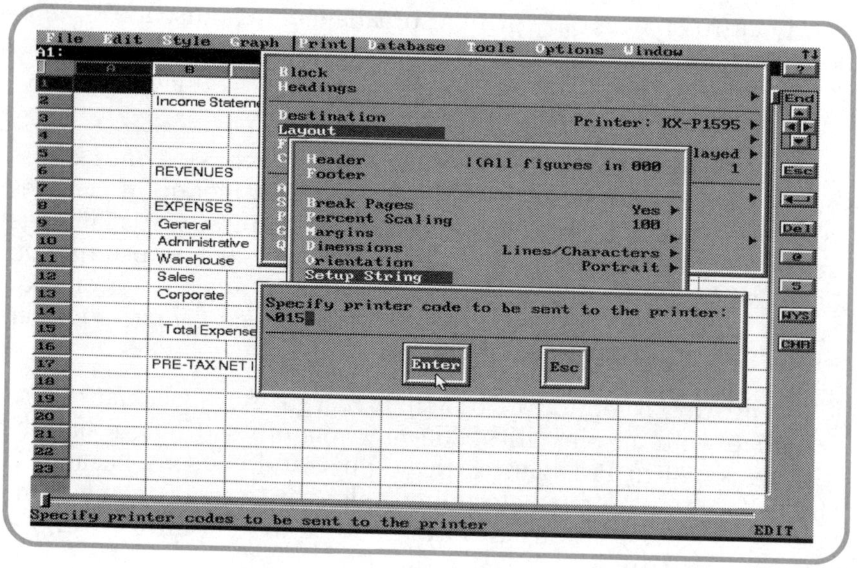

Figure 5.13 Entering a setup string that causes a printer to print in compressed mode.

You can create various combinations of printing styles by entering multiple setup strings. The **S**etup String dialog box, in fact, accepts up to 39 continuous characters—this gives you plenty of room to enter two, three, or more setup strings.

You also can *embed* a setup string in a spreadsheet cell. To do this, type two vertical bars followed by the setup string (for example, ||\015). Apply this technique when you need to use two different print styles in a spreadsheet. Suppose that you wish to switch to compressed printing in the middle of a spreadsheet. Just embed the compressed print setup string in a cell directly above the text block you want to print in compressed characters. When Quattro Pro encounters the embedded setup string, it switches to compressed style printing.

> **Tip:** An embedded setup string affects all the spreadsheet text appearing below the embedded string. To switch back to the original print mode, type another embedded setup string at the cell location where you wish to switch back to the original print mode—or to another print mode.

Updating and Resetting Layout Options

You can save customized print settings and use them for all future printouts if you wish. To do so, change the settings on the **L**ayout menu, and then select the **U**pdate command. To restore Quattro Pro's default printer settings, select the /**P**rint **L**ayout **R**eset command.

Reviewing the Layout Submenu Settings

Now that you've learned how to manage your printouts with the **L**ayout commands, you may be wondering if there's an easy way to review all of the current settings. Well, when you select /**P**rint **L**ayout **V**alues, Quattro Pro displays the screen shown in Figure 5.14. This screen summarizes the current layout settings and displays the current printer destination.

The screen shown in Figure 5.14 is for review purposes only. You cannot change the setting directly on this screen.

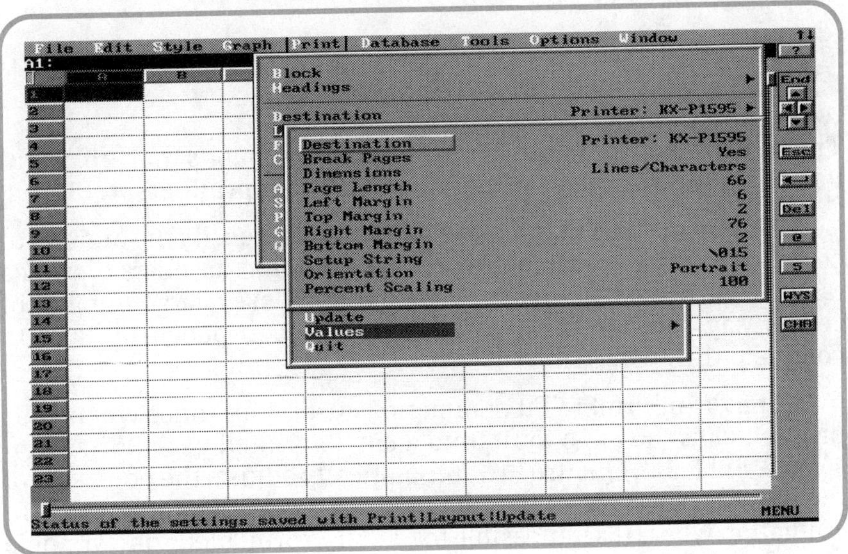

Figure 5.14 Reviewing the current page layout settings.

Changing A Printout's Display Format

Quattro Pro can print using two different display formats. The **A**s Displayed format option prints your spreadsheets pretty much as they appear on your screen. Print your document "as displayed" when you want a rough draft or a final copy. Quattro Pro's default format setting is **A**s Displayed.

The second display format is useful when you want to troubleshoot formulas and document a spreadsheet application. This format prints the cell address, the numeric format, the column width settings, and the contents of each cell in the selected print block. With this feature, you can check the integrity of the data entered into your spreadsheet. To use this display format, select /**P**rint **F**ormat **C**ell-Formulas.

Note that when you print a spreadsheet in the **C**ell-Formulas format, Quattro Pro still applies format settings such as headers, footers, margins, and setup strings. It does, however, ignore hard page breaks. Figure 5.15 shows a Cell-Formulas display printout of the income statement spreadsheet.

Printout Management Extras

The /**P**rint menu contains two additional commands that are useful for controlling the quantity and quality of your printouts.

The /**P**rint **C**opies command allows you to specify the number of copies to print of a particular spreadsheet. Valid numbers of copies range from 1 (the default) to 1000. If you choose a large number of copies, say 750, be sure that you have enough paper on hand to complete the operation.

The /**P**rint **P**rint to Fit command is useful for times when your print block is too large to fit onto a single printed page. When you select **P**rint to Fit, Quattro Pro automatically adjusts the point size of the spreadsheet fonts so that the printout fits onto a single page. In a situation where it's impossible to fit a large print block onto a single page Quattro Pro will print on as few pages as possible.

This command is operative only when **G**raphics Printer is the selected print destination.

It's worth noting that the shrinking of font point sizes takes place behind the scenes. You won't actually see your spreadsheet data shrinking on-screen. Also, this command operates in both WYSIWYG and text (or extended text) display modes.

```
B2: 'Income Statement
E4: 33269
F4: 33297
G4: 33328
B6: 'REVENUES
E6: (CO) 344567
F6: (CO) 454559
G6: (CO) 521276
B10: ' Administrative
E10: (,0) 25843
F10: (,0) 34092
G10: (,0) 39096
B11: ' Warehouse
E11: (,0) 46517
E11: (,0) 61365
F11: (,0) 70372
B12: ' Sales
E12: (,0) 93033
F12: (,0) 1227371
G12: (,0) 140745
B13: ' Corporate
E13: (,0) 8614
E13: (,0) 11364
G13: (,0) 13032
E14: \-
F14: \-
G14: \-
B15: '   Total Expenses:
E15: (CO) +E9+E10+E11+E12+E13
F15: (CO) +F9+F10+F11+F12+F13
G15: (CO) +G9+G10+G11+G12+G13
E16: \-
F16: \-
G16: \-
B17: 'PRE-TAX NET INCOME
E17: (CO) +E6-E15
F17: (CO) +F6-F15
G17: (CO) +G6-G15
E18: \=
F18: \=
G18: \=
```

Figure 5.15 Printing a spreadsheet using the Cell-Formulas display format.

Finally, you can not use the /**P**rint **L**ayout **P**ercent Scaling command in conjunction with the /**P**rint **P**rint to Fit command. You must use one or the other. When you use the **P**rint to Fit command, Quattro Pro ignores the scaling setting for the **P**ercent Scaling command.

What You've Learned

This chapter demonstrated many of Quattro Pro's printing capabilities. To develop a feel for the full extent of the /**P**rint menu options, experiment with each of the commands introduced in this chapter. Specifically, try adjusting the command settings on the **L**ayout submenu to learn more about how easy it is to control and manage your printouts.

- Quattro Pro prints basic spreadsheets using the default printer settings you specified during installation, and page layout defaults. You can modify both types of settings.
- The /**P**rinter **D**estination command allows you to print to a text printer, to a graphics printer, to a file, and to the screen.
- Adjust page layout options (such as headers, footers, page breaks, margins, page length, and dimensions) using the /**P**rint **L**ayout command.
- Change the display format of your printouts with the /**P**rint **F**ormat command.

Chapter 6

Understanding Formulas and @function Commands

In This Chapter

- *What makes a formula?*
- *Understanding how Quattro Pro calculates*
- *Using @function commands*
- *Learning about cell address reference formats*
- *Troubleshooting spreadsheet formulas*
- *Sampling the @function commands*
- *Solving formulas in reverse*

This chapter introduces you to methods for building Quattro Pro formulas. Formulas are the "brains" of your spreadsheet applications—they produce all the answers to your questions. Until now, you've worked with basic formulas. In Chapter 3, for instance, you learned how to build a spreadsheet formula to sum a group of numbers. This chapter shows you how to build formulas that go beyond basic math operations like addition and subtraction. This chapter also introduces you to Quattro Pro's built-in formulas, called *@function* commands. Instead of building complicated formulas, use the @function commands to perform specific, complex tasks.

What Makes a Quattro Pro Formula?

Enter +1+2+3 into any cell on a spreadsheet, and you've created one type of Quattro Pro formula. This formula does not rely upon data stored in other cells. Instead, this formula calculates an answer using three *arguments*—the numbers 1, 2, and 3. All Quattro Pro formulas use arguments to indicate which numbers to include in the calculation. Text, numbers, cell addresses, cell block references, and block names all are examples of valid arguments. Now enter the formula +B5-100 into another cell. This formula subtracts 100 from the number stored in cell B5. Quattro Pro knows to use the number stored in cell B5 because you specified it as an argument when you typed B5. To be a formula in Quattro Pro, a cell entry must begin with a plus (+) or minus (–) and can contain the following characters:

```
0 1 2 3 4 5 6 7 8 9 . + - ( @ $
```


A formula that begins with the @ symbol is called an *@function* (pronounced "at function"). @functions require specifically ordered arguments to perform calculations correctly. You'll learn about this special type of formula later in this chapter.

Quattro Pro recognizes three types of formulas: *arithmetic formulas, text formulas,* and *logical formulas.* Each type of formula meets different needs in your spreadsheet applications. The next several sections demonstrate how to build and use all three types of formulas.

Arithmetic Formulas

An *arithmetic formula* uses numbers, cell addresses, and even @function commands to perform calculations. The expressions *+5250*.25*, *–(D10/D2)*4*, and *+B5*@SUM(D2..D101)* are all arithmetic formulas.

In Quattro Pro, arithmetic formula cell entries use *arithmetic operators*. The eleven arithmetic operators are

```
+ - * / ^ = < > <= >= <>
```

Every arithmetic formula must begin with either the plus (+) or minus (–) operators so that Quattro Pro immediately recognizes the entry as a formula. Then Quattro Pro performs its computations based on the other operators in the formula. Figure 6.1 shows examples of how to use arithmetic formulas in a spreadsheet. The formula in cell E11 adds the contents of cells B3, B4, and B5. The formula in cell E12 adds B3 to B4 and then divides by B5. The @function in cell E13 calculates the average of the same three values.

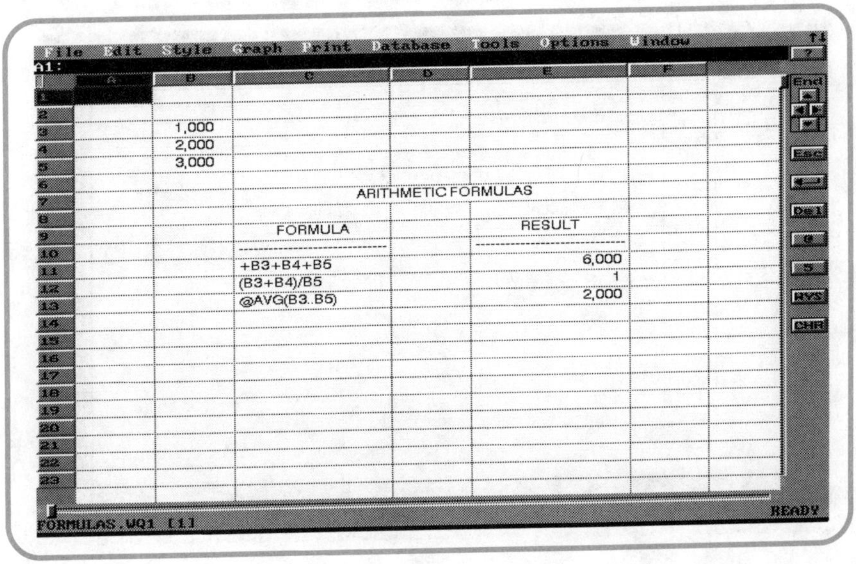

Figure 6.1 Using arithmetic formulas in a spreadsheet.

Text Formulas

A *text formula* performs "mathlike" operations on letters and words using a special operator, the *ampersand (&)*. An ampersand tells Quattro Pro to expect a *literal string*—words or letters enclosed within quotation marks. Because they operate on strings of text, text formulas sometimes are called *string formulas*. Although most spreadsheet users may never need to use text formulas, macro programmers frequently use text formulas.

You could create a text formula that "adds" two words together. The formula + (plus sign) *"Good"&"bye"* is a text formula. When you enter this formula into a spreadsheet cell, Quattro Pro displays `Goodbye`. Quattro Pro does not show the quotation marks or the ampersand when it displays a text formula result in a cell. Quattro Pro leaves the operators out, much like it leaves operators out in displaying the result of an arithmetic formula.

Figure 6.2 shows examples of text formulas. The formula in cell E11 displays the contents of cell B4. The formula in cell E12, however, uses the ampersand to join the contents of cells B3 and B5. The formula in cell E13 uses several ampersands to join all three labels stored in cells B3, B4, and B5.

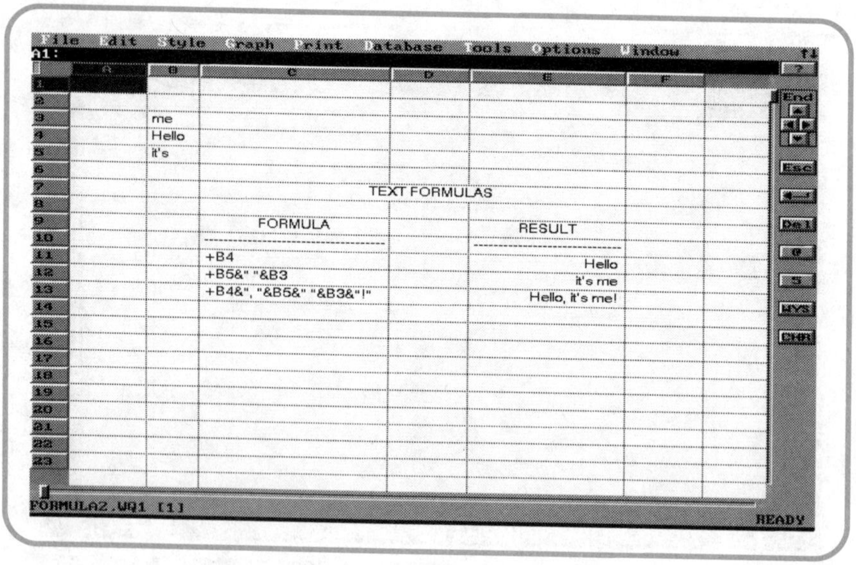

Figure 6.2 *Using text formulas in a spreadsheet.*

> **Tip:** You can use quotation marks to add extra characters to a text formula (as in cell C13 above). For instance, to add spaces between two labels that you join in a text formula, insert a blank space surrounded by quotations (“ ”) between the labels. You can add other text (such as an exclamation mark or a comma) to a text formula simply by placing the text within quotation marks.

Logical Formulas

A *logical formula* compares two or more pieces of data and returns a *true* or *false* result. For example, the formula *+D5<D6* compares the value in cell D5 to the value in cell D6. If D5's value is less than

D6's value, then the comparison is *true*, so Quattro Pro displays a 1. If D5's value is greater than D6's, the comparison is *false*, so Quattro Pro displays a 0. You can use any of the following operators to construct logical formulas:

= < > <= >= <> #AND# #OR# #NOT#

The last three operators are special. They allow you to create complex logical formulas to compare more than one set of data. For the formula *+D5<D6#AND#D6<D7* to be *true*, for instance, D6 must be both greater than D5 and less than D7.

Figure 6.3 shows examples of logical formulas. The formula in cell E11 asks the question, "Does the value in B3 equal the value in B4?" Because the answer is *false*, Quattro Pro displays a 0 in cell E11. The formula in cell E12 is similar. It asks, "Is B3 less than B5?" The answer to this question is *true*, so Quattro Pro displays a 1 in cell E12. The formula in cell E13 asks two questions, "Is the value in B3 less than the one in B4?" and "Is the value in B4 less than the one in B5?" Because the answer to both of these questions is *true*, Quattro Pro displays a 1 in cell E13.

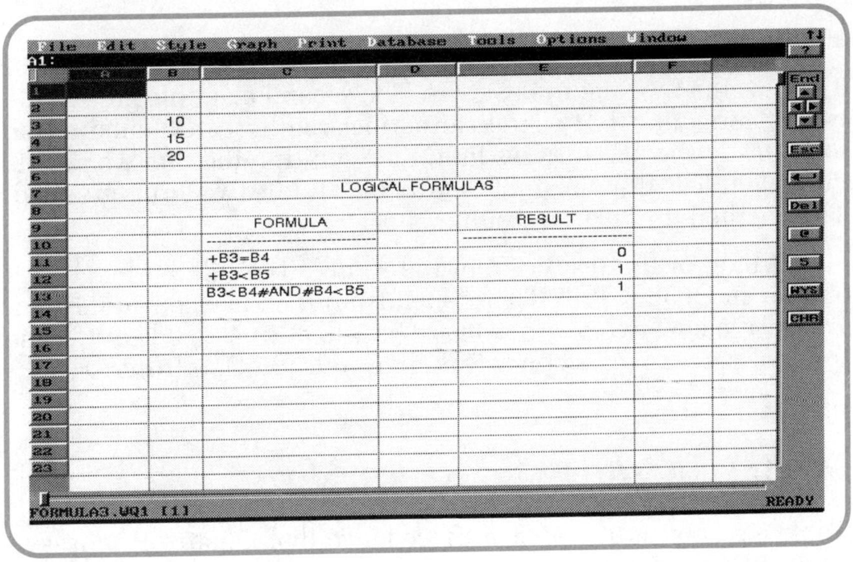

Figure 6.3 *Using logical formulas in a spreadsheet.*

Understanding How Quattro Pro Calculates

Before Quattro Pro displays an answer to a formula, it evaluates the formula according to its *mathematical order of precedence*. Quattro Pro's order of precedence determines which formula calculations it performs first, second, third, and so on. You need to know which math operations always take place before others to construct accurate formulas. Let's see how this important math property affects a typical Quattro Pro calculation.

Without an order of precedence rule, a formula could produce many different answers, depending on the order in which you perform formula calculations. Consider the formula *+10+2*5^2*. This formula can return three different answers if you use different orders of precedence, as follows:

Order of Precedence Used	Result
Left to right	3,600
(10+2) * (5^2)	300
10 + (2*5) ^ 2	400

Calculating the formula operations from left to right results in 3,600, as the first example shows. The second example groups the two left terms and the two right terms in parentheses. Calculating the formulas in the parentheses first, then multiplying the two results yields 300. The third example shows the middle two terms grouped. This method produces a result of 400.

Which of the results from the sample formula is the correct answer in Quattro Pro? That depends on the answer you desired. Follow the next two sections to see how to evaluate and control the order of precedence when creating formulas in Quattro Pro.

Quattro Pro's Order of Precedence Rule

Table 6.1 shows the order of precedence that Quattro Pro uses to evaluate spreadsheet formulas. Note that some of the operators listed in Table 6.1 have the same order of precedence. When a formula contains operators with the same order of precedence, Quattro Pro evaluates the operators from left to right.

Table 6.1 Reviewing Quattro Pro's order of precedence.

Operator	Operation	Order of Precedence
^	Exponentiation	1st
+, -	Positive and Negative	2nd
*, /	Multiplication and Division	3rd
+, -	Addition and Subtraction	4th
= <>	Equal To or Not Equal To	5th
<, >	Less Than and Greater Than	5th
<=	Less Than or Equal To	5th
>=	Greater Than or Equal To	5th
#NOT#	Logical NOT Test	6th
#AND#	Logical AND Test	7th
#OR#	Logical OR Test	7th
&	String Union	7th

Creating Formulas with Nesting Parentheses

In the earlier section's example, you saw that using parentheses to group formula terms can affect the result Quattro Pro returns. You can control how Quattro Pro calculates a formula by grouping formula terms in parentheses. When you use *nesting parentheses* in a formula, Quattro Pro calculates the terms inside the parentheses first, then it calculates the terms outside the parentheses. If the formula has nesting parentheses within nesting parentheses, Quattro Pro performs the operations enclosed in the innermost parentheses first, as follows:

Formula	Answer	Order of Calculation
5*(12/3)+4	24	(12/3) * 5 + 4
24*(12*(4/2))+4	580	(4/2) * 12 * 24 + 4
5+((3*(6/3)+1))	12	(6/3) * 3 + 1 + 5

Note that the order of precedence rule also holds for formula terms that appear within nesting parentheses. In the last example, for instance, Quattro Pro would multiply 3 times the expression (6/3) before adding 1 because multiplication always comes before addition.

One final note about nesting parentheses. Formulas must contain pairs of parentheses. If you type three left parentheses in the formula, then you also must type three right parentheses. If parentheses are not balanced, Quattro Pro displays an error message.

Recalculating Your Spreadsheet Formulas

Quattro Pro recalculates a spreadsheet formula when you edit or erase data referenced by the formula. There are three recalculation modes: *Automatic*, *Background*, and *Manual*.

Automatic recalculation takes place "behind the scenes" while you continue to work on your spreadsheet. Every time you edit or erase data used in a formula, Quattro Pro immediately supplies you with a new answer.

The `BKGD` mode indicator on the status line shows when Quattro Pro is in *Background recalculation* mode. In this mode, Quattro Pro recalculates formulas between keystrokes—you must wait for it to finish before you can continue typing.

Use *Manual recalculation* mode when you build a lot of complex formulas into your spreadsheets. The more formulas you use, the longer it takes Quattro Pro to recalculate. With other calculation modes active, you would spend a lot of time after edits waiting while Quattro Pro performs computations. However, using Manual mode, when you change cell data referenced in a formula, Quattro Pro displays `CALC` on the status line to remind you to issue a command to update the spreadsheet's displayed results. To recalculate the formulas, press F9, the Calc key. The following Quick Steps illustrate how to change to Manual mode.

Q Setting Manual Mode and Recalculating Formulas

Step	Result
1. Press /ORM to select the **O**ptions **R**ecalculation **M**ode command.	Quattro Pro displays the Mode menu, which has three choices.
2. Press M to select **M**anual.	Quattro Pro returns to the **R**ecalculation menu.
3. Press Q twice to exit the **O**ptions menu.	Quattro Pro returns to the active spreadsheet.
4. Change data referenced in spreadsheet formulas.	Quattro Pro displays `CALC` on the status line.
5. Press F9 to recalculate the formulas.	Formulas on the spreadsheet display new values. □

(Be sure to reset the recalculation mode to Automatic before moving on.)

What Is an @function Command?

An *@function command* is a built-in spreadsheet formula. These commands perform calculations that are difficult to complete using only simple arithmetic formulas. @function commands turn spreadsheets into multipurpose analytical tools. With @function commands, Quattro Pro can calculate mortgage payments, add and average groups of numbers, count the number of items in a long list, and more.

All @functions have three parts: the @ ("at") symbol, the *command name*, and one or more *arguments*. An *argument* tells the @function command which number or cell to use in the calculation. When an @function uses more than one argument, you must separate the arguments with commas.

For instance, the @PV command, which computes present value, uses three arguments to perform its calculation, as follows:

```
@PV(pmt,rate,term)
```

The first argument, *pmt*, is the amount of the payment for each period. The second argument, *rate*, is the interest rate per period. The third argument, *term*, gives the number of periods for the investment. You must use the same period for each argument—days, months, or years. Note that commas separate the three arguments.

All @functions return some value. The @PV command returns the present value of an investment, a function easily performed by most financial calculators. Imagine how difficult it would be to create an arithmetic formula to compute present value.

Entering @function Commands

There are two ways to enter an @function command into a cell. You can type it on the input line, or you can build it by pressing Alt-F3, the Functions key. As you become comfortable with entering @function commands, familiarize yourself with the following five rules:

1. Do not enter spaces between the @ symbol and the function name. *@AVG(B1..B4)* is correct, *@ AVG(B1..B4)* is not.
2. You can use both uppercase or lowercase characters when entering an @function. *@sum(A1..A5)* returns the same answer as *@SUM(a1..a5)*.
3. Always enclose arguments in parentheses. *@SUM(B12..B25)* is correct, *@SUM B12..B25* is not.
4. Every @function command requires different numbers and types of arguments.
5. You may use one @function command as an argument in another @function command. For example, *@SQRT(@AVG(D5..D10))* computes the average of the numbers stored in cells D5..D10 and displays the square root of that average.

To enter an @function manually, press @ (the "at" key), type the function name, enter the arguments, and press Enter. Quattro Pro recognizes @functions when you type them in uppercase or lowercase letters. The Quick Steps below show how to use Alt-F3, the Functions key, to enter an @function command.

Entering an @function by Pressing Alt-F3

1. Press Alt-F3 once.

   Quattro Pro displays a complete list of its @function commands (see Figure 6.4).

2. Scroll through the list by pressing the (↑) and (↓) keys.

   Quattro Pro highlights each @function command as you scroll.

3. Highlight an @function command and press Enter.

   The @function command appears on the input line next to an open parenthesis.

4. Type in all valid arguments, type a right parenthesis, and press Enter. (See the Quattro Pro documentation for a complete listing of valid arguments.)

   Quattro Pro enters the formula into the cell, evaluates the arguments, and displays the @function command result.

To display the @functions list using your mouse, click once on the @ symbol in the middle of the mouse palette. Quattro Pro immediately displays the list on your screen.

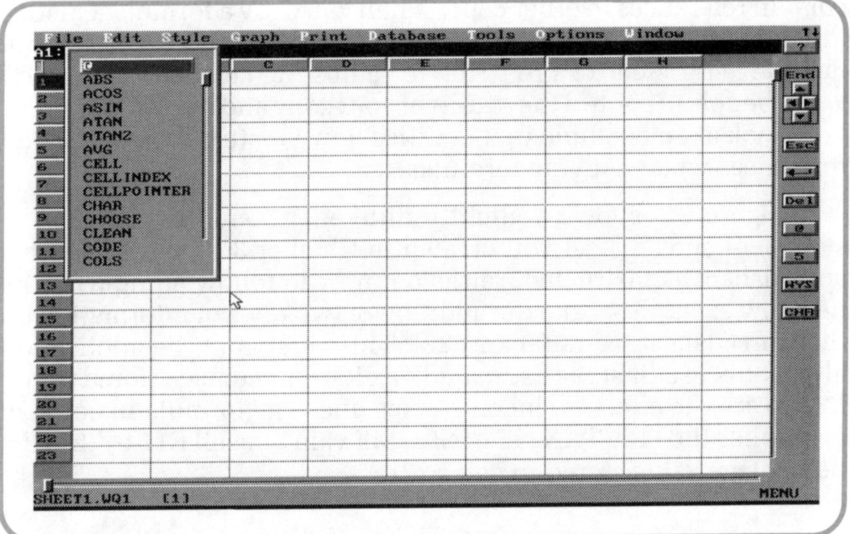

Figure 6.4 Displaying a list of the @function commands.

When you create an invalid @function entry, Quattro Pro displays an error message and beeps at you. This can happen for several reasons. You may have supplied too many or too few arguments. Or you may have used the wrong type of argument (such as entering text when Quattro Pro requires a value). When an error message appears, press F1 to display context-specific help about the error. Correct the error and press Enter, and Quattro Pro displays an answer.

Copying @function Commands

Chapter 3 showed you how to use the /**E**dit **C**opy command to duplicate and move labels and numbers around on a spreadsheet. The sample exercise in Chapter 3 illustrated how easy it is to build spreadsheets when you don't have to retype labels and numbers over and over again.

Well, the same holds true for spreadsheets that use formulas and @functions. It's much easier to build spreadsheets when you can create one formula and copy it to other cells. The mechanics for copying formulas and @functions are the same as for copying labels and numbers—with one exception. Formulas and @functions often contain references to other cells. When you copy a formula, Quattro Pro adjusts the cell references in the formula copy. If you are not familiar with Quattro Pro's rule for adjusting cell references, you won't be able to control the results of your copy and move operations. Let's look at an example that clarifies how Quattro Pro adjusts cell references when copying formulas.

Figure 6.5 shows a slightly different version of the income statement spreadsheet you created in Chapter 3. If you saved this spreadsheet as instructed, retrieve it now to follow along with the next few examples. Note the addition of two rows of information on this spreadsheet (rows 20 and 22). This version of the application allows you to adjust the Estimated Tax Rate percentage stored in cell E22 to see the effect on income taxes due. The formula in cell E20 multiplies the PRE-TAX NET INCOME value in cell E17 by .28 (the percentage value stored in cell E22).

File Edit Style Graph Print Database Tools Options Window

E20: (,0) +E17*E22

	A	B	C	D	E	F	G	H
2		Income Statement						
4					01/31/91	02/28/91	03/31/91	
6		REVENUES			$344,567	$454,559	$521,276	
8		EXPENSES						
9		General			34,457	45,456	52,128	
10		Administrative			25,843	34,092	39,096	
11		Warehouse			46,517	61,365	70,372	
12		Sales			93,033	122,731	140,745	
13		Corporate			8,614	11,364	13,032	
14					------------	------------	------------	
15		Total Expenses:			$208,464	$275,008	$315,373	
16					------------	------------	------------	
17		PRE-TAX NET INCOME			$136,103	$179,551	$205,903	
18					=====	=====	=====	
20		Income Taxes			38,109			
22		Estimated Tax Rate:			28.00%			

INCOME.WQ1 [1] READY

Figure 6.5 An income statement spreadsheet application.

To complete this spreadsheet, you could copy the formula in cell E22 to cell block F20..G20 using the /**E**dit **C**opy command. Figure 6.6 shows the result of the copy operation.

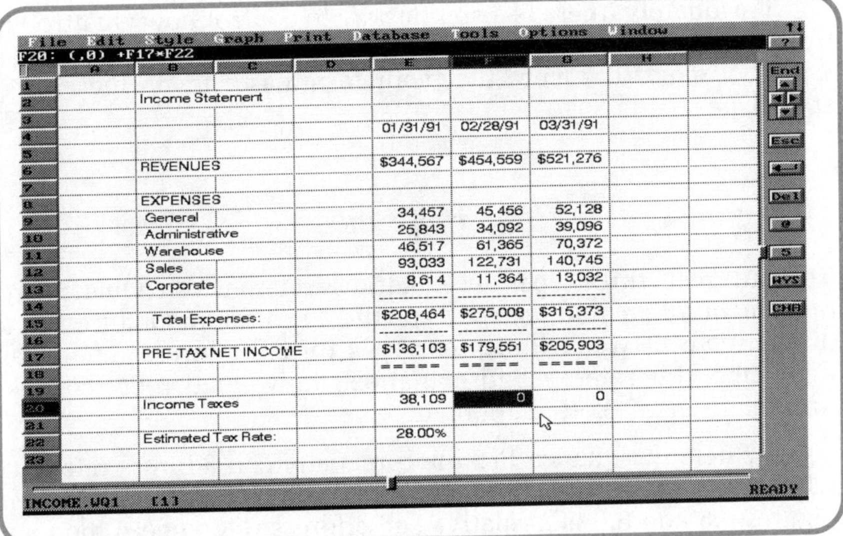

Figure 6.6 Copying a spreadsheet formula into cells F20..G20.

Quattro Pro displays the value 0 in cells F20 and G20—not the income tax figures that you might expect. Now look at the formula in cell F20. (It's displayed on the input line at the top of the spreadsheet shown in Figure 6.6.) This copied formula multiplies the correct PRE-TAX NET INCOME value (cell F17) by the value stored in cell F22. Because cell F22 is blank, Quattro Pro returns the value 0. There's the problem!

When you copy a formula, Quattro Pro adjusts cell addresses relative to the new cell location. The adjusted cell addresses are known as *relative cell address references*. Suppose a formula contains a relative reference to the next cell to the right. All copies of that formula will reference the data in the cell immediately to the right of the formula copy location.

Relative copying is fine for the first half of the tax formula, because you want the copied formulas to reference the PRE-TAX NET INCOME values in cells F17 (February) and G17 (March). But you don't want the second half of the formula to refer to cells F22 and G22 for the income tax percentage—the formula copies should refer to cell E22. You must tell Quattro Pro not to change the reference to cell E22 when copying the formula. To do this, you would use an *absolute cell address reference* for the address, E22, in the formula.

Fortunately, there is a simple way to control how Quattro Pro treats cell addresses when copying formulas. Use the techniques described next to ensure that your formulas refer to the correct spreadsheet cells.

Managing Cell Address References

You can create three types of cell address references in Quattro Pro: *relative*, *absolute*, and *mixed*. Type the $ symbol in Quattro Pro to differentiate between the three types of cell address references. Remember, the reference format affects how Quattro Pro copies a formula from one cell to another.

By default, Quattro Pro interprets any cell address reference without $ signs as a *relative reference*. Each cell address shown in Figures 6.5 and 6.6 is a relative cell address reference. When you copy a formula with relative cell address references, Quattro Pro adjusts each cell address in the formula copy to be an equal number of rows and columns away from the cells referenced in the original formula. A formula that contains only relative cell address references looks like

```
+A5–B25*(D55+E55)
```

An *absolute cell address reference* anchors a cell address in a formula. When you copy the formula to another cell, Quattro Pro doesn't adjust the cell address at all. To create an absolute reference, place the $ symbol in front of a cell address's row number and column letter. A formula that contains only absolute cell address references looks like

```
+$A$10+$A$20*($B$20/$D$50)
```

You also can create formulas that use both relative and absolute cell address references. These combination cell addresses are called *mixed cell address references*. Use mixed references if you wish to anchor some, but not all, of the cell addresses in a formula. Think back to the original formula shown in cell E20 of Figure 6.5. We now know that the first part of the formula should change when copied, and the second part of the formula should always refer to cell E22. So, we need to use mixed cell address references in this formula, and change it to be

```
+E17*$E$22
```

Now, when you copy the formula into cells F20 and G20, Quattro Pro correctly adjusts the original formula to create the formulas +F17*$E$22 and +G17*$E$22.

Changing a Cell Address Reference

To change a cell address reference to a new format, use F4, the Absolute key. This key changes relative references to absolute references. The Quick Steps below demonstrate how to change cell address reference formats.

Q Changing a Cell Address Reference to a New Format

1. Highlight the cell you want to edit, and press F2 once. — Quattro Pro enters EDIT mode and displays the contents of the cell on the input line.
2. Press the ← until the edit cursor is next to the cell address you wish to change. Or click your mouse once on the cell address. — Watch the input line to track your location.
3. Press F4 four times in a row. — Quattro Pro toggles the format of the cell address so it displays different styles.
4. Use steps 1-3 to make changes to other cell address references in the formula as needed.
5. Press Enter once. — Quattro Pro stores the formula in the cell with the new reference formats intact. □

Troubleshooting Spreadsheet Formulas

Quattro Pro evaluates formulas you enter before it displays answers. The program does this to make sure that you create valid formulas. A valid formula meets two conditions: it adheres to basic mathematical principles, and Quattro Pro can interpret it. Fortunately, if a formula meets the first condition, it usually meets the second condition. But there are times when you will need to troubleshoot your formulas to get correct answers.

Correcting ERR Values

If Quattro Pro encounters a formula error, it displays ERR in the cell holding the incorrect formula. You must correct the error so Quattro Pro can display the correct result.

Quattro Pro may display ERR in a formula cell for a number of reasons. For example, if you enter +50/0 into cell A1, Quattro Pro displays ERR because dividing by zero is an illegal math operation. Now enter the formula +100/B5 into cell A1. If cell B5 is blank, Quattro Pro displays ERR because there is no number by which to divide 100.

Quattro Pro also displays ERR when you delete a row or column referenced in a formula. For instance, if cell A1 contains the formula *+100/B5* and you delete row 5 or column B, Quattro Pro loses its link to the data stored in cell B5. In this case, Quattro Pro replaces the original B5 reference with ERR and converts the formula to *+100/ERR*. To see this effect, you could highlight cell A1 and look at its contents on the input line.

If you enter a formula that references a cell that contains ERR, Quattro Pro also displays ERR. For example, enter the formula 100+A1 into any empty cell other than A1 on the same spreadsheet. Because cell A1 currently contains ERR, the formula in the new cell also displays ERR. Once you correct the ERR in cell A1, Quattro Pro automatically corrects the ERR in the other formula.

Correcting these errors is easy. Go to the cell with the error message. Press F2 to enter EDIT mode. Now backspace over the ERR and type in a new cell address reference.

Correcting Circular References

Circular references, another type of formula error, have nothing to do with math properties or Quattro Pro's inability to calculate formulas that contain ERR. This type of error usually can be traced to typographical errors.

A formula that contains a *circular reference* uses its own cell address in the formula. Consider the spreadsheet application shown in Figure 6.7. This spreadsheet tallies personal expenses using the

@SUM command. Notice that cell D13 contains the formula *@SUM(D5..D13)*. This formula includes its own cell address in the argument range. The first time you enter this formula, Quattro Pro displays the correct answer, `$1,125`. The program also tells you that you've created a circular reference by displaying `CIRC` on the status line.

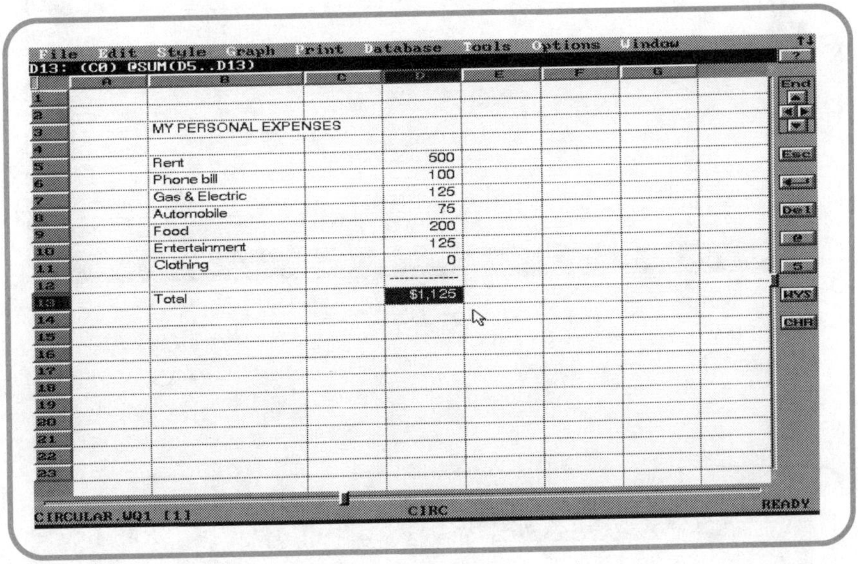

Figure 6.7 Cell D13 has a formula that contains a circular reference.

Formulas that contain circular references have more than one answer. If you press F9 to recalculate the spreadsheet, Quattro Pro displays a new value in cell D13, as shown in Figure 6.8. Take a look at the formula in cell D13. Nothing has changed in the formula, yet Quattro Pro displays the value `$2,250` in cell D13. This happened because Quattro Pro included the value $1,125 in the second calculation, and $1,125 plus $1,125 is $2,250.

You can easily pinpoint the location of a circular reference once you know one exists. In the case of the spreadsheet shown in Figure 6.8, the trouble spot is obvious—there is only one formula that could contain a circular reference. When there are several formulas on a spreadsheet, select /**O**ptions **R**ecalculation, and Quattro Pro displays the menu shown in Figure 6.9. Notice that the Circular Cell status line displays the cell address of the circular reference (`D13`).

Figure 6.8 Formulas that contain circular references have more than one answer.

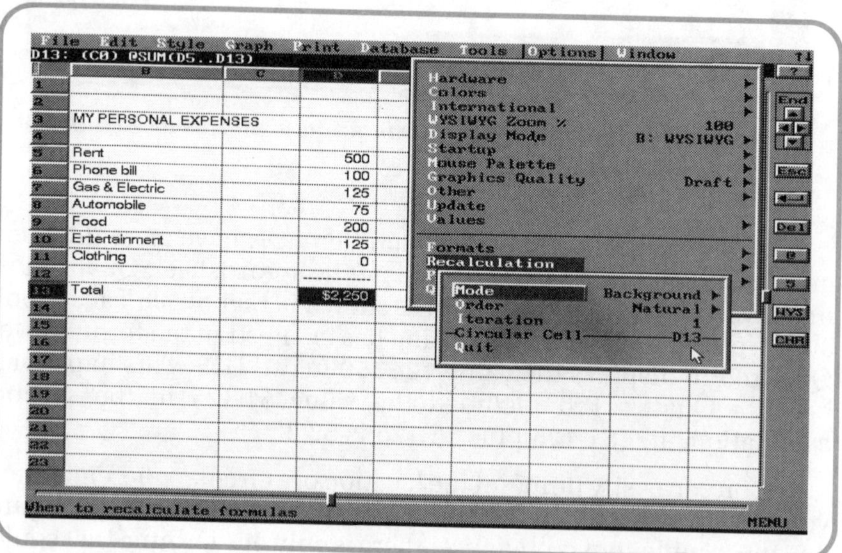

Figure 6.9 The Recalculation submenu displays the exact location of the circular reference on the active spreadsheet.

It's easy to correct a circular reference error. Just edit the original formula, and retype the cell block reference that the formula uses in its calculation. In the spreadsheet shown in Figures 6.7 and 6.8, you would enter `@SUM(D5..D11)` in cell D13. Once you correct the error, Quattro Pro displays the value $1,125 and removes the CIRC indicator from the status line.

> **Tip:** If you have trouble pinpointing the location of a circular reference in a large spreadsheet, select /**W**indow **O**ptions **M**ap View **Y**es. In MAP VIEW mode, Quattro Pro shrinks all column widths to a single character and displays special codes for each type of cell entry. Look for a cell that contains a lowercase `c`—this is the location of the circular reference. Note its cell address, and then select /**W**indow **O**ptions **M**ap View **N**o to return to the original display mode.

An Overview of Quattro Pro's @function Commands

Quattro Pro has 114 @function commands. These built-in formulas are organized into eight categories:

Mathematical
Statistical
String
Miscellaneous
Logical
Financial
Date and Time
Database Statistical

The next few sections offer you a sampling of @functions from all eight categories.

> **Tip:** Select the `Functions` and `Function Index` keywords from the main help window, then select Function Index Keyword to learn more about the arguments used in a particular @function command.

Mathematical @function Commands

There are two types of *mathematical* @functions: *arithmetic* and *trigonometric*. These @functions duplicate many of the operations found on scientific and financial calculators. Figure 6.10 illustrates how to use the @SQRT function in a spreadsheet. Following are six of the mathematical @function commands and brief descriptions of how they work.

@SQRT(x)—Where x is a numeric value >= 0; returns the square root of a number.

@ABS(x)—Where x is a numeric value; returns the absolute value of a number.

@RAND—Displays a random number between 0 and 1.

@INT(x)—Where x is a numeric value; deletes the fractional part of a number.

@PI—Returns the value 3.14159265.

@DEGREES(x)—Where x is a numeric value in radians; converts radians to degrees.

Statistical @function Commands

The *statistical* @function commands perform basic math operations on large groups of numbers. They also calculate statistical measures using sample and population data sets. Figure 6.11 illustrates how to use the @AVG function in a spreadsheet application. Following are six of the statistical @function commands and brief descriptions of how each works.

@AVG(List)—Where List is one or more numeric values; averages a block of cell values.

@SUM(List)—Where List is one or more numeric values; sums a block of cell values.

@VARS(List)—Where List is two or more numeric values; computes variance for a sample data set.

@STDS(List)—Where List is one or more numeric values; computes standard deviation for a sample data set.

@MAX(List)—Where List is one or more numeric values; returns the maximum value in a block of cells.

@MIN(List)—Where List is one or more numeric values; returns the minimum value in a block of cells.

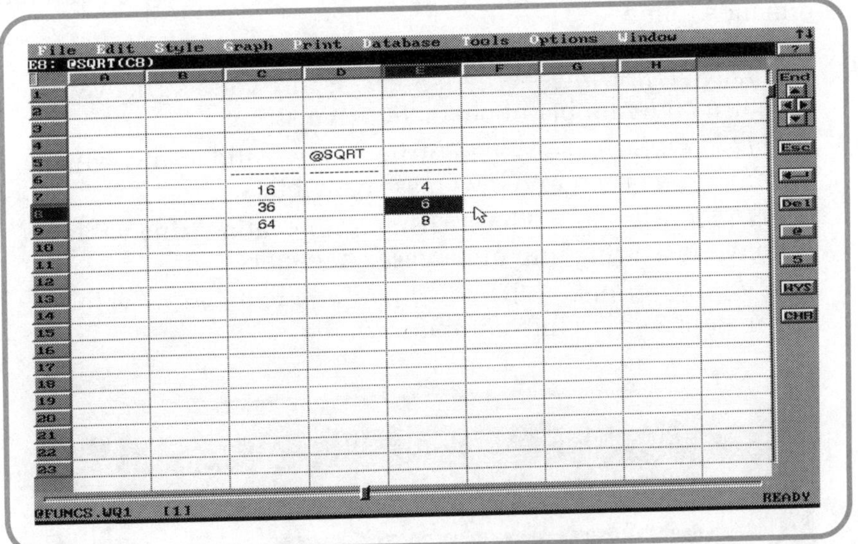

Figure 6.10 *Using @SQRT in a spreadsheet application.*

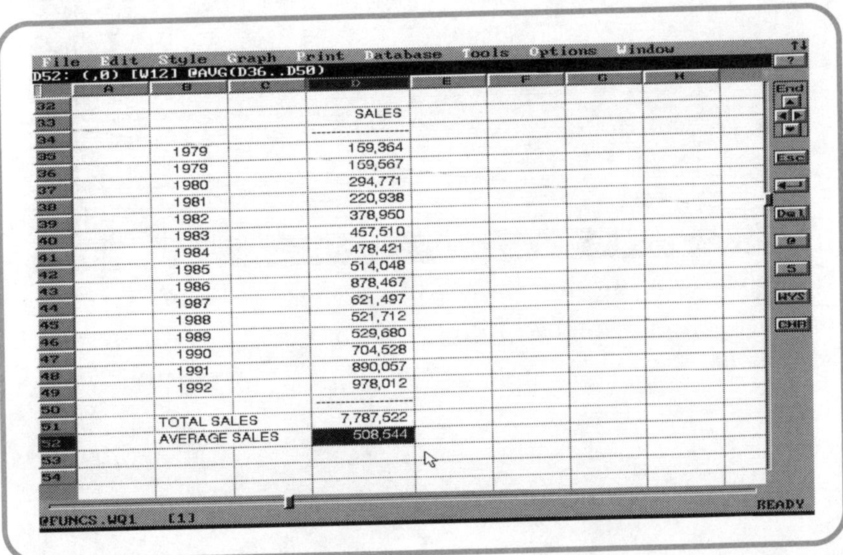

Figure 6.11 *Using @AVG in a spreadsheet application.*

String @function Commands

The *string* @function commands manipulate letters and numbers appearing in a string. These commands only work on strings—not values. Figure 6.12 illustrates how to use the @LENGTH and @UPPER functions in a spreadsheet application. (Cell B65 contains the @UPPER command to convert the contents of cell B62 to uppercase letters.) Descriptions of four of the string @function commands follow.

@LENGTH(String)—Where String is any valid string value; returns the number of characters in a string.

@LOWER(String)—Where String is any valid string value; converts a string into lowercase characters.

@UPPER(String)—Where String is any valid string value; converts a string into uppercase characters.

@VALUE(String)—Where String is any valid string value; converts a string into a numeric value.

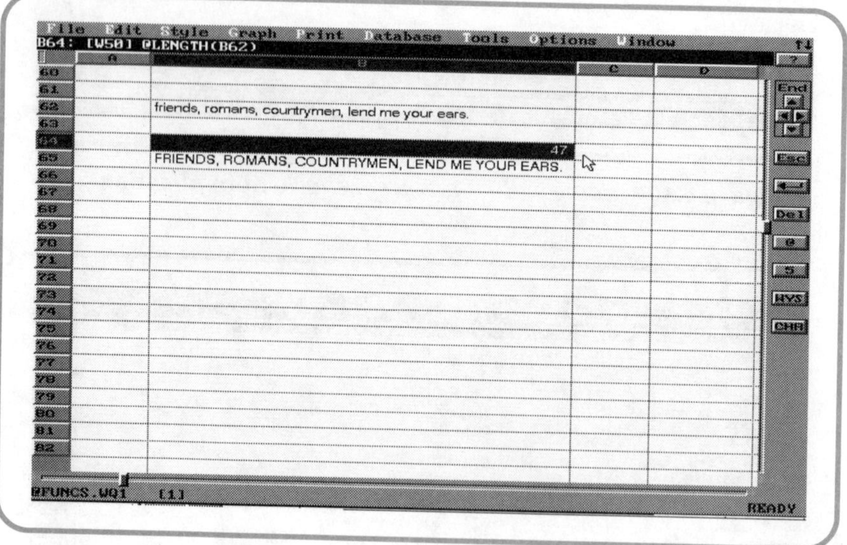

***Figure 6.12** Using @LENGTH and @UPPER in a spreadsheet application.*

Miscellaneous @function Commands

The *miscellaneous* @function commands tell you about your spreadsheet and the current work session. For example, these commands tell you about formula errors and the amount of RAM memory available for Quattro Pro. Figure 6.13 illustrates how to use the @NA function in a spreadsheet application. (The formula in cell F98 says, "If the value in D98 is blank, then display NA; otherwise display the product of C98 times D98.") All five of the following @functions operate without arguments.

> *@ERR*—Returns ERR in a cell and in any other cell which uses that cell in its formula.
>
> *@MEMAVAIL*—Displays the amount of available extended memory.
>
> *@NA*—Displays NA (not available) in the current cell, and in all cells that reference the current cell in a formula.
>
> *@VERSION*—Displays the Quattro Pro version number.

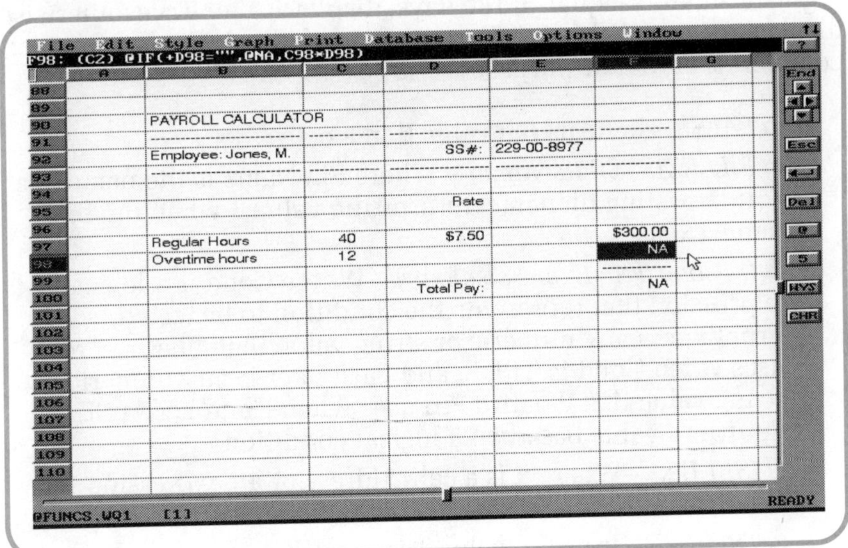

Figure 6.13 Using @NA in a spreadsheet application.

Logical @function Commands

The *logical* @function commands test *true-false* conditions and return values depending upon the outcome. Use logical @function commands to troubleshoot formulas.

One of the most important uses for logical @functions is to *error-trap*. For example, when a formula returns ERR, every other cell that references the original cell also displays ERR. It's possible to prevent this "trickle-down" effect with logical @function commands. Suppose you type the formula `@IF(@ISERR(D10),@NA,D10)` into cell A1. This formula says, "If cell D10 displays ERR, then display NA in A1; otherwise display the value of cell D10." Other formulas that reference cell A1 react in a similar manner. When cell D10 displays `ERR`, cell A1 displays `NA`—and so do all other cells that reference A1. This formula shows one way to control the "trickle-down" effect of displaying ERR on a spreadsheet.

Figure 6.14 illustrates how to use the @FALSE, @IF, and @TRUE functions in a spreadsheet application. (The formula in cell D128 says, "If the difference between today and the last review date is greater-than-or-equal-to 180 days, display a 1 for True; otherwise display a 0 for False.") Here are five of the logical @function commands and their purposes.

@FALSE—Returns the value 0 in a cell.

@FILEEXISTS(FileName)—Where FileName is the name of a valid, existing filename; returns the value 1 when the file name exists.

@IF(Cond,TrueExpr,FalseExpr)—Where Cond is a logical expression that represents the condition to be tested, TrueExpr is any numeric or string value that Quattro Pro uses when Cond is TRUE, and FalseExpr is any numeric or string value that Quattro Pro uses when Cond is FALSE. Returns a value based on a logical condition.

@ISERR(x)—Where x is a cell address or an expression for Quattro Pro to test; checks the contents of cells for errors.

@TRUE—Returns the value 1 in a cell.

Financial @function Commands

Quattro Pro's *financial* @functions help you analyze a loan, manage your business assets, and evaluate the worth of an investment. Figure 6.15 illustrates how to use the @IPAYMT function in a spreadsheet application.

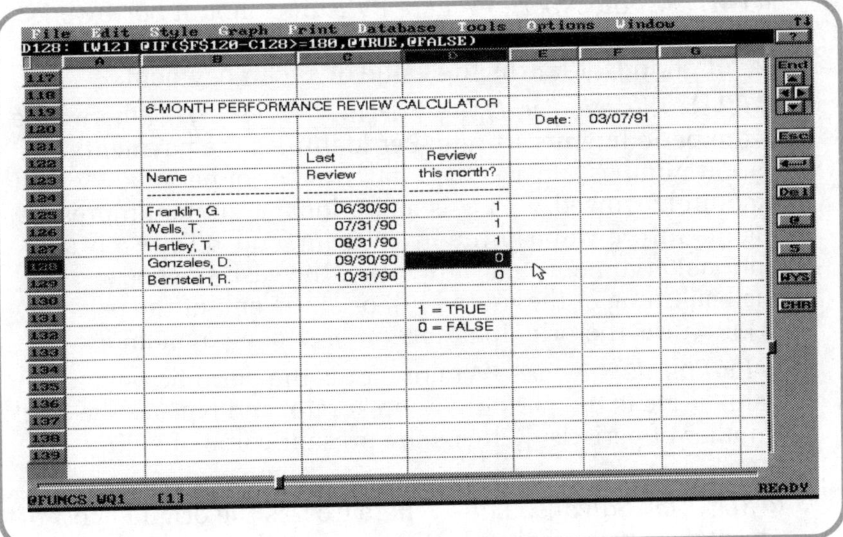

Figure 6.14 Using @FALSE, @IF, and @TRUE in a spreadsheet application.

> **Caution:** @function arguments must appear in a specific order for the calculation to be correct. Note that you do not need to arrange the argument data in a specific order on the spreadsheet, as long as you reference each @function argument in the correct order.

Following are six financial @function commands and brief descriptions of what each does.

@FV(Pmt,Rate,Nper)—Where Pmt is the periodic payment value, Rate is the periodic interest rate, and Nper is the total number of periods. Returns the future value of an investment.

@IPAYMT(Rate, Per, Nper, Pv,<Fv>,<Type>)—Where Rate is the periodic interest rate, Per identifies the payment period number, Nper is the total number of periods, Pv is the amount borrowed, <Fv> is an optional argument representing the future value of the investment, and <Type> is an optional argument that indicates if the cash flow occurs at the beginning of the period (0), or at the end of the period (1). Returns the interest portion of a loan payment.

@PMT(Pv,Rate,Nper)—Where Pv is the amount borrowed, Rate is the periodic interest rate, and Nper is the total number of periods. Returns the value of a loan payment.

@PPAYMY(Rate, Per, Nper, Pv,<Fv>,<Type>)—Where Rate is the periodic interest rate, Per identifies the payment period number, Nper is the total number of periods, Pv is the amount borrowed, <Fv> is an optional argument representing the future value of the investment, and <Type> is an optional argument that indicates if the cash flow occurs at the beginning of the period (0), or at the end of the period (1). Returns the principal portion of a loan payment.

@PV(Pmt,Rate,Nper)—Where Pmt is the periodic payment value, Rate is the periodic interest rate, and Nper is the total number of periods. Returns the present value of an investment.

@SLN(Cost,Salvage,Life)—Where Cost is the original cost of an asset, Salvage is the asset's salvage value, and Life is the depreciable life of the asset. Computes straight-line depreciation.

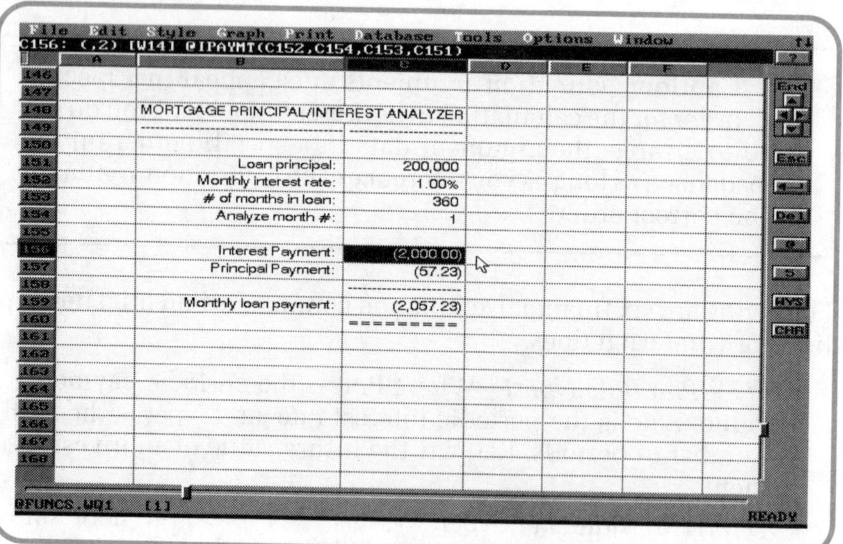

Figure 6.15 Using @IPAYMT in a spreadsheet application.

Date and Time @function Commands

Quattro Pro's *date and time* @function commands help you to keep track of time. Use them to display the current time or the amount of time that has elapsed between two dates. Use these @functions in all of your "time-sensitive" spreadsheet applications. Figure 6.16 illustrates how to use the @NOW function in a spreadsheet application. Descriptions of three of the date and time @functions follow.

> *@DATE(Yr,Mo,Day)*—Where Yr is a numeric value between 0 and 199, Mo is a numeric value between 1 and 12, and Day is a numeric value between 1 and 31. Displays a date serial number.
>
> *@NOW*—Displays today's date serial number.
>
> *@TODAY*—Enters the numeric value of the system's date.

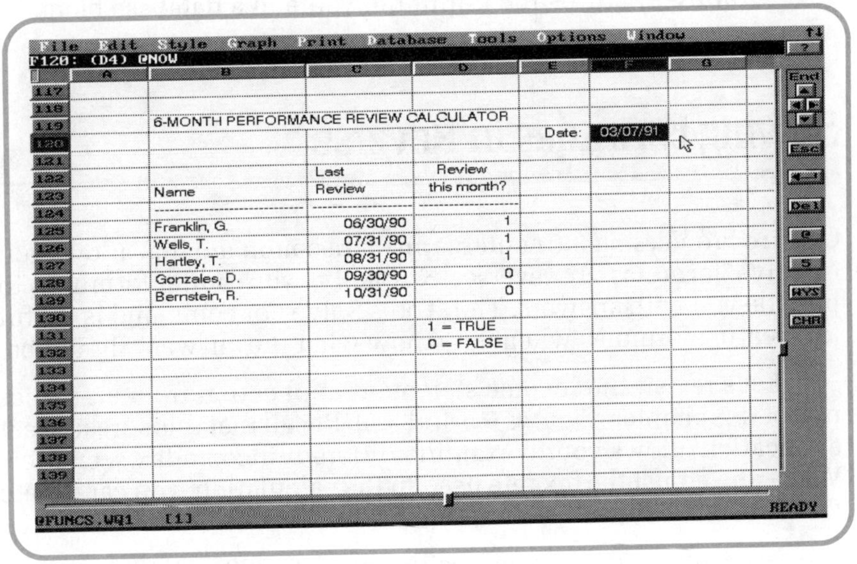

Figure 6.16 Using @NOW in a spreadsheet application.

Database Statistical @function Commands

The *database statistical* @function commands are just like the statistical @function commands. These @functions return information about data in a Quattro Pro database. All Database Statistical @functions use the same arguments. The arguments syntax is as follows:

(Block,Column,Criteria)

Block is the cell block that contains the database and the database field names, where Column is the number of the column containing the field upon which the operation is being performed (the first column in Block is 0, the second is 1, and so on). Criteria is the cell block containing the search criteria.

Following are six of the database statistical @function commands and how they work.

@DAVG—Averages a block of values in a database.

@DSUM—Sums a block of values in a database.

@DVARS—Computes variance for a sample data set.

@DSTDS—Computes standard deviation for a sample data set.

@DMAX—Returns the maximum value in a database block.

@DMIN—Returns the minimum value in a database block.

Solving Formulas in Reverse

Quattro Pro Version 3.0 contains an extra command that allows you to solve formulas in reverse. Normally, you build formulas to provide you with answers. The /**T**ools **S**olve For command is useful for creating formulas when you know what the answers should be.

Let's revisit the income statement application from an earlier part of this chapter (Figures 6.5 and 6.6). Recall that this spreadsheet application allows you to examine different income-tax scenarios. When you adjust the tax rate used in the calculation, you can create different tax amounts.

Now suppose that you decide that $25,000 is the maximum amount that you wish to pay in taxes. You might ask yourself the question, "What tax rate produces a tax bill of exactly $25,000?" The following Quick Steps show how to solve a formula in reverse, such as finding the desired tax rate.

Solving a Formula in Reverse

1. Press /TS to select the /**T**ools **S**olve For command. — Quattro Pro displays the blank **S**olve For menu.

2. Press F to activate the **F**ormula Cell option, type `E20`, and press Enter. — Quattro Pro accepts E20 as the location of the tax formula.
3. Press T to activate the **T**arget Value option, type `25000` without commas, and press Enter. — Quattro Pro accepts 25000 as the targeted income tax value.
4. Press V to activate the **V**ariable Cell option, type `E22`, and press Enter. — Quattro Pro accepts E22 as the location of the value that it will vary in an attempt to produce the answer 25000. The Solve For menu on your screen should appear exactly like the one shown in Figure 6.17.
5. Press G to select the **G**o command. — Quattro Pro executes the **S**olve For command. It varies the value in cell E22 until the value in cell E20 equals 25,000.
6. Press Q to **Q**uit the **S**olve For and return to the active spreadsheet. — Your screen should appear exactly like the one shown in Figure 6.18. □

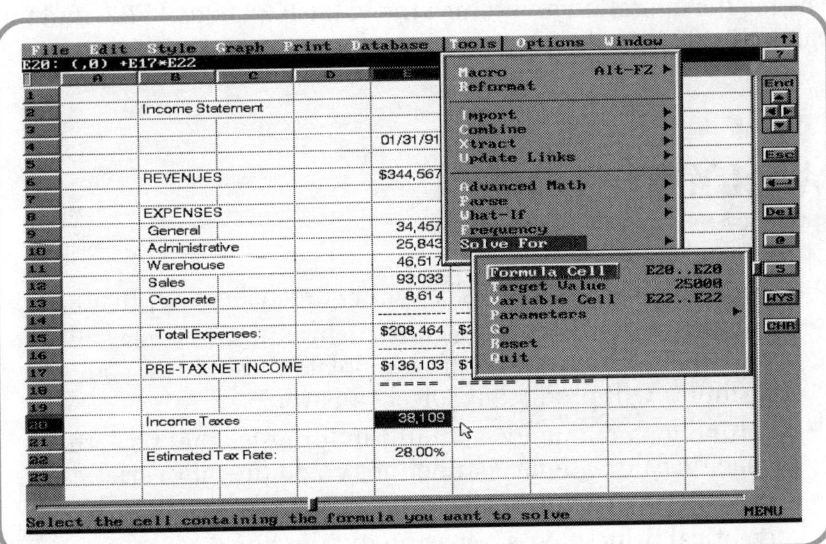

Figure 6.17 Entering the values that Quattro Pro will use to solve the income-tax formula backwards.

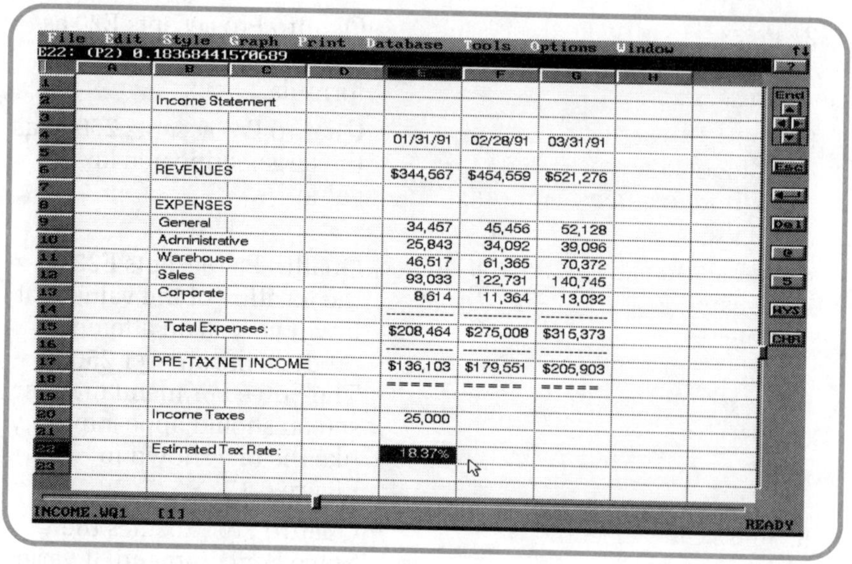

Figure 6.18 Quattro Pro calculates that a tax rate of 18.37% produces a $25,000 tax bill for January.

Once Quattro Pro locates the target tax rate, it places the value into cell E22, replacing the original value of 0.28. Quattro Pro also substitutes the Target Value into cell E20. These are the only two cells on your spreadsheet that Quattro Pro changed. Press Alt-F5 to reverse the operation and return the value 0.28 to cell E22, and the value 38,109 to cell E20.

What You've Learned

- Formulas are the "brains" of your spreadsheet applications.
- Quattro Pro calculates formulas using specific rules called the order of precedence. If you violate these rules, your formulas will produce incorrect answers.
- @function commands are built-in formulas that perform specific calculations. @functions come in eight varieties.
- Quattro Pro displays ERR when your formulas violate mathematical principles, such as no dividing by 0.

- Formulas containing circular references have multiple answers because they include the answer in the calculation.
- Version 3.0 lets you solve formulas in reverse using the **S**olve For command.

Chapter 7

Improving Your Spreadsheet Style

In This Chapter

- *Changing global formats*
- *Aligning values and labels in a cell*
- *Formatting numbers*
- *Protecting spreadsheet cells*
- *Working with rows and columns*
- *Drawing lines and shading cells*
- *Turning off gridlines*
- *Experimenting with different fonts*
- *Style enhancement extras*

This chapter shows you how to turn a basic spreadsheet into a great looking spreadsheet, or into a professional-looking report. You've already learned how to use labels, numbers, and formulas to create "mathematically accurate" applications. Sometimes, though, having data in neat columns and rows just isn't enough. You may need to enhance an application's appeal, magnify its impact, or create a final-draft output to include in an important report.

With Quattro Pro's WYSIWYG mode, you can enhance the style of your spreadsheets and immediately see results on-screen. Now more than ever it's a breeze to create attractive, presentation-quality spreadsheets that go far beyond the basics.

Changing Global Format Settings

While using Quattro Pro, you may have noticed that certain spreadsheet activities produce the same results every time. For example, each time you enter data into a spreadsheet, Quattro Pro right-aligns values and left-aligns text in cells. Quattro Pro uses a set of rules called *global format settings* to control the display of cell data. You can modify Quattro Pro's global format settings with the /**O**ptions **F**ormats command. Select this command now, and you'll see the menu displayed in Figure 7.1.

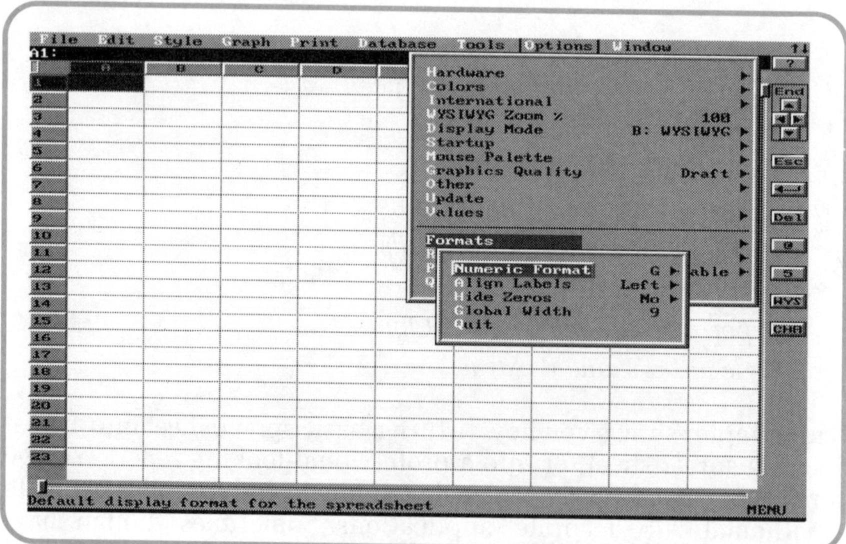

Figure 7.1 Reviewing the commands on the /Options Formats menu.

The **N**umeric Format option defines how Quattro Pro displays every number that you enter into a cell. The default setting for this option, **G**eneral, basically displays cell data in the form you entered it. Using the **N**umeric Format option, you can display numbers as dollars, percentages, dates, or times. Or you can choose to hide all labels and values as you enter them into cells.

The **A**lign Labels option tells Quattro Pro which default alignment to use for labels. This option allows you to left-align (the default), right-align, or center-align labels as you enter them into a spreadsheet cell.

The **H**ide Zeros option tells Quattro Pro to display a cell as a blank when the cell contains a zero value. Turn on this option when you prefer not to show zeros in spreadsheet cells. Initially, **H**ide Zeros is set to **N**o.

The **G**lobal Width option lets you select the column width that Quattro Pro uses for every new spreadsheet. The default setting is nine (9) characters. If your applications use a lot of large numbers and long labels, select this option and choose a wider default column width.

The default global settings affect the format *only* for new spreadsheets you create in Quattro Pro. Once you create, save, and retrieve a spreadsheet, the commands on /**O**ptions **F**ormats menu no longer affect the format settings for that spreadsheet. If you wish to use your new default global settings for all new spreadsheets, select the /**O**ptions **U**pdate command to save your changes as the new default global format settings. If you don't use the /**O**ptions **U**pdate command, Quattro Pro will revert to the original global format settings the next time you load a spreadsheet.

You easily can override Quattro Pro's global format settings for individual cells using the commands found on the /**S**tyle menu.

The /Style Menu Commands

A typical spreadsheet created with global formatting contains lots of labels, formulas, and values—but not much else. Quattro Pro's /**S**tyle menu commands allow you to customize specific cell blocks without disturbing the global format settings for the rest of the spreadsheet.

For example, you can draw boxes around text and values, draw double lines under financial statement figures, and shade important cells. You also can change the cell width of a column or a block of columns, or hide columns that contain private data. To give your reports and graphs that "published" look, you can select unique *fonts* (lettering styles) for different types of data. For instance, you might use a large font for a report title, a medium-sized font for column and row labels; and a smaller font for numbers and legends.

Figure 7.2 shows the final version of a special application, a timeclock calculator spreadsheet. This spreadsheet calculates the total number of work hours for workers at a fictitious company called SayCo Corporation.

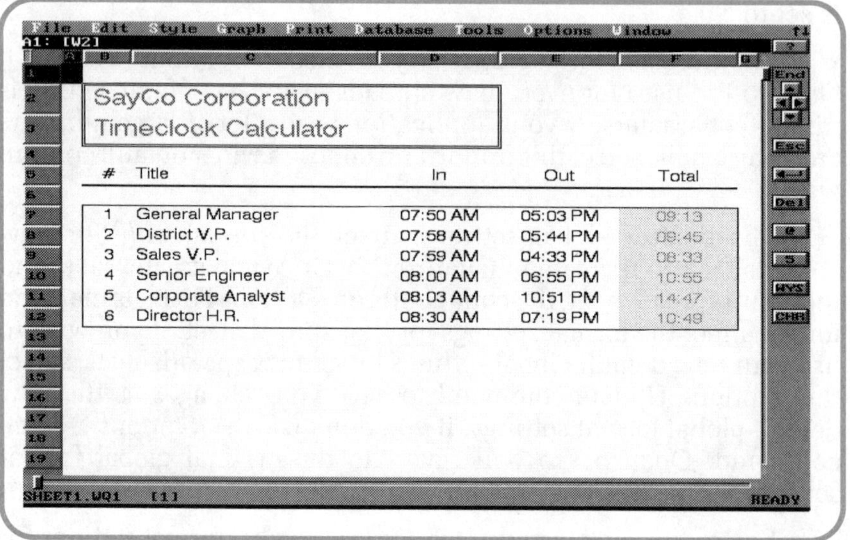

Figure 7.2 The Timeclock Calculator spreadsheet.

Create this spreadsheet now so you can follow along in this chapter to learn all about improving spreadsheet style. Review the following guidelines for insights into how the timeclock calculator spreadsheet works. For now, concentrate on the process of entering report labels and data only. Later in this chapter you will actually perform the steps necessary to create the spreadsheet shown in Figure 7.2.

1. Enter report titles into cells B2 and B3. Use the titles shown in Figure 7.2 or create titles of your own.
2. Enter the label headings, `#`, `Title`, `In`, `Out`, and `Total` into cells B5 through F5.
3. Enter each employee's record one row at a time, beginning on row 7. To make the first entry, for example, type `1` into cell B7, then type `General Manager` into cell C7.

4. Use the Ctrl-D shortcut described in Chapter 5 to enter each employee's In and Out times. For instance, to enter the In time for employee #1, move the cell selector to cell D7, press Ctrl-D, type `07:50`, and press Enter. You must enter the Out times using 24-hour military time. It's easy to calculate military time—just add 12 to the value of any time after 12 noon. So, to enter an Out time of 5:03 p.m. in cell E7, you must type `17:03`. Quattro Pro correctly displays the **AM** or **PM** indicator when you format the time entry later in this chapter.
5. The values in column F actually are formula results. That is, to arrive at the total hours that each employee worked, simply subtract the In time from the Out time. (The formula in cell F7 is *+E7–D7*, which returns an answer of nine hours and 13 minutes for employee #1.)

Once you've finished creating this application, your screen should resemble the one shown in Figure 7.2. The only difference will be the lack of "spreadsheet style."

The /**S**tyle menu organizes its commands in roughly the order you should use them. For example, when you align and format cell data, you may need to increase the width of a column to accommodate the formatted data. It makes sense to add final stylistic touches such as drawn lines, shaded cells, and customized fonts *after* you can see full cell entries. Press /S to pull down the /**S**tyle menu shown in Figure 7.3.

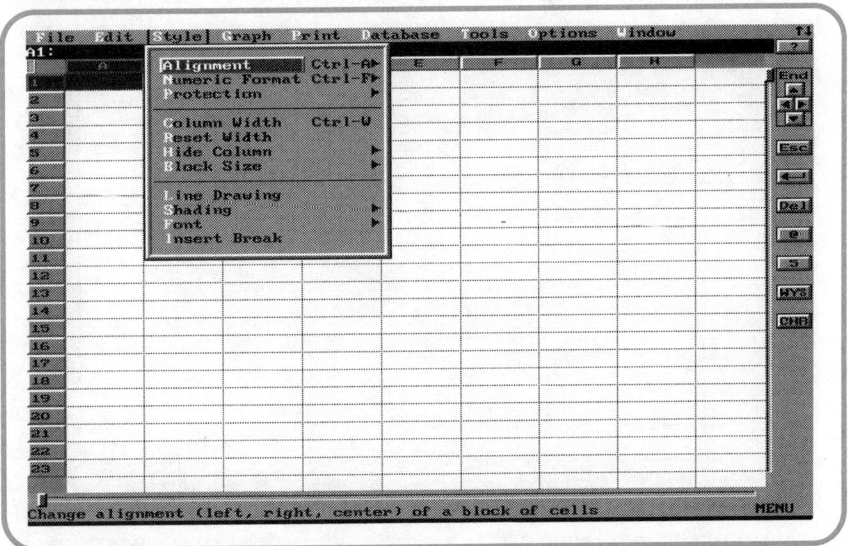

Figure 7.3 Reviewing the commands on the /Style menu.

> **Tip:** You already know that pressing Alt-F5 (the Undo key) reverses many Quattro Pro spreadsheet operations. Except for **I**nsert Break, the Undo key cannot reverse effects created with the /**S**tyle menu commands.

Aligning Data in a Cell

Experience and common sense have taught you the importance of properly spacing words when you write or type a paragraph of text. It's equally important to space spreadsheet entries properly. Your spreadsheets will make little sense if your labels and numbers appear in one continuous line, with no spacing.

In Chapter 3, you learned that when you enter data into a cell, Quattro Pro decides what type of data it is (value or label). Earlier in this chapter, you saw that Quattro Pro automatically aligns data according to the global format settings (labels left and values right). Look at the spreadsheet shown in Figure 7.4. This figure illustrates that some applications just don't look right when built using the default global format settings (if you built your own spreadsheet and are following along, your screen should resemble the one shown here).

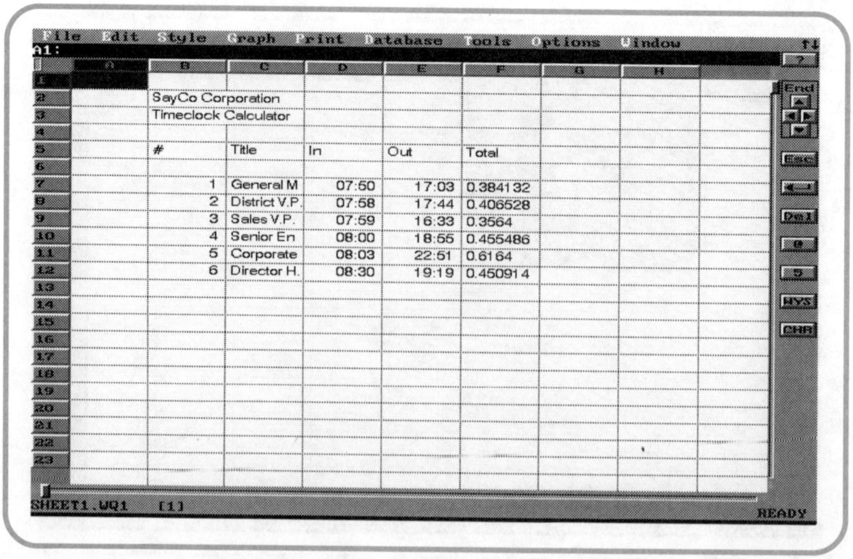

Figure 7.4 A basic, unformatted Quattro Pro spreadsheet.

The following Quick Steps show how to use the /**S**tyle **A**lignment command to help improve the alignment of the labels and values on our timeclock spreadsheet.

Aligning a Block of Data on the Spreadsheet

1. Move the cell selector to the cell in the upper left corner of the cell block you want to align (cell B5).	The mode indicator displays READY. The contents of the active cell appear on the input line.
2. Press /SA (or press Ctrl-A) to select the /**S**tyle **A**lignment command.	Quattro Pro displays a menu showing four alignment options: **G**eneral, **L**eft, **R**ight, and **C**enter.
3. Press the boldface letter of the alignment option you wish to use. For our example, press C to select Center.	Quattro Pro prompts you to type in the cell block you wish to align.
4. Highlight the target cell block by pressing End-↓ twice to highlight B5..B12.	Quattro Pro highlights the target cell block.
5. Press Enter to align the target cell block.	Quattro Pro aligns the data in the target cell block and places the cell selector back in the first cell of the highlighted cell block (cell B5). The mode indicator displays READY. ☐

It's a breeze to add stylistic touches to a spreadsheet when you use a mouse. With a mouse, you can preselect (highlight) a cell block before you choose a /**S**tyle menu command. This way, Quattro Pro knows ahead of time which spreadsheet area to improve. For instance, if you highlight cell block B5..B12 and press Ctrl-A then C, Quattro Pro immediately center-aligns the data in the highlighted block. Compare this lightning-fast operation to the time it took you to do the preceding Quick Step and you'll be pleasantly surprised!

Figure 7.5 shows how aligning cell data improves the organization and clarity of a spreadsheet. Notice that the center-aligned label in cell B5 now lines up exactly with the numbers beneath it. In the figure, the data in columns D, E, and F are also center-aligned.

> **Tip:** Use the /**O**ptions **F**ormats **A**lign Labels command to change the global label alignment setting to **R**ight or **C**enter.

Formatting the Display of Cell Data

Recall from Chapter 3 that Quattro Pro uses special symbols called label prefixes to define a label's alignment. Type the caret (^) prefix, for example, to center-align a label (see the input line at the top of the spreadsheet in Figure 7.5). You can manually edit a label's alignment by entering EDIT mode and then replacing the existing prefix with a new one. You *cannot* manually set the alignment of a value, because Quattro Pro doesn't store alignment prefixes with values. Likewise, there is no way to set the global alignment setting for values—you must change the alignment for a block of values using the /**S**tyle **A**lignment command.

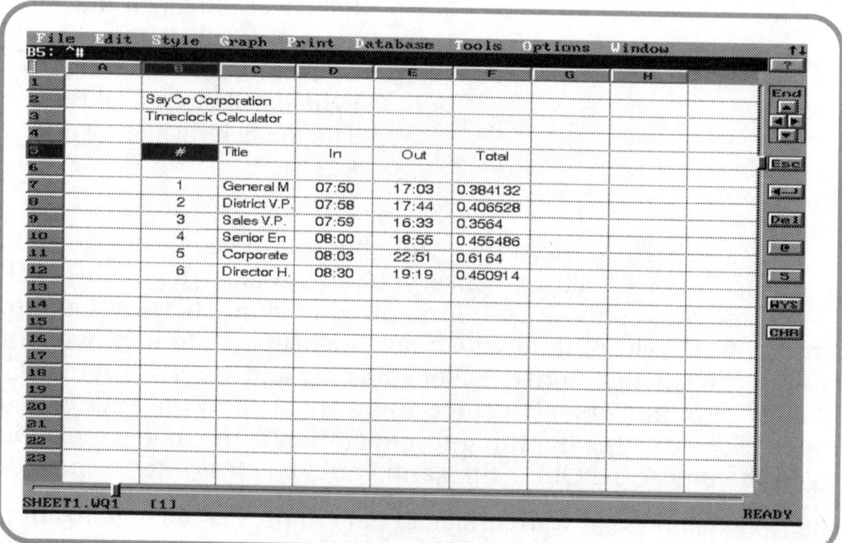

Figure 7.5 Properly aligned data makes it easier to understand a spreadsheet.

Quattro Pro can work with values that contain up to 16 significant digits. A *significant digit* is any integer in any position in a number, except a leading zero. Quattro Pro does not count decimals, commas, dollar signs, and percentage signs as significant digits.

The **S**tyle **N**umeric Format command alters the display of values in spreadsheet cells. (In some cases, this command also affects the display of labels.) Use the **N**umeric Format command when your values are longer than the width of the cells. Altering a value's display does not change the number itself, just the way it looks on-screen. Suppose that cell A1 contains the value 5, and you format it to display as $5.00. Doing so does not change the value in A1 to $5.00 or 5.00—the new format only alters the value's on-screen appearance.

This is an important point to remember. If you format the number 9.95 to display as 10, Quattro Pro still uses 9.95 in all calculations. Quattro Pro's mathematical operations work on entire numbers, and not their abbreviated, on-screen equivalents.

In certain cases (say, when a value is longer than the width of its cell), Quattro Pro may automatically show a rounded value. For instance, Quattro Pro would display the value 0.9999999 as 1 in a cell nine characters wide (the default width), because Quattro Pro cannot display the entire number in the cell. In this case, Quattro Pro still uses 0.9999999 in calculations.

Table 7.1 summarizes the options available on the /**S**tyle **N**umeric Format menu.

Table 7.1 The /Style Numeric Format options.

Format	Description	Examples
Fixed	Displays values with leading zeros and decimal places.	0.00 –543.21 54321.00
Scientific	Displays values in scientific notation format.	0.0E+00 –2.1E+02
Currency	Displays values with currency symbol, and commas to separate thousands. Shows negative numbers in parentheses.	$0.00 ($432.10) $65,432.10
,(comma)	Displays values with commas to separate thousands, and shows negative numbers in parentheses.	0.00 432.10 65,432.10

(continued)

Table 7.1 (continued)

Format	Description	Examples
General	Displays numbers in the general form they were entered.	0 –543.2 54321
+/–	Transforms values into a horizontal bar graph where the plus symbol (+) represents a positive integer, the minus symbol (–) represents a negative integer, and the decimal point (.) represents zero.	++++ –––– ....
Percent	Displays values as percentages.	0.00% 22.00% 1.5%
Date	Displays values in various date and time formats.	23-SEP-62 09/23/62 17:24:33 PM
Text	Displays formulas as text instead of calculated results.	@AVG(A1..F100) +35+(B2/C3)
Hidden	Conceals the display of cell entries. Entries still appear on the input line when you select the cell.	
Reset	Returns the numeric format for a cell block to the default format (specified with the /**O**ptions **F**ormats **N**umeric Format command). Redisplays entries hidden with the **H**idden format.	

Many of the format options listed in Table 7.1 require that you specify the number of displayed decimal places. Quattro Pro can display up to 15 decimal places for these numbers when permitted by the column width.

Let's return to the sample timeclock spreadsheet to learn how to format the number display. Use the following Quick Steps.

Formatting a Block of Values on a Spreadsheet

Step	Result
1. Move the cell selector to the cell in the upper left corner of the cell block that you want to format (cell D7).	The mode indicator displays READY. The contents of the active cell appear on the input line.
2. Press /SN (or press Ctrl-F) to select the /**S**tyle **N**umeric Format command.	Quattro Pro displays a menu showing the numeric format options (see Table 7.1).
3. Press the boldface letter of the numeric format option you wish to use (choose D for **D**ate, T for **T**ime, and then **2**).	Quattro Pro prompts you to type in the cell block you wish to modify.
4. Highlight the target cell block by pressing End-↓ then → to highlight D7..E12.	Quattro Pro highlights the target cell block.
5. Press Enter to format the target cell block.	Formats the data in the target cell block and places the cell selector back in the first cell of the highlighted cell block (cell D7.) The mode indicator displays READY. □

After you change the numeric format of a cell, Quattro Pro displays a format code in parentheses on the input line (for example (D7) for Date format number 7).

The format option you choose may create a number longer than the width of the column. For instance, look at the data in column F of Figure 7.6. The values in this column were formatted using the Date Time **1**-(HH:MM:SS AM/PM) format. Because the formatted display is longer than the width of the column, Quattro Pro fills each cell with asterisks. Asterisks tell you that you need to adjust the column width or the cell format—asterisks do not affect the values stored in the cells. To correct this problem, select /**S**tyle **N**umeric Format **D**ate **T**ime and choose the **4**-(Short intl.) option.

You may edit or delete data in a formatted cell without destroying or erasing its format. Also, when you copy or move formatted values, Quattro Pro reproduces the cell format in the new location.

> **Tip:** Use the /**O**ptions **F**ormats **N**umeric Format command to change the global numeric format setting to any of the options listed in Table 7.1.

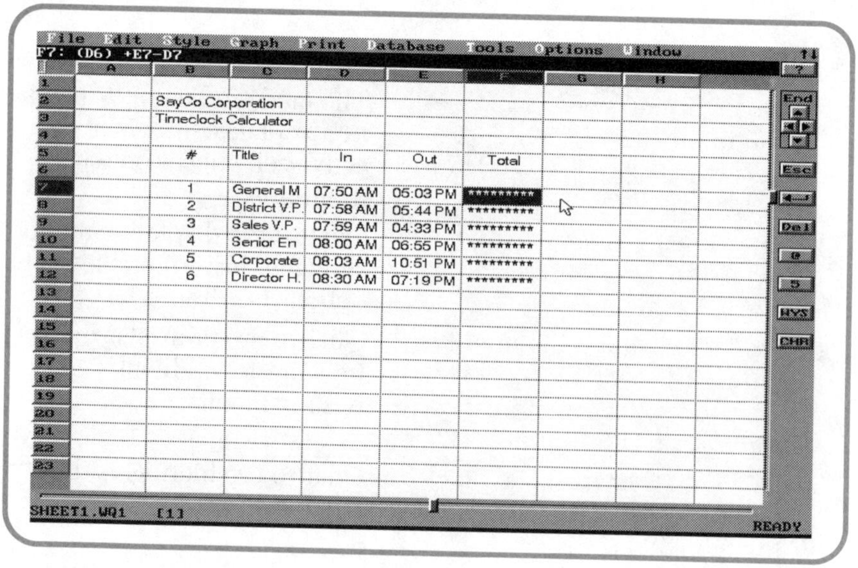

Figure 7.6 Quattro Pro displays asterisks in a cell when a column's width can't accommodate a numeric format.

Hiding Labels

Use the /**S**tyle **N**umeric Format options for formatting values, dates, and times. You can choose the **H**idden and **R**eset options to format labels. Formatting a label with any other numeric format option command has no effect.

Use the **H**idden command to hide a label on a spreadsheet. The **H**idden command only removes it from view—it is still there and you can still overwrite the contents of a hidden cell. To avoid accidentally overwriting or erasing a hidden cell, use the protection commands covered in the next section.

When the cell selector is in a hidden cell, the cell contents appear on the input line. To redisplay a label in a spreadsheet, choose /**S**tyle **N**umeric Format **R**eset.

Protecting Spreadsheet Cells

Protecting cells is a bit different from other Quattro Pro enhancement operations. When you protect a cell, you do not enhance its display. You just prevent anyone using the spreadsheet from altering the cell data. Quattro Pro won't allow you to edit, replace, or delete entries in protected cells. Also, you can't delete columns or rows that contain protected cells.

You can protect the whole spreadsheet, then unprotect or protect individual cells. By default, each spreadsheet loads with global protection disabled.

Protecting the Entire Spreadsheet

Select /**O**ptions **P**rotection **E**nable to protect spreadsheet cells—this command activates global spreadsheet protection. When global protection is enabled, Quattro Pro shows `PR` on the input line for every protected cell that you select. When you try to alter a protected cell, Quattro Pro beeps and displays an error message. Press Esc to cancel the error message. Unless you turn on global spreadsheet protection, you can erase, overwrite, or otherwise alter data in any spreadsheet cell.

Unprotecting Individual Cells

It's relatively easy to remove the protection from individual cells to change data stored in the cells. To unprotect a cell, place the cell selector in the cell and select /**S**tyle **P**rotection **U**nprotect. After you've unprotected a cell, Quattro Pro displays a `U` on the input line when that cell is active.

> **Tip:** Quattro Pro makes unprotected cells easy to see by displaying them in reverse color on a color display, and in high intensity on a monochrome display. You may have to adjust the foreground and background intensity knobs on a monochrome display to see this effect.

You can protect a block of cells that previously has been unprotected by choosing the /**S**tyle **P**rotection **P**rotect command.

Working with Columns

There are four column adjustment commands on the /**S**tyle menu: **C**olumn Width, **R**eset Width, **H**ide Column, and **B**lock Width. These commands allow you to set and reset the column width of a single column or the column widths in a block of columns. These commands also allow you to set and reset the height of a single row or the row height in a block of rows. You can also hide columns that contain private information.

Setting the Width of a Single Column

Quattro Pro lets you set the width of an individual column with the /**S**tyle **C**olumn Width command. Valid column widths range from 1 to 254 characters. Although you may never need a column 254 characters wide, it's nice to know you can adjust a column to fit nearly any size label or value. The following Quick Steps explain the procedure for changing a column's width.

Q Changing the Width of a Single Column

1. Place the cell selector in any cell in the column you want to make wider or narrower. (Choose cell C7 in our example spreadsheet.)
   The mode indicator displays READY. The contents of the active cell appear on the input line.
2. Press /SC (or press Ctrl-C) to select the /**S**tyle **C**olumn Width command.
   Quattro Pro prompts you to enter a desired column width.
3. Type a number that represents the desired character width for the target column (the default setting is 9, so for our example, type 25).
4. Press Enter.
   Quattro Pro adjusts the width of the target column, as shown in Figure 7.7. □

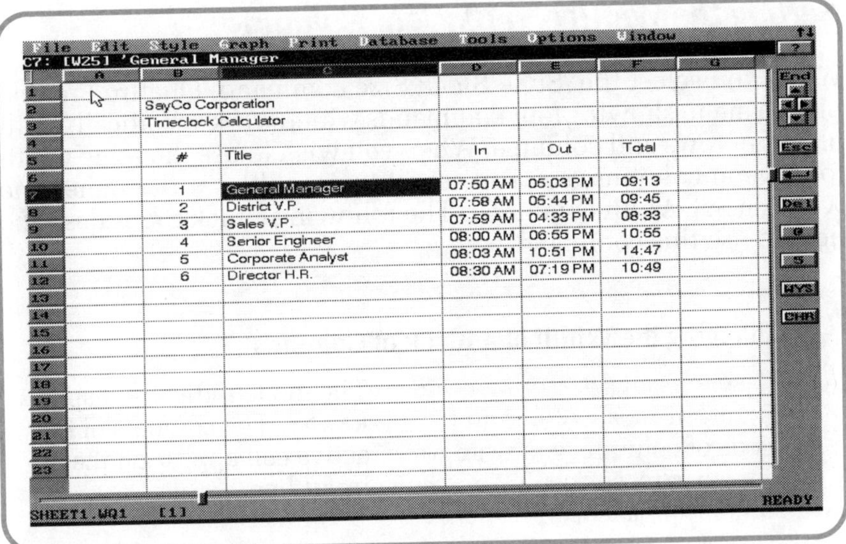

Figure 7.7 Changing column widths makes it easier to see long labels and values.

After you change the width of a column, Quattro Pro displays the new width in brackets on the input line (for example, `[W25]`). (See Figure 7.7.)

It's sometimes difficult to pick the correct width for a column just by looking at the spreadsheet. Could you have guessed that the best width for column C is 25? If you're unsure of the column width you want, you can use a second method for changing column widths. Start by selecting a column. Now press Ctrl-W, the shortcut key for the /**S**tyle **C**olumn Width command. Instead of typing a width value, press the ← or → keys until the column is wide enough to display the values and labels it contains. Press Enter once to save that width for the active column.

To change a column's width with a mouse, click and hold the mouse pointer on the target column's letter at the top of the spreadsheet. Now drag the mouse right to widen (or drag it left to narrow) the column width. Release the mouse button when you get the correct width.

Now use the preceding Quick Steps to change the width of column A to 2, and B to 5.

Setting the Width of a Block of Columns

When you select the /**S**tyle **B**lock Size command, Quattro Pro displays a menu showing four commands which work specifically with blocks of rows and columns. When you wish to use the same width for several columns, you can set all their widths at the same time with the **S**et Width command. The following Quick Steps describe how to use this command.

Changing the Width of a Block of Columns

1. Place the cell selector in a cell in the left-most column in the block of columns you want to change (choose cell D7 in our sample spreadsheet).
   The mode indicator displays READY. The contents of the active cell appear on the input line.
2. Press /SBS to select the /**S**tyle **B**lock Size **S**et Width command.
   Quattro Pro prompts you to enter the block containing the target columns.
3. Highlight the cell block that contains the columns you wish to alter and press Enter. (Or type in block name coordinates that include those columns.) Press the → twice to highlight cell block D7..F7.
   Quattro Pro prompts you to type a number for the new column width.
4. Enter a number for the new column width (Type 12 for our sample spreadsheet).
5. Press Enter.
   Quattro Pro adjusts the width of the block of columns, as shown in Figure 7.8. □

You also may reset the widths of all columns in a block by choosing the /**S**tyle **B**lock Size **R**eset Width command. Quattro Pro resets the width of all columns in the block to the default value. Remember, the default column width is always nine characters, unless you change the global column width setting with the /**O**ptions **F**ormats **G**lobal Width command.

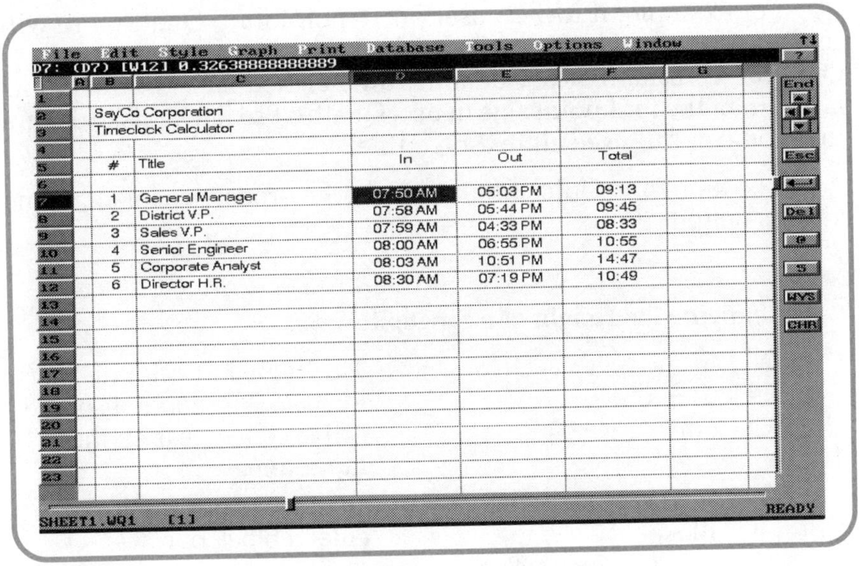

Figure 7.8 Adjusting the width of a block of columns.

The /**S**tyle **B**lock Size **A**uto Width command resets the width of a column to accommodate the longest entry in the column. When you choose this command, Quattro Pro prompts you to enter a number for the amount of "extra spaces" to tack on to the longest column entry so there is some vacant space between columns of entries. For instance, if the longest entry in column A were 10 characters, and you chose 5 extra spaces, Quattro Pro would set the width of column A to 15 characters (10 + 5).

Managing Spreadsheet Row Height

In WYSIWYG display mode, Quattro Pro automatically manages spreadsheet row height for you. If, for example, you add a font with a large point size to a spreadsheet, Quattro Pro automatically adjusts the height of the current row to accommodate the new font.

If you wish, you can manually modify spreadsheet row height with the /**S**tyle **B**lock Size **H**eight command. Valid row heights range from 1 to 240. The default height of a row (unlike in the case of column widths) is determined by the point size of the font in use on each row. In general, Quattro Pro sets the default height of a row to be slightly taller than the largest point size in use on that row.

For example, if row 25 uses an 18 point font, Quattro Pro will set the default height of that row to at least 18 points. In some cases Quattro Pro establishes a default row height that is a few points larger than the font point size in use. Quattro Pro does this to ensure that you can fully see all text on a line.

The following Quick Steps explain the procedure for changing a row's height.

Changing the Height of a Single Row

1. Place the cell selector in any cell in the row you want to make taller or shorter.

   The mode indicator displays READY. The contents of the active cell appear on the input line.

2. Press /SBHS to select the /**S**tyle **B**lock Size **H**eight **S**et Row Height command.

   Quattro Pro prompts you to enter a block of rows.

3. Press Enter to accept the current row as the the target row.

   Quattro Pro prompts you to alter height of the row.

4. Type a number that represents the desired point size for the target row.

5. Press Enter.

   Quattro Pro adjusts the height of the target row. □

You use the same procedure to set the height for a block of rows. In Step 3, instead of pressing Enter to accept the current row, press the ↓ or ↑ and highlight all of the rows you wish to adjust. In Step 4, instead of typing in a point size value try pressing the ↑ or ↓ keys to enlarge or shrink the height of the target row.

To change a row's height with a mouse, click and hold the mouse pointer on the target row's number at the left edge of the spreadsheet. Now drag the mouse up to enlarge (or drag it down to shrink) the row height. Release the mouse button when you get the correct height.

As with column widths, Quattro Pro saves all custom row heights with the spreadsheet when you choose the /**F**ile **S**ave command.

> **Caution:** if you shrink the height of a row below the default height, Quattro Pro may truncate text on that row. In this event you will need to use the **S**et Row Height command to reveal the top portion of the truncated text.

To reset the height of a single row, substitute the **R**eset Row Height command for the **S**et Row Height command in the preceding Quick Steps.

Hiding Columns

In some cases, you may want to hide certain columns to keep them from being seen by unauthorized people (payroll figures are a good example). You can hide, then unhide columns on a spreadsheet with the /**S**tyle **H**ide Column command. When you hide a column, Quattro Pro keeps that column's data in memory so you can show the data again when you need to.

To hide one or more columns from view, choose /**S**tyle **H**ide Column **H**ide. When prompted, type a cell block address that contains the letters of the columns to hide. By typing D5..E5, for example, you can hide columns D and E. Press Enter, and Quattro Pro hides the selected column(s).

Quattro Pro does not reletter the column names when you execute this command. Instead, it joins the bordering columns (to the right and left of the hidden columns) so there are no blank areas on the spreadsheet. It looks as if Quattro Pro erased the target columns, but they weren't erased, just hidden. Hidden formulas still figure in the spreadsheet totals.

The /**S**tyle **H**ide Column command creates a screen that looks very much like the one you get when you split a spreadsheet into two vertical window panes—but without the annoying vertical border from the second pane. Figure 7.9 shows what the sample spreadsheet looks like when you hide columns D and E.

To expose hidden columns, choose /**S**tyle **H**ide Column **E**xpose. Quattro Pro temporarily redisplays each hidden column on your screen, and places an asterisk (*) next to the column letter. This allows you to see which columns were hidden. Type in a cell or block address that contains the letters of the columns you wish to expose. Once you press Enter, the hidden columns you selected become permanently visible. Quattro Pro rehides any hidden columns that you choose not to expose.

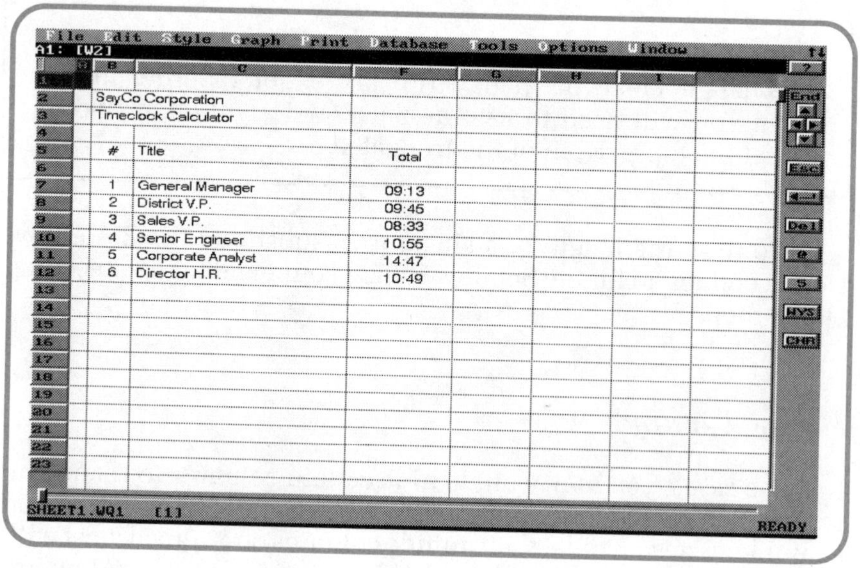

Figure 7.9 The letters of hidden columns D and E do not show on the spreadsheet.

Quattro Pro does not show hidden columns on a printout of a spreadsheet that contains hidden columns.

> **Tip:** The use of certain Quattro Pro commands (such as /**E**dit **M**ove and /**E**dit **C**opy) temporarily exposes all hidden columns on the active spreadsheet, in case you need to perform operations on cells in the hidden columns. When you're finished with the operation at hand, Quattro Pro rehides the columns.

Drawing Lines and Shading Cells

In WYSIWYG display mode, Quattro Pro exactly reproduces all /**S**tyle menu features on-screen for you. When you add custom fonts, draw lines, or shade cells in WYSIWYG display mode, you already know what your spreadsheet will look like on a printed page. In fact, with WYSIWYG display mode you can fine-tune a spreadsheet's presentation-quality appearance prior to printing the final copy.

Drawing Lines

When you select the /**S**tyle **L**ine Drawing command, Quattro Pro offers you several line options. After you press /SL to see the Line Drawing menu, press Enter once to review the line drawing options, defined as follows:

All draws a box around the target cell block and adds vertical and horizontal lines between all cells.

Outside draws a box around the perimeter of the target cell block.

Top draws a horizontal line on top of the first row in the target cell block.

Bottom draws a horizontal line underneath the last row in the target cell block.

Left draws a vertical line along the left edge of the cells in the leftmost column in the target cell block.

Right draws a vertical line along the right edge of the cells in the rightmost column of the target cell block.

Inside draws vertical and horizontal lines between all cells in the target cell block.

Horizontal draws lines between each row in the target cell block. This command does nothing if the target cell block contains only one row.

Vertical draws lines between each column in the block. This command does nothing if the target cell block contains only one column.

Quit returns to the spreadsheet without making any changes.

Press Q to quit the /**S**tyle menu after you've finished reviewing the options. The following Quick Steps show you how to draw lines on a Quattro Pro spreadsheet, such as the thick line in Figure 7.10, which is more attractive than repeating hyphens.

Q Drawing Lines on a Spreadsheet

1. Press /SL to execute the /**S**tyle **L**ine Drawing command. — Quattro Pro prompts you to type the block address of the cells around which you wish to draw lines.
2. Type the cell or block address of the target cell(s). (For the sample spreadsheet, type `B5..F5`.) — The address appears on the input line as you type.

3. Press Enter once to record the target cell block.

   Quattro Pro displays the Placement menu listing the 9 placement options.

4. Scroll through the dialog box until you highlight the `Bottom` option, or click on `Bottom` with the mouse.

   Quattro Pro displays the Line types menu listing four options, as shown in Figure 7.11.

5. Scroll through the dialog box until you highlight the `Thick` option, or click on this option once with a mouse.

   Quattro Pro draws a thick line on the bottom of the target cell block (see Figure 7.10), and displays the Placement menu again.

6. Modify the Placement and Line type options for the target cell block as desired. Or press Esc once, type in a new target cell block, and press Enter.

   Quattro Pro redraws lines around the target cell block.

7. While the Placement menu appears, press Q to Quit and return to the active spreadsheet.

   The last versions of the drawn lines remain on the spreadsheet. □

#	Title	In	Out	Total
1	General Manager	07:50 AM	05:03 PM	09:13
2	District V.P.	07:58 AM	05:44 PM	09:45
3	Sales V.P.	07:59 AM	04:33 PM	08:33
4	Senior Engineer	08:00 AM	06:55 PM	10:55
5	Corporate Analyst	08:03 AM	10:51 PM	14:47
6	Director H.R.	08:30 AM	07:19 PM	10:49

Figure 7.10 A thick double underline created with the /Style Line Drawing command is more attractive than using repeating hyphens (\-).

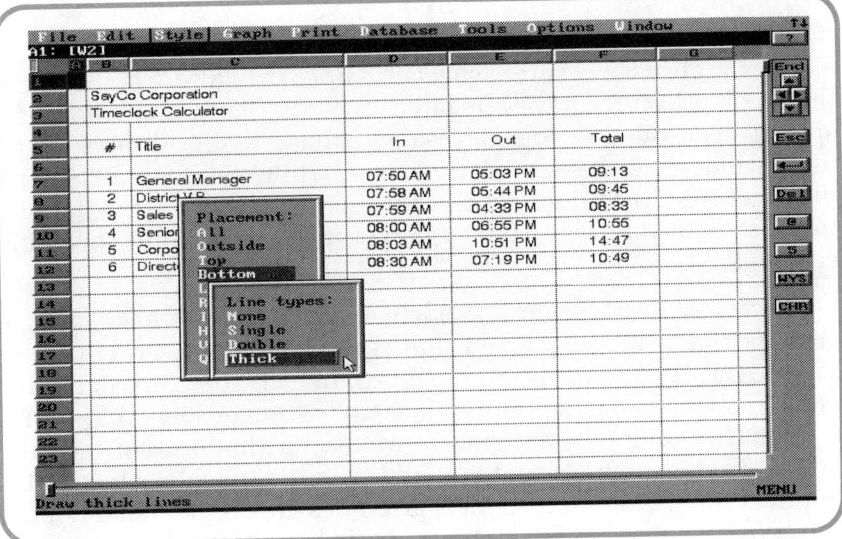

Figure 7.11 Adding graphically drawn lines to a spreadsheet report.

It's just as easy to erase drawn lines as it is to draw them. To remove lines from the spreadsheet, choose **S**tyle **L**ine Drawing, reselect the target cell block, choose All on the Placement menu, and choose None on the Line types menu. Quattro Pro immediately removes the drawn lines from the spreadsheet.

You also can partially remove lines from a spreadsheet. For example, to remove the bottom line from a box, highlight the target cell block and choose /**S**tyle **L**ine Drawing **B**ottom **N**one. Or to remove the top line from a box, choose /**S**tyle **L**ine Drawing **T**op **N**one.

> **Tip:** When you print a spreadsheet that contains drawn lines, you must first select /**P**rint **D**estination **G**raphics Printer. If you use the default destination, Quattro Pro replaces the drawn lines with the +, –, and l characters. When you print to a graphics printer, Quattro Pro correctly interprets the drawn lines and prints them as smooth lines and boxes (see Chapter 5 for complete information about printing to a graphics printer).

Figure 7.12 shows a final version of the timeclock calculator spreadsheet, illustrating how drawn lines improve the organization and the presentation quality of a basic spreadsheet report.

Removing Spreadsheet Grid Lines

Notice the absence of spreadsheet grid lines in Figure 7.12. So far, in this book grid lines have appeared in every figure that contains a spreadsheet. By now you may have realized that grid lines are an invaluable spreadsheet development tool while you are in WYSIWYG display mode. Grid lines act as an on-screen ruler, making it easier to enter data into cells and organize information into rows and columns.

Beyond these basic spreadsheet-building activities though, grid lines have little practical value. If you prefer to see grid lines on-screen, by all means continue to do so. In fact, you can even select your grid lines color with the /**O**ptions **C**olors **S**preadsheet **W**YSIWYG Colors **G**rid Lines command. However, so that we can see the stylistic enhancements that you added to the timeclock calculator application, we turn spreadsheet grid lines off. For the remainder of the book, you'll only see spreadsheet grid lines when they are useful to the topic at hand.

To remove spreadsheet grid lines, select the /**W**indow **O**ptions **G**rid Lines **H**ide command. To redisplay grid lines, select the /**W**indow **O**ptions **G**rid Lines **D**isplay command.

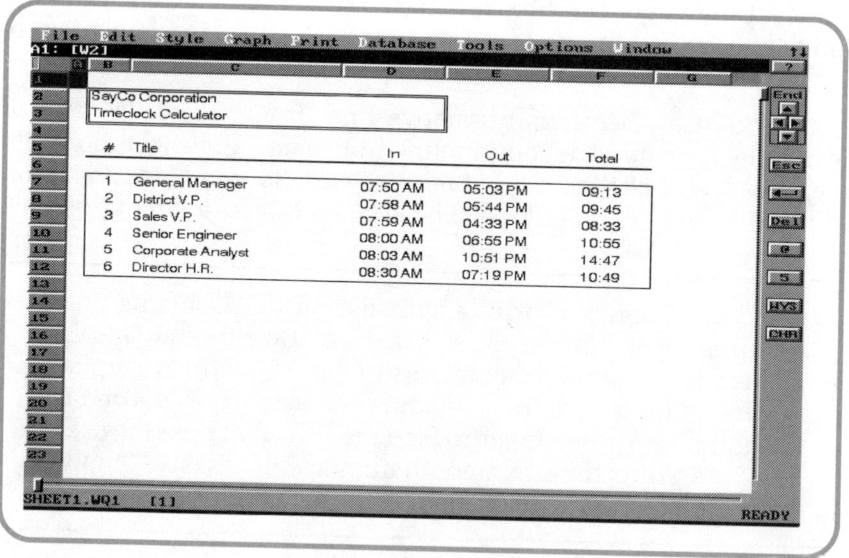

Figure 7.12 A presentation-quality version of the timeclock spreadsheet, complete with adjusted columns, formatted cells, and drawn lines.

Shading Cells

Add another useful style enhancement tool in Quattro Pro with the /**S**tyle **S**hading command. Shade cells when you need to make important data stand out on a spreadsheet, as shown in Figure 7.13. Shaded cells also can point out an area where a viewer should enter data into a spreadsheet. When you select the /**S**tyle **S**hading command, Quattro Pro offers you two shading options: **G**rey and **B**lack. The **N**one option is used to remove grey or black shading from a cell.

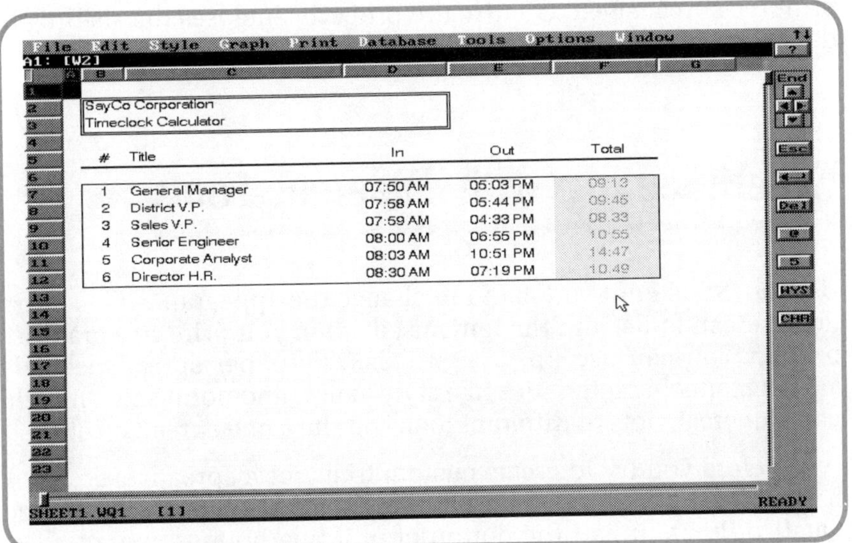

Figure 7.13 Adding shaded cells to the Timeclock Calculator spreadsheet.

To shade cells on a spreadsheet, press /SS to select the /**S**tyle **S**hading command. Select a shade option from the Shading submenu. Quattro Pro prompts you to type the coordinates of the cell block you wish to shade. Type the coordinates, then press Enter to shade those cells.

Notice that Quattro Pro shades the entire width of a cell when you use the **S**hading command. In Figure 7.13, for example, the shading in cell block F7..F12 exactly matches the width of column F. If you widen or narrow column F, Quattro Pro adjusts the shading accordingly.

> **Tip:** Quattro Pro allows you to select your own color preferences for shaded cells with the /**O**ptions **C**olors **S**preadsheet **S**hading command.

As with drawn lines, you must print to a graphics printer destination if you want to show shaded cells on a printout. If you don't, Quattro Pro won't print the shaded cells. When you shade cells bordered by drawn lines, Quattro Pro sometimes overlaps the lines. Don't worry, this is simply an on-screen quirk—when you print the spreadsheet, Quattro Pro properly encloses the shading in the lined cells.

Experimenting with Different Fonts

Use the /**S**tyle **F**ont command to change the appearance of Quattro Pro's screen fonts, and the fonts used when you print to a graphics printer. You can use up to eight basic fonts per spreadsheet. By altering font characteristics like style, color, and point size, though, you can create lots of different looks on the same spreadsheet.

Before you try to create custom fonts for a spreadsheet, think back to when you first installed the program. When you installed Quattro Pro, you had the option of building none, some, or all of Quattro Pro's fonts. If you installed none or some, then you'll only be able to access a few fonts with the /**S**tyle **F**ont command. But fear not, this is not a permanent condition. If you use a font that has not been installed, Quattro Pro will pause while it builds the font, as long as the /**O**ptions **G**raphics Quality command is set to **F**inal. In this state, Quattro Pro will build uninstalled fonts when it encounters them on a spreadsheet, on an "as-needed" basis. If you originally installed the entire font library, then you can instantly access and edit all of the screen fonts using the /**S**tyle **F**ont **E**dit Fonts command.

Adding Fonts to a Spreadsheet

Quattro Pro uses the Bitstream Dutch 12-point Black font as the global default font for every cell in a new spreadsheet. To use a different font in a cell, make that cell active and select the /**S**tyle **F**ont command.

Quattro Pro displays the **F**ont menu as shown in Figure 7.14. Select a new font by pressing the number next to that font name.

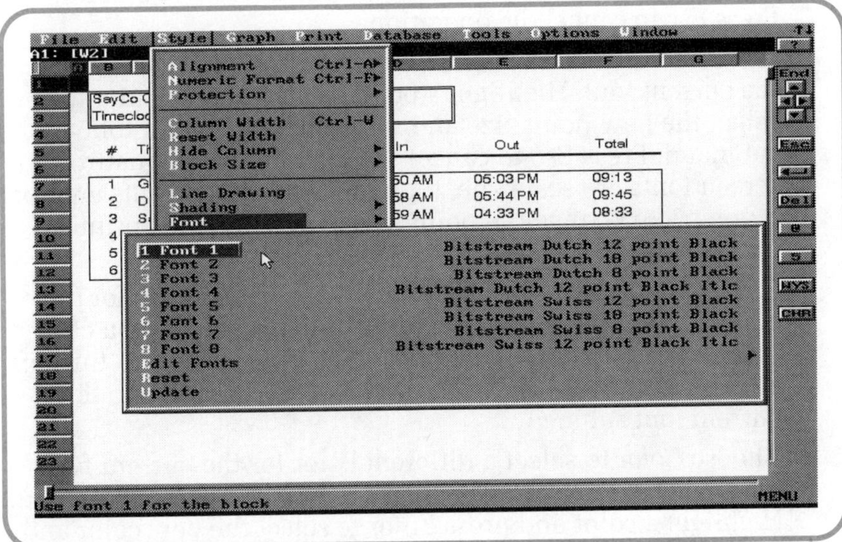

Figure 7.14 Adding fonts to a spreadsheet.

If you are in WYSIWYG display mode you can view a new font on-screen as soon as you press **Q** to quit and return to the active spreadsheet.

To check the number of a font for a cell, make that cell active and review the code displayed on the input line. If you see [F2], for example, the cell is displaying (and will be printed with) font #2. Quattro Pro does not display default font codes on the input line. You also can inspect a font's appearance on-screen by printing the spreadsheet to the Screen Preview tool, covered in Chapter 5.

Editing Spreadsheet Fonts

You can edit the display attributes of all eight fonts listed on the **F**onts menu by changing typeface, point size, style and color from the /**S**tyle **F**ont **E**dit Fonts submenu. When you select this command, Quattro Pro displays a menu very similar to the one shown in Figure 7.14. Press the number of the font you wish to edit, and Quattro Pro reveals attributes which offer five options:

Choose *Typeface* to display a list of the screen and printer fonts currently available to you. Using the arrow keys, highlight a different font name on the list and press Enter to select the new typeface and return to the current font submenu. Press Esc to cancel the operation.

Choose *Point Size* to display a list of point sizes available for the current font. Highlight a point size and press Enter to select the new point size and return to the current font submenu. Press Esc to cancel the operation. All Quattro Pro screen fonts are scaleable, though some printer fonts are not. If you try to change the point size of a fixed-point printer font, Quattro Pro displays an error message.

Choose *Style* to choose additional display attributes for the current font. Depending upon the individual font, you can choose **B**old, **I**talics, and **U**nderlined. Select **R**eset to turn off all **S**tyle submenu selections. Select **Q**uit to return to the current font submenu.

Choose *Color* to select a different color for the current font. Once selected, Quattro Pro displays the color selection menu. Highlight a color and press Enter to select the new color and return to the current font submenu. Press Esc to cancel the operation.

Choose *Quit* to return to the **E**dit Fonts submenu.

Figure 7.15 shows how to edit the typeface for Font #1 on the timeclock calculator spreadsheet. The font shown in Figure 7.15 (Scaleable Universe Roman8) is available only when you install a LaserJet printer.

Tip: Even if you do not own a LaserJet printer you can still display the screen version of a font. Select the /**O**ptions **H**ardware **P**rinters command, and install the HP III printer as your second printer. Now make that printer the default printer (see Chapter 5 for complete instructions on installing printers). Now return to the **E**dit Fonts menu and reselect Font #1. Select **T**ypeface and scroll through the list of fonts. This time, notice that there are many more choices on this menu—that's because Quattro Pro thinks that you have a LaserJet printer connected to your PC.

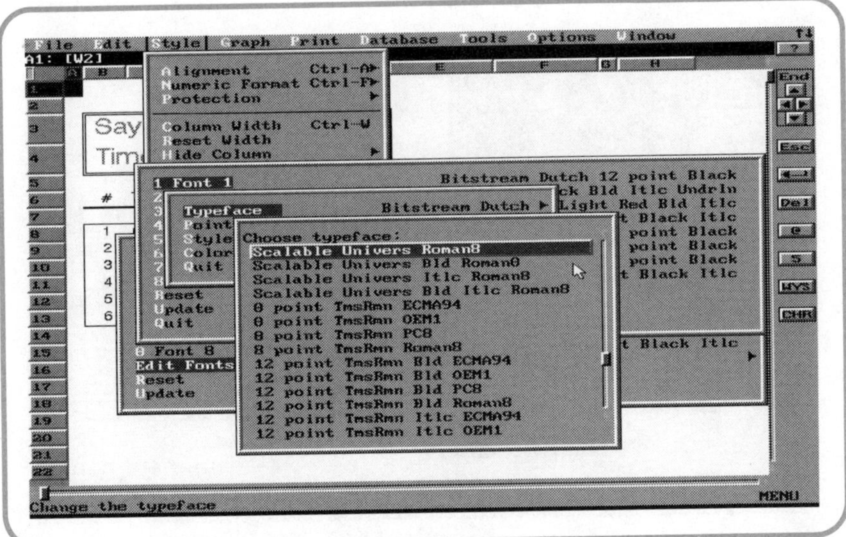

Figure 7.15 *Creating custom fonts for a spreadsheet.*

> **Caution:** Be sure to reset your own printer as the default printer before you attempt to print this spreadsheet.

Figure 7.16 shows how to select a different point size for new Font #1 on the timeclock calculator spreadsheet. Not all Quattro Pro fonts support all of the features available on the **E**dit Fonts submenu. For example, the Bitstream Courier font does not support the bold style option. If you choose **B**old on the **S**tyle submenu, the formatted character will not print bold.

On the **F**ont menu, choose **U**pdate to store all font edits as the new default for the current spreadsheet. Choose /**S**tyle **F**ont **R**eset Fonts to reset all fonts to Quattro Pro's default settings.

Figure 7.17 shows the enhanced version of the Timeclock Calculator application.

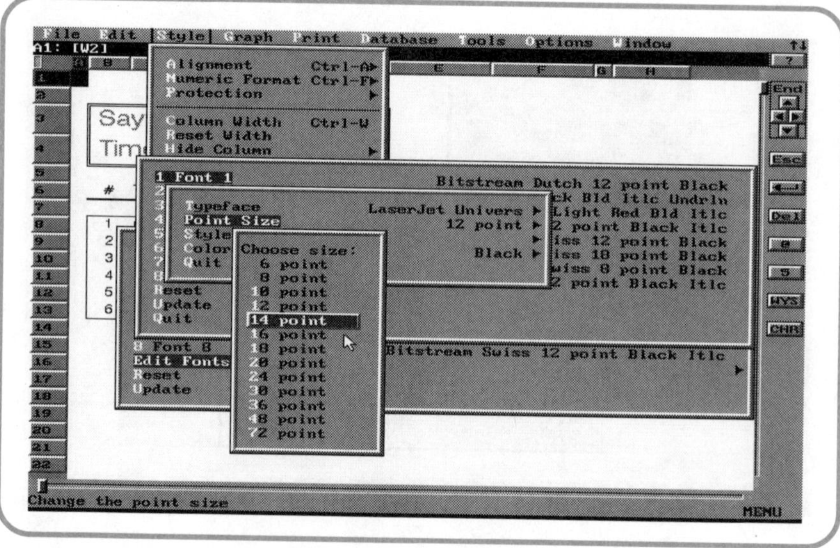

Figure 7.16 Selecting a different point size for new Font #1 on the Timeclock Calculator spreadsheet.

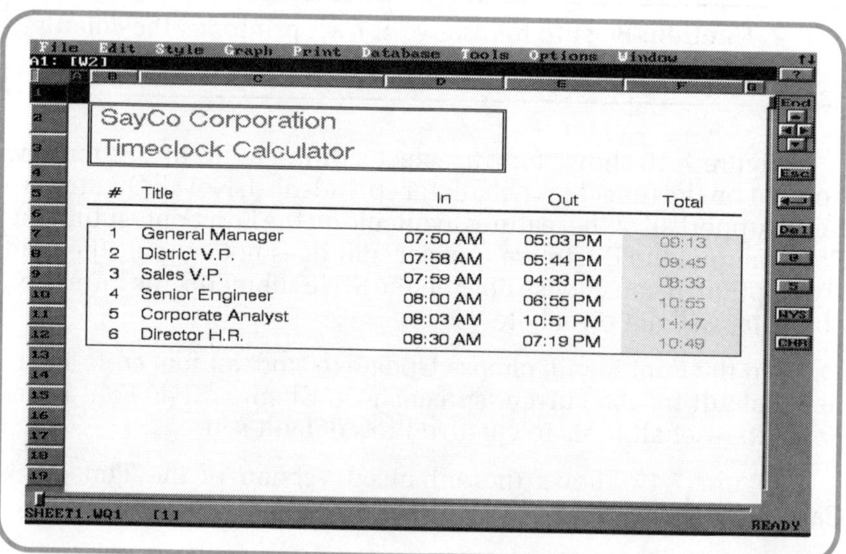

Figure 7.17 The enhanced version of the Timeclock Calculator spreadsheet.

To achieve this same look on your version of the spreadsheet, change the point size of the report titles to 20 and the color to Light Red, and change the point size of the remaining data to 14. Feel free to experiment with any of the other options on the font attribute menus to enhance this report even further.

> **Tip:** Drawn lines occasionally spill off-screen into other columns. To correct this problem, decrease the width of a column just outside the target cell block. For instance, to achieve the look shown in Figure 7.17, column G was narrowed to a width of six characters.

Style Enhancement Extras

Recall from Chapter 5 that Quattro Pro automatically inserts soft page breaks into a spreadsheet. Soft page breaks tell Quattro Pro when to move to a new page in a printout. Occasionally, you may find the need to control spreadsheet printing with even greater precision. For instance, you may wish to print a graph at the bottom of the first page of a printout before printing the rest of the spreadsheet. It's during such occasions that you'll find the /**S**tyle **I**nsert Break command a useful spreadsheet enhancement tool.

To add a hard page break to a spreadsheet, place the cell selector in a cell on the row where you wish the break to occur, and select /**S**tyle **I**nsert Break. Quattro Pro adds a hard page break symbol (**: :**) at the location of the cell selector. Be sure to insert the hard page break into an empty row, because Quattro Pro does not print data that is on the same row as a hard page break.

To delete a hard page break, move the cell selector to the cell where the hard page break resides, and press Del on the numeric keypad. Quattro Pro erases the hard page break symbol, but does not delete the row.

Spreadsheet bulleting is another enhancement extra that you use to add that final touch to a spreadsheet report. In Quattro Pro, *bulleting* is the process of attaching circles, boxes, shadowed boxes, and checked boxes to your spreadsheets. This option is not available on any Quattro Pro menu—you must use the special codes shown in Table 7.2 to create this effect. To create a bullet graphic, simply enter `\bullet #\` in the blank cell in which you want the bullet to appear (see Figure 7.18).

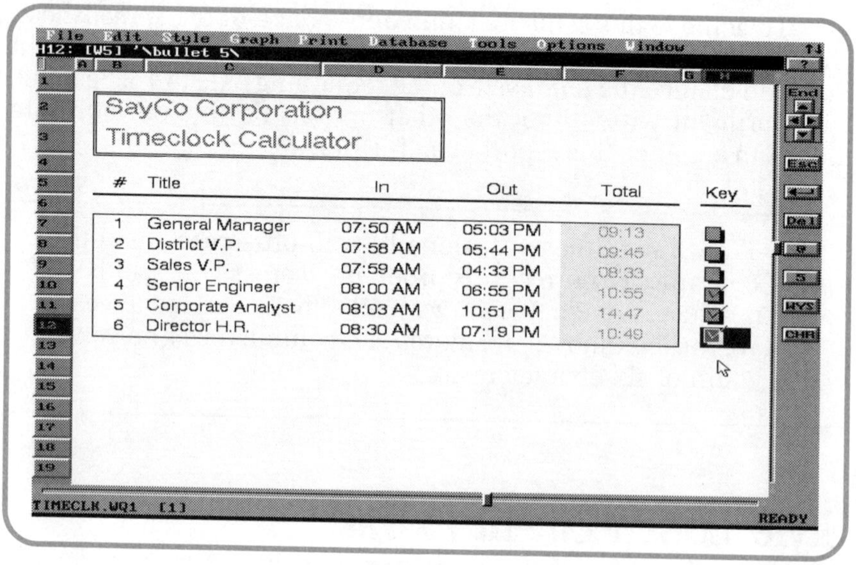

Figure 7.18 Adding bullet graphics to the Timeclock Calculator spreadsheet.

The bullet code used to display the checked, shadowed box in Figure 7.18 appears on the input line, at the top of the spreadsheet. In this expression, # stands for the bullet style number listed in Table 7.2. As with all other /**S**tyle menu enhancements, you can immediately view a bullet graphic as soon as you return to the active spreadsheet. You also can examine the bullet graphic on-screen by printing the spreadsheet to the Screen Preview tool.

Table 7.2 The Bullet Character Code Designations.

Code	Bullet Effect
0	Box
1	Filled box
2	Checked box
3	Check
4	Shadowed box
5	Shadowed, checked box
6	Filled circle

To enter a bullet graphic in a cell by itself, precede the bullet code with a label prefix (', ", or ^). Otherwise, Quattro Pro interprets the first \ as a repeating label prefix, and repeats the entry in the cell.

Figure 7.19 shows the look of the updated, presentation-quality form of the timeclock calculator spreadsheet. Notice that a legend has been added to the bottom of the spreadsheet to clarify the meaning of the bullet graphics.

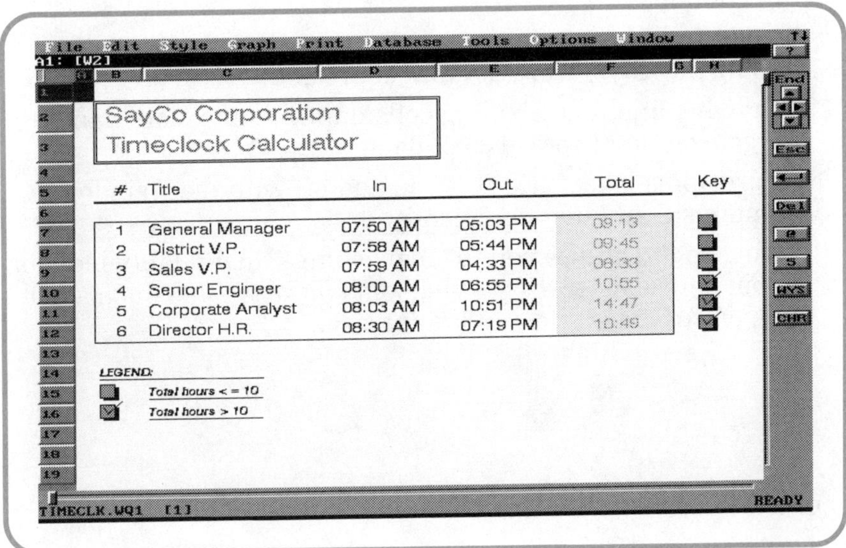

Figure 7.19 Reviewing the Timeclock Calculator spreadsheet in the Screen Preview environment.

What You've Learned

This chapter showed you how to turn a basic, unformatted spreadsheet into a finished-quality document to use in a report, show at an important meeting, or display during a business presentation.

- You change Quattro Pro's *default global format settings* on the /**O**ptions menu.
- To align values and labels in a cell, use the /**S**tyle **A**lignment command.

- Select meaningful and appropriate *numeric formats* for values, labels, dates, and times with the /**S**tyle **N**umeric Format command.
- You can *protect* and *unprotect* cell data, and enable and disable *global spreadsheet protection* with the /**S**tyle **P**rotection and /**O**ptions **P**rotection commands.
- There are several column adjustment commands to let you set, reset, and autoset the width of a single column or a block of columns.
- You can hide private or sensitive spreadsheet information using the /**S**tyle **H**ide Column command.
- Drawing lines and shading cells improves the clarity and organization of spreadsheet data.
- Turn spreadsheet grid lines on and off with the /**W**indow **O**ptions **G**rid Lines command.
- Quattro Pro allows you to create a published-quality look for your spreadsheets by varying *font characteristics* such as the typeface, style, color, and point size.

Chapter 8

Designing Graphs

In This Chapter

- *What is a graph?*
- *What you need to display a graph*
- *The 11 types of graphs*
- *Creating a graph*
- *Customizing a graph*
- *Annotating a graph*
- *Managing and printing graphs*
- *Building graph slide shows*

In previous chapters, you learned how to create a spreadsheet and then improve its appearance using Quattro Pro's style enhancement commands. This chapter introduces you to a more dramatic way of presenting your spreadsheet data. In this chapter, you'll learn how to convert spreadsheet entries into graphs. As you'll soon discover, graphs are useful for uncovering trends, for comparing various sets of numbers, and for analyzing the individual parts of a whole.

What Is a Graph?

A graph is a visual representation of numbers. In Quattro Pro, the numbers that you graph are from a spreadsheet. Putting numbers into graph form helps to clarify relationships among sets of data. Graphs are an extremely effective medium for driving home an important point. It's easy, for example, to look at the spreadsheet in Figure 8.1 and see that, in terms of dollars, California produces more grapes than Texas. The graph shown in Figure 8.2 dramatically illustrates this point.

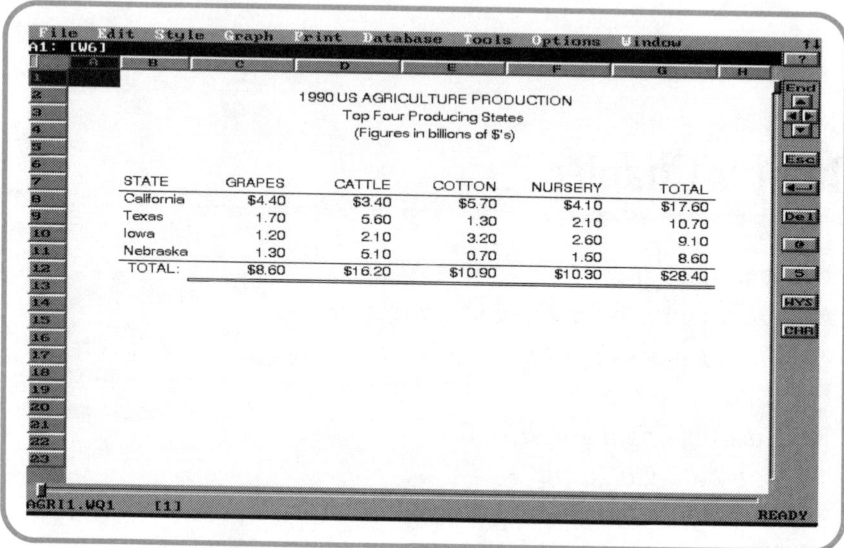

1990 US AGRICULTURE PRODUCTION
Top Four Producing States
(Figures in billions of $'s)

STATE	GRAPES	CATTLE	COTTON	NURSERY	TOTAL
California	$4.40	$3.40	$5.70	$4.10	$17.60
Texas	1.70	5.60	1.30	2.10	10.70
Iowa	1.20	2.10	3.20	2.60	9.10
Nebraska	1.30	5.10	0.70	1.50	8.60
TOTAL:	$8.60	$16.20	$10.90	$10.30	$28.40

Figure 8.1 A spreadsheet showing the four largest food-producing states.

To create a graph, use the commands found on the /**G**raph menu. Like most Quattro Pro commands, the /**G**raph menu commands are intuitive—the command name tells you what the command is supposed to do. If you press /G to pull down the /**G**raph menu, you'll notice that the menu is divided into three sections. The commands in each section are organized by function.

The top section of the /**G**raph menu contains the commands that you'll use to create a graph. The **G**raph Type command allows you to select from among 11 graph styles available in Quattro Pro. The **S**eries command tells Quattro Pro which spreadsheet data to include in a graph. The **T**ext command adds titles and legends to a basic graph.

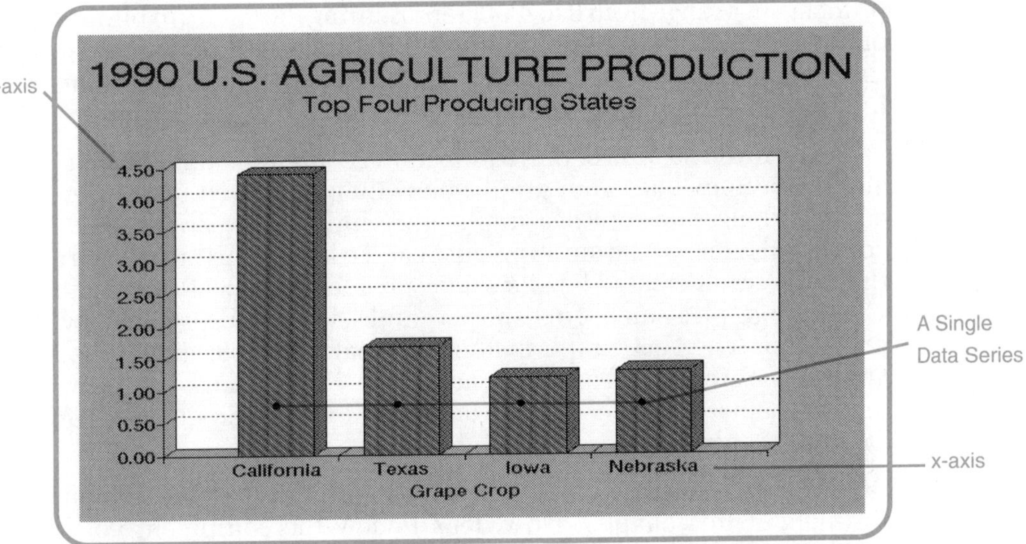

Figure 8.2 A bar graph shows the relative sizes of grape crops for four states.

To enhance the appearance of a basic graph, use the commands found in the middle section of the /**G**raph menu. The **C**ustomize Series command changes the appearance of the individual parts of a graph. The **X**-Axis and **Y**-Axis commands control the display and scaling of the x-axis and y-axis data. The **O**verall command lets you add lines, patterns, and colors to the entire graph.

Before we continue, let's define three important graph terms: data series, x-axis, and y-axis. These terms describe the three basic elements of a Quattro Pro graph. Take a closer look at Figure 8.2 to see exactly where each element is located.

Figure 8.2 contains a single data series. A *data series* is a grouping of numerical data that originates from two or more unique sources. The numerical data on the graph in Figure 8.2 are the dollar values of the grape crops (cell block C8..C11 on the spreadsheet in Figure 8.1 contains the values) for the four states with the largest agricultural output. If you added the cattle production values to this graph (in cell block D8..D11 of Figure 8.1), there would be two data series: one for grapes and one for cattle.

The *x-axis* is the horizontal line appearing at the bottom of the graph. In Figure 8.2, the x-axis displays the names of each state appearing on the agricultural spreadsheet. The *y-axis* is the vertical line at the left side of the graph. In Figure 8.2, this axis displays numbers in a range from 0 to 4.50, representing the value (in billions of dollars) of each state's grape crop for 1989. The y-axis is *scaled* so that both the highest (4.40) and lowest (1.30) values—and all values in between—can display on the same graph.

The lower section of the /**G**raph menu contains commands that allow you to manage your graphs once they're created. The **I**nsert command inserts a copy of a graph onto a spreadsheet, and the **H**ide command removes it from a spreadsheet. To help keep track of more than one graph created for the same spreadsheet, select **N**ame and give your graph a name. To display a graph at any time, use the **V**iew command. The **F**ast Graph command creates a basic, unadorned graph. The **A**nnotate command adds text, lines, arrows, and geometric shapes to help create a professional, published-quality look for your graphs.

We will examine these commands and others in more detail throughout this chapter. Now, let's review the equipment you'll need to be able to display Quattro Pro graphs on your screen.

What You Need To Display a Graph

To display a Quattro Pro graph, your computer must have a graphics display system. This means that you must have a graphics card, and a display monitor that supports graphics images (today, nearly all do). If your computer is an older PC or XT system, you may be able to create and print a graph, but not view it on-screen. Quattro Pro works with the following graphics systems:

Hercules monochrome graphics card
Color Graphics Adapter (CGA)
Enhanced Graphics Adapter (EGA)
Video Graphics Adapter (VGA)

A Hercules graphics display system shows graphs in black and white. The CGA, EGA, and VGA systems display in color. EGA and VGA display systems have sharper resolution than the monochrome or CGA adapters.

> **Tip:** To take full advantage of your display system's capabilities, select the /**O**ptions **H**ardware **S**creen **R**esolution command and choose the highest resolution setting shown on the menu. Usually, Quattro Pro automatically does this for you. It's worth a look, however, to insure that your graphs will display with the highest clarity.

Even if you don't have a graphics display system, you may be able to print a graph if you own a dot-matrix or laser printer. These printers print graphs in various shades of gray. The end of this chapter covers the procedure for printing graphs.

The Eleven Types of Graphs

Quattro Pro lets you create 11 different types of graphs. This section presents an overview of each style and discusses the types of data that work best with each graph type. You'll quickly discover that it's possible to display data using two or three graph types and still make the same impact. Other times, your data will be so specific that only one graph type will work.

Each example presented in this section is just one way to use the graph type. You'll discover many other ways for using Quattro Pro graphs because your data is unique and different from the data graphed here. In any case, use the example graphs as a yardstick for choosing when to use a particular graph type. Later in this chapter, you'll have an opportunity to see exactly how to construct two of the graph types.

Line Graphs

The *line graph* is the most common type of graph. Use the line graph to track changes in values over a period of time. For example, Figure 8.3 shows a line graph that tracks the growth of two children from kindergarten through high school.

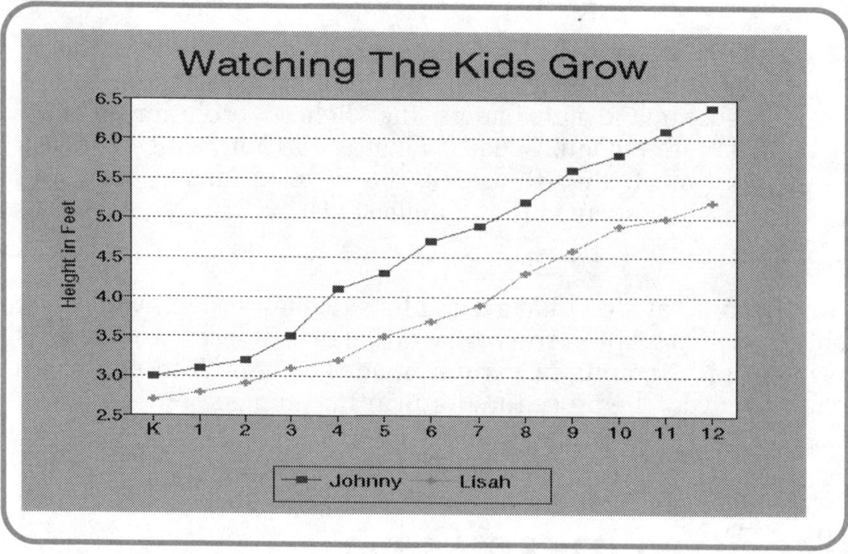

Figure 8.3 A sample line graph.

Bar Graphs

Bar graphs are good for comparing the values of various items at one point in time. A bar graph makes it easy to spot differences in values because the higher the bar, the higher the value. For example, Figure 8.4 shows a bar graph that compares the average price of each car built by four automobile manufacturers.

XY Graphs

An *XY graph* shows the correspondence between two sets of values. Although it looks like a line graph, the XY graph is not time-dependent. The data on an XY graph can represent one moment in time, or it can show changes in data over time. Figure 8.5 shows the correlation between water and air temperatures on a sunny day in San Diego.

Stacked Bar Graphs

The *stacked bar graph* is Quattro Pro's default graph type. This graph type is good for comparing individual statistics while also showing contributions made to an overall trend. For example, in Figure 8.6, each bar shows total sales by territory for an advertising agency. Each bar, in turn, is divided into service categories so you can see how much each service category contributed to overall sales in each territory.

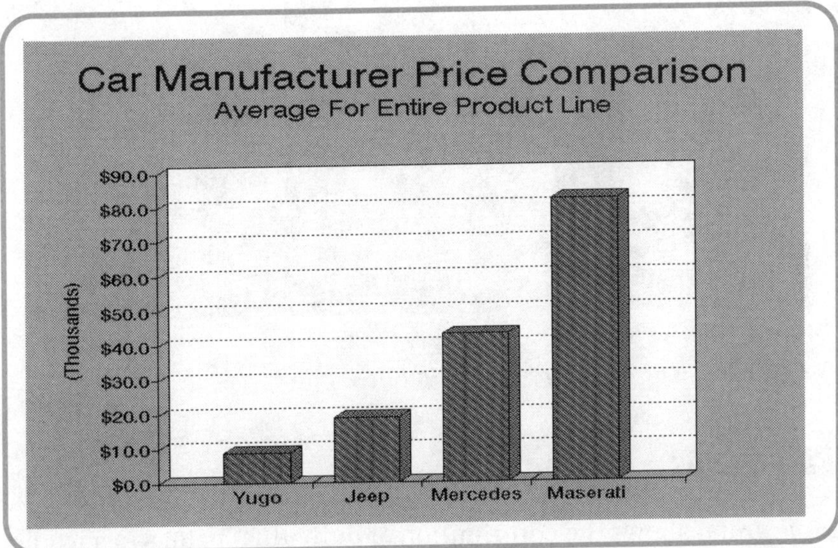

Figure 8.4 A sample bar graph.

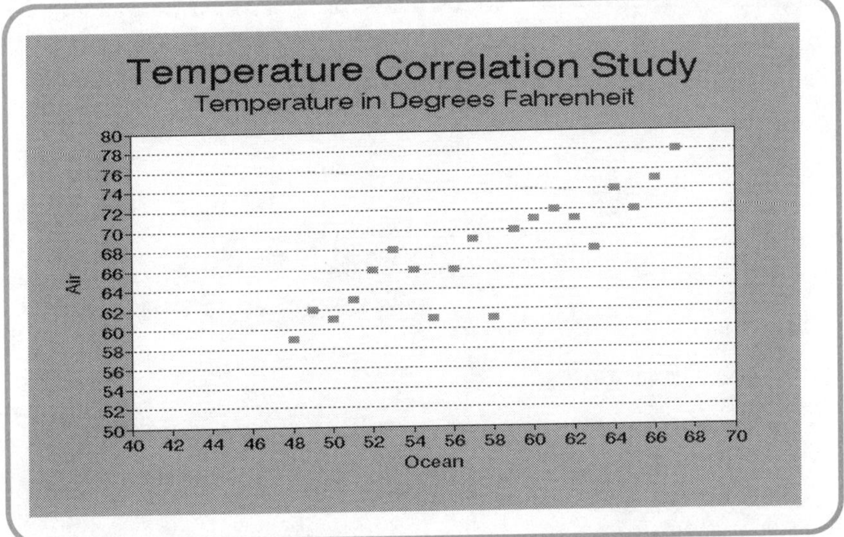

Figure 8.5 A sample XY graph.

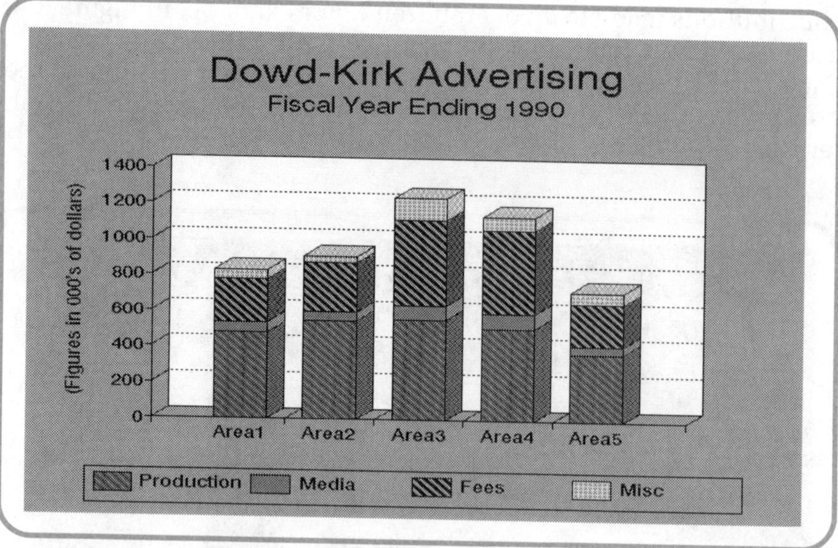

Figure 8.6 A sample stacked bar graph

Pie Graphs

A *pie graph* shows the contribution of individual values to a whole. A *wedge*, sometimes referred to as a "slice of the pie," represents each individual value. In Figure 8.7, you can see that of the five expense categories shown, Entertainment is the largest slice of the pie.

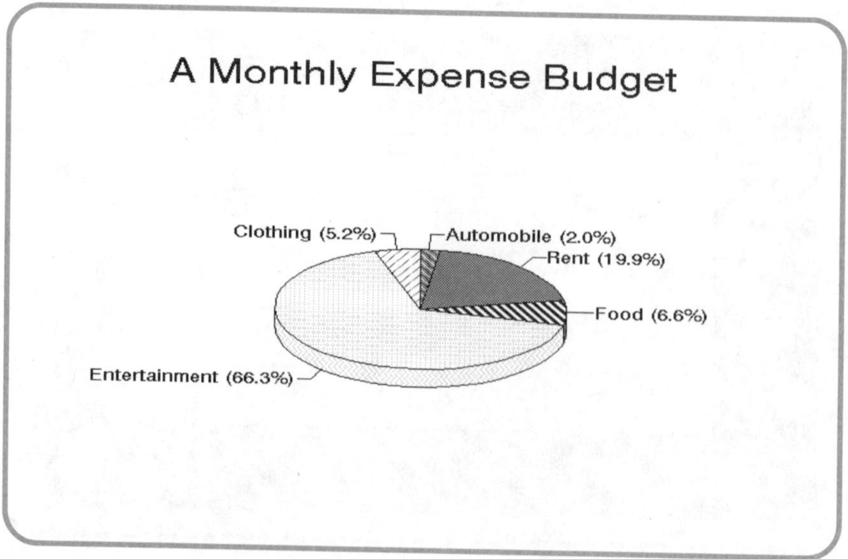

Figure 8.7 A sample pie chart.

Area Graphs

An *area graph* reveals trends like a line graph, and makes value comparisons like a bar graph. When plotting two or more data series, Quattro Pro stacks the series on top of each other to convey a sense of "total area" for the graph. For example, the area graph in Figure 8.8 is used to monitor a firm's productiion schedule. This graph tracks total production by product line (varieties of hamburgers, in this case) and also monitors total quarterly production.

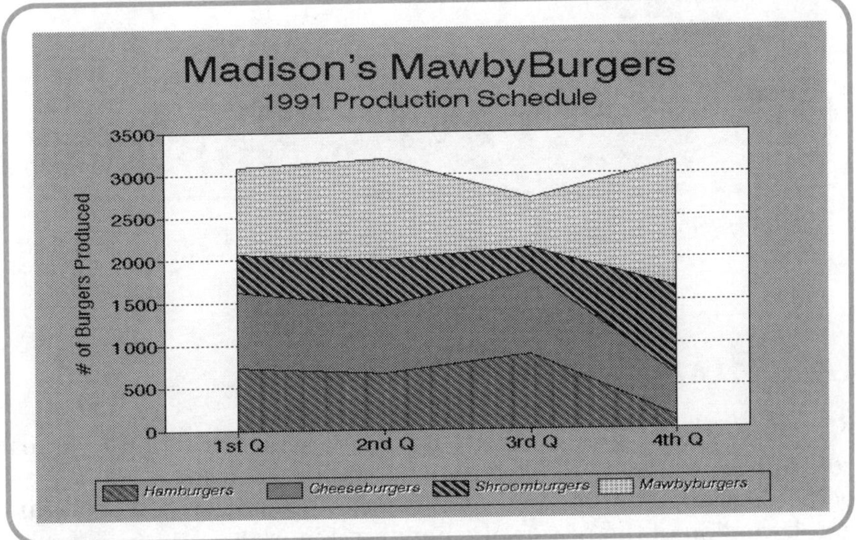

Figure 8.8 A sample area graph.

Rotated Bar Graphs

Flip a bar graph on its side, and you have a *rotated bar graph*. The x-axis and y-axis on a rotated bar graph are reversed. This graph type is good for displaying the results of athletic events like a footrace, election results, and even sales. Figure 8.9 is the rotated bar graph version of the bar graph shown in Figure 8.4.

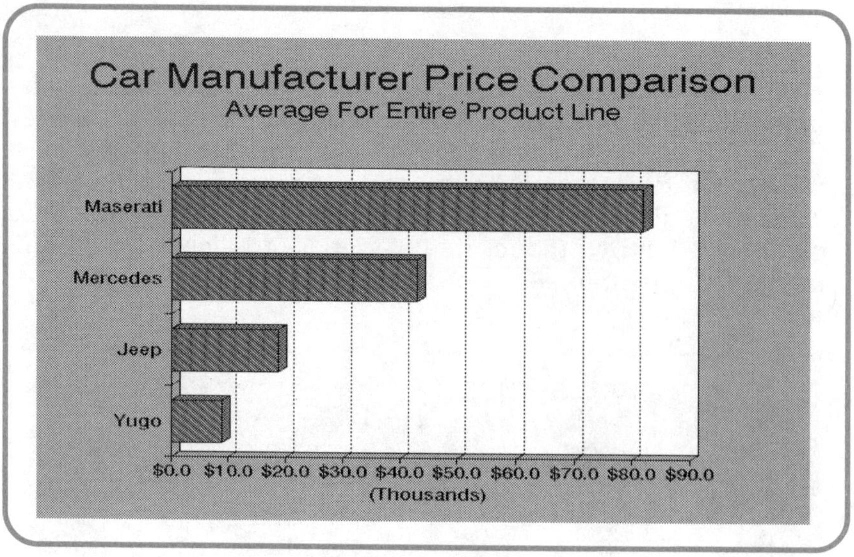

Figure 8.9 A sample rotated bar graph.

Column Graphs

A *column graph*, like a pie graph, shows how individual values contribute to a whole. This type of graph can show values as percentages or as numbered quantities. Figure 8.10 is the column graph version of the pie graph shown in Figure 8.7.

High-Low (Open-Close) Graphs

The *high-low (open-close)* graph is an example of a data-specific graph. You've probably seen this type of graph commonly used to plot high, low, open, and close prices for stocks, precious metals, and other commodities. Figure 8.11 shows how to plot high and low stock prices during five key periods of a trading day. With a little imagination, you can use this graph type to plot other data such as interest rates, average temperatures, or even body weight.

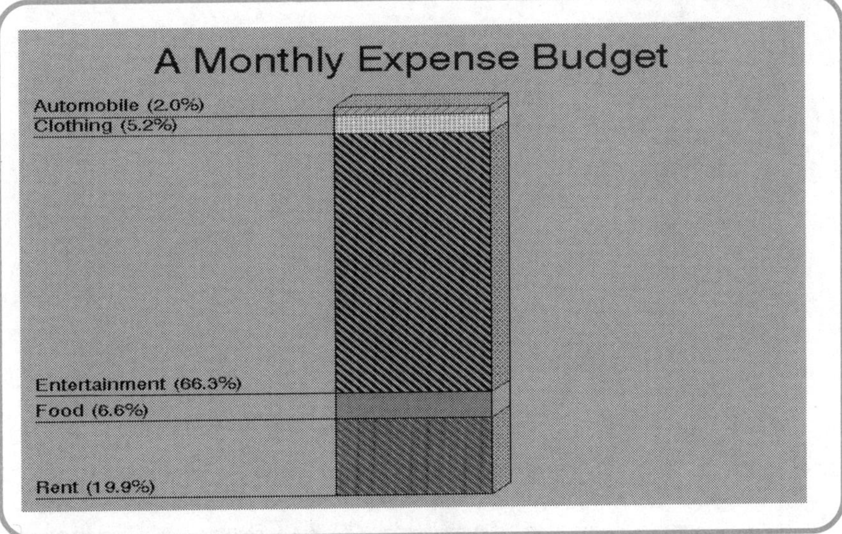

Figure 8.10   A sample column graph.

Text Graphs

A *text graph* does not rely on spreadsheet data. Choose the text graphs type when you need to draw a graph freehand. For example, you could create a text graph that depicts a firm's organizational structure (see Figure 8.12), or a flowchart that shows the passage of information through a computer program. You create a text graph using Quattro Pro's graph Annotator tool (covered later in this chapter).

3-D Graphs

Quattro Pro Version 3.0 allows you to create *three-dimensional (3-D) graphs*. There are four types of 3-D graphs: bar, ribbon, step, and area. Unlike other Quattro Pro graphs, the 3-D graph contains an extra axis (the z-axis) that projects outward from your viewing perspective. The z-axis creates the illusion that the graph is three-dimensional.

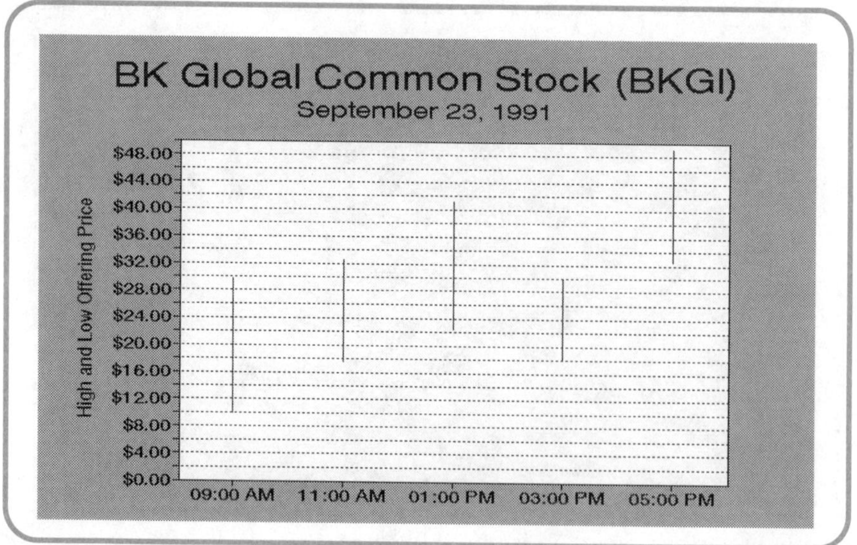

Figure 8.11 A sample high-low graph.

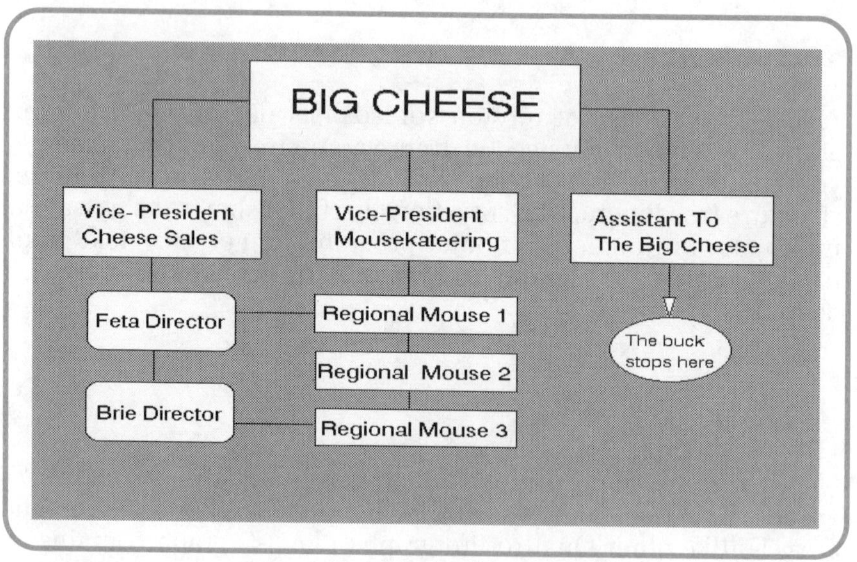

Figure 8.12 A sample text graph.

Each 3-D graph corresponds to one of the graph types discussed already. For instance, the 3-D bar graph resembles a regular bar graph with the bars standing in front of each other instead of side-by-side. The 3-D step graph is similar to a 3-D bar graph, except the bars touch, creating a step effect. The 3-D ribbon graph essentially is a line graph on a 3-D grid with each line widened into a segmented ribbon. Figure 8.13 is the three-dimensional version of the graph shown in Figure 8.3. The 3-D area graph is a ribbon graph with the area below each line filled in.

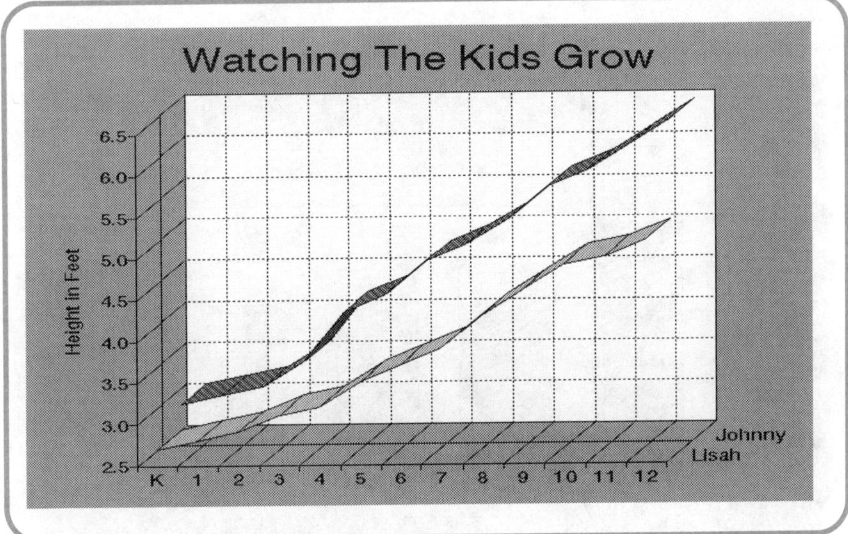

Figure 8.13 A sample 3-D ribbon graph.

Creating a Fast Graph

There are two ways to create a graph with Quattro Pro: from the ground up or using the **F**ast Graph command. Building a fast graph is the easiest and fastest method for constructing a graph, one that requires very little effort on your part. (Later, this chapter covers the procedure for creating a graph.)

Use the following Quick Steps to create a "bare-bones" fast graph using the agriculture spreadsheet from Figure 8.1. Recreate the agriculture spreadsheet in Figure 8.1 now for yourself so you can follow along with this graph-building example and others in this chapter.

Creating a Fast Graph

1. Choose Fast Graph from the /Graph menu (or press Ctrl-G, the shortcut key).

   Quattro Pro prompts you to type the fast graph block— the spreadsheet cell block that you wish to graph.

2. Type in the cell coordinates of the fast graph block and press Enter. (I typed cell block B7..F11.)

   Quattro Pro immediately displays the graph, shown in Figure 8.14. Press Enter once to return to the spreadsheet. □

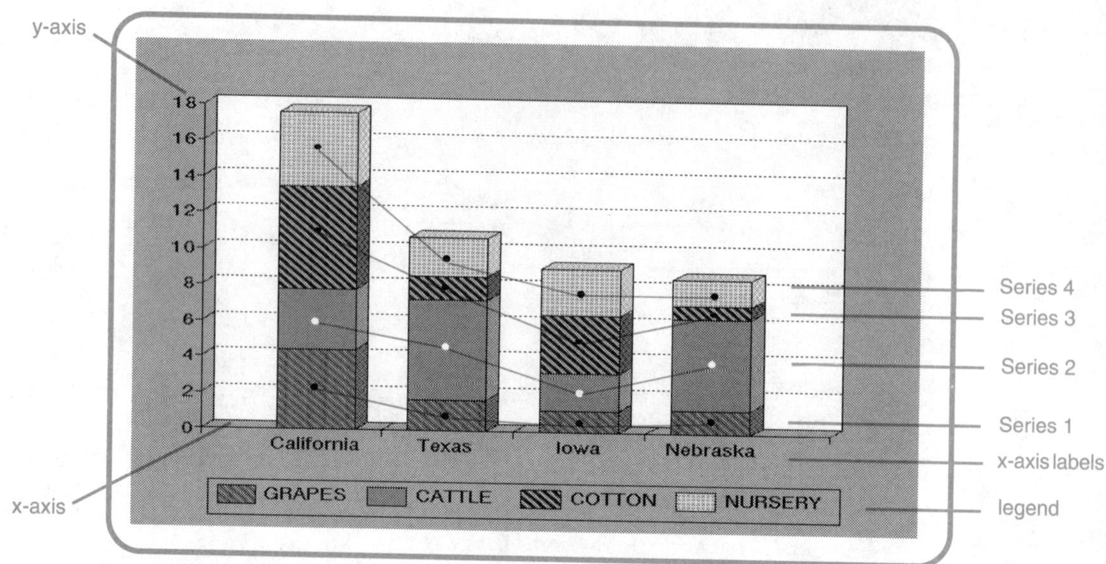

Figure 8.14 Creating a fast graph using data on the agriculture spreadsheet.

On a fast graph, Quattro Pro shows only the basic graph elements: a scaled x-axis, a scaled y-axis, and the data. If the fast graph block contains labels in the first row and column, Quattro Pro also displays axis labels and a legend. Figure 8.14 shows that there are four data series on this fast graph. Series #1 comes from cell block C8..C11 on the agriculture spreadsheet. Series #2, #3, and #4 come from cell blocks D8..D11, E8..E11, and F8..F11 respectively.

The following rules describe how Quattro Pro evaluates a fast graph block when the cell block contains more rows than columns, or when the number of columns equals the number of rows:

1. Each column is a single series.
2. Labels in the first column become the x-axis labels.
3. Labels in the first row become the graph legend labels.
4. When there are no labels in the first column or row, Quattro Pro creates a graph without labels or legends.

These rules apply when the columns in the fast graph block are equal to or greater than the number of rows:

1. Each row is a single series.
2. Labels in the first row become the x-axis labels.
3. Labels in the first column become the graph legend labels.
4. When there are no labels in the first column or row, Quattro Pro creates a graph without labels or legends.

If the block you graph contains any blank cells, they'll show up as gaps in the graph. To remove the gaps, return to the spreadsheet and delete all blank rows and columns from the selected data block. Reselect the data block and choose **F**ast Graph to redisplay the same graph without gaps.

Now let's review the four-step process that Quattro Pro used to create the fast graph in Figure 8.14. Your fast graphs will always make sense if you apply this same logic when building graphs:

1. When the number of rows in the fast graph block is equal to or exceeds the number of columns, Quattro Pro follows the first set of rules outlined previously.
2. Quattro Pro creates x-axis labels using the labels appearing in the first column of the block (B8..B11 in the example).
3. Quattro Pro creates a legend using the labels appearing in the first row of the block (C7..F7 in the example).
4. Quattro Pro uses the remaining row data (C8..F11 in the example) to create four unique data series.

Once you have finished viewing the fast graph, press Enter to return to the active spreadsheet. Now, if you need to, modify values in your data block, then press F10 to redisplay a fast graph showing the new figures.

The Basic "From-the-Ground-Up" Graph

You can create a graph from the ground up using just three /**G**raph menu commands: **G**raph Type, **S**eries, and **T**ext.

The commands located on the **S**eries menu allow you to specify the cell block address of the data that you wish to graph. Press /GS now and review the commands on this menu (see Figure 8.15).

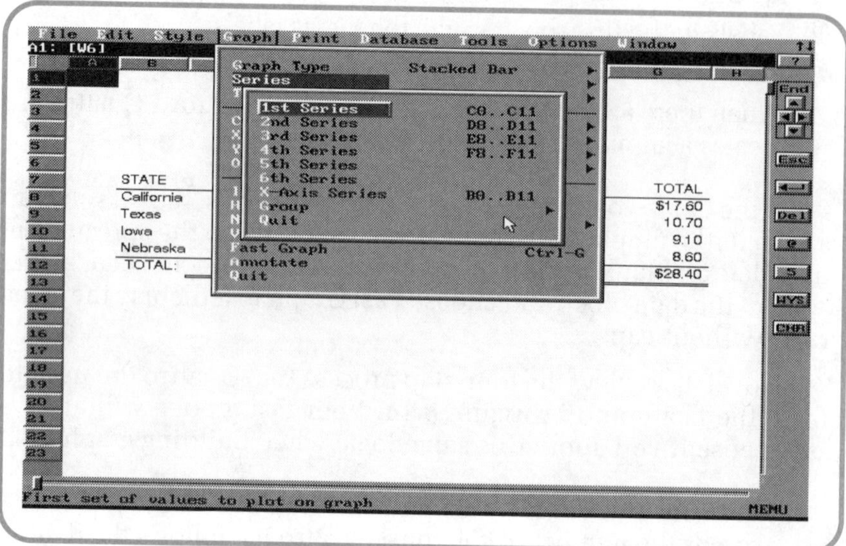

Figure 8.15 Reviewing the commands on the Series menu.

You can add as many as six data series to a graph with the **1**st Series through **6**th Series commands. Generally, you create series using data appearing in adjacent rows or columns. In Figure 8.15, you can see that the block coordinates for all four series from the fast graph example appear at the right side of the **S**eries menu.

Quattro Pro also allows you to define series using data appearing in nonadjacent cell blocks. For example, on the sample spreadsheet you could define cell block C8..C11 as the first data series, cell block E8..E11 as the second series, and cell block F8..F11 as the third series. This graph, then, would not display the data appearing in D8..D11 (the Cattle data), because you didn't define it as a series.

Select the **X**-Axis Series command to define the block that contains the labels you want to display as the x-axis labels. On an XY graph, the **X**-Axis Series command defines a series rather than a block containing labels as it does for all other graph types.

Use the **G**roup command to avoid having to define individual series—this command defines every series on the graph at once. When you select this command, Quattro Pro prompts you to define a group of columns or rows that contains the series. If you choose the **C**olumns option, Quattro Pro assigns columns of values to each series; the **R**ows option causes Quattro Pro to assign rows of values to each series.

Now let's create a Quattro Pro graph from the ground up. This graph will rely on data from the agriculture spreadsheet. Before you begin, press /GCRGQQ to select the /**G**raph **C**ustomize Series **R**eset **G**raph **Q**uit **Q**uit command. This returns all of the /**G**raph menu commands to their default settings and returns you to the active spreadsheet.

Creating a Quattro Pro Graph "From the Ground Up"

1. Press /G to pull down the Graph menu. — Quattro Pro displays the **G**raph menu.
2. Press G to select the **G**raph Type command. — The **G**raph Type menu shows the different types of graphs.
3. Highlight the graph type you wish to use and press Enter. (I selected the Area graph.) — Quattro Pro writes the graph type name next to the **G**raph Type command at the right margin of the /**G**raph menu.
4. Press S to select the **S**eries command. Press 1 to select the **1**st Series command. — Displays the **S**eries menu, then prompts you for the first series block.
5. Type the block coordinates and press Enter (I typed C8..C11). — Quattro Pro records the first series at the right side of the **S**eries menu next to the **1**st Series command.
6. Repeat Step 5 for the second, third, and fourth series (I typed D8..D11, E8..E11, and F8..F11). — Quattro Pro writes the rest of the series definitions on the **S**eries menu.
7. Press X to choose the **X**-Axis Series command. — Quattro Pro prompts you for the cell block containing the x-axis labels.

8. Type the coordinates of the block containing the labels you wish to display on the x-axis, and press Enter (I typed B8..B11).

   Quattro Pro records the x-axis labels on the **S**eries menu.

9. Choose Q to **Q**uit the **S**eries menu.

   Quattro Pro exits the **S**eries menu and returns you to the /**G**raph menu.

10. Press V to select the **V**iew command.

    Quattro Pro displays the graph on-screen. Your screen now should resemble the one pictured in Figure 8.16. □

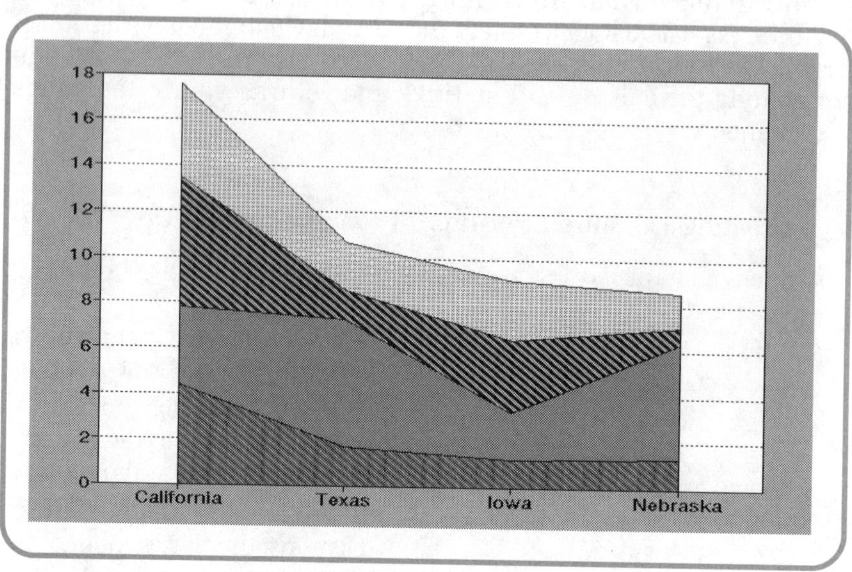

Figure 8.16 Building an area graph from the ground up using the data on the agriculture spreadsheet.

Enhancing the Appearance of the Basic Graph

Adding some enhancements to the graph in Figure 8.16 will clarify the data. These finishing touches are important when your objective is to create high-quality, professional-looking graphs.

Adding Titles and Legends

When a spreadsheet is displayed, press /GT to select the /**G**raph **T**ext command, and Quattro Pro displays the **T**ext menu. Using the commands on this menu, you can add report titles, axis labels, and a legend to any graph. You even can customize the fonts used to display words and letters on a graph.

The **1**st Line command adds the primary title to a graph. The *primary title* appears at the top of a graph. By default, the primary title uses the Bitstream Swiss 36-point font. Select this command and type `\D2`, a special code consisting of the backslash character and a cell address, which describes the location on the spreadsheet of the label you wish to use as the primary title. Or if you wish, just type in the title text.

> **Tip:** To later remove a title from a graph, reselect the particular **T**ext menu command, backspace over the description, and then press Enter to record a blank space in place of the old text.

The **2**nd Line command adds a secondary title to a graph. The *secondary title* appears at the top of a graph, just below the primary title. By default, the secondary title uses the Bitstream Swiss 24-point font. Select this command and type `\D3`. Again, you may type in a title freehand if you wish.

The **X**-Title command adds descriptive text directly below the x-axis. For our example, no x-axis label is necessary because it should be obvious to the viewer that California, Texas, Iowa, and Nebraska all are states.

Select the **Y**-Title command to add a descriptive label to the y-axis. Select this command and type `\D4`. Again, you may type in the title text if you wish.

The **L**egends command inserts and positions a legend on the graph. A legend is an important addition to a graph. It helps you identify the data series, much the same way as a legend on a map distinguishes between roads and highways. Select this command now and review the **L**egends menu. Although you could type in legend descriptions by hand, let's continue to use the cell location code. Figure 8.17 shows the final version of the **L**egends menu with all of the cell location codes entered. These codes refer to the labels appearing on row 7 on the agriculture spreadsheet. Your screen should now resemble the one pictured below in Figure 8.17.

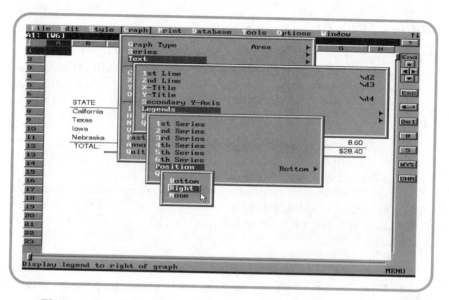

Figure 8.17 Entering the cell locations of the labels to include in the graph legend.

Press F10 and view the graph. It should look like the one shown in Figure 8.18.

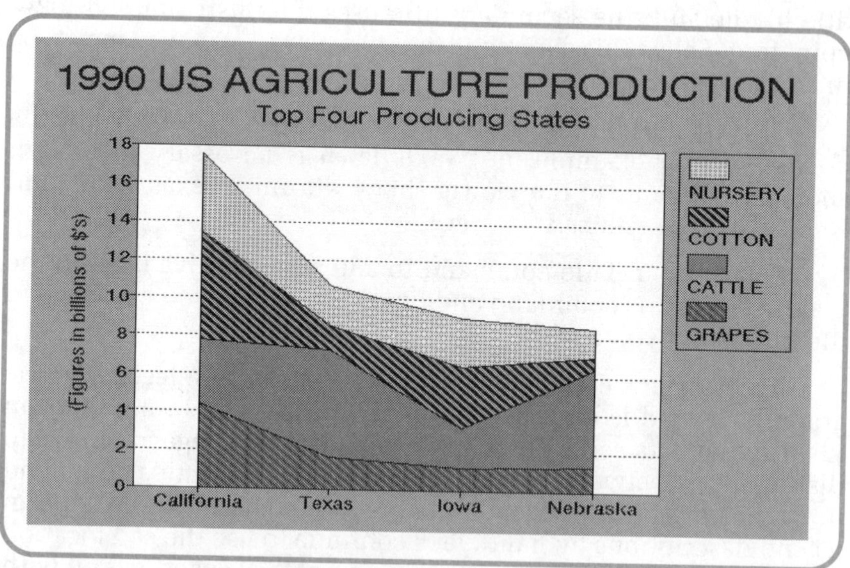

Figure 8.18 The basic graph complete with titles, a legend, and a y-axis label.

If you would like to experiment further, use the **F**ont command to modify the typeface, point size, color, and style of any fonts appearing on a graph.

Customizing a Data Series

The /**G**raph **C**ustomize Series command contains a whole slew of other graph customizing commands. These commands are fun to experiment with, because they affect very specific parts of a graph. Take a few minutes now and review the options on the **C**ustomize Series menu.

The ***C**olors* option allows you to choose different colors for each graph series.

The ***F**ill Patterns* command adjusts the patterns used to display bars and areas on a graph.

The ***M**arkers & Lines* command alters the line style and marker symbols used to display series on line and XY graphs.

The ***B**ar Width* command increases and narrows the width of bars on bar graphs, rotated bar graphs, stacked bar graphs, and column graphs.

The ***I**nterior Labels* command attaches labels or values from a spreadsheet directly onto a graph data series.

The ***O**verride Type* command allows you to create a combination graph that displays both a line and bar graph.

The ***Y**-Axis* command adds a second y-axis to a combination graph so it can accommodate two sets of data with different scales.

The ***P**ies* command helps you to manage and customize the appearance of pie and column graphs. With this command you can explode a wedge from the rest of the pie, display percentages or whole values, and modify the patterns and colors used to display these two types of graphs.

The ***U**pdate* command saves all current /**G**raph **C**ustomize Series settings as the new defaults. These settings remain in effect for future work sessions.

The ***R**eset* command allows you to reset individual series definitions, or return the entire graph to its default settings.

Use the following Quick Steps to customize the appearance of the graph shown in Figure 8.18. In this exercise, you learn how to change the fill pattern for a single data series.

Q Customizing a graph data series

1. Press /GC to select the /**G**raph **C**ustomize Series command. — Quattro Pro displays the Customize Series submenu.
2. Press F to select the **F**ill Patterns option. — Reveals the Fill Patterns submenu.
3. Press the number that corresponds to the data series you wish to customize (I pressed **4** to select the **4**th Series option). — Quattro Pro displays the Select Pattern palette, listing the available fill pattern designs.
4. Using the arrow keys, highlight the fill pattern you wish to use, or just point your mouse at a design box (I highlighted the Bricks design located in the righthand column, second from the bottom).
5. Press Enter, or click your mouse once. — Quattro Pro writes the name of the new setting at the right edge of the **F**ill Patterns submenu, next to the selected data series.
6. Press F10 to review the new fill pattern on the current graph. Press Enter when you are finished viewing the graph. — Quattro Pro returns you to the **F**ill Patterns submenu.
7. Press Q three times to return to the active spreadsheet.

□

To quickly close all active menus, point the mouse arrow anywhere on the active spreadsheet and click once.

The best way to learn which series-customizing commands create the most attractive graph display is to take time and experiment with each command. Press F10 at any time to view the current graph, even when several menus are pulled down. Then press Enter to return to the active spreadsheet—it'll look exactly as it did before you displayed the graph.

Customizing the Axes

Quattro Pro automatically scales the axes when it first creates a graph. First it looks at the range of values in each data series. Then it records the highest and lowest values. Finally, it draws each axis by creating a range of values that encompasses the high and low values. Use the **X**-Axis and **Y**-Axis commands on the /**G**raph menu to alter the scale and format of the graph axes. When you select either command, Quattro Pro displays a menu listing the parts of each axis you can modify, as follows:

The ***Scale*** command is set to **A**utomatic by default. Select **M**anual to place all ensuing command settings into effect. For instance, Quattro Pro will use the values stored next to the **L**ow and **H**igh commands to create the scale for each axis.

The ***Increment*** command indicates the number of divisions you want along an axis.

The ***Format of Ticks*** command permits you to choose a numeric display format for each value that corresponds to a tick on a graph axis. These formats are the same ones available when you select the /**S**tyle **N**umeric Format command.

The ***No. of Minor Ticks*** command helps to prevent labels from overlapping on a graph. If you experience overlapping labels (usually because the labels are too long to fit under the graph without overlapping), choose this command to replace every other label with a tick mark. This command works on all graph types except pie and column graphs.

The ***Alternate Ticks*** command also controls overlapping labels. After you select this option, Quattro Pro displays every other tick label slightly below the x-axis labels so Quattro Pro can fully display longer labels.

The ***Display Scaling*** command shows a scale next to an axis when Quattro Pro abbreviates the axis numbers.

The *Mode* command enables you to display a graph on a **L**ogarithmic scale. The default mode setting is **N**ormal.

Note that the **Y**-Axis menu differs slightly from the **X**-Axis menu. On the **Y**-Axis menu, there is no **A**lternate Ticks command, but there is a **2**nd Y-Axis command. This extra command enables you to change the display characteristics of a second y-axis, when one is added to a graph. The **2**nd Y-Axis menu looks exactly like the **Y**-Axis menu except that it does not show the **2**nd Y-Axis command.

The following Quick Steps demonstrate how to create a custom scale for the y-axis on the graph shown in Figure 8.18. In this exercise, you learn how to manually scale a Quattro Pro graph to control the display size of graph data.

Scaling a graph axis

1. Press /G to pull down the /**G**raphmenu. — Quattro Pro displays the **G**raph menu.
2. Press Y to select the **Y**-Axis command. — The **Y**-Axis command reveals a list of the features that you can change on the y-axis.
3. Press SM to select **S**cale **M**anual. — This sets y-axis scaling to manual, and tells Quattro Pro to scale the y-axis according to the values listed next to the **L**ow and **H**igh options.
4. Press L to select the **L**ow option. Type a number for Quattro Pro to use as the lowest value on the y-axis (I typed 0) and press Enter. — Quattro Pro writes the number next to **L**ow option on the **Y**-Axis submenu.
5. Press H to select the **H**igh option. Type a number for Quattro Pro to use as the highest value on the y-axis (I typed 26) and press Enter. — Quattro Pro writes the number next to **H**igh option on the **Y**-Axis submenu.
6. Press F10 to review the new y-axis scaling on the current graph. Press Enter when you are finished viewing the graph. — Quattro Pro returns you to the **Y**-Axis submenu.
7. Press Q two times to return to the active spreadsheet.

□

Figure 8.19 shows the customized version of the graph, complete with a new fill pattern for data series #4 and a manually scaled y-axis.

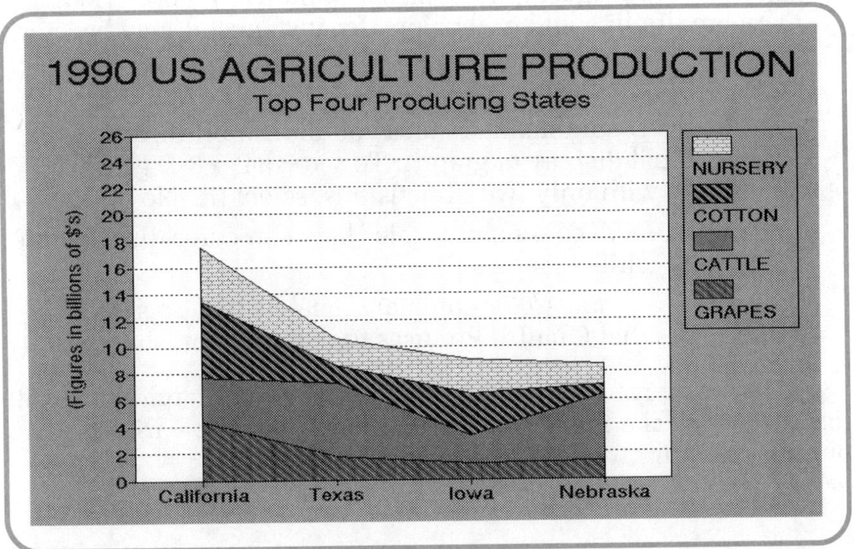

Figure 8.19 Customizing the appearance of the basic graph.

The best way to learn which axis-customizing commands create the most effectual and well-ordered graph axes is to experiment with each command. Press F10 at any time to view the current graph, even when several menus are pulled down. Press Enter to return to the active spreadsheet.

Customizing the Overall Graph

After you've customized the individual parts of a graph, you still may need to do a little more to enhance the overall appearance of a graph. For these times, you can use the commands on the /**G**raph **O**verall menu. Pull down this menu now and take a moment to review its commands.

> The ***Grid*** command adds vertical, horizontal, or both types of grid patterns to the graph background. This makes it a bit easier to identify values, for example, on a bar graph.

The ***Outlines*** command draws lines and drop shadow boxes around graph title text, the legend, and around the entire graph area.

The ***Background Color*** command selects the color that Quattro Pro displays in the background of a graph. When you modify line and grid colors, for instance, it may become necessary to adjust the graph's background color so that you can see the lines and grids.

The ***Three-D*** command enables you to turn off three-dimensional display of graphs. To see what a 3-D graph looks like with only two dimensions, select the **N**o option.

The ***Color/B&W*** command toggles between color display and black and white display.

The ***Drop Shadow Color*** command enables you to select the color pairs that Quattro Pro uses to display drop shadows.

The best way to learn which customizing commands work well together is to take the time to experiment with the various menu options on your own.

Annotating a Graph

Quattro Pro has a built-in graph editor to help you add the final stylistic touches to any graph. To use this editor, select the /**G**raph **A**nnotate command, and Quattro Pro displays the current graph in the Graph Annotator environment (see Figure 8.20). Or while a graph is in full-screen display, press the / (forward slash) key to do the same.

In the Graph Annotator environment, you can add descriptive text, boxes, lines, and other geometric shapes to a graph using the commands found on the menu bar at the top of the screen. Figure 8.20 shows how you could add boxed text and an arrow to point out significant data on the graph.

The following Quick Steps demonstrate how to annotate the boxed text. Using similar techniques, you can also add the arrow if your wish.

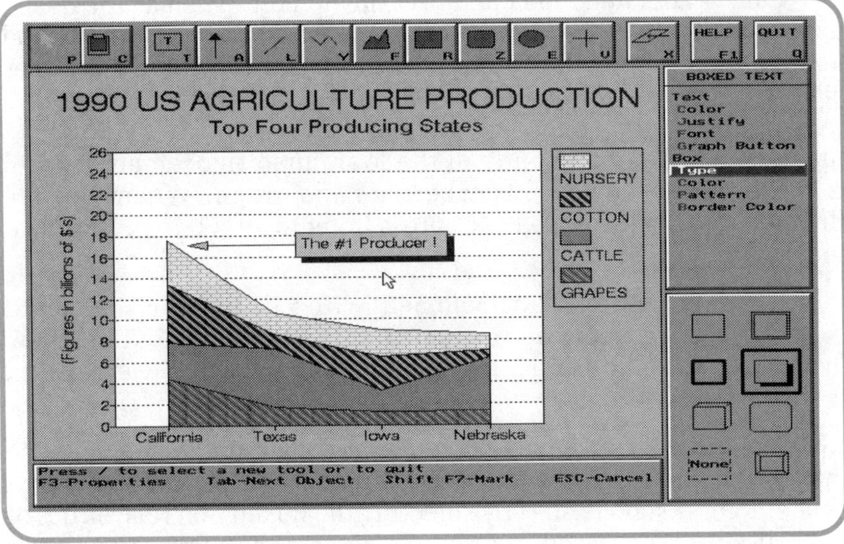

Figure 8.20 Modifying a graph while in Quattro Pro's Graph Annotator environment.

Adding boxed text to a graph

1. Press /GA to execute the Graph Annotate command.

   Quattro Pro loads the current graph into the Annotator environment. If you have a mouse, Quattro Pro displays the arrow pointer.

2. Press /T to activate the Boxed Text element, or click once on the Boxed Text element box at the top of the screen with your mouse.

   Quattro Pro highlights the Boxed Text element, and a cross-hair appears on top of the graph.

3. Press Enter.

   Quattro Pro draws the outline of a text box on the graph.

4. Type the text you wish to appear in the box (I typed *The #1 Producer !*) and press Enter.

   Quattro Pro affixes the text box, including the text you typed, to the graph. The cross-hair (or mouse arrow) reappears. □

Once annotated, you can move an element (such as the boxed text) anywhere on the current graph. Start by selecting the boxed text. To do this, press the Tab key repeatedly until Quattro Pro places eight small boxes around the outside edge of the boxed text. Or if you have a mouse, click once anywhere inside the boxed text to select that element. Now press any of the four cursor-movement keys to relocate the boxed text elsewhere on the graph. When you are finished moving the boxed text, press Enter to affix it to the graph at the current position.

To move any annotated element with a mouse, click and hold the mouse arrow on the element. Drag the element to a new location on the graph and release the button when you want to affix the element.

Occasionally, you may wish to resize an annotated element so that it blends in better with your graph. To resize the boxed text element, for instance, start by selecting the boxed text (use either of the procedure discussed in previous paragraphs). Press the period key (.) once. Quattro Pro draws a thin box around the boxed text. A small square appears in one corner of the thin box. Press any of the four cursor-movement keys to resize the boxed text starting at the location of the small square. If you wish to resize the boxed text from a different location on the element, continue pressing the period until the small square appears at the desired corner of the thin box. When you finish resizing the element, press Enter to permanently store the new size for that element.

To resize any element using a mouse, select the element. Click the mouse pointer on one of the small boxes that appears on the outline of the selected element. Drag the small square until you create the ideal size for the element. Release the mouse button to store the new size for the element.

Tip: To edit text in a boxed text element, select the element and press F2. Quattro Pro enters EDIT and places the edit at the end of the text. To edit text in the box use the same keys and procedures you use for editing spreadsheet cells. When you finish editing the text, press Enter to save the new text and reaffix the element to the graph.

In the Graph Annotator environment, you also can import clip art from Quattro Pro clip art files. Quattro Pro copies these files into your \QPRO directory during program installation. Clip art files have the .CLP file name extension. To bring a clip art file into the Graph Annotator environment, select the /**C**lipboard **P**aste From command.

Quattro Pro displays a file name prompt box that, by default, lists all files whose file name extension begins with the letter C. This list includes the clip art (.CLP) files that arrive with your Quattro Pro package, as well as any computer graphics metafile (.CGM) files you may have purchased from a third-party vendor and placed into this directory.

To display only the clip art files in the file name prompt box, backspace over the default wildcard (*.C*), type **.CLP* and press Enter. To import clip art into the Annotator environment, highlight a file name and press Enter.

In Figure 8.21, the filename CLAPHAND.CLP is highlighted. This clip art file displays a pair of clapping hands—the perfect addition to the sample graph.

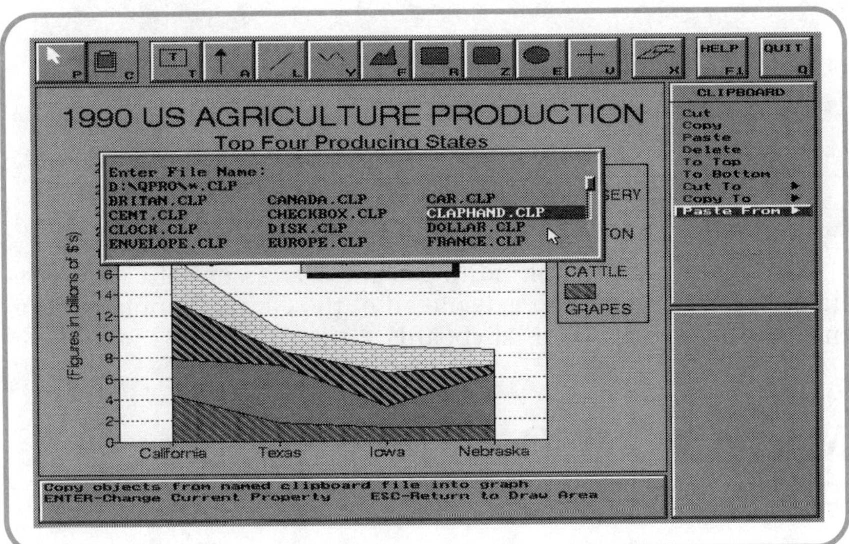

Figure 8.21 Retrieving a Quattro Pro clip art file into the Annotator environment.

Once you import clip art into the Annotator environment you can modify it as you would any other annotator element. For instance, you can create a custom color scheme, modify a line style, or even scale the entire graphic so that it fits into a particular area on a graph. When clip art first arrives into the Annotator environment, Quattro Pro selects the entire graphic element (the small boxes and thin lines surround the graphic).

Figure 8.22 shows the final, scaled version of the clapping hands clip art placed strategically on the sample graph. Use the steps outlined in the previous section to scale and place clip art on your own graphs.

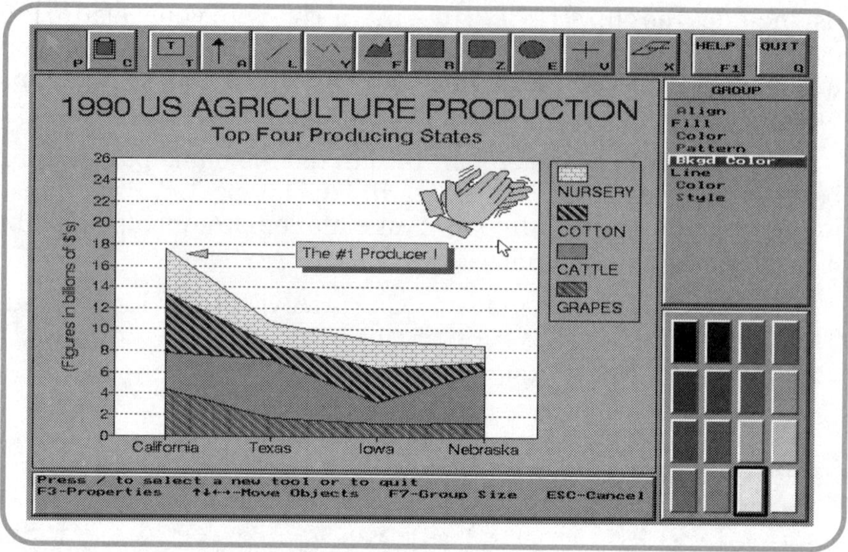

Figure 8.22 Clip art enhances a graph when it is properly sized and strategically located.

Although this graph editing feature is essentially a mouse-driven tool, you also can execute all of the Graph Annotator commands directly from your keyboard.

Managing Your Quattro Pro Graphs

Let's say you're busily building graphs to use in an important meeting. You may be wondering how to keep track of them. In Quattro Pro, it's critical to remember that if you intend to create multiple graphs for the same spreadsheet, assign a unique name to each graph. If you don't, Quattro Pro discards the current graph settings as soon as you begin creating another graph.

Creating, Displaying, and Deleting Graph Names

When you save a spreadsheet, Quattro Pro also saves the current graph settings for that spreadsheet. It's a good idea to also save your graphs using unique names so you don't accidentally overwrite them later.

To build and keep more than one graph with a spreadsheet, select the /**G**raph **N**ame **C**reate command. Quattro Pro prompts you for a name. Type in a unique name, and press Enter to assign that name to the current graph.

To later display the graph, select the /**G**raph **N**ame **D**isplay command. When Quattro Pro displays the graph name prompt box, highlight the graph name and press Enter. The graph immediately displays on your screen.

When you create several graphs from data on the same spreadsheet, the **A**utosave Edits command helps you manage your graphs. This command prevents you from accidentally overwriting one graph with another graph. This command has two settings: **Y**es (auto-saving is on) and **N**o (auto-saving is off). By default, the **A**utosave Edits command is set to **N**o.

With auto-saving on, Quattro Pro saves the current graph's settings as soon as you make another graph's settings current. If the first graph has no name, Quattro Pro prompts you to name the graph before it makes the second graph current.

> **Caution:** When **A**utosave Edits is set to **N**o, be extremely careful if you are working with multiple graphs. Always remember to save the current graph's settings (with the **S**ave command) before you make another graph current (with the **D**isplay command).

Use the /**G**raph **N**ame **E**rase command to erase individual graphs from a spreadsheet. Quattro Pro displays the graph name prompt box containing all of the graph names assigned to the active spreadsheet. Highlight a name and press Enter to erase that graph. To erase all of the saved graph names assigned to the active spreadsheet, select /**G**raph **N**ame **R**eset. Quattro Pro displays a dialog box asking if you wish to `Delete all named graphs?` Select **Y**es to do so, or **N**o to cancel the operation.

Creating a Graph Slide Show

Graph slide shows are an exciting way to display the results of all your graph-building efforts. When you view a slide show, you can analyze and make comparisons between data on the different graphs as they flash on-screen. Graph slide shows are an effective way to shed the best light on your graphs during a meeting.

To create a slide show, you first must create and name at least two (or more) graphs for the current spreadsheet. Now create a data table somewhere on the current spreadsheet. This table is made up of two columns, as shown in Figure 8.23. In the first column, type the names of the graphs you wish to appear in the slide show. In the right column, type a number that represents the number of seconds to display each graph. Enter `0` next to the graph name or omit this column entirely if you want a slide to remain on-screen until you press a key on the keyboard.

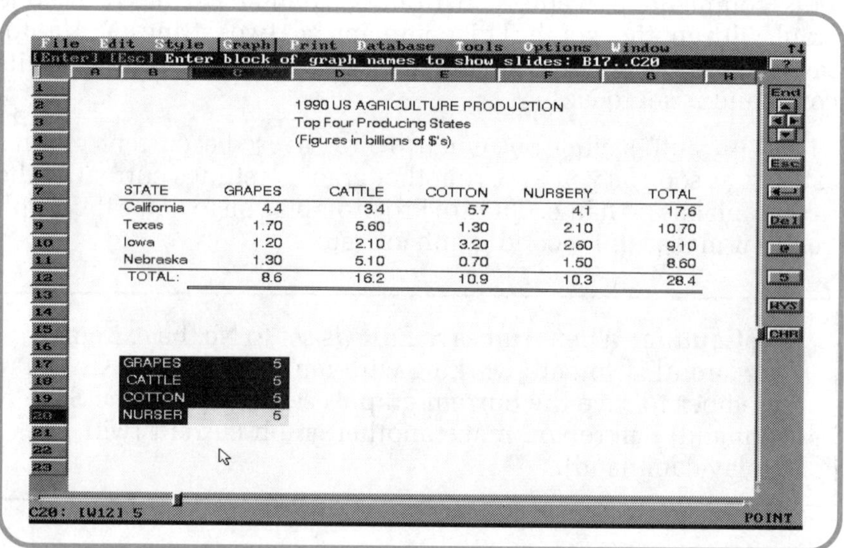

Figure 8.23 Entering the instructions for a slide show onto a spreadsheet.

To start the slide show, select the /**G**raph **N**ame **S**lide command. When Quattro Pro prompts you for the slide show block, type in the cell coordinates for the data table. Press Enter to begin the slide show.

You can enhance the impact of your slide shows by adding transitional effects and sound effects.

A transition is a special screen effect that Quattro Pro uses to smooth the transition from one slide to another. Quattro Pro has 24 slide transition effects—they are numbered 1 to 24. To use a transition, add the transition effect number (from 1 to 24) to the third column in the slide show. In the fourth column, enter the number of seconds you wish each transition to last.

> **Tip:** The best way to review all of the transition effects at one time is to create a 24-graph slide show, and apply one transition effect to each slide in the show. Note that you do not necessarily have to create 24 separate graphs to accomplish this test. Simply create a few, and reuse them (add their names to the slide data block) several times.

To add sound effects to a slide show, create a fifth column in the slide show block. In this column you enter the name of a special digitized sound file. Your Quattro Pro package includes 3 sound effect files: FANFARE.SND, THANKYOU.SND, and APPLAUSE.SND. The filename describes the sound effect. Also, the ProView Power Pack that arrives with Quattro Pro includes other sound effect files.

Placing a Graph onto a Spreadsheet

The **I**nsert command allows you to simultaneously view a graph and a spreadsheet on-screen, as shown in Figure 8.24. For this command to work, however, you must have an EGA or VGA graphics display system. You also must set your system to WYSIWYG display mode by selecting the /**O**ptions **D**isplay Mode **B**: WYSIWYG Mode command.

To insert a graph, start by selecting the /**G**raph **I**nsert command. Quattro Pro displays the graph name prompt box. Highlight the name of the graph you wish to insert and press Enter. When prompted, type in the address of a cell block into which Quattro Pro can insert the graph (in Figure 8.24, the insert block is C13..F23). Quattro Pro immediately redraws the spreadsheet with the inserted graph.

By default, Quattro Pro draws an inserted graph according to a special scaling procedure. So, even if your target cell block is very large, the graph probably will not fill the entire cell block. To cause an inserted graph to entirely fill up the target cell block, select /**P**rint **G**raph Print **L**ayout **4**:3 Aspect **N**o before you place the graph onto the spreadsheet.

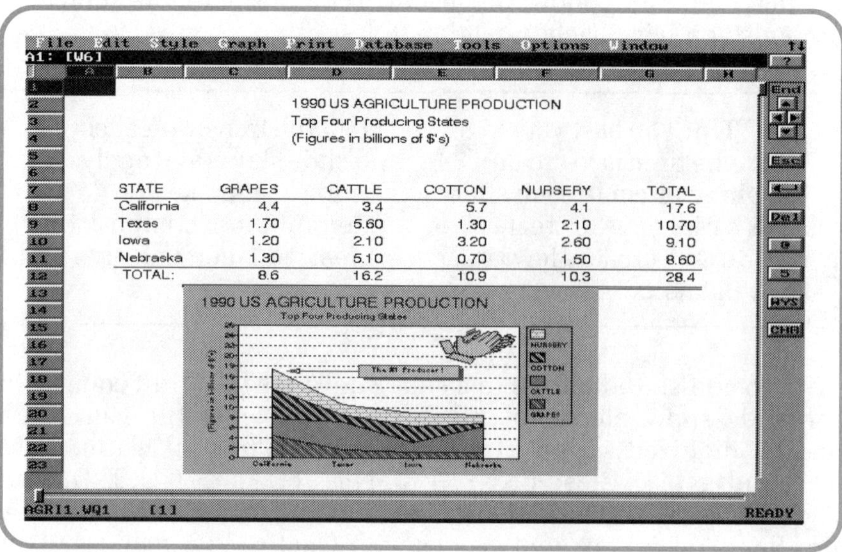

Figure 8.24 Inserting a graph onto the agriculture spreadsheet.

If the target cell block area is too small for the graph, the inserted image may be unreadable. To fix this, select a larger target block and repeat the insert operation again. Continue to do this until the inserted graph is appropriately sized. Press F10 to display the graph in full-screen mode.

To print a spreadsheet containing an inserted graph, add the inserted graph to the print block with the /**P**rint **B**lock command. Before printing, set the /**P**rint **D**estination command to **G**raphics Printer, and align the paper to top-of-form with the /**P**rint **A**djust Printer **A**lign. When you're ready to print, select /**P**rint **S**preadsheet Print.

To remove an inserted graph from the spreadsheet, place the cell selector anywhere inside the cell block containing the graph. Now select the /**G**raph **H**ide command and Quattro Pro will display the graph name prompt box. Highlight the graph name in the box and press Enter. The inserted graph disappears from the spreadsheet.

Printing a Quattro Pro Graph

You can print any Quattro Pro graph as long as your printer supports a graphics character set. Check the owner's manual that came with your printer if you aren't sure.

The /**P**rint **G**raph Print menu appears in Figure 8.25. Review the commands on this menu and the following definitions to learn how to print a Quattro Pro graph.

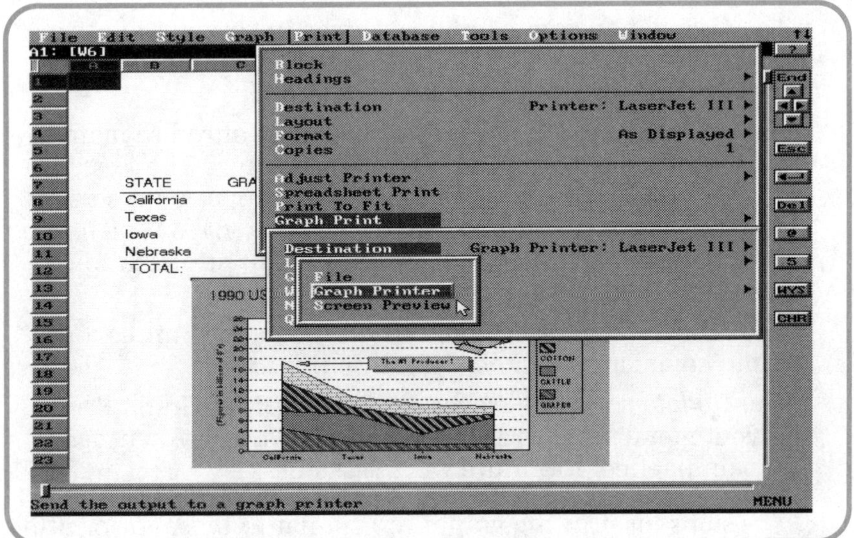

Figure 8.25 Reviewing the commands on the /Print Graph Print menu.

The **D**estination command allows you to print a graph to a **F**ile, to a **G**raph Printer, or into the **S**creen Preview environment. As with spreadsheets, the Screen Preview function gives you a chance to examine a graph's final print form on-screen before you actually print it.

The **L**ayout command allows you to determine the exact scaling of your graph prior to printing it. The options on this menu control the left and right margins of the graph, as well as the height and width of the graph itself. You can print the graph sideways if you wish. Pull down this menu now and take a moment to review its commands.

The *Left Edge* option sets the number of inches (or centimeters) from the left edge of the paper to the printed graph.

The *Top Edge* option sets the number of inches (or centimeters) from the top edge of the paper to the printed graph.

The *Height* option determines the printed height of the graph in inches (or centimeters).

The *Width* option determines the printed width of the graph in inches (or centimeters).

The *Dimensions* command specifies the measurement system that Quattro Pro uses to manage graph layout settings. The options are **I**nches (the default setting) and **C**entimeters.

The *Orientation* command determines the orientation that Quattro Pro uses to print a graph. The two options are **P**ortrait (the default) and **L**andscape.

The *4:3 Aspect* command determines if Quattro Pro maintains a 4:3 aspect ratio when printing a graph. The **Y**es option forces a graph to print much as it appears on-screen, and so may cause Quattro Pro to ignore the **L**ayout menu settings. The **N**o option tells Quattro Pro to print a graph using the **L**ayout menu settings.

The *Reset* command restores all /**P**rint **G**raph Print **L**ayout menu commands to their default settings.

The *Update* command saves all current /**P**rint **G**raph Print **L**ayout menu settings as the new defaults. These settings remain in effect for future work sessions.

The steps for printing graphs are similar to those for printing spreadsheets. Use the following Quick Steps.

Printing a Quattro Pro Graph

1. Select /**P**rint **G**raph Print **D**estination **G**raph Printer. — Quattro Pro records your graph printer as the print destination.

2. Make necessary changes to the graph on the **L**ayout menu. Select **Q**uit and then **Q**uit again to return to the /**P**rint menu.

3. Select **A**djust Printer **A**lign from the /**P**rint menu to align your printer to the top-of-form.
4. Select **G**raph Print **G**o from the /**P**rint menu. Select **Q**uit to return to the spreadsheet.

Quattro Pro begins printing the selected graph.

□

What You've Learned

Quattro Pro graphs display important spreadsheet data in a visually appealing manner. Using the commands on the /**G**raph menu you can create and customize graphs, and display graphs on-screen, in the Screen Preview environment. The /**P**rint menu contains a command that you use to print a graph. Following are some points to remember from this chapter:

- There are 11 types of Quattro Pro graphs. Among the most popular of these are the *pie graph*, the *line graph*, and the *bar graph*.
- There are two ways to create a graph: using the **F**ast Graph command, and building one from the ground up.
- Add *titles*, *legends*, and *customized fonts* to your graphs to create custom, presentation-quality graphs.
- Managing graphs is important when you wish to build more than one graph for the same spreadsheet.
- You can build *slide shows* using Quattro Pro graphs.
- Quattro Pro allows you to insert a graph directly onto a spreadsheet.
- You can print your Quattro Pro graphs on any printer that supports graphics. You also can print a graph to the screen, or to a disk file for later processing.

Chapter 9

Writing Macros To Automate Spreadsheet Tasks

In This Chapter

- *Writing, naming, and executing a basic macro*
- *Recording a macro*
- *Debugging a macro*
- *Managing your macros*

This chapter teaches you how to automate repetitive spreadsheet tasks using *macros*. Now, instead of executing the same menu commands over and over again, you can store them in a macro that will duplicate actions at the touch of a key.

What Is a Macro?

A *macro* is a collection of special instructions that you store in spreadsheet cells. These special instructions tell Quattro Pro to perform spreadsheet operations as if you weren't there pressing keyboard keys or clicking mouse buttons. Macro instructions direct Quattro Pro to pull down a menu, enter a label into a cell, build a formula, display a graph, and more.

To create a macro, enter each instruction into a column of cells on the active spreadsheet. When you execute a macro, Quattro Pro performs the instruction in the first cell of the macro column, and next moves down the column one cell at a time, performing each ensuing instruction.

A macro can duplicate every possible Quattro Pro menu selection or command execution. A macro also can reproduce keystrokes, cursor movements, and other keyboard actions that you normally perform by hand. For instance, the macro shown in Figure 9.1 enters your name into a cell on the active spreadsheet. Just replace the label in cell B5 (`YOUR NAME HERE`) with your own name.

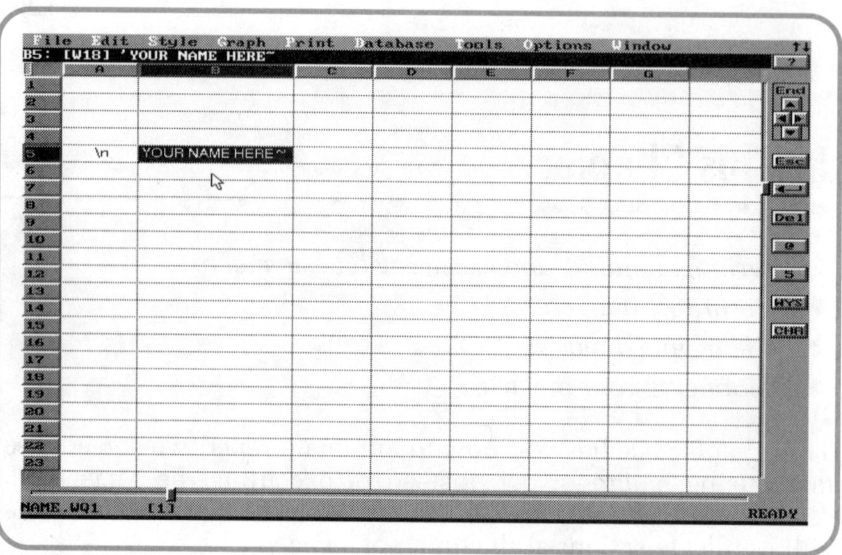

Figure 9.1 The macro in cell B5 enters your name into a spreadsheet, at the location of the cell selector.

The label in cell A5 (`'\n`) is known as an *instant macro name*. Assign this special name to the first (and only) line of the macro (cell B5 in the example) using the /**E**dit **N**ames **L**abel **R**ight command. It's a good practice to place a macro name in the cell directly to the left of the first instruction—that way, you'll always know which macro you're executing. To execute an instant macro, press Alt plus the letter appearing in the macro name. For example, to execute the macro in Figure 9.1, move the cell selector to cell A1, then press Alt-n. Quattro Pro immediately executes the macro in cell B5. This macro enters your name into the current cell.

The macro shown in Figure 9.2 is a bit more involved than the one-line macro we just saw. This macro moves the cell selector into cell E8, enters an @SUM formula, and then changes the width of column E to five spaces. Let's take a closer look at the different parts of this macro.

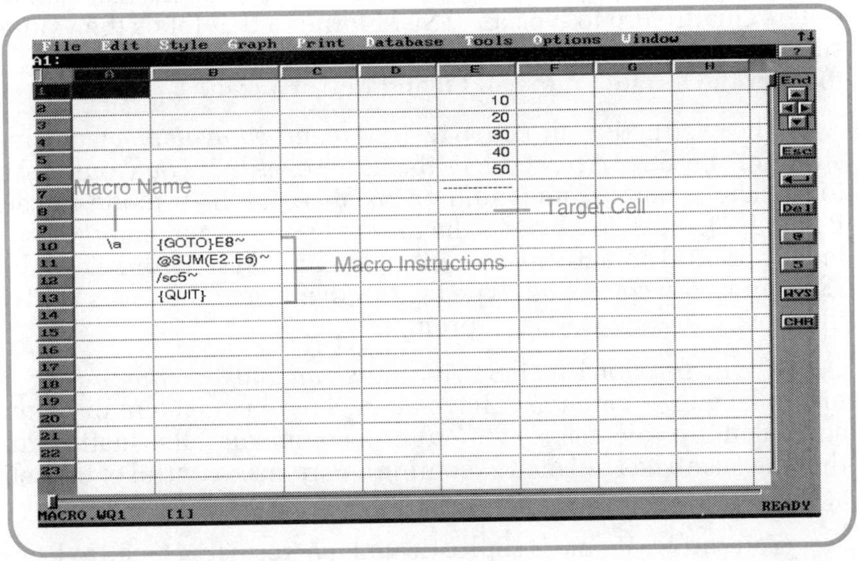

Figure 9.2 The macro in cells B10..B13 performs three specific tasks.

The label in cell A10 (`' \a`) is the instant macro name. Assign this special name to the first line of the macro (cell B10 in the example) using the /**E**dit **N**ames **L**abel **R**ight command. To execute this instant macro, press Alt plus the letter appearing in the macro name. For example, press Alt-a to execute the macro in Figure 9.2. Quattro Pro immediately begins to execute the macro at cell E8.

Each macro instruction appears in a cell of its own, starting with cell B10 and ending with cell B13. Let's take a closer look at the four instructions that appear in this macro.

The instruction in cell B10 has three distinct parts: a keyboard-equivalent macro (`{GOTO}`), a cell address (`E8`), and the tilde (`~`) character. A *keyboard-equivalent* macro instruction reproduces keystrokes that you would take during a work session. In this macro, {GOTO} reproduces the action of pressing F5 on the keyboard (Quattro Pro's GoTo key). The cell address E8 is the macro's response to the Quattro Pro prompt asking for the cell to go to. The tilde character tells Quattro Pro to issue a carriage return, exactly as if you had pressed the Enter key. When Quattro Pro has executed the command in this macro cell, the cell selector immediately moves to cell E8 on this spreadsheet.

The instruction in cell B11 has two distinct parts: a formula and a tilde character. While the cell selector is in cell E8, this instruction orders Quattro Pro to type an @SUM formula that totals the values stored in cells E2 through E6. The tilde character causes Quattro Pro to enter the formula into cell E8 and return a result.

The instruction in cell B12 is a *menu-equivalent* macro instruction, because it reproduces the keystrokes that you would take to execute a menu command. For instance, the instruction in cell B12 tells Quattro Pro to press the forward slash (/) and enter MENU mode, press S to activate the /**S**tyle menu, press C to select the **C**olumn Width command, type the number 5, and then press Enter in response to the command prompt.

The instruction in cell B13 is a *macro language command*. Most macro language commands have no keyboard equivalent or menu equivalent. In this macro, the `{QUIT}` command tells Quattro Pro that the macro has finished executing and returns control of the cell selector to you.

You can create more sophisticated macros using Quattro Pro's macro language commands. Macro commands tell Quattro Pro to do things that you can't accomplish simply by pulling down a menu or executing a command. You could create a macro, for instance, that asks the macro user to type Y or N in response to a Yes/No question. Then, based on the response, the macro would continue executing one of two sets of commands.

Tip: You also can stop a macro from executing by pressing Ctrl-Break. Pressing Ctrl-Break ends a macro prematurely; {QUIT} indicates that Quattro Pro has concluded the normal execution of the macro. The macro language command for pressing Ctrl-Break is {BREAK}.

How To Create a Basic Macro

Creating and using macros is fun and easy when you follow four general steps:

1. *Design* the macro. Decide what the macro is to do. Jot these thoughts down on paper so you can refer to them while writing the macro.
2. *Write* the macro. Type each instruction into a cell on the same spreadsheet. Assign a name to the first instruction cell once you've finished writing the macro.
3. *Test* the macro by executing it. If the macro doesn't work properly, or if Quattro Pro finds a program error, *debug* the macro. The word *debug* means to proofread the macro, find the macro error, and then correct the error before executing the macro again.
4. *Document* the macro and save the spreadsheet. Other people may wish to use macros you create. To *document* the macro, type text on the spreadsheet that identifies the name of the macro and offers a word or two about what each instruction does.

Writing the Basic Macro

To design a macro, start by jotting down on paper the spreadsheet activities you wish to automate. Do you want to write a macro that changes column widths for you? Would you like the macro to format numbers for you? Perhaps you just want to automate the process of saving and replacing a spreadsheet file. Give careful thought ahead of time to the spreadsheet activities the macro will accomplish for you—good planning is the key to successful macro development.

A basic macro uses keyboard-equivalent and menu-equivalent commands almost exclusively. List the keystrokes you use most often during a normal work session. Then, figure out which activities you wish to automate, and type the keystrokes for each activity into one column of cells.

You can automate other keyboard actions, such as moving the cell selector around the spreadsheet or pressing the Esc key to cancel a command, using keyboard-equivalent commands. You already know that {GOTO} in a macro is just like pressing F5 on your keyboard. Likewise, {ESC} in a macro works just like pressing the Esc key on your keyboard. Table 9.1 lists the keyboard-equivalent commands you'll use most often in basic macros.

Table 9.1 Using keyboard-equivalent commands.

Keyboard Key	Macro Command Equivalent
←	{LEFT} or {L}
→	{RIGHT} or {R}
↑	{UP} or {U}
↓	{DOWN} or {D}
Ctrl-Break	{BREAK}
Ctrl-D	{DATE}
End	{END}
Enter	{CR} or ~
Esc	{ESC}
Home	{HOME}
Pg Up	{PGUP}
Pg Dn	{PGDN}
/	/ or {MENU}

> **Tip:** You can amplify the effect of the cell selector movement commands by adding a number inside the braces, next to the command name. The number represents the number of times in succession you wish Quattro Pro to perform that command. For instance, the command to move the cell selector 10 spaces to the right is {RIGHT 10}, the equivalent of pressing the → arrow 10 times in a row.

As you become more accustomed to using Quattro Pro, you'll undoubtedly find yourself using the function key commands more and more. Table 9.2 lists four commonly-used function keys and the equivalent macro command you'll use most often in basic macros.

Table 9.2 Using function key-equivalent commands.

Keyboard Key	Macro Command Equivalent
F2	{EDIT}
F5	{GOTO}
F9	{CALC}
F10	{GRAPH}

> **Note:** Refer to your Quattro Pro documentation for a complete list of the keyboard-equivalent and menu-equivalent macro commands.

Use the following Quick Steps to write a basic macro.

Writing a Basic Macro

1. Think of the spreadsheet activity you wish to automate. Jot down a list of the keys that you'll press to accomplish this task.

   Be sure to create this list—it makes writing the macro much easier.

2. Press /FN to select the /File New command and open a new, blank Quattro Pro spreadsheet. Pick a cell where you wish to begin writing the macro. Move the cell selector there, then move it one cell to the left. Type in the macro name as a label. Now move the cell selector one cell to the right. (I typed '\s into cell D2, then pressed → to move the cell selector to cell E2.)

   A macro name consists of the backslash character (\) and any letter in the alphabet. Be sure to type a label prefix in front of the \ so that Quattro Pro does not interpret the entry as a repeating label.

3. Type the first macro instruction. Press ↓ to move the cell selector to the next cell down. (I typed {GOTO}B1~ then pressed ↓ and moved to cell E3.)

   If the instruction is a menu-equivalent command (such as /FS) or a value such as @SUM(E2..E6), be sure to type a label prefix before you type the first character.

4. Repeat Step 3 until you've entered all the instructions that you wish to automate.

   Be sure to enter only one instruction per cell. Do not leave a blank cell between any two macro instructions.

5. Move the cell selector back to the cell containing the macro name. (I moved to cell D2.) Press /ENLR to select the **/Edit Names Label Right** command, then press Enter to name the macro.

   Quattro Pro assigns the name to the cell that contains the first macro instruction. □

Figure 9.3 shows a basic macro that automates several of the formatting steps required to prepare a sales spreadsheet for data input. Write this macro for yourself if you find it of value—it appears as the example throughout the remainder of this section.

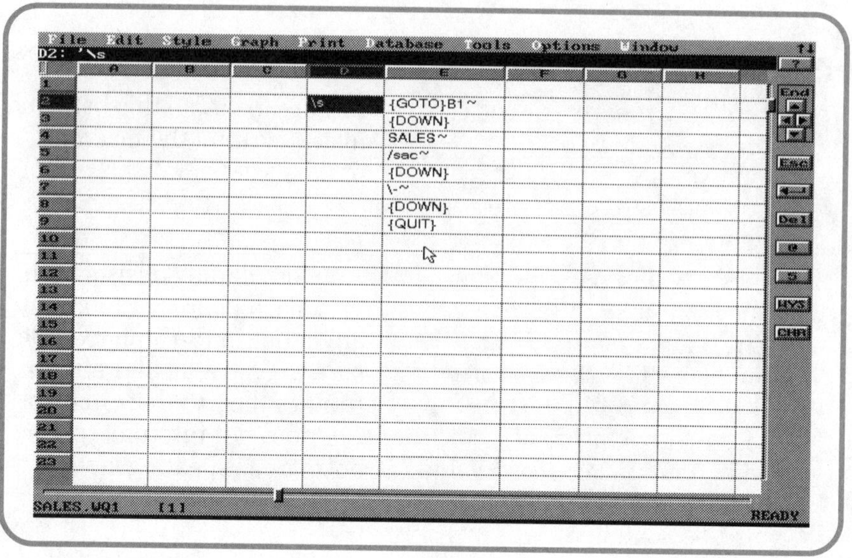

Figure 9.3 A basic macro that formats a sales spreadsheet in preparation for data entry.

Executing the Basic Macro

It's simple to execute an instant macro. Simply press the Alt key and then its name letter. For example, to execute the sales macro, just press Alt-s (the S stands for "sales"). It doesn't matter if the macro name letter is an uppercase or lowercase letter. Quattro Pro automatically stores a macro name (and any block name for that matter) in uppercase letters.

You also can assign longer names to a macro. Suppose that you want to assign the name SALES to the macro in Figure 9.3. To do so, just enter the word `SALES` into cell D2 and assign the name using the /**E**dit **N**ames **L**abel **R**ight command. (Do this now if you are following along with your own macro.) Keep in mind that you can't execute this macro by typing Alt-SALES—that won't work. Instead, you must access the commands located on Quattro Pro's /**T**ools **M**acro menu.

To execute a macro with a long name, press /TM to select the /**T**ools **M**acro command. Quattro Pro displays the Macro menu, shown in Figure 9.4. Or just press the Alt-F2 shortcut key to reveal the same menu.

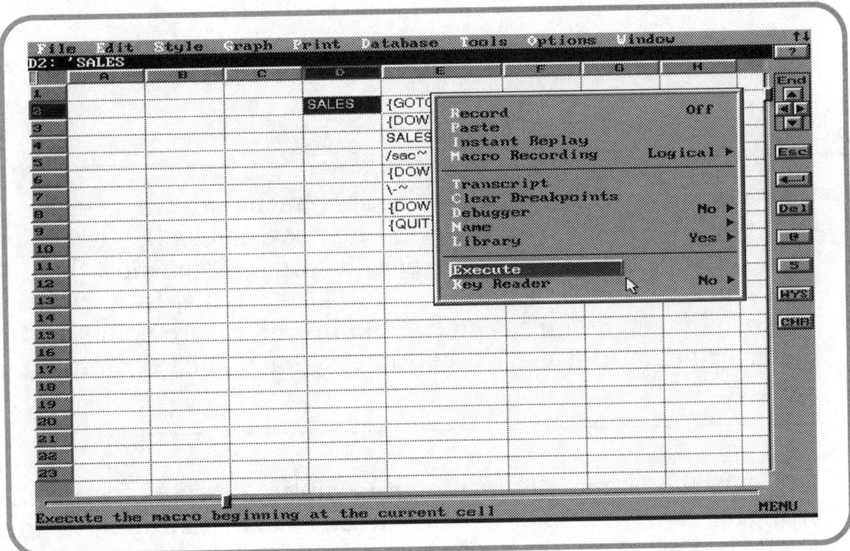

Figure 9.4 Reviewing the commands on the Macro menu.

Press E to select the **E**xecute command. Quattro Pro prompts you for the first cell in the column of macro instructions you wish Quattro Pro to execute. Type `E2` and press Enter or type `SALES` and press Enter—both entries accomplish the same objective. If you don't know the name of the macro you want to execute, press F3 and Quattro Pro will display the block names list, like the one shown in Figure 9.5. Highlight a name on the list and press Enter to execute that macro. Quattro Pro displays the `MACRO` mode indicator on the status line while it executes the macro.

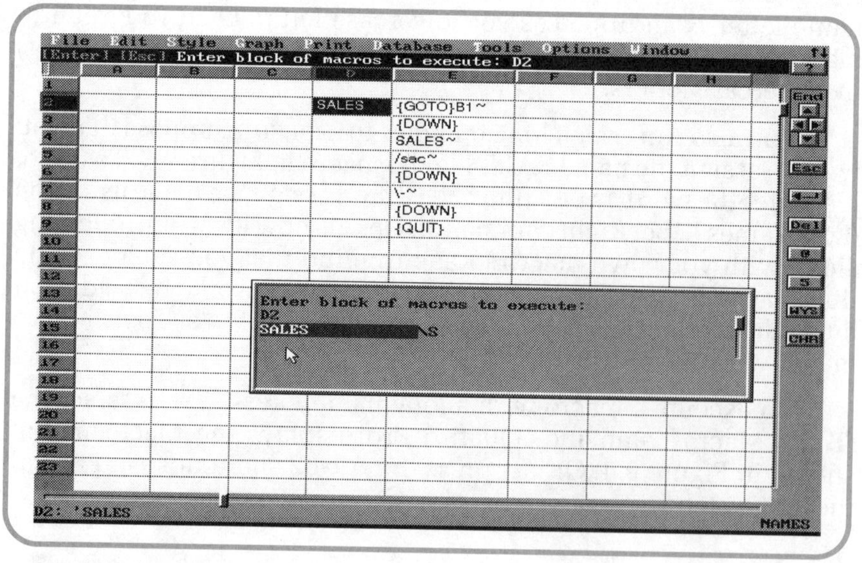

Figure 9.5 Choosing the name of a macro to execute from the block names list.

> **Tip:** Figure 9.5 reveals that both of the names we used for the SALES macro appear on the block names list. Recall from Chapter 3 that Quattro Pro permits you to assign more than one name to a cell block. This rule also applies to naming macros. In fact, if you assign both an instant macro name and a longer name to a macro, you have your choice of how to execute the macro.

Figure 9.6 shows the results of executing the SALES macro. Starting in cell E2, see if you can match each macro instruction to the formatted data that now appears in cell block B2..B4. Before continuing, change the macro name in cell D2 back to \s to remind yourself that the easiest way to execute this macro is by pressing Alt-s. Doing so does not change the fact that you may execute this macro using either name. In practice, you'll come to prefer the convenience and quick response of an instant macro name.

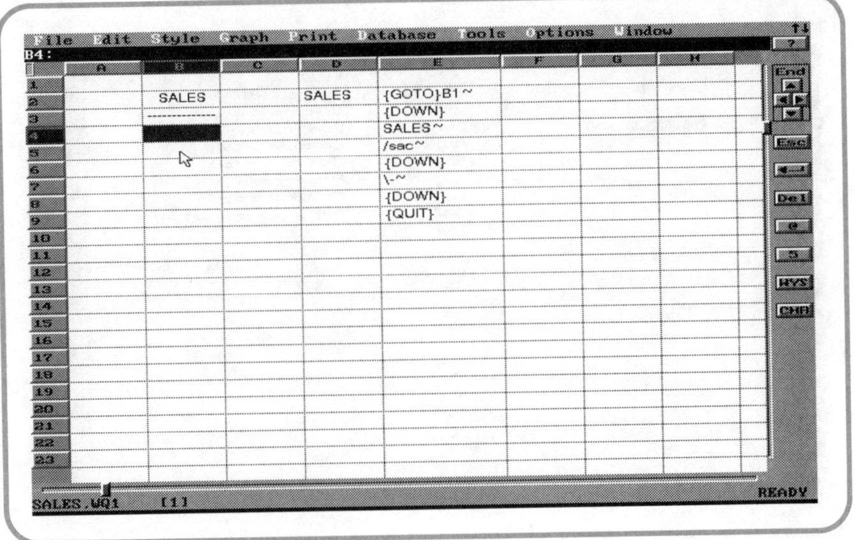

Figure 9.6 Executing the SALES macro.

Documenting the Basic Macro

As mentioned, documentation is an important final step in creating a basic macro. To get a feel for how important documentation can be, imagine if you had to learn all about creating macros without the benefit of this book (or any other book). Do you think you could do it?

Macro documentation is particularly important for another reason. Although you could figure out how to use a spreadsheet program by toying with the menu commands, it would be nearly impossible to decipher a set of macro instructions without some type of guidance.

Fortunately, documenting a macro is a fairly straightforward and painless task. Of course it's up to you to determine how thorough your documentation will be. For now, let's examine how to provide the minimum amount necessary to properly document the SALES macro. Figure 9.7 shows basic documentation added to the SALES macro.

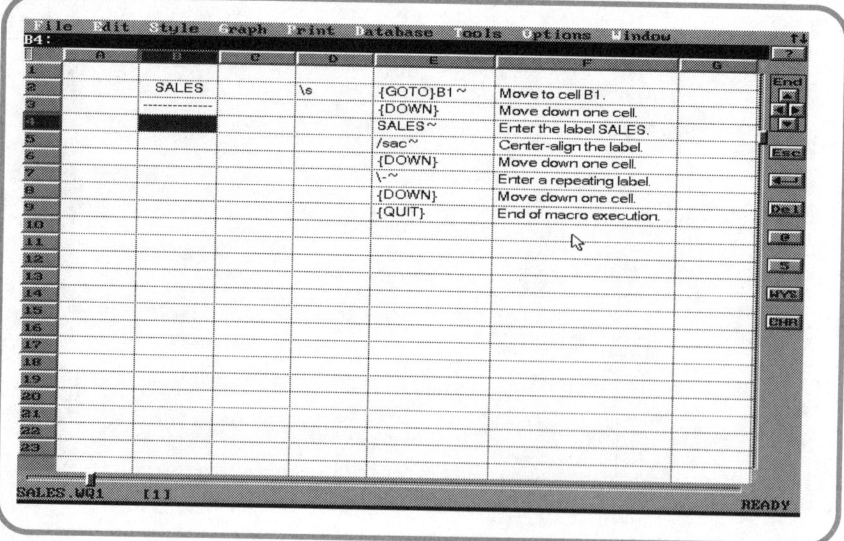

Figure 9.7 Documenting the Sales macro.

As you can see in Figure 9.7, documenting a macro isn't so hard after all. Think of how the addition of this information now makes it easier for others to use and understand the SALES macro. After a few months or years go by, you may forget the purpose of a macro you created. It happens to the best of us! As your macros become longer and more involved, keep in mind that the more complex the macro instructions, the greater the need for good documentation.

Recording a Macro Program

Quattro Pro has a built-in macro recorder that, when turned on, keeps track of keystrokes and menu and command selections that you make during a work session. You use this tool to create longer, more complex macros. Using the macro recorder saves you the time normally spent entering individual macro instructions into spreadsheet cells.

Creating and using a recorded macro involves five steps, only one step more than if you wrote the macro out by hand. These steps are:

1. *Design* the macro. Visualize what the macro is to do. You don't have to jot these thoughts down, though, because you act them out as you press keystrokes and execute commands.
2. *Record* the macro. When the recorder is on, simply prepare and format a spreadsheet as you normally do when building a new application.
3. *Paste* the macro. To transfer a recorded macro from Quattro Pro's memory onto a spreadsheet, you must paste it. Once pasted, you can modify the macro as you please.
4. *Test* the macro by executing it. Again, this step involves the process of debugging (identifying problem areas and correcting them before attempting to execute the macro again).
5. *Document* and *save* the macro.

Recording and Pasting the Macro

To record and paste a macro onto a spreadsheet, use the following Quick Steps:

Recording and Pasting a Macro onto a Spreadsheet

1. Press /FN to select the /File New command.	A new, blank Quattro Pro spreadsheet opens. The READY mode indicator appears on the status line.
2. Press /TMMK to execute the /Tools Macro Macro Recording Keystroke command.	Quattro Pro will record all spreadsheet activity as keystrokes.
3. Press /TMR to select the /Tools Macro Record command.	Quattro Pro turns the Macro Recorder on and displays the REC mode indicator on the status line.
4. Build the spreadsheet as you normally would. Type in the title and column headings, change column widths, enter data, etc. (I created the report headings shown in Figure 9.8, and changed the width of column B to 21.)	Quattro Pro stores each keystroke—even miskeys and cancelled command selections—in memory.

5. Press /TMR to reselect the /**T**ools **M**acro **R**ecord command.

Quattro Pro turns the Macro Recorder off.

6. Press /TMP to select the /**T**ools **M**acro **P**aste command.

Quattro Pro prompts you to type a name for the macro you just recorded.

7. Type an instant macro name, or type a long macro name. (I typed \l, for log.) Press or click Enter (see Figure 9.9).

Quattro Pro prompts you to type the cell block where you want Quattro Pro to paste the macro.

8. Type a cell address or a block address. (I typed G3.)

Quattro Pro pastes the macro into the cell block that you specify (see Figure 9.10).

9. Move the cell selector to the cell that will contain the macro name. (I moved to cell F3.) Press /ENLR to select the /**E**dit **N**ames **L**abel **R**ight command, then press Enter to name the macro.

Quattro Pro assigns the name to the cell that contains the first macro instruction.

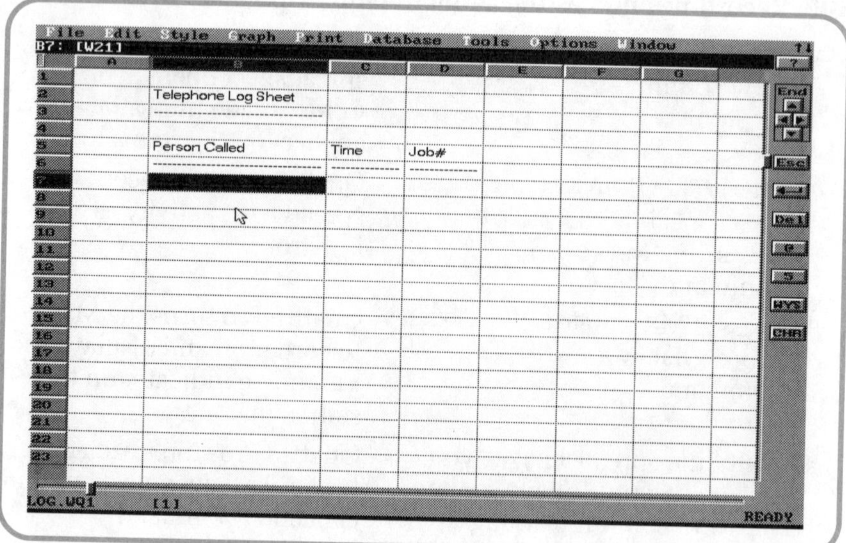

Figure 9.8 Creating the report title and headings for a Telephone Log Sheet macro.

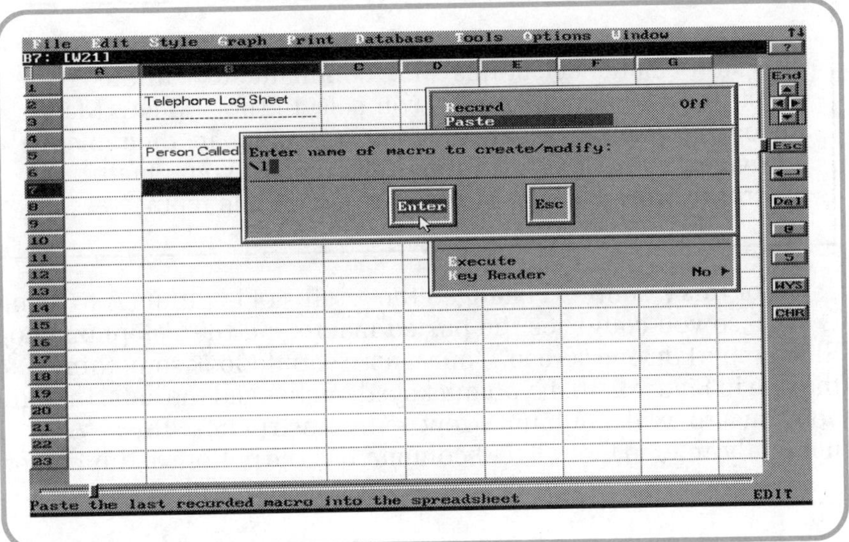

Figure 9.9 Naming the macro \l for "log".

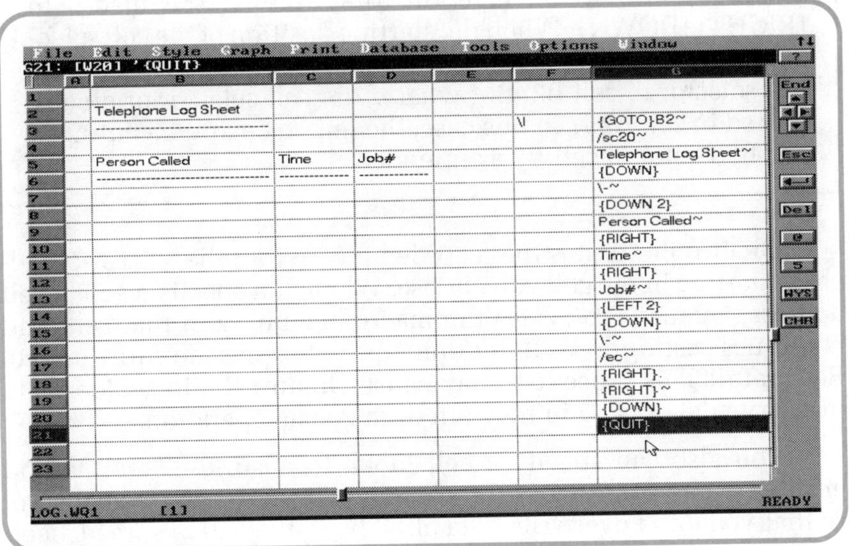

Figure 9.10 Pasting a recorded macro into a block on the active spreadsheet.

> **Tip:** In step 2 of the Quick Steps, you told Quattro Pro to store menu selections and command executions in a keystroke-equivalent form. If you select /**T**ools **M**acro **M**acro Recording **L**ogical, Quattro Pro stores them in their menu-equivalent form. Use this form if you require your Quattro Pro macros to work with Quattro Pro's compatible menu trees.

For this example, I changed the widths of columns A to 3 and G to 20 so you could see the pasted macro and the Telephone Log Sheet report on one screen. Your macro should look something like the one in Figure 9.10. If you miskeyed or changed the data, though, your macro will contain a few extra instruction lines. Also, I manually entered the {QUIT} command at the bottom of this macro.

> **Tip:** It's a good idea to always begin your macros with the {GOTO} command. Use the {GOTO} command to place the cell selector in a starting position before you execute any menu commands. Let's see why this is so. Look back to Figure 9.10. Suppose we change the first line of the macro to {RIGHT}{DOWN}. When the starting position of the cell selector is A1, the {RIGHT}{DOWN} commands properly move the cell selector to cell B2. But what if the cell selector originally started in cell A25? In this case, the macro begins executing at cell B26—not in cell B2 as intended.

Quattro Pro pastes the recorded macro into the active spreadsheet starting in the cell you choose. When you specify a single cell address, Quattro Pro pastes the macro beginning in that cell, and continues pasting down the column until it copies the entire macro. Be careful! This procedure may cause Quattro Pro to accidentally overwrite data that is in the path of the paste operation.

You also can specify a cell block to paste to. This method enables you to control exactly where Quattro Pro pastes the macro, so that you don't overwrite data already on the active spreadsheet. When you paste a macro into a cell block, be sure that the block is large enough to accommodate all of the recorded macro instructions. Otherwise, Quattro Pro will lop off the bottom portion of the macro so that it fits into the target cell block.

Replaying a Recorded Macro

The **I**nstant Replay command lets you execute the last recorded macro stored in Quattro Pro's memory. This is useful for testing a macro prior to pasting it into a block on a spreadsheet. To show an instant replay of the last macro recorded, select the /**T**ools **M**acro **I**nstant Replay command.

Managing Your Macros

There's one problem associated with storing a macro on a spreadsheet. When you execute the macro, it may accidentally overwrite itself. For instance, suppose that you store a macro in cell block A1..B25. Now imagine that the macro contains several instructions that tell Quattro Pro to enter labels and values into the same cell block. This causes Quattro Pro to overwrite the macro itself. As a rule, you should store your macros near the spreadsheet area that the macro will alter, but not so close that it'll overwrite itself.

Creating a Macro Library Spreadsheet

An alternative to this method for managing macros is to store all of your macros in a special file called a *macro library spreadsheet*. While a macro library spreadsheet is open in Quattro Pro's memory, you can open a new, blank spreadsheet with the /**F**ile **O**pen command. Quattro Pro overlays the macro library spreadsheet with a new, blank spreadsheet. Now, when you execute a macro stored on the macro library spreadsheet, the macro will affect the active spreadsheet, and not the macro library spreadsheet.

Following are several reasons for storing macros in a macro library rather than on individual spreadsheets:

- When Quattro Pro can't locate a macro you want to execute on the active spreadsheet, it automatically searches through all macro libraries open in memory.
- You can eliminate the possibility of a macro accidentally overwriting itself on the active spreadsheet.

- You reduce spreadsheet file sizes by not having to copy macros over and over again onto new spreadsheets.
- A macro library is a permanent reference source, whereas spreadsheets often outlive their usefulness.

The following Quick Steps illustrate how to create a macro library spreadsheet.

Q Creating a Macro Library Spreadsheet

1. Press /FN to execute the /**F**ile **N**ew command.	Quattro Pro opens a new, blank spreadsheet into memory.
2. Retype existing macros onto the blank spreadsheet, or type new macros directly onto the spreadsheet. (I retyped the \s and \l macros.)	Be sure to leave at least one blank row in between macros that are in the same column (see Figure 9.11).
3. Press /TML to select the /**T**ools **M**acro **L**ibrary command.	Quattro Pro displays the Library menu.
4. Press Y to select the **Y**es option.	Quattro Pro designates the spreadsheet as a macro library (see Figure 9.12).
5. Press /ENLR to execute the /**E**dit **N**ames **L**abel **R**ight command and assign the names in column B to the macros in column C.	
6. Press /FS to select the /**F**ile **S**ave command.	Quattro Pro prompts you to type a file name for the macro library spreadsheet.
7. Type a name and press Enter. (I typed LIBRARY 1.)	Saves the macro library spreadsheet. □

> **Tip:** Notice that the macros on LIBRARY1.WQ1 reside in cell block B2..E11. Now recall that the SALES macro writes data into cell block B2..B3. Should you be concerned? Not really. The benefit of using a macro library is that the macro commands affect only the active spreadsheet. So as long as you use /**F**ile **O**pen to load a new, blank spreadsheet atop of LIBRARY1.WQ1, you do not run the risk of overwriting the macros.

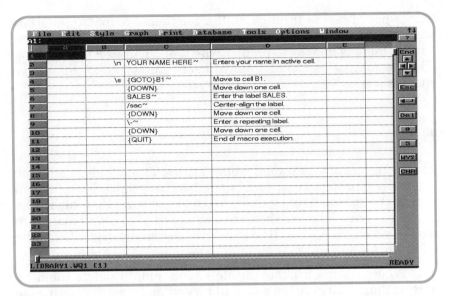

Figure 9.11 Retyping your macros on a blank spreadsheet for easier maintenance and management.

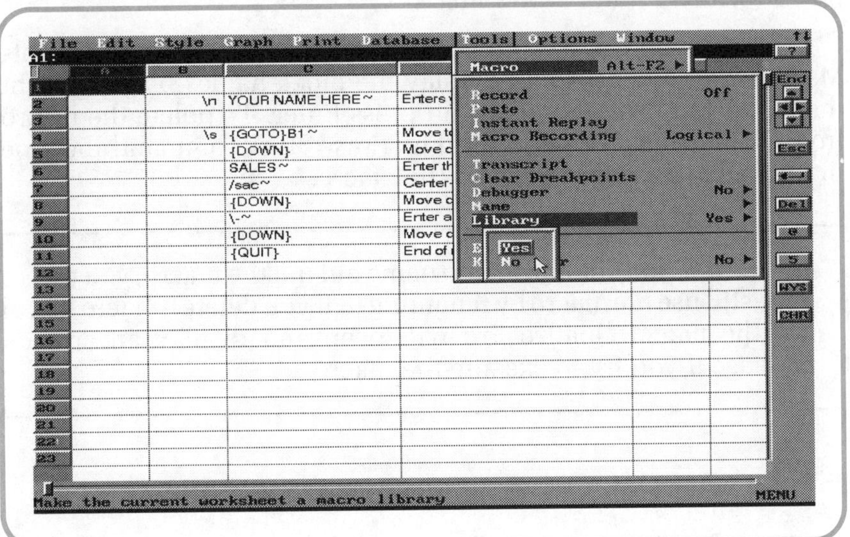

Figure 9.12 Creating a macro library spreadsheet.

You may create as many macro libraries as you wish. The rules that apply to one macro library apply to all. You may create as many unique macro names as you wish but are limited to 26 instant macro names per library (a through z). If more than one macro library is open at one time and the open libraries contain duplicate macro names, there is no way to predict which one will execute, if any at all. The macros executed from a macro library affect the active spreadsheet only.

Deleting Macros and Macro Names

As your library of macro applications grows, it's inevitable that some macros will become obsolete. As you become more adept at macro programming, you'll find it easier to develop macros that can handle a wider variety of tasks. Then, instead of writing several macros to handle several tasks, you'll be able to write a single macro to handle all of the tasks.

When macros become obsolete, you should delete them by erasing the macro from the macro library spreadsheet or deleting the spreadsheet that contains the macro. Doing so conserves disk space on your hard disk drive and on the macro library spreadsheet. It also reduces the number of names on the block names list. More importantly, deleting old instant macros frees up that letter of the alphabet for use with another, newer macro.

To delete a macro name, select /**E**dit **N**ames **D**elete or /**T**ools **M**acro **N**ame **D**elete—both display the block names list. Highlight the name you want to delete and press Enter. To delete the macro from the spreadsheet, select the /**E**dit **E**rase Block command and type in the cell block coordinates of the macro.

> **Tip:** If you delete a macro name but not the macro, you can still use the macro by renaming it. If you delete a macro but not the name, Quattro Pro will beep and display an error message if you try to execute the macro.

Using the Macro Debugger

Debugging is the process of isolating problems that cause macro execution errors. You'll know when you've encountered a macro error, because Quattro Pro beeps at you and stops executing the macro. When this happens, it's a good idea to use the Macro Debugger to help you locate the problem.

To debug a macro, you execute it while Quattro Pro is in DEBUG mode. To enter DEBUG mode, press /TMDY to select the /**T**ools **M**acro **D**ebugger **Y**es command. Quattro Pro displays the DEBUG mode indicator on the status line.

When you execute a macro while in DEBUG mode, Quattro Pro displays the Debug Window, as shown in Figure 9.13. Initially, this window shows the first several instructions in the macro. Press the Space Bar or one of the Arrow keys twice in succession. As you do this, Quattro Pro moves through the first macro line one character at a time, executing the instruction on the input line at the top of the screen. The highlighted cursor in the Debug Window indicates the exact point of execution in the macro.

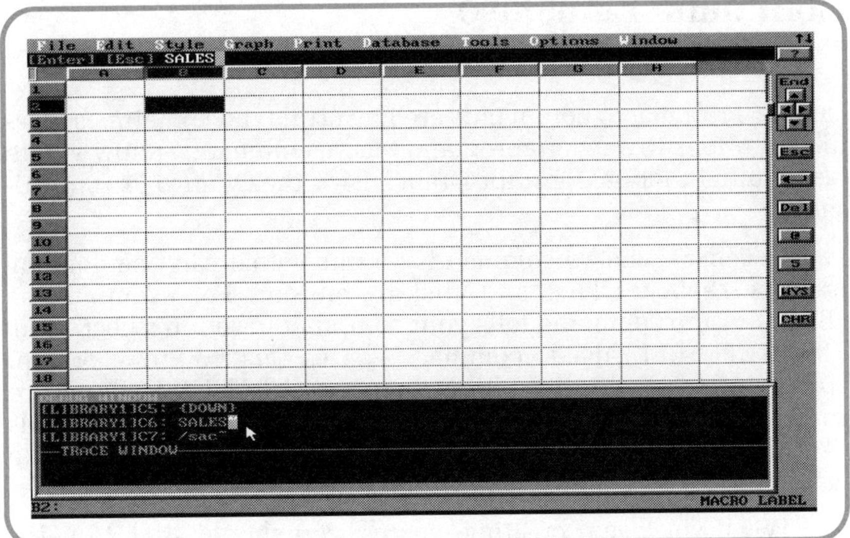

Figure 9.13 Debugging a macro to locate a program error.

In Figure 9.13, for instance, you can see that Quattro Pro is about to enter into the active cell the label appearing on the input line at the top of the screen. Continue pressing the Space Bar or an Arrow key until Quattro Pro again encounters the error. It will beep and stop executing the macro. Now you can look inside the Debug Window to see exactly where the error occurred. Return to the spreadsheet and correct the error. Now restart the macro while in

DEBUG mode. If Quattro Pro does not encounter an error, your macro will execute completely. Turn the Macro Debugger off by pressing /TMDN to select the /**T**ools **M**acro **D**ebugger **N**o command. Remember to save your macro.

> **Tip:** Press Enter once during a Debug operation to continue executing a macro at full speed. This technique is useful if you locate a program error at the beginning of a macro and wish to correct it immediately.

Using Quattro Pro's Macro Command Language

Quattro Pro's macro commands are powerful (and sometimes volatile) additions to a macro program. Macro commands allow you to make fully-functional miniprograms using the Quattro Pro spreadsheet.

In general, macro commands do things that can't be done by pressing keyboard keys and clicking buttons. For example, the {BEEP} macro command tells your computer to sound a beep tone. The {GETLABEL} macro command causes Quattro Pro to prompt you to type a label on the input line; the {GETNUMBER} macro command prompts you for a value. Additionally, macro commands like {BRANCH} and {DISPATCH} control the execution flow of a macro—just like with other programming languages.

When you begin creating macros, you should stick to using keystroke macros. The following information, provided for your review, conveys a sense of the potential power of a Quattro Pro macro. To display a menu that lists all seven macro commands categories, press Shift-F3. Highlight a category name and press Enter to view a list of the commands available within that category. The seven categories of macro commands are as follows:

The *Keyboard* macro commands reproduce the action of pressing keys on your keyboard. These are the commands that you should experiment with the most as a beginning macro programmer.

The *Screen* macro commands affect how Quattro Pro displays information on your screen while a macro is executing.

The *Interactive* macro commands pause a macro's execution and prompt a user to enter data from the keyboard. Experiment with these commands in your macros once you are fully comfortable with creating and managing keystroke macros.

The *Program Flow* commands control the flow of data through your macro. These commands are extremely powerful, and require extensive planning and thought before they can be used in a macro. These commands allow Quattro Pro macros to make use of program flow features more commonly found in advanced programming languages, such as Borland's C.

The *Cell* macro commands control spreadsheet activity at the cell level.

The *File* macro commands manipulate data stored in unopened files.

> **Caution:** The File macro commands can be extremely volatile to your spreadsheet files if you are not completely familiar with their use. These commands are better left to expert macro programmers.

The / macro commands are menu-equivalent commands. Menu-equivalent commands have a one-to-one correspondence to Quattro Pro's menu and command names. These commands are special, though, because they can be used with any of Quattro Pro's menu trees.

What You've Learned

Chapter 9 showed you how to create, edit, execute, and debug macros. In this chapter, you learned about

- Recording, naming, documenting, and executing basic *macros*.
- The value of macros, especially for automating mundane and repetitive spreadsheet operations.
- Using commands on the /**T**ools **M**acro menu to record, paste, execute, name, debug, and delete macros.
- Managing macros with a *macro library spreadsheet*.
- Debugging macros so that they execute perfectly.

Chapter 10

Managing and Linking Spreadsheet Files

In This Chapter

- *What is a file?*
- *Working with spreadsheet files*
- *Password-protecting spreadsheet files*
- *Using the File Manager*
- *Linking spreadsheets with formulas*
- *File management extras*

This chapter explains how to manage your Quattro Pro spreadsheet files. Along the way, you should gain some insight into how your computer actually saves and retrieves spreadsheet files. The /**F**ile menu commands in Quattro Pro help you manage your files. Several commands on the /**W**indow menu also assist with spreadsheet management operations.

What Is a File?

Your personal checkbook is an example of a file. It stores the following information for you: the check issue date, the name of the check recipient, and the amount of the check. Your address book is another type of file. This type of file stores the names, addresses, and phone numbers of your business associates, family, and friends. While attending a conference or meeting, you may take notes which you keep in a folder—you've created another type of file.

In general, a *file* is anything that stores information in an organized manner so you can easily get to it later. In Quattro Pro, a *spreadsheet file* on a hard disk or floppy diskette stores all of the information that you enter into a spreadsheet.

Creating and Accessing Spreadsheet Files

As you know, the /**F**ile **N**ew command opens a new, blank Quattro Pro spreadsheet into your computer's random-access memory (RAM). While you build a spreadsheet application, Quattro Pro stores your work in RAM. Your system's RAM, though, is only a temporary storage area. If you turn off your computer before saving the spreadsheet, you lose all your work.

When you wish to create a permanent copy of a spreadsheet, you tell Quattro Pro to save it in a file on your hard disk drive (or to a diskette in your floppy drive, if you choose). For instance, when you select the /**F**ile **S**ave command, Quattro Pro makes a permanent record by transferring all of the spreadsheet data from the spreadsheet in RAM into a file. This procedure is known as a *write-to-disk operation*. Your computer also can retrieve data stored on a disk, or perform a *read-from-disk operation*. When you select the /**F**ile **R**etrieve command, Quattro Pro asks you for the name of the file you wish to retrieve. After you supply the name of the file, Quattro Pro copies that spreadsheet data back into your computer's RAM. At the same moment, the spreadsheet appears on your screen in exactly the same form it had just before the last save operation.

While your spreadsheet data is in RAM, you can modify it and then resave it to the same spreadsheet file. Doing so replaces the old version of the saved spreadsheet file with the new version. This operation is akin to opening up a file folder, pulling out a sheet of paper, typing a few numbers, and then closing the folder and putting it back into the filing cabinet.

Managing Spreadsheet Files

In Quattro Pro, the commands on the /**F**ile menu provide you with the means to manage your spreadsheet files. *File management* is an easy task when you only have a few files. However, it won't always be that simple. Eventually, you'll have difficulty locating a particular spreadsheet because you've created so many. That's when file management becomes important. Take the time now to learn file management techniques—the job of organizing your data becomes much more complex when you have a larger number of spreadsheet files to work with.

When you installed Quattro Pro, recall that the installation procedure copied all the program files into a directory called \QPRO on your hard disk drive. A *directory* is an area on your hard disk drive reserved for a particular type of file, like Quattro Pro's program files. Whenever you see a name preceded by the backslash (\) key, it usually means that you're working with a directory path name. (The Quattro Pro exception to this rule is instant macro names, such as \a. The backslash here indicates you should press the Alt key plus a letter to execute the macro.)

Today, most application programs create a separate program directory during program installation. For example, when you install WordPerfect 5.1, it creates a directory named \WP51 on your hard disk drive. Suppose that you install five application programs on your hard disk drive, and that each of these creates its own program directory. Sometimes, programs (like Quattro Pro and WordPerfect) create secondary level directories, called *subdirectories*, to store other specialized files.

Figure 10.1 illustrates one type of directory structure. Notice that each program directory is an offshoot of the root directory. The *root directory* is the basic directory level on your hard disk drive; it functions like the root of a tree. As you know, it is from a tree's roots that all branches (directories) and leaves (subdirectories) originate.

You can use directories to manage your own spreadsheet files. For instance, placing spreadsheet files in separate application directories makes it easier to find and retrieve the files later. For example, you might store all of your personal financial spreadsheets in a directory called \PERSFIN and all of your accounting spreadsheets in a directory called \ACCTG. If you have several consulting clients, then you might create directories for each of them using a sequential naming style like \CLIENT1, \CLIENT2, and so on. Or just create directory names using company names. In fact, you'd be smart to create unique directories for each application grouping that you work with.

To make a directory named \CLIENT1, start by returning to DOS. At the DOS command prompt type `cd\` to make the root directory active. Now type `md\client1` and press Enter to make the new directory. To verify that you created the directory, type cd\client1 and press Enter. Now type cd and press Enter. Your screen will display something like C:\CLIENT1>. If your DOS prompt looks like C>, type prompt pg and press Enter. Now press cd\ again. This time your prompt will look like C:\CLIENT1>.

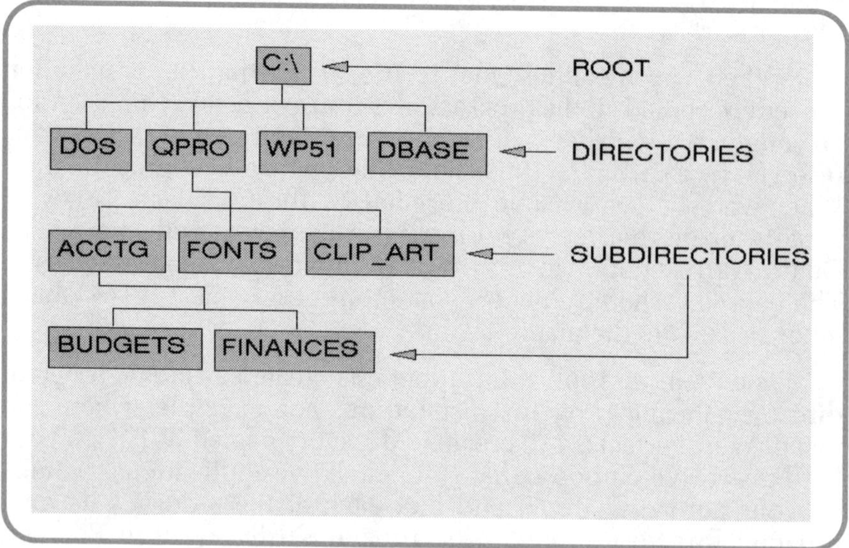

Figure 10.1 A sample directory tree structure.

To create a subdirectory named \BILLINGS in the \CLIENT1 directory, type cd\client1 to make the \CLIENT1 directory active. Now type md billings and press Enter. Type cd billings. Now the prompt will look like C:\CLIENT1\BILLINGS>.

When you create application directories, you also must supply the directory path name with the spreadsheet file name when you retrieve files. Otherwise, Quattro Pro will look in the wrong place on your hard disk drive for the file. The convention for naming files is as follows: the drive letter comes first, followed by a colon, then the directory path name (if any), and then the spreadsheet file name. To retrieve a spreadsheet file named EXPENSES that was saved in the \ACCTG directory on the C: drive you would specify the full path and file name as

C:\ACCTG\EXPENSES

The letter C is the name of the hard disk drive (C is the default drive on most hard drive systems). \ACCTG is the path name of the directory that contains a spreadsheet file named EXPENSES.WQ1.

Keep the following rules in mind when creating directories and subdirectories.

- A directory name may contain up to eight characters.
- You can add an extension to a directory name much like you do to a file name. A directory name extension may contain up to three characters. Be sure to separate the directory name and the extension with a period.
- All lowercase letters are automatically converted to uppercase letters.
- When creating a directory name, you may use any letter of the alphabet, any number from 0 to 9, and any of the following symbols:

  @ # $ & ( ) - _ { } ‘ ~

  Spaces, commas, and all other symbols are not allowed.
- It's a good idea to make directory names that are easy to remember.

Although this review has been brief and the explanations quite simple, it will help you understand what happens to your spreadsheet files when you execute the commands explained in the rest of this chapter.

The File Menu Commands

Let's take a moment to review some basic Quattro Pro spreadsheet terminology before we learn about the /**File** menu commands.

A *spreadsheet* is the screen display area containing the *columns* and *rows* of cells into which you enter data. Quattro Pro allows you to have as many as 32 spreadsheets open at once, although only one spreadsheet can be active at a time. A Quattro Pro *window* contains a spreadsheet. The window that contains the *active spreadsheet* is the *active window*. The term *workspace* describes all of the spreadsheets currently open in your computer's RAM (remember, that's up to 32 spreadsheets at a time).

The 13 commands on the /**File** menu enable you to create, retrieve, and save files, and to manage the directories where you save your files. Quattro Pro displays all of the Ctrl-key shortcuts and current command settings at the right margin of the /**File** menu, as shown in Figure 10.2.

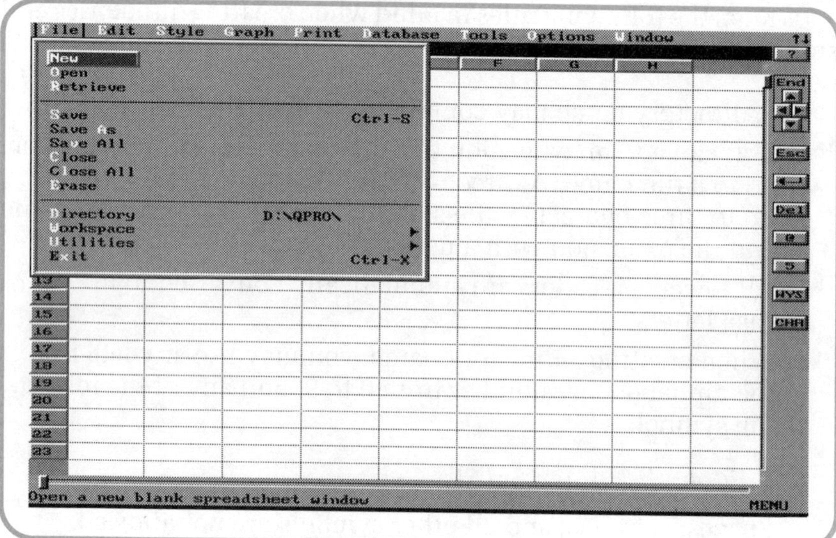

Figure 10.2 Reviewing the commands on the /File menu.

Saving Spreadsheet Files

Use the **S**ave command to save a spreadsheet file. Quattro Pro will prompt you to type a file name. If you previously saved the spreadsheet, Quattro Pro tells you that the `File already exists`, then allows you to take one of three actions. You can **C**ancel the operation, you can **R**eplace the old spreadsheet with the new version, or you can create a **B**ackup of the current spreadsheet.

> **Tip:** You can save a Quattro Pro spreadsheet in several other popular file formats simply by adding a special extension to the file name when you save it. For instance, to save the EXPENSES spreadsheet as a 1-2-3 Version 2.01 or Version 2.2 spreadsheet, use the file name EXPENSES.WK1. To save the same spreadsheet as a Quattro spreadsheet, use the file name EXPENSES.WKQ.

The Save **A**s command prompts you for a file name and saves the current spreadsheet using that name. Use this command to assign new names to files that you've saved before.

The Save All command first prompts you for a file name and saves the current spreadsheet using that name. Then, Quattro Pro activates the next window open in memory and again prompts you to save the spreadsheet. This process continues for all spreadsheets open in memory.

Occasionally, you may wish to password-protect a spreadsheet to prevent others from viewing private data. A good example of this would be a spreadsheet containing employee payroll earnings, or your business expense ledger. Once a spreadsheet is password-protected, the only way to load it back into Quattro Pro is by supplying the correct password. The following Quick Steps describe how to save a spreadsheet file with password protection.

Password-Protecting a Spreadsheet File

Step	Result
1. Press /FA to select the /File Save As command.	Quattro Pro displays the file name prompt box.
2. Type a valid file name, press Space Bar once to insert a space, then type P. If the spreadsheet was saved at least once before, Quattro Pro displays the file name in the file name prompt box. In this case, just type a space followed by the letter P after the file name.	The file name, a blank space, and the letter P appear in the file name prompt box (see Figure 10.3).
3. Press Enter once (or click on Enter with a mouse).	Quattro Pro displays the password entry screen.
4. Type a password that is up to 15 characters long (I typed SECRET).	As you type each character in the password, Quattro Pro displays a single square bullet.
5. Press Enter once.	Quattro Pro prompts you to verify the password you just typed (see Figure 10.4).
6. Retype the password.	Again, square bullets appear in place of each character that you type.

7. Press Enter once.

If the spreadsheet was saved at least once before, Quattro Pro prompts you to **R**eplace, **C**ancel, or **B**ackup the current spreadsheet. If you select **R**eplace, or if the spreadsheet has not yet been saved, Quattro Pro assigns the password to the spreadsheet. □

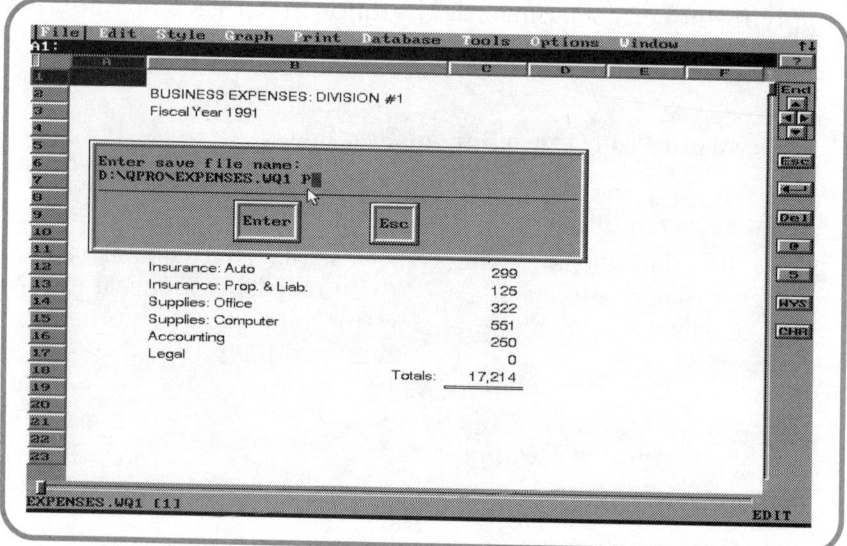

Figure 10.3 Creating a spreadsheet password.

Each time you select /**F**ile **R**etrieve or /**F**ile **O**pen, Quattro Pro prompts you to type the password for a password-protected spreadsheet.

There are two important things to remember when you use passwords. First, to successfully open a password-protected spreadsheet, you must type the password in exactly the same case as it was originally typed. The password *secret*, therefore, will not open a spreadsheet with the password *SECRET*. Second, there is no way to retrieve a password if you forget it. Once you lose the password, you lose your spreadsheet (unless you later remember the password).

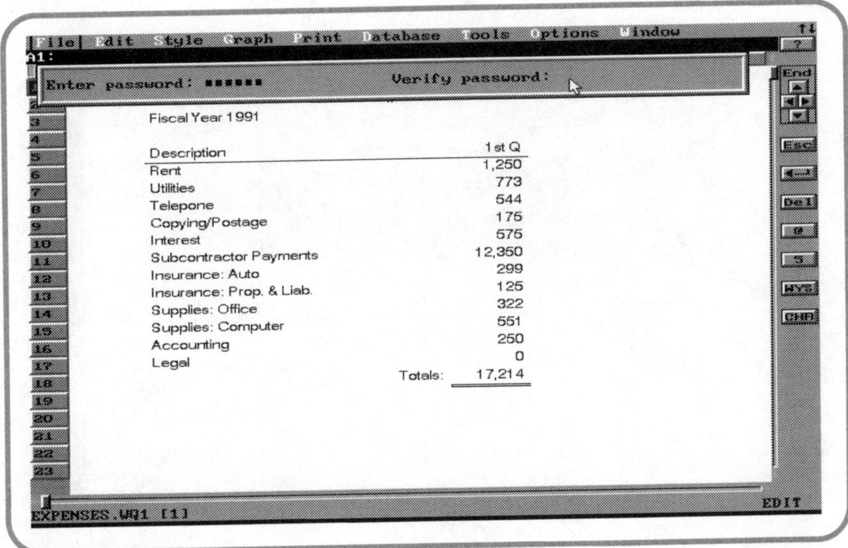

Figure 10.4 Validating a spreadsheet password prior to saving it with a spreadsheet.

If you wish, you also can rename or remove a spreadsheet password. To do so, start by making a password-protected spreadsheet active. Select the /**F**ile Save **A**s command. Quattro Pro displays the file name prompt box. You'll notice the expression `[Password protected]` appears in the prompt box next to the file name, as shown in the example in Figure 10.5. Press the Backspace key once to erase the `[Password protected]` indicator. Your spreadsheet is no longer password protected. Press Enter and select **R**eplace to make the change permanent. If you wish to assign a new password, type the letter P after the file name in the file name prompt box and press Enter once. Quattro Pro again prompts you for a new password. Enter the new password, verify it, and then press Enter to save the spreadsheet with the new password.

Retrieving Spreadsheet Files

When you wish to load a saved spreadsheet file back into Quattro Pro, you have two options. You can *open* it, or you can *retrieve* it, depending upon whether or not you need to work with several spreadsheets open in memory at the same time.

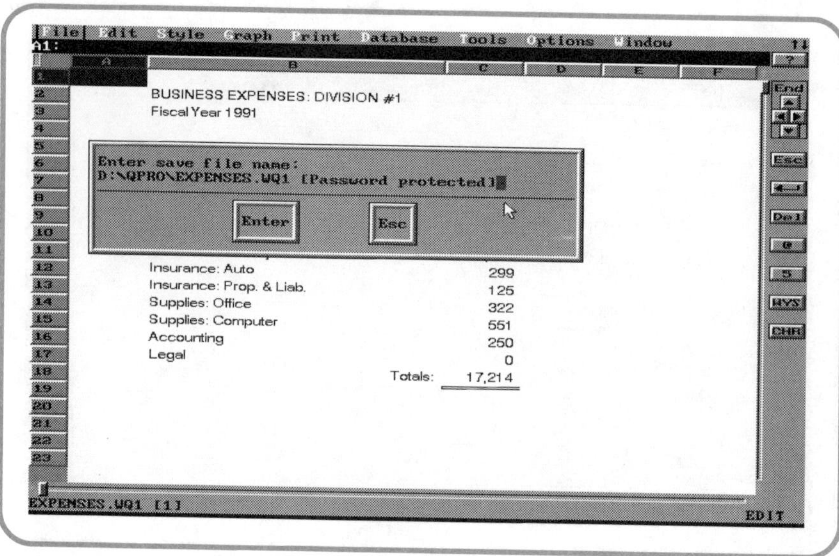

Figure 10.5 Removing the password from a spreadsheet.

Select the **O**pen command to load a previously saved spreadsheet file back into Quattro Pro. Use this command when you wish to load more than one spreadsheet into memory. When you select the Open command, Quattro Pro prompts you for the name of the file to open. There are three ways to open an existing spreadsheet file: you can type the name and press Enter, you can highlight the name in the file name prompt box and press Enter, or you can click on the name once with a mouse. Quattro Pro loads the spreadsheet into its own window. If only one other spreadsheet was open before you issued the **O**pen command, the newly opened spreadsheet window number is [2]. Quattro Pro displays the window number on the status line at the bottom of the spreadsheet. The next spreadsheet you open will load into window number [3].

The **R**etrieve command closes the active spreadsheet and loads a saved spreadsheet file into the active window. The active window number is [1].

> **Tip:** While Quattro Pro displays a file name prompt box, press the plus (+) or minus (–) key on the numeric keypad to display more information about your files. Quattro Pro tells you the file size and the date and time the file last was modified. Press F3 once to enlarge this display to fill half your screen, as shown in Figure 10.6.

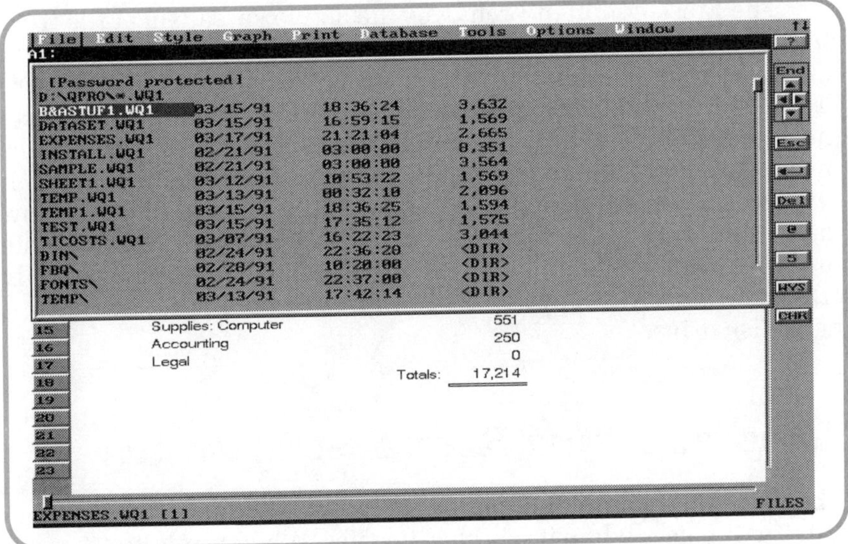

Figure 10.6 Displaying full information about your spreadsheet files.

Closing Spreadsheet Files

When you wish to close a Quattro Pro spreadsheet, you have three options. You can close a single spreadsheet, close all spreadsheets open in memory, or erase the active spreadsheet from memory.

The **C**lose command closes the current spreadsheet. If you modified the spreadsheet before selecting this command, Quattro Pro asks if you wish to `Lose your changes?` Select **N**o to cancel the operation and return to the active spreadsheet, or **Y**es to close it without saving the changes.

The C**l**ose All command closes all spreadsheets open in memory. Use this command if you used the **O**pen command to load several spreadsheets into memory. Then, rather than issuing a series of **C**lose commands, you can close all open spreadsheets with one command. Before closing each spreadsheet, Quattro Pro asks if you wish to `Lose your changes and Close Window?` Select **N**o to cancel the operation and return to the active spreadsheet, **Y**es to close the active spreadsheet without saving any changes, or **S**ave & Close to save and then close the active window.

The **E**rase command removes the active spreadsheet file from RAM memory. Use this command to erase a spreadsheet that you have not yet saved, or one with changes you wish to discard. Quattro Pro asks if you wish to `Lose your changes?` Select **N**o to cancel the command and return to the active spreadsheet, or **Y**es to erase the spreadsheet. Once Quattro Pro erases the active spreadsheet, it displays a new, blank spreadsheet in its place—regardless of how many other spreadsheets may be open in memory at the time. Note that if you erase a previously saved spreadsheet, Quattro Pro only erases the current changes—not the spreadsheet file stored on your hard disk drive.

Changing the Default Spreadsheet File Directory

The **D**irectory command temporarily defines the directory that Quattro Pro uses when it searches for files. When prompted, type in a new directory path name and press Enter. If the directory does not exist, Quattro Pro beeps to tell you so. Press Esc and enter a valid directory name.

Changing the directory name this way is only temporary. Once you end the current work session, Quattro Pro resets the directory name to the one defined on the /**O**ptions **S**tartup **D**irectory menu. To permanently change the default directory name, select this command and type in a new name. Then select /**O**ptions **U**pdate to save the new setting for all future work sessions. (See Appendix A for complete coverage of Quattro Pro's startup options.)

Using the File Manager

Quattro Pro's File Manager offers the same flexibility and power available in stand-alone file management programs such as XTreePro and DESQview. Select /**F**ile **U**tilities **F**ile Manager to load the File Manager into a Quattro Pro window. You'll see a screen similar to the one shown in Figure 10.7. In this figure, Quattro Pro has loaded the File Manager into its own window atop the active spreadsheet.

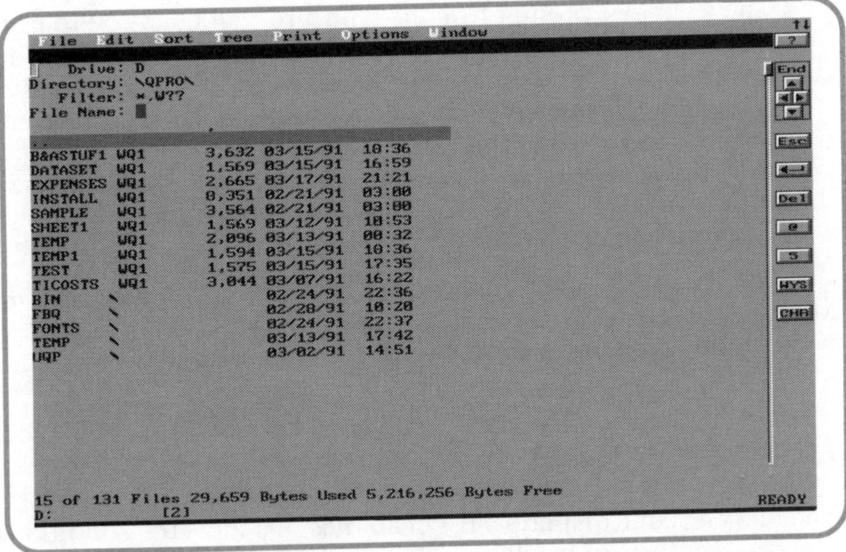

Figure 10.7 Reviewing the different parts of the File Manager.

The File Manager window has three sections: the Control pane, the File List pane, and the Tree pane. Quattro Pro performs all the File Manager operations inside one of these three panes. Before you can work in a pane, you must make that pane active. By default, the Control pane is the active pane each time you load the File Manager.

Using the Control Pane

The Control Pane contains four prompts which manage the display of data elsewhere in the File Manager. To move from prompt to prompt in this pane, press the ↑ and ↓ keys.

The `Drive:` prompt specifies the disk drive Quattro Pro currently is reading. To read a different disk drive, type the drive letter at this prompt and press Enter. Quattro Pro immediately displays files from the new disk drive in the File Name pane.

The `Directory:` prompt lists the directory path name that Quattro Pro searches when it displays file names in the File Name pane. You may specify any valid directory path name at this prompt to search a different directory.

The Filter: prompt lists the wildcard that Quattro Pro uses in its file name search. The default wildcard (*.W??) searches for all files in the current directory with file name extensions beginning with W, and displays them in the File Name pane. To use a different wildcard, move the cell selector to this prompt and type in a new wildcard, then press Enter. The wildcard *.* searches for all files in the current directory. The *.WQ1 wildcard searches for all files with a .WQ1 file name extension.

The File Name: prompt is blank each time you load the File Manager. You can make any spreadsheet file active by typing a file name in this field and pressing Enter.

Using the File List Pane

The File List pane displays a list of all files that meet the conditions specified on the Control Pane. The File List pane displays the full name, size in bytes, and last alteration date for each file. You can erase, rename, select, move, copy, and paste files from the File List pane.

Use the keys listed in Table 10.1 to manage the files displayed in the File List pane.

Table 10.1 Using the File List pane keys.

Use	To
F2	Execute the /**E**dit **R**ename command.
Shift-F7	Select and unselect a highlighted file name.
Alt-F7	Select and unselect all file names in the list.
Shift-F8	Transfer selected files into the paste buffer.
Del	Delete all highlighted or selected files.
F9	Execute the /**F**ile **R**ead Dir command.
Shift-F9	Copy selected files into the paste buffer.
Shift-F10	Move all files from the paste buffer to the current directory, at the location of the cursor.

Using the Tree Pane

The Tree Pane displays when you select the /**T**ree **O**pen command. Quattro Pro displays the tree pane in the right portion of the File Manager window, as shown in Figure 10.8. A tree pane displays the names of all files stored in the current directory. To remove a tree pane from the active window, select the /**T**ree **C**lose command.

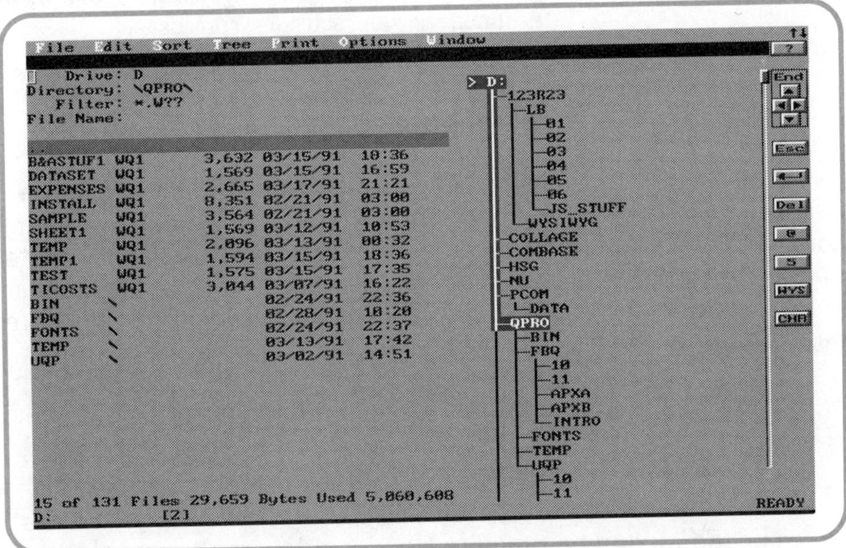

Figure 10.8 Displaying a Tree Pane in the File Manager window.

Use the keys shown in Table 10.2 to move around the File Manager panes and to move from the File Manager to the active spreadsheet.

Table 10.2 The window keys in the File Manager.

Use	To
Alt-# (Alt plus a window number)	Activate the specified window.
Alt-0	Display a list of all spreadsheets open in memory.
Shift-F5	Display a list of all spreadsheets open in memory.

(continued)

Table 10.2 (continued)

Use	To
F6	Activate the next pane in the File Manager window.
Alt-F6	Enlarge and shrink the active File Manager window (works only in text display mode).
Shift-F6	Activate the next open File Manager Window, or if none is open, activate a spreadsheet.
Tab	Activate the next pane in the File Manager Window.

The best way to learn how to use the File Manager is to experiment with its menu commands. You'll notice that many of the commands on the File Manager menu are the same ones you use to manipulate spreadsheets. There are also a few other commands that perform operations not available with spreadsheets. Following are descriptions of the File Manager's menus.

The /***F**ile* menu in the File Manager offers two additional commands. The **R**ead Dir command reads a new directory, and the **M**ake Dir creates a new directory anywhere on your hard disk drive.

The /***E**dit* menu commands allow you to simultaneously perform operations on many files. You can copy, move, and erase all of the files in the current directory. Or you can rename a group of files and simultaneously copy them to another location on the same disk drive.

The /***S**ort* menu sorts files by name, date and time, file name extension, and file size.

The /***T**ree* menu opens, resizes, and closes the tree pane.

The /***P**rint* menu is an abbreviated version of the one you see when a spreadsheet is active. The commands on this menu allow you to print a list of the files in the displayed directory, and print a list of the entire directory tree.

The /***O**ptions* menu looks much the same as the menu available on an active spreadsheet. One extra command, **F**ile List, allows you to display a wider version of the File List pane.

The /***W**indow* menu allows you to change the size or shape of a window, and reorganize and pick active windows.

Linking Spreadsheets with Formulas

Spreadsheet linking is an effective technique for sharing data between spreadsheets. Sharing data between spreadsheets is possible if you create *linking formulas*, formulas that contain special cell references. Linking formulas enable you to summarize data from several locations on one spreadsheet.

In an ordinary formula, you use cell references to tell Quattro Pro where to find data. For instance, the formula *@SUM(B1..D1)* tells Quattro Pro to sum all of the values stored in cell block B1..D1. The result of this calculation displays in a cell on the active spreadsheet. In a linking formula, the cell references can refer to data on the active spreadsheet, data on another spreadsheet open in memory, and even data on a closed spreadsheet.

In its most basic application, spreadsheet linking involves two files. The first file is the *supporting spreadsheet.* This spreadsheet contains the data that you wish to summarize on a second spreadsheet, called the *primary spreadsheet.* For illustration purposes, let's assume that our supporting spreadsheet is the EXPENSES spreadsheet first shown in Figure 10.3. The primary spreadsheet, then, will be one that summarizes the business expenses for several other departments, or people, if you wish.

Figure 10.9 shows two spreadsheets. The EXPENSES spreadsheet is the supporting file, and the TOTALS spreadsheet is the primary file. Notice that the primary spreadsheet only shows the row and column headings. Values do not yet appear on this spreadsheet, because that's the job that our linking formulas will handle. As you can see, the primary spreadsheet summarizes first quarter business expense data for three divisions in a firm. Although the example only shows you how to build linking formulas to summarize Division #1's totals, you can use the same procedure to create the linking formulas for Division #2 and Division #3.

There are two items in Figure 10.9 you should take note of. First, notice that the layout of both spreadsheets is identical. When both the primary and secondary spreadsheets look the same, it's much easier to create the linking formulas. Second, note that the spreadsheets appear in a modified *tiled* view. To accomplish this view you must do three things. First, be sure that you are operating in WYSIWYG display mode. Select /**O**ptions **D**isplay Mode **B**: WYSIWYG to switch if need be. Second, select the /**W**indow **T**ile command and Quattro Pro displays each spreadsheet in one half of the current window. Third, because it is difficult to view the areas of each spreadsheet pertinent to the exercise at hand, shrink the display size of the spreadsheet text. To do this, select the /**O**ptions **W**YSIWYG Zoom % command. When Quattro Pro prompts you for a percent zoom value, type 85 and press Enter. Because the zoom value is less than 100%, Quattro Pro shrinks the point size of text on the spreadsheets, making it easier to see what is going on.

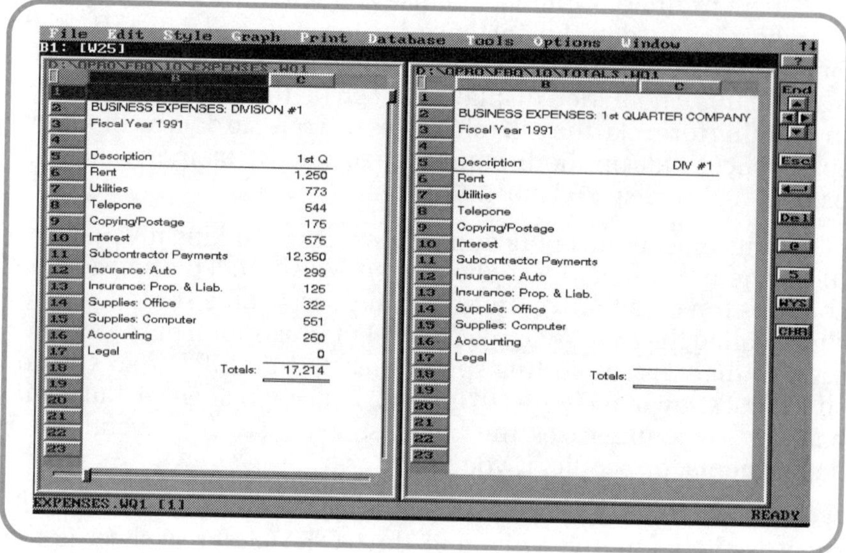

Figure 10.9 Creating a basic spreadsheet linking application.

In text display mode (/**O**ptions **D**isplay Mode **A**: 80x25), it's easy to duplicate this style if you own a mouse.This display style makes it much easier to track the progress of numbers from one spreadsheet to another.

Just point, click, and hold on the double lines that frame every spreadsheet, and drag the border until the spreadsheet is properly shaped. If you don't have a mouse, then select the /**W**indow **T**ile command, and Quattro Pro places the two spreadsheets side by side. To place them one on top of the other, use the following steps:

1. Select the /**W**indow **M**ove Size command, and Quattro Pro highlights the outer edge of the active spreadsheet.
2. Press the period (.) key once (this illuminates the Scroll Lock light on your keyboard), or press the Scroll Lock key.

3. Press the ↑ key to shrink the height of the active spreadsheet until it fills the top half of the screen.
4. Press the → key until the spreadsheet entirely fills up the top half of your screen display and press Enter.
5. Press Shift-F6 to activate the second spreadsheet.
6. Repeating steps 1 through 4, move and size the other spreadsheet so it entirely fills up the bottom half of your screen display.

The following Quick Steps describe how to create a linking formula.

Q Linking Two Spreadsheets with Linking Formulas

1. Create primary and supporting spreadsheets, and arrange them as shown in Figure 10.9. — If you wish, use the information from Figure 10.4 to create your own spreadsheet.
2. Press Shift-F6 until the primary spreadsheet is active (the TOTALS spreadsheet in the example in Figure 10.9). — Pressing Shift-F6 moves the cell selector from spreadsheet to spreadsheet.
3. Make the first blank formula cell on the primary spreadsheet active (cell C6 in the example).
4. Type `+[`, type the name of the supporting spreadsheet, type `]`, type the source cell address on the supporting spreadsheet, and press Enter to record the first linking formula. (In the example, this formula looks like `+[EXPENSES]C6`, as shown in Figure 10.10.) — Quattro Pro stores the linking formula on the primary spreadsheet, and then displays the formula result.
5. Press /EC to select the /Edit Copy command. — Quattro Pro prompts you for the source cell block.
6. Press Enter to select the active cell. — Quattro Pro prompts you for the destination cell block.
7. Type the cell block into which you wish to copy the linking formula, and press Enter (cell block C7..C18 in the example). — Quattro Pro copies the linking formula into the destination cell block and immediately returns results for all of the linking formula copies. □

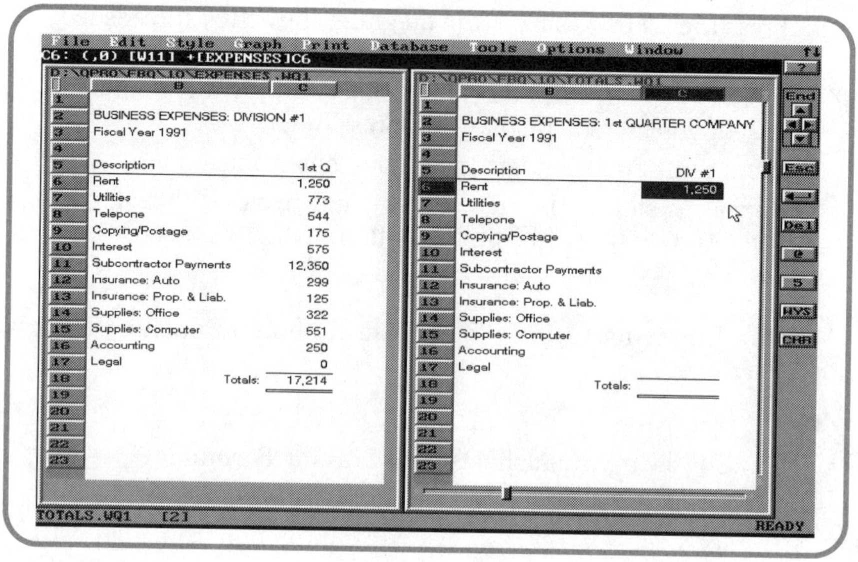

Figure 10.10 Entering the first linking formula onto the primary spreadsheet.

Creating linking formulas is extremely simple when you own a mouse. After arranging the two spreadsheets in a tiled fashion, activate the first blank formula cell on the primary spreadsheet. Press the plus (+) symbol to enter VALUE mode, then point and click the cell on the supporting spreadsheet to which you wish to link the primary spreadsheet. (In the example, that would be cell C6 on the EXPENSES.WQ1 spreadsheet.) Quattro Pro automatically creates the linking formula syntax for you on the input line at the top of the primary spreadsheet. Press Enter to store the linking formula and return a result.

Figure 10.11 shows the final version of the example primary spreadsheet. Here, the cell selector appears in cell C18 to illustrate the final formula that you need to create to complete this linking application.

Congratulations! You've successfully built your first spreadsheet linking application. You also can use wildcard characters to link spreadsheets. 3-D consolidation, another linking method, takes advantage of Quattro Pro's cell block operations. You can use POINT mode to create linking formulas, too. Just as you can move and copy formulas within an individual spreadsheet, you can move and copy linking formulas from spreadsheet to spreadsheet.

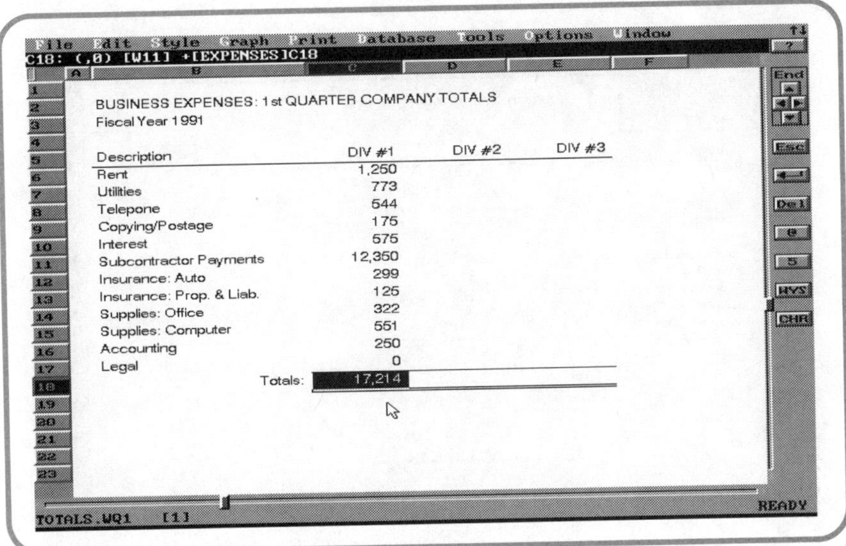

Figure 10.11 Adding the first set of linking formulas to the primary spreadsheet.

You must pay special attention when loading spreadsheets that are linked by formulas. When the first document you retrieve is the supporting spreadsheet (such as the EXPENSES spreadsheet), nothing will seem out of the ordinary. When you retrieve a primary spreadsheet first, though, Quattro Pro displays the Link options menu as shown in Figure 10.12. You now have three options.

Select the **L**oad Supporting option, and Quattro Pro opens all the supporting spreadsheets before updating the linking formula references on the primary spreadsheet. This way, the linking formulas on the primary spreadsheet will display their formula results.

Select the **U**pdate Refs option to open the primary spreadsheet and display all of the correct formula results without having to open the supporting spreadsheets.

Select the **N**one option to open the primary spreadsheet without updating the linking formula references and without opening the supporting documents. Quattro Pro displays `NA` in each cell that contains a linking formula. If you later open the supporting documents, Quattro Pro immediately recalculates the linking formulas.

Although other linking operations are too advanced for this book, the basics presented here should give you great insight into the power of linking formulas.

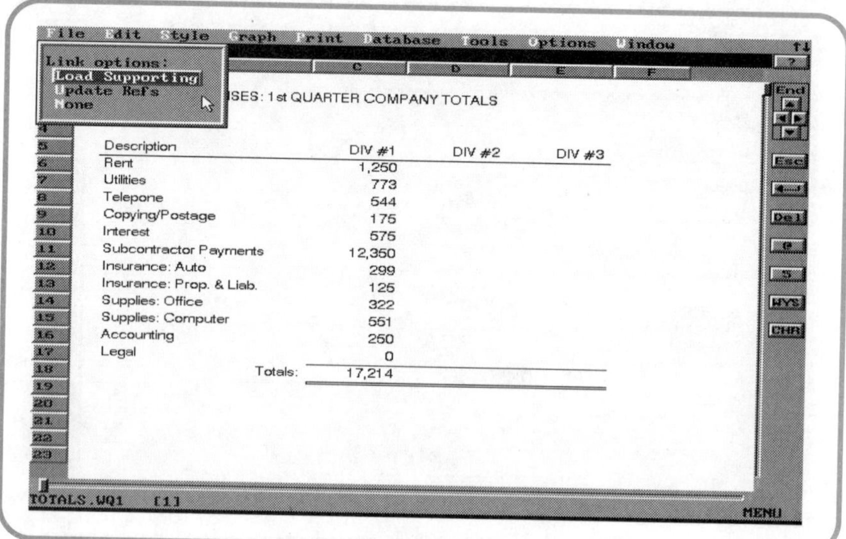

Figure 10.12 The Link options menu.

Spreadsheet File Management Extras

As long as you have a couple of spreadsheets open in Quattro Pro's memory, let's explore a couple of the file management commands found on the /**W**indow menu. As you know, Quattro Pro allows you to have as many as 32 spreadsheets open at one time. The status line displays the number of the spreadsheet in the active window. Press /W to pull down the /**W**indow menu so you can review its commands.

Three of the first four commands on this menu work only when you are in text display mode (**Z**oom, **S**tack, and **M**ove/Size). As you've already seen, the **T**ile command works fine in WYSIWYG display mode (see Figure 10.9).

Switch to text display mode for a moment so you can review the operation of the other three commands. To do this, select the /**O**ptions **D**isplay Mode **A**: 80x25 command. Now select the /**W**indow **S**tack command and watch as both spreadsheet files open in memory. You can press Shift-F6 to move from spreadsheet to spreadsheet. Or press Alt and the window number to go directly to a particular spreadsheet. Before continuing, switch back to WYSIWYG display mode (select the /**O**ptions **D**isplay Mode **B**: WYSIWYG command).

Now select the /**W**indow **O**ptions **R**ow & Col Borders **H**ide command. This command removes the row and column borders from the spreadsheet display (see Figure 10.13). This display technique is useful for applications where you wish to present a user with a report-quality view of a spreadsheet. To restore the row and column borders, select the /**W**indow **O**ptions **R**ow & Col Borders **D**isplay command.

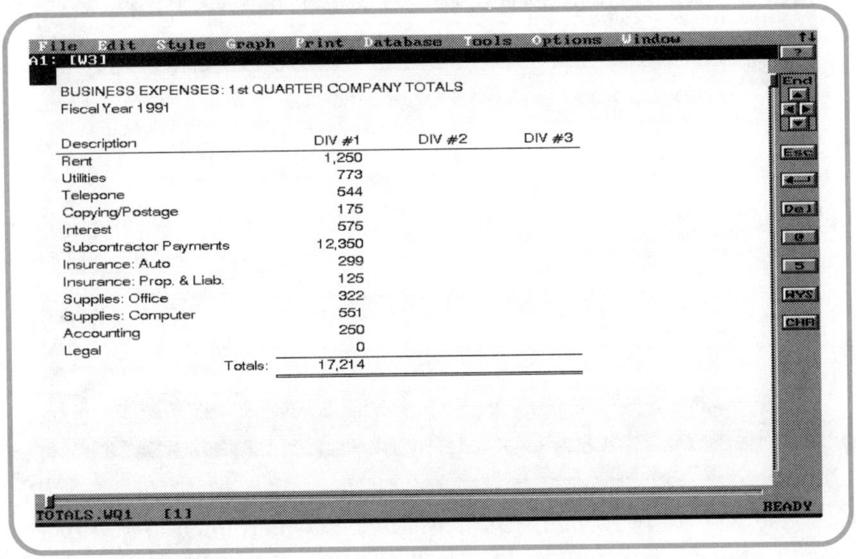
File Edit Style Graph Print Database Tools Options Window
A1: [W3]
BUSINESS EXPENSES: 1st QUARTER COMPANY TOTALS
Fiscal Year 1991
Description DIV #1 DIV #2 DIV #3
Rent 1,250
Utilities 773
Telepone 544
Copying/Postage 175
Interest 575
Subcontractor Payments 12,350
Insurance: Auto 299
Insurance: Prop. & Liab. 125
Supplies: Office 322
Supplies: Computer 551
Accounting 250
Legal 0
Totals: 17,214
TOTALS.WQ1 [1]
READY

Figure 10.13 Removing the row and column borders from a spreadsheet exposes a larger spreadsheet.

Finally, let's take a look at a /File menu command that helps you to manage applications that rely on two or more spreadsheets.

Now select the /**W**indow **S**tack command and watch as both spreadsheets reorganize themselves on your screen, as shown in Figure 10.14. As you can see, the advantage to this type of display is that it allows you to quickly scan the names and window numbers of all spreadsheet files open in memory. You can press Shift-F6 to move from spreadsheet to spreadsheet. Or press Alt and the window number to go directly to a particular spreadsheet.

To create a *workspace file*, select the /**F**ile **W**orkspace **S**ave command. At the prompt, type `totals` and press Enter. This command saves all spreadsheets open in memory in a workspace file named TOTALS.WSP. The next time you want to open up both of these spreadsheets, select the /**F**ile **W**orkspace **R**estore command.

When prompted, type `totals` and press Enter. Quattro Pro immediately loads both spreadsheets back into memory. This valuable file management tool eliminates the need for issuing consecutive /**F**ile **O**pen commands—a real plus when you enjoy creating and working with linking applications.

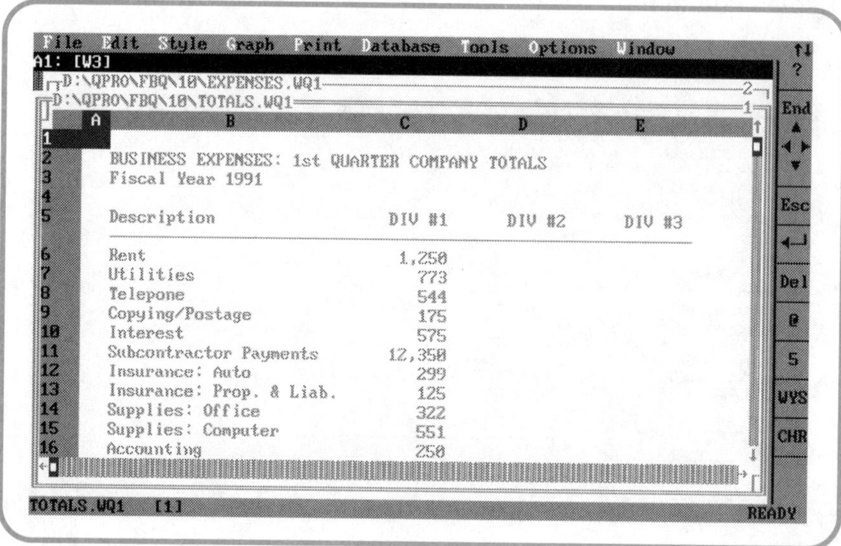

Figure 10.14 Stacking all spreadsheets open in Quattro Pro's memory. (This figure is displayed in text display mode.)

What You've Learned

This chapter introduced you to some basic spreadsheet file management strategies. At this point, you should be familiar with the following Quattro Pro concepts:

- Your computer's RAM is only a temporary storage area for spreadsheet data. To permanently store a spreadsheet, use the /**F**ile **S**ave or /**F**ile Save **A**s commands to create a spreadsheet file and store it on your hard or floppy disk drive.
- You can protect private data by assigning *passwords* to your spreadsheet files.

- *Spreadsheet linking formulas* make it easy to summarize data from several supporting sources onto one *primary spreadsheet.*
- A *workspace file* is an index that keeps track of a group of spreadsheets. To simultaneously load all of the spreadsheets into memory, select the /**F**ile **W**orkspace **R**estore command.

Chapter 11

Managing Databases

In This Chapter

- *What is a database?*
- *Designing a database*
- *Entering data into a database*
- *Sorting and searching through a database*

The Quattro Pro *database* is a terrific information management tool. In this chapter, you will learn how to turn a spreadsheet into an information manager using the commands on the /**D**atabase menu. Once you create and enter data into a database, you can sort the data any way you want, and search for and find specific records.

What Is a Database?

A database gives you the means to quickly store and retrieve information. Usually, the information in a database is related somehow. For instance, if you own a card file, you're already using one type of database. A card file is a manual database. You type information on index cards (as shown in Figure 11.1) that you arrange, and then insert into the card file.

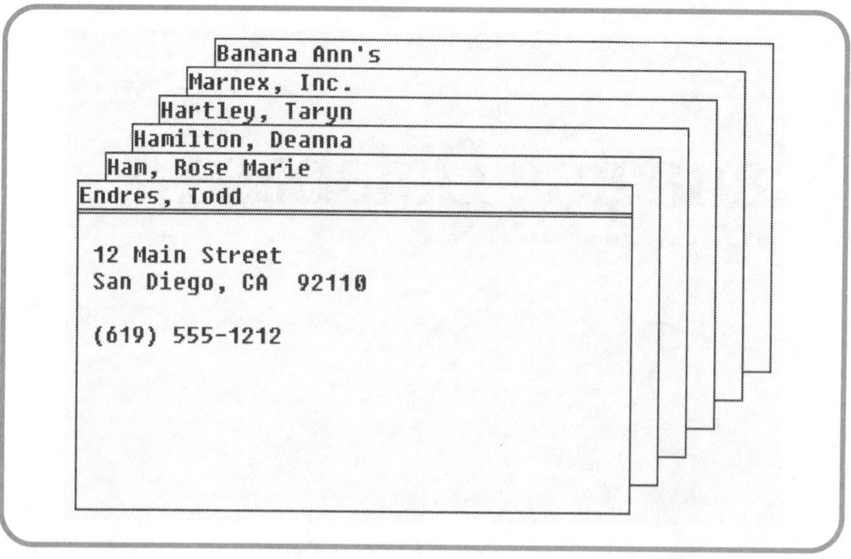

Figure 11.1 A card file that contains six address cards.

To retrieve an address or phone number from a card file, you simply thumb through the index cards until you find the one you're looking for. If the index cards are in alphabetical order, then finding a particular card is easy. You may even arrange the card file into two separate sections: one for business contacts, the other for friends and family. Organizing a card file this way makes searching for and finding a particular card even easier.

The method you use to organize your card file determines how easy it is to later retrieve a particular card. Even so, the best-laid data management plans sometimes go awry. Have you ever flipped through a phone book, hunting for an address for John Smith or Bill Jones? In most large cities, it's not uncommon to find five, 10, or even 20 or more listings with the same name. Some listings may not even show an address, making it even more difficult to find the correct John Smith or Bill Jones.

It's time-consuming, tedious, and often costly to change the organization of a manual database (like a phone book) that contains a large number of listings. This can be particularly annoying when the database contains many listings with similar data. Under these circumstances, your options for using the database are very limited and may seem a bit impractical. Do you call every single Smith and Jones in the phone book until you find the correct one?

Fortunately, a Quattro Pro database is extremely flexible. You decide exactly how to organize your data. Once you enter the data into the database, you can reorganize it any way you wish instantly. If you decide to reorganize your card file, you must pull out all of the cards, reorder them, and then reinsert them into the file. It's easy to do this with only six cards, like those shown in Figure 11.1, but can you imagine having to rearrange 100 or 1,000 cards manually?

In Quattro Pro, the /**D**atabase menu contains the commands you use to manage a database. Press /D, and Quattro Pro pulls down the /**D**atabase menu. A brief description of each of the commands on this menu follows.

The ***Sort*** command lets you reorganize database entries in a virtually unlimited number of ways.

The ***Query*** command allows you to ask questions about the entries stored in a database. Use this command to locate unique entries, delete duplicate entries, and extract entries that meet specific conditions.

The ***Restrict Input*** command confines movement of the cell selector to unprotected cells only. Use this command to simplify the process of entering data into a database.

The ***Data Entry*** command restricts the type of data that Quattro Pro accepts as an entry into a block of cells. You can choose **L**abels Only or **D**ates Only. The **G**eneral option accepts all types of data (it is the default setting).

The ***Paradox Access*** command enables you to run Quattro Pro from within Paradox, Borland's powerful relational database program. If you do not own Paradox, you will not have the occasion to use this command during a work session.

Use the following three steps to create a Quattro Pro database:

1. Design the database. Type a database title and label headings onto a spreadsheet.
2. Enter data into the database. Type each entry into a separate row on a spreadsheet.
3. Create database reports. Using commands on the /**D**atabase menu, you can manipulate the entries to create many unique reports.

The next three sections illustrate how to create a database, and enter and manipulate database entries.

Designing a Database

The spreadsheet shown in Figure 11.2 is an example of a Quattro Pro database. This database replaces the manual card file for a fictitious company called HotShot Sports Shop. The database contains one entry on row 6.

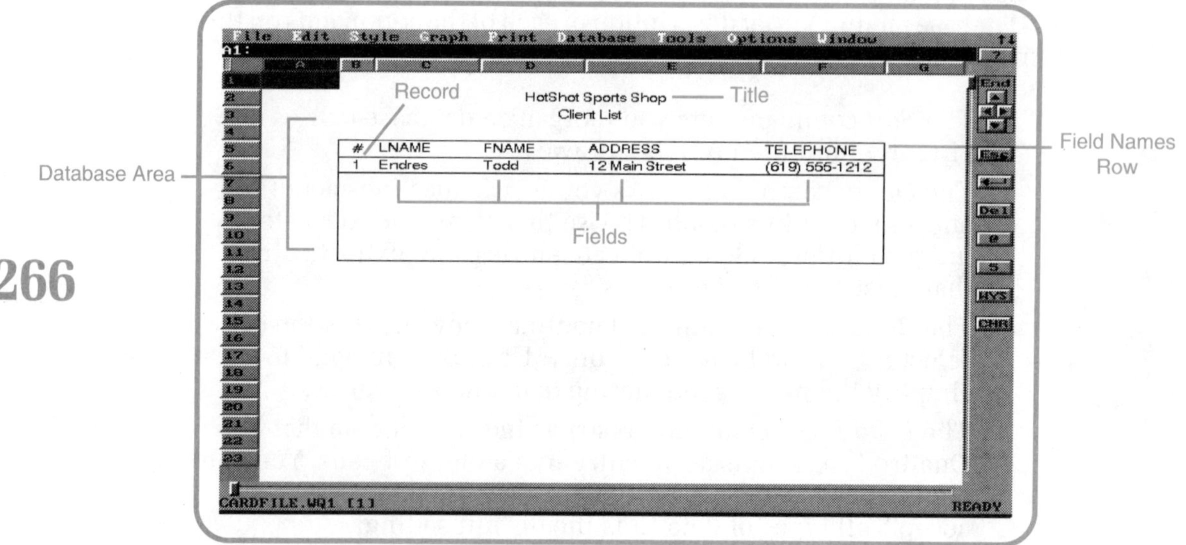

Figure 11.2 Creating an electronic database for HotShot Sports.

In a database, each row stores a single entry called a *record*. Each individual piece of data in a record is called a *field*. Cell block B5..F5 in Figure 11.2 contains very special data. This area, the *field names row*, displays the names that correspond to each field in a record. The field names row is an important player in all /**D**atabase menu operations. As you can see, this database stores records that consist of five fields (pieces of information): a record number (`#`), a last name (`LNAME`), a first name (`FNAME`), an address (`ADDRESS`), and a telephone number (`TELEPHONE`). The *database area* is the part of the spreadsheet where you store records (cell block B6..F11.)

Use the following Quick Steps to design a Quattro Pro database.

Designing a Database

1. Press /FN to select the /**F**ile **N**ew command. — Quattro Pro opens a new, blank spreadsheet. The READY mode indicator appears on the status line.
2. Select a spot near the top of the spreadsheet and type in a database title. — I typed HotShot Sports Shop in cell D2, and Client List in cell D3.
3. Select a spot just below the title and type in the field names row labels. — I typed '#, LNAME, FNAME, ADDRESS, and TELEPHONE into cell block B5..F5.
4. Press /SL to select the /**S**tyle **L**ine Drawing command, and draw a single line around the field names row and the database area.
5. Press /ENC to select the /**E**dit **N**ames **C**reate command and assign a name to the database area. — I assigned the name DATABASE to cell block B6..F11.The database area includes all columns across and possible rows down with data. Assigning the name to this area will make it easy to work with later.
6. Use the /**S**tyle **C**olumn Width command to adjust column widths as you see fit. — I changed the width of B to 4, C to 12, E to 20, and F to 14.
7. Press /FS to select the /**F**ile **S**ave command, and name the spreadsheet. — I named the spreadsheet CARDFILE.WQ1.

□

The spreadsheet on your screen now should resemble the one shown in Figure 11.2. The only difference is that your database does not contain any records yet. Let's take a close look at this spreadsheet, because it illustrates several important Quattro Pro database concepts.

1. *A database should have a simple design.* The more complex the design, the more difficult it will be to enter, locate, and work with records.
2. *The database structure closely resembles the format of a phone book, or a card file.* A Quattro Pro database is most useful when you organize it to resemble the manual databases that you are

most familiar with. That's not to say you can't be creative when designing a database, but if you want to create a Quattro Pro database to replace a card file, create one that organizes the records in much the same way.

3. *The database contains two name fields: one for the first name, and one for the last name.* Quattro Pro's database management abilities are only as good as the database structure you create. If you wish to be able to sort a database by first and last name, you must create a separate field for each name.
4. *The database field names appear on the same row, in a block of adjacent cells.* It's okay to enter a partially complete record (a record where one or more fields of data is missing), but never place an entire blank column anywhere inside the database area.

Adding Data and Controlling Data Entry

The easiest way to enter data into a database is simply to begin typing away. This method works just fine for smaller databases (less than thirty records). You use exactly the same techniques for entering data into a database as you do for a spreadsheet. Like a spreadsheet, a database record can contain labels, numbers, and even formulas.

When your database contains 30 or more records, you may wish to use Quattro Pro's /**D**atabase **R**estrict Input command to streamline the data entry process. The **R**estrict Input command limits the movement of the cell selector to unprotected cells only. This will come in handy when you wish to delegate the data entry task to another person, someone who may be less familiar with using Quattro Pro than you.

In all, you must execute three different commands to prepare for the following Quick Steps. While it may seem like a lot to do just to prepare for data entry, once you see the **R**estrict Input command in action, you'll understand why the extra steps are well worth the effort. Use the following Quick Steps to prepare a database for record entry using the /**D**atabase **R**estrict Input command.

Entering Data into a Database

1. Press /SPU to select the /**S**tyle **P**rotection **U**nprotect command. — Quattro Pro prompts you for a block of cells to unprotect.

2. Type the block name assigned to the database area and press Enter. (I typed DATABASE and pressed Enter.)

   Quattro Pro unprotects each cell in the database area. These cells show as Cyan on a color display, or in high intensity on a monochrome display.

3. Place the cell selector in the upper left corner of the database area (cell B6 on the sample database).

4. Press /WOLB to execute the /**W**indow **O**ptions **L**ocked Titles **B**oth command.

   Quattro Pro creates locked titles at the location of the cell selector. Now you only can move the cell selector into cells that are to the right, or below, the active cell (see cell B6 in Figure 11.3). All text above the location of the active cell now appears in Cyan on a color monitor, or in high intensity on a monochrome display.

5. Press /DR to select the /**D**atabase **R**estrict Input command.

   Quattro Pro prompts you for the block of unprotected cells, as shown in Figure 11.4.

6. Type the block name assigned to the database area and press Enter. (I typed DATABASE and pressed Enter.)

   Quattro Pro enters INPUT mode, which restricts cell selector movement to the database area. The cell selector appears in the upper left corner of the restricted cell block. □

After executing the /**D**atabase **R**estrict Input command you can begin entering records. The cell selector appears in the first field of the first record in the database. To enter the first record, type the number 1 and press Enter to store the data in the active cell (cell B6). Press the → key to move to the next field in the record (cell C6), type Endres, and press Enter to store the data in the active cell. Repeat this procedure until you've entered all the data for the first record.

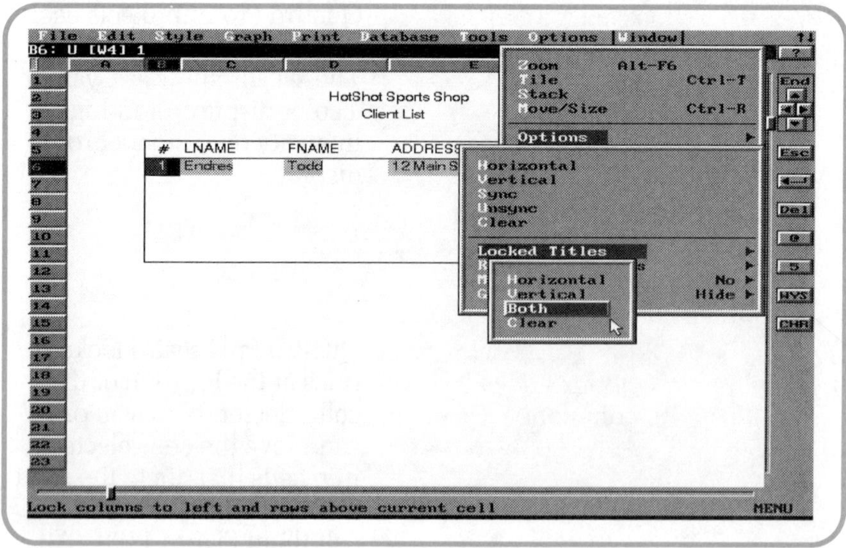

Figure 11.3 Locking titles provides a further measure of control when entering data into a database.

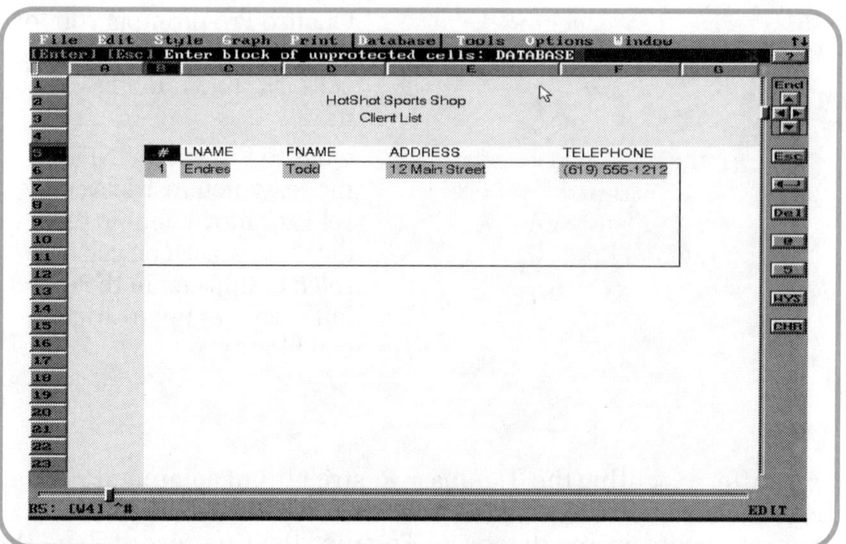

Figure 11.4 Restricting input to the database area.

> **Tip:** The final two fields in this database require labels that start with a number, or a value symbol. Although the ADDRESS field entry `12 Main Street` is a label, attempting to enter it into a cell without first typing a label prefix causes Quattro Pro to sound its error tone. Be sure to precede all ADDRESS and TELEPHONE field entries with a label prefix.

Enter the remaining records shown in Figure 11.5 into the database.

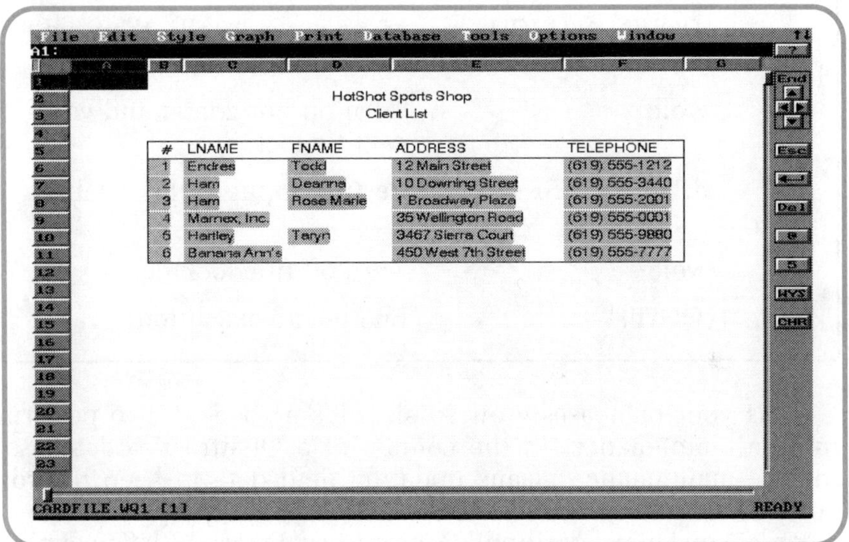

HotShot Sports Shop
Client List

#	LNAME	FNAME	ADDRESS	TELEPHONE
1	Endres	Todd	12 Main Street	(619) 555-1212
2	Ham	Deanna	10 Downing Street	(619) 555-3440
3	Ham	Rose Marie	1 Broadway Plaza	(619) 555-2001
4	Marnex, Inc.		35 Wellington Road	(619) 555-0001
5	Hartley	Taryn	3467 Sierra Court	(619) 555-9880
6	Banana Ann's		450 West 7th Street	(619) 555-7777

Figure 11.5 The completed version of the CARDFILE database.

To exit restricted data entry, press Enter once from INPUT mode, or press Enter twice from VALUE or LABEL mode. Quattro Pro now allows you to move the cell selector to cells outside the database area. Remember, though, you created locked titles, so you will not be able to move the cell selector above or to the left of the locked title. To remove locked titles, select the /**W**indow **O**ptions **L**ocked Titles **C**lear command. You now have complete freedom to move anywhere on the spreadsheet.

You may change entries in a database using the same editing commands you learned for editing spreadsheet entries. These editing commands work even when you restrict input to a database with the /**D**atabase **R**estrict Input command. Use the arrow keys or your mouse to highlight the cells you wish to edit and press F2. Make the necessary changes on the input line and press Enter once to record them.

Tip: The following six-line macro automates the previous Quick Steps for you. If you later expand the size of the database area to accommodate more records, be sure and unprotect all cells in the new database area before executing this macro.

\d	{GOTO}A1~	Make cell A1 the active cell.
	{DOWN 5}{RIGHT}	Move down 5 cells, then right 1 cell.
	/wolb~	Turn on horizontal and vertical title locking.
	/drDATABASE~	Restrict input to the database area.
	/wolc~	Turn off title locking.
	{QUIT}	End macro execution.

As your databases grow in size, it's a good idea to perform routine maintenance. In the context of a Quattro Pro database, routine maintenance means updating field data to keep records current, and deleting inactive records to free up space for new records. You know how to add records to a database, so let's examine how to delete them from a database. Before you delete a database record, think about why you are deleting it. The reasons for removing records from a database vary, so the following four examples should give you food for thought.

To delete a database record in order to make room for a new record, use the /**E**dit **E**rase Block command. This technique erases only a record's field data—all cell formats and style enhancements remain intact for the current row.

To delete a database record in order to shrink the size of the database, use the /**E**dit **D**elete **R**ows command. This approach is excellent for removing many records that reside in an adjoining block of rows. Be careful though—do not delete either the first or the last record in a database. Doing so will erase the name that you assign to the database area (DATABASE, in the example).

To delete a record that resides in the first or last row in a database, use the /**E**dit **E**rase Block command. This operation leaves a blank row at the top and bottom of the database. The next time you perform a sort operation (covered in the next section) Quattro Pro will move all blank rows to the bottom of the database.

It's easy to quickly delete a database record with a mouse. Simply highlight the target record and press the Del key once. Quattro Pro removes only the field data for the target record. All cell formats and style enhancements remain intact for the current row. To reverse this operation, press Alt-F5.

These four techniques provide you with the tools to meet all basic database maintenance needs. For more specialized record removal needs, you will need to use the commands found on the /**D**atabase **Q**uery menu, covered later in this chapter.

Sorting a Database

One of the most interesting manipulations you can perform on a database is a sort operation. Over time, this single procedure can save you hundreds of hours of time that you might spend manually reorganizing your databases.

In Quattro Pro, you can sort a database in an unlimited number of ways. The only limitation to sorting, in fact, is the structure of your database. You could not sort the CARDFILE database both by last name and first name, for example, if you only had a single name field.

You can sort the CARDFILE database many different ways. You can sort it by record number, by last name, by first name, by address, or by telephone number. In fact, you can even sort the database using combinations of several, or even all, of the field names. Plus, Quattro Pro sorts in either ascending or descending order, so you can even sort your data in those two ways.

Sorting a Database Using a Single Sort Key

Quattro Pro sorts database records according to sort keys. A *sort key* is a cell address that describes the column containing the field by which you wish to sort. To sort the LNAME field in the CARDFILE database, for instance, you could specify cell C1, C5, or C124. All three of these sort key definitions tell Quattro Pro the same thing: sort the database using the data in column C.

The following Quick Steps show how to sort a database using a single sort key.

Sorting a Database

1. Press /DS to select the /**D**atabase **S**ort command.	Quattro Pro displays the **S**ort menu.
2. Press B to select the Block option.	Quattro Pro prompts you for the block you wish to sort.
3. Type DATABASE and press Enter.	Quattro Pro records the **B**lock definition on the **S**ort menu.
4. Press 1 to select the **1**st Key option.	Quattro Pro prompts you for the cell address of the first sort key.
5. Type C5 and press Enter.	Quattro Pro displays the Sort Order submenu, which prompts you for the sort order.
6. Press A to select the **A**scending option, then press Enter.	Quattro Pro records the **1**st Key definition on the **S**ort menu, as shown in Figure 11.6.
7. Press G to select Go and start the sort operation.	Quattro Pro immediately rearranges the records in ascending alphabetical order, as shown in Figure 11.7. □

You can reverse the effects of a sort operation by pressing the Undo key. Try pressing Alt-F5 now to see this. Press Alt-F5 again to restore the database to its newly sorted order.

Sorting a Database Using Multiple Sort Keys

You may define up to five sort keys per sort operation. When you use multiple sort keys, Quattro Pro sorts the database in order according to each key's priority. This way, a database is first sorted according to the **1**st Key definition, then the **2**nd Key definition, and so on.

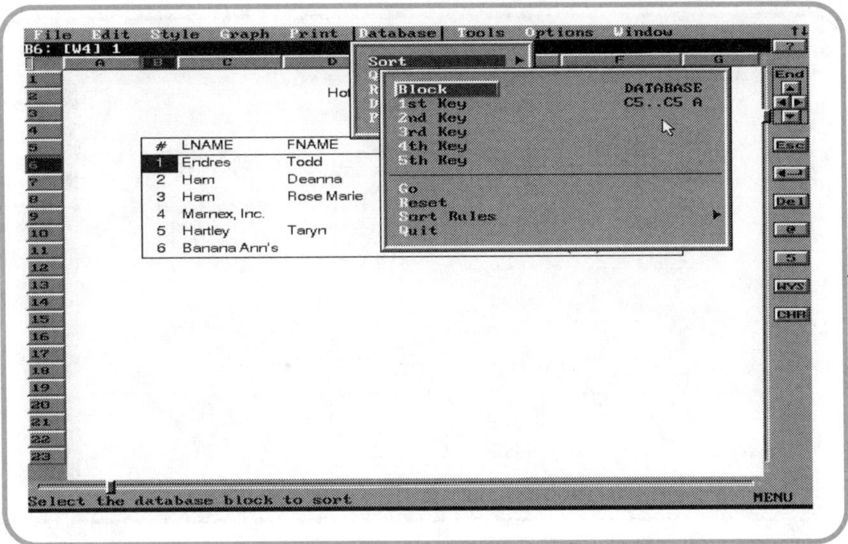

Figure 11.6 Preparing the Sort menu options for a single sort key operation.

Let's now sort the CARDFILE database by last name first, then by first name. Figure 11.8 shows the **S**ort menu definitions to achieve this objective. Before you enter these definitions on your screen, notice that Quattro Pro retained the block and sort key definition from the previous sort. Quattro Pro does so as long as you work with the same spreadsheet. Using the previous Quick Steps as a guideline, make the menu entries shown in Figure 11.8 for yourself.

When you're ready, select **G**o and sort the database. Figure 11.9 shows the result of this sort. At first, it may appear that nothing has changed. Look closely, and you'll notice that records 3 and 2 switched their order of appearance. Remember, the **1**st Key definition tells Quattro Pro to alphabetize by last name in ascending order (the same as in the previous example). The **2**nd Key definition, though, offers new guidance. This sort key specifies that Quattro Pro should alphabetize any records with the same last name in ascending order according to the first name. Because *Deanna* comes before *Rose Marie*, Quattro Pro switches the order of these two database records.

HotShot Sports Shop
Client List

#	LNAME	FNAME	ADDRESS	TELEPHONE
6	Banana Ann's		450 West 7th Street	(619) 555-7777
1	Endres	Todd	12 Main Street	(619) 555-1212
3	Ham	Rose Marie	1 Broadway Plaza	(619) 555-2001
2	Ham	Deanna	10 Downing Street	(619) 555-3440
5	Hartley	Taryn	3467 Sierra Court	(619) 555-9880
4	Marnex, Inc.		35 Wellington Road	(619) 555-0001

CARDFILE.WQ1 [1] READY

Figure 11.7 The results of sorting the CARDFILE database alphabetically by last name.

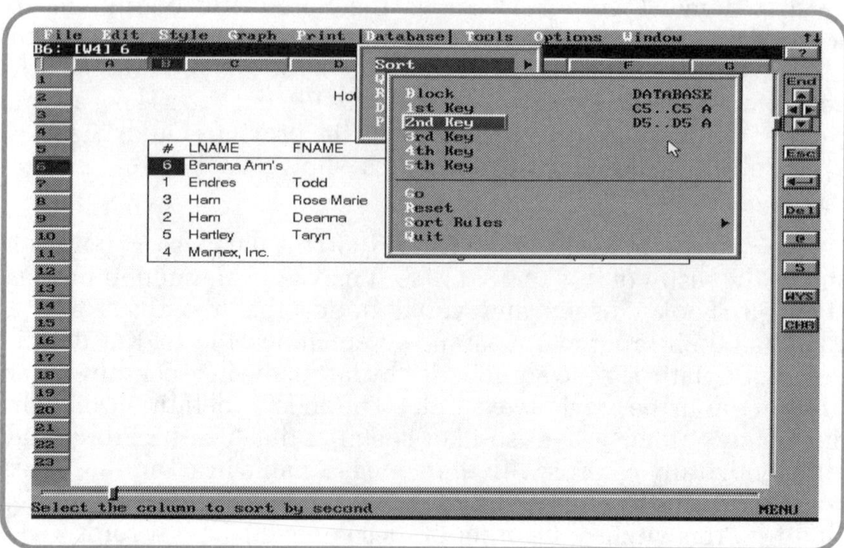

Figure 11.8 Preparing the Sort menu options for a multiple sort key operation.

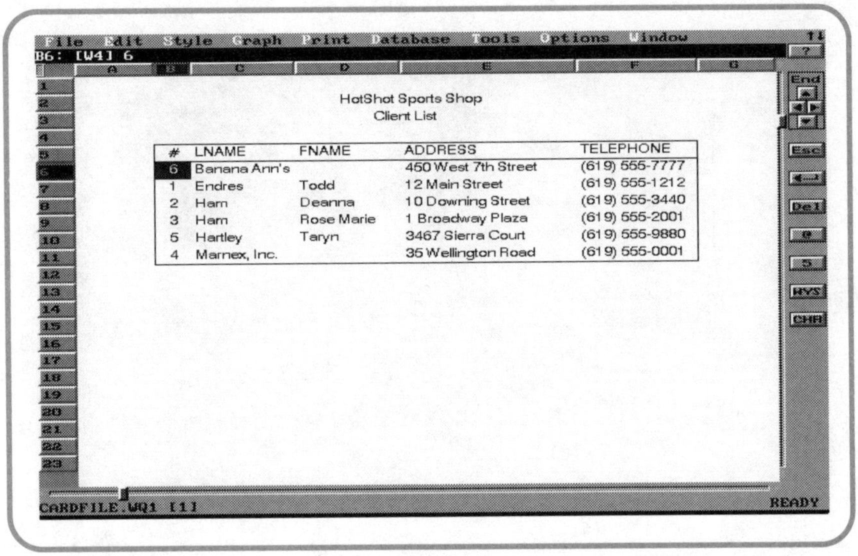

HotShot Sports Shop
Client List

#	LNAME	FNAME	ADDRESS	TELEPHONE
6	Banana Ann's		450 West 7th Street	(619) 555-7777
1	Endres	Todd	12 Main Street	(619) 555-1212
2	Ham	Deanna	10 Downing Street	(619) 555-3440
3	Ham	Rose Marie	1 Broadway Plaza	(619) 555-2001
5	Hartley	Taryn	3467 Sierra Court	(619) 555-9880
4	Mamex, Inc.		35 Wellington Road	(619) 555-0001

CARDFILE.WQ1 [1] READY

Figure 11.9 The results of sorting the CARDFILE database alphabetically by last name, then alphabetically by first name.

Returning a Database to its Original Order

So far, I haven't said much about the number (#) field of the CARDFILE database. The sole reason for including this field in a database is to preserve the original order of the database records. By including a number (#) field in every database you create, and then sequentially numbering the records as you enter them, you can use this field as the sort key whenever you wish to return the database to its original order.

Figure 11.10 displays the **S**ort menu definitions that enable you to return any database to its original order. Here, the database shown behind the **S**ort menu is back in its original order of entry. To return a database to its original order, just sort the number (#) field in ascending order.

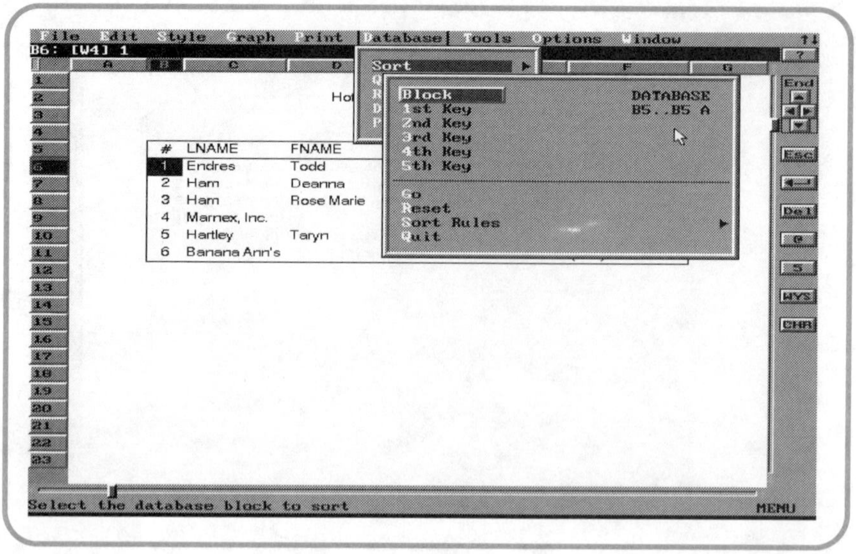

Figure 11.10 Returning a database to its original order.

Modifying Quattro Pro's Sort Rules

The /**D**atabase **S**ort **S**ort Rules command allows you to control the method Quattro Pro uses to sort a database. By default, Quattro Pro sorts a database as follows:

1st	Blank cells
2nd	Labels that start with numbers
3rd	Labels that start with letters or special characters
4th	Values

To change how Quattro Pro sorts values, for instance, select /**D**atabase **S**ort **S**ort Rules **N**umbers before Labels **Y**es. This command causes Quattro Pro to sort according to the following rules:

1st	Blank cells
2nd	Values
3rd	Labels that start with numbers
4th	Labels that start with letters or special characters

To change how Quattro Pro sorts labels, select /**D**atabase **S**ort **S**ort Rules **L**abel Order **D**ictionary. The dictionary sort rule disregards case when Quattro Pro sorts labels, so that the word "france" would appear before "Friendly." By default, Quattro Pro sorts according to the **ASCII** rule. This rule states that labels beginning with uppercase characters (like Friendly) appear before labels beginning with lowercase characters (like france).

As one final note, use the /**D**atabase **S**ort **R**eset command to erase all definitions from the **S**ort menu, and as always, select the /**O**ptions **U**pdate command to save any changes made to default settings (that is, new **S**ort Rules command settings) so that they're active for future work sessions.

Searching Through a Database

The /**D**atabase **Q**uery command is another powerful data management tool. To *query* means to ask a question. In Quattro Pro, a *query operation* enables you to ask a question and then affect the database in some way based on the answer. You can define a query, for instance, that searches through a database, locates all records of a certain type, then copies the records elsewhere on the spreadsheet. As you can see, a query operation allows you to create mini-databases from larger ones.

Imagine a database that contains 3,000 records. Each record includes, among other things, a client's date of birth. At the end of May, you could define a query that searches for all clients with a June birth date, copies their records, and then prints out a list which you can use as a birthday card mailing list.

Querying a database is a four-step procedure, as follows:

1. Define a block to search in the database. This step is as simple as defining a sort block.
2. Create a criteria table. A *criteria table* contains the *query definitions*—these are the questions you're asking.
3. Create an output block. An *output block* is where Quattro Pro copies records that meet the query definitions.
4. Perform a *query operation*. In Quattro Pro, you can **L**ocate, **E**xtract, **D**elete, and identify **U**nique records in a database.

Defining the Search Block

There is only one rule to remember when you define a search block in a query operation. *The search block absolutely must include the field names row.* This rule is completely different from the one used in sort operations. To sort, you intentionally omitted the field names row so it was not sorted into the database area. Here, the field names row enables Quattro Pro to search through the database correctly.

In a search operation, Quattro Pro does not rearrange records, it just looks at the individual parts of each record. To do this, though, Quattro Pro first must be able to distinguish between each field in a record. That's why the field names row is so important. Imagine a query that tells Quattro Pro to search for all records with the label "Bob" in the FNAME field. Quattro Pro first locates the FNAME label on the field names row. Then it begins its search by looking down the column that contains the FNAME fields.

There is a simple way to ensure that you'll always correctly define the search block. Just think of a block name that you can remember, and assign it to the entire database (the database area plus the field names row). Use the /**E**dit **N**ames **C**reate command to name the database. For example, use the name SHELL for the search block. A shell is the outer casing of something, and here describes the outer shell of the database (including the field names row). Returning to the CARDFILE database, assign the name SHELL to cell block B5..F11.

Creating a Criteria Table

Next, create the criteria table, where you record your "queries" about the records in your database. I'll describe more about that soon. First, let's review some background on the design of a criteria table.

A criteria table must include at least one field name label, and at least one query. You type the query in the cell directly below the field name label. Look at the criteria table shown in Figure 11.11. This table looks just like a duplicate of the field names row (and it is!). To create this criteria table, copy the data from cell block B5..F5 into B14..F14. Next, enter the label `CRITERIA TABLE` into cell B13 so you know the purpose of this block of data. This criteria table lists all the field name labels so you may quickly create and enter queries about any of these fields. When Quattro Pro encounters a field name label in the criteria table that has no query definition below it, Quattro Pro ignores that field during the search operation.

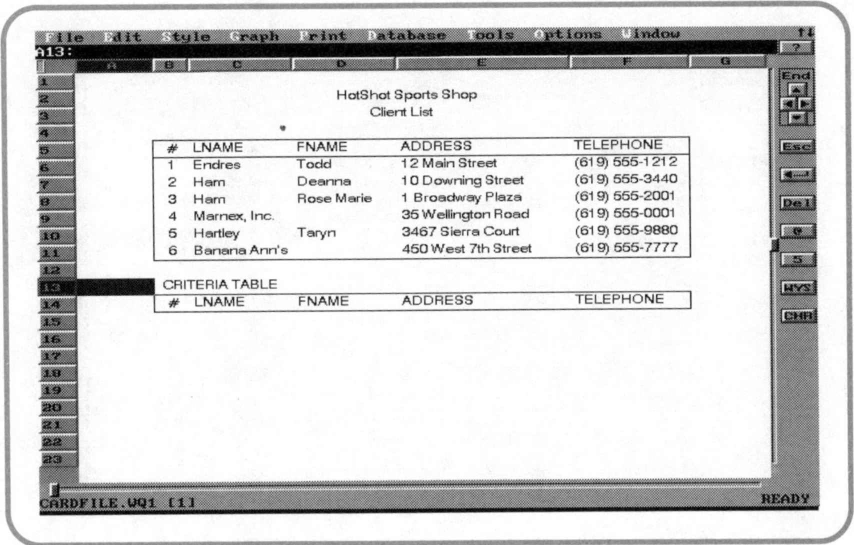

Figure 11.11 A sample criteria table.

Before Quattro Pro can recognize a criteria table (and read your query) you must name the table. Select /**E**dit **N**ames **C**reate and assign the name `CRITERIA` to block B14..F15. This block name includes the row containing the field names and the row containing the query definitions.

Now let's create our first query for the CARDFILE database. Suppose that we wish to locate every record where the LNAME field contains the label Hartley. To create the query for this task, look at the spreadsheet shown in Figure 11.12. Cell C15 contains a single query: `Hartley`. Type that label into cell C15, and that's it! Querying is that simple. This query tells Quattro Pro to search through the LNAME column in the search block until it finds the label Hartley. The criteria table now is complete, and we're ready to move on.

Searching Through a Database

Are you ready to perform a search operation? Good. Start by selecting the /**D**atabase **Q**uery command. Quattro Pro displays the **Q**uery menu. Select the **B**lock command. When prompted, type `SHELL` and press Enter. Quattro Pro records the block definition on the **Q**uery menu, next to the **B**lock command.

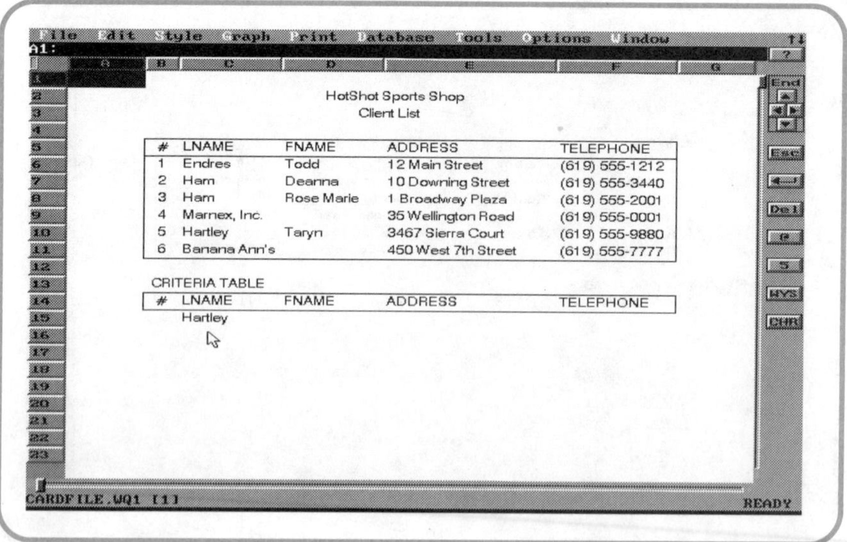

Figure 11.12 Enter a query under the appropriate field name label in the criteria table.

Next, select the **C**riteria Table command. When prompted, type `CRITERIA` and press Enter. Quattro Pro records the criteria table definition on the **Q**uery menu next to the **C**riteria Table command, as shown in Figure 11.13.

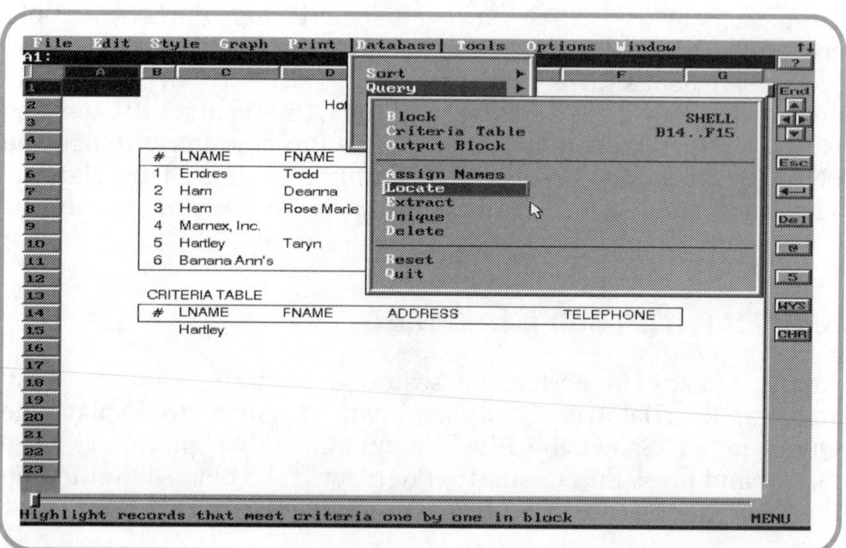

Figure 11.13 Quattro Pro stores the search conditions on the Query menu.

To begin a search operation and locate all records that meet your criteria conditions, select **L**ocate. Figure 11.14 illustrates how Quattro Pro highlights the first field in the first record in the search block with the label Hartley in the LNAME field.

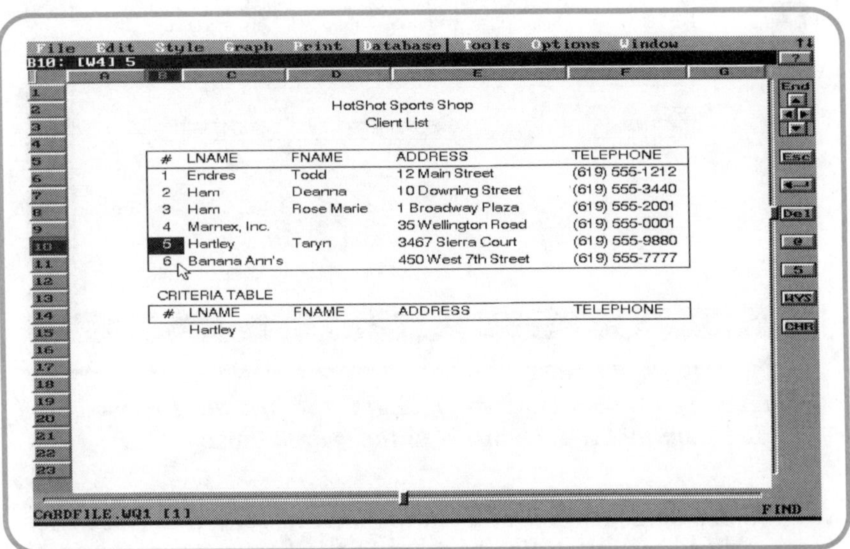

Figure 11.14 Quattro Pro locates the first record in the search block containing the label specified in the criteria table.

You can edit the contents of any record found through a search operation. Press F2 to enter EDIT mode, and Quattro Pro displays the contents of the active cell on the input line. When you've finished editing, press Enter to insert the data to the cell. While a record is highlighted, you may press the ← and → keys to move the cell selector into a different field within that record.

Now let's perform another search operation using different criteria. Return to the criteria table and change the entry in cell C15 to `Ham`. Reselect the /**D**atabase **Q**uery **L**ocate command to start a new search operation. This time, Quattro Pro highlights record #2—the first record with the label `Ham` in the LNAME column, as shown in Figure 11.15. Notice, however, that there are two entries in this database that display the label `Ham`.

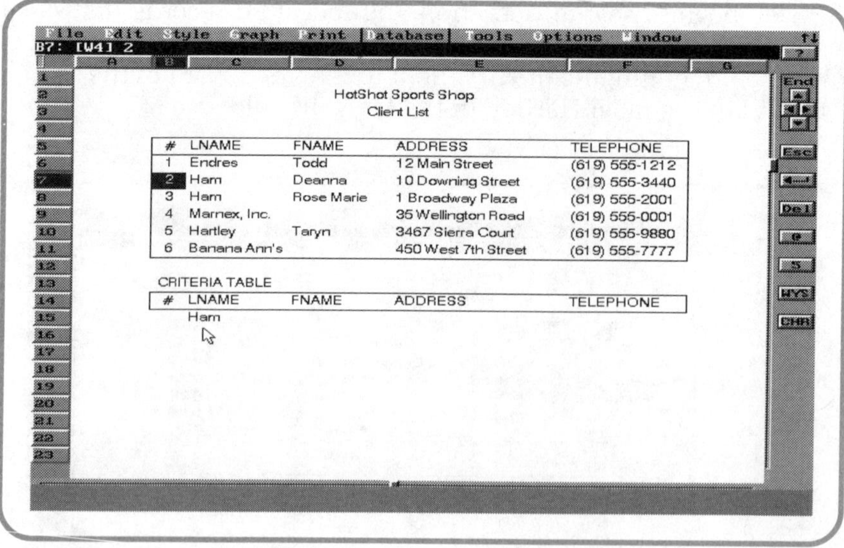

Figure 11.15 Quattro Pro highlights the first occurrence of the label Ham that it encounters in the search block.

When a database contains more than one record that satisfies a search criteria, Quattro Pro highlights the first occurrence in the search block. Press the ↓ key to highlight other records that satisfy the search criteria. Press Home to highlight the first matching record in the database, and press End to highlight the last.

Let's perform one final search operation. Return to the criteria table and enter the number 3 into cell B15. Reselect the /**D**atabase **Q**uery **L**ocate command to start a new search operation. This time, Quattro Pro highlights record #3. There is only one record that meets both of the conditions listed in the criteria table, as shown in Figure 11.16.

> **Tip:** When searching for different records in the database, you need not keep using the menu commands, such as /**D**ata **Q**uery. You can make a change in the criteria area and just press the F7 key. This key works for all the /**D**ata **Q**uery functions, repeating the most recent series of commands you've used.

You now are familiar with two of the most handy database management tools: the /**D**atabase **S**ort command and the /**D**atabase **Q**uery **L**ocate commands. With these two commands alone, you can rearrange and locate data using a Quattro Pro database.

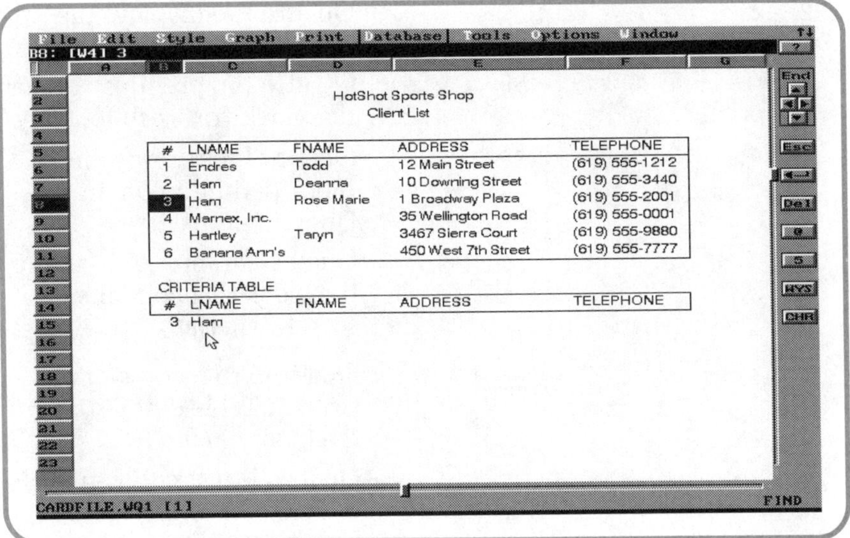

Figure 11.16 Multiple criteria definitions can streamline a search and locate operation.

Deleting Records From a Database

In an earlier section in this book we discussed the importance of performing routine maintenance on a database. This section demonstrated four basic techniques for deleting database records. When you have specialized record removal needs (for example, removing all records with a ZIP code equal to 92075) use the commands on the /**D**atabase **Q**uery menu.

The /**D**atabase **Q**uery **D**elete command removes records satisfying your search criteria from a database. Quattro Pro shifts up other database records to fill in gaps left by deleted records. The following Quick Steps demonstrate how to use the **D**elete command to perform very specific record removals from a database.

Deleting records from a database that satisfy search criteria

1. Enter search criteria into your Criteria Table (I entered 3 into cell B15 and Ham into cell C15).

   The search criteria must be very specific to guard against the accidental removal of active records from the database.

2. Press /DQ to select the /**D**atabase **Q**uery command.	Quattro Pro displays the **Q**uery menu.
3. Press B to select the **B**lock option.	Quattro Pro prompts you for the block you wish to query.
4. Type *DATABASE* and press Enter.	Quattro Pro records the **B**lock definition on the **Q**uery menu.
5. Press C to select the **C**riteria Table option.	Quattro Pro prompts you for the block that contains the search criteria.
6. Type *CRITERIA* and press Enter.	Quattro Pro records the **C**riteria Table definition on the **Q**uery menu.
7. Press D to select the **D**elete option.	Quattro Pro asks if you wish to *Delete Record(s)?* (see Figure 11.17)
8. Press C to **C**ancel the operation, or press **D**elete to delete all records satisfying the search criteria.	This is your last opportunity to cancel the delete operation, so proceed carefully. If you press D, Quattro Pro immediately deletes matching records from the database. If you press C, Quattro Pro returns you to the **Q**uery menu. □

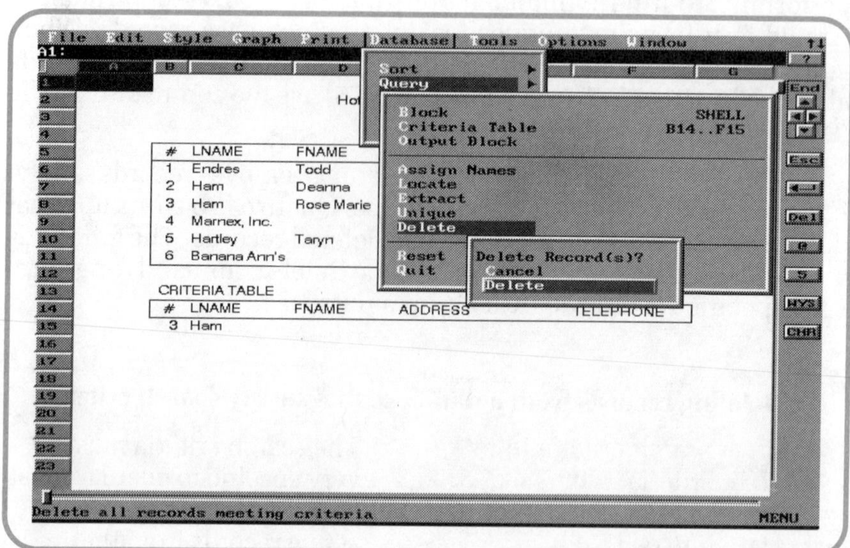

Figure 11.17 Specifying the search criteria for a delete operation.

Figure 11.18 shows the result of the delete operation. Here, Quattro Pro removes the only record from the database that meets the search criteria—record #3. After removing the record Quattro Pro shifts up records #4, #5, and #6 to fill in the gaps left from the delete operation.

Suppose that the search criteria did not include the entry in cell B15 (see Figure 11.17). In this case, Quattro Pro would have deleted records #2 and #3 because both records contain the label Ham in the LNAME field.

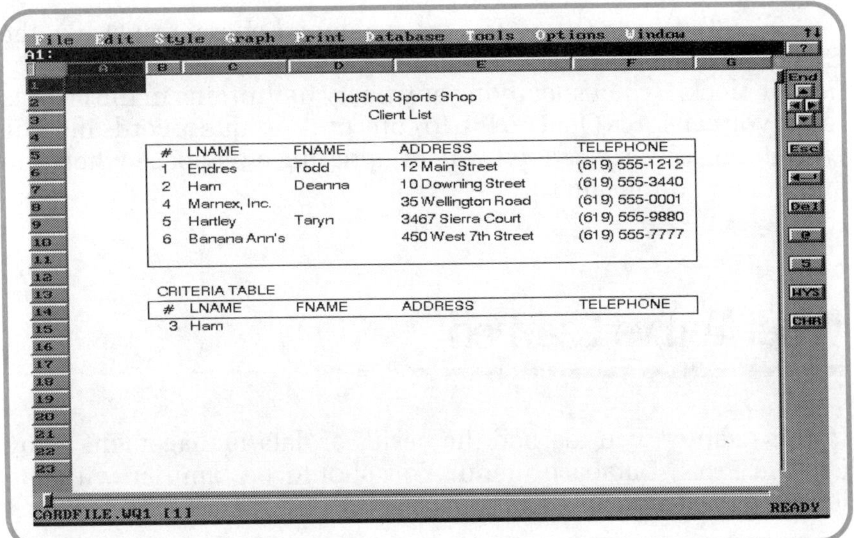

Figure 11.18 Reviewing the results of a delete operation.

When Quattro Pro is unable to locate matching records in a delete operation, the program does nothing to the database and returns you to the **Q**uery menu. Press Q twice to **Q**uit the **Q**uery menu and return to the active spreadsheet. Make any needed changes to the search criteria in the Criteria Table, and restart the delete operation.

As always, you can press Alt-F5 to reverse a /**D**atabase operation.

Other Query Operations

Although the balance of the commands on the **Q**uery menu are beyond the scope of this book, they merit some mention here.

The /**D**atabase **Q**uery **E**xtract command copies all records matching your query definitions into an output block. An *output block* is similar to a criteria table. In an extract operation, Quattro Pro copies from each matching record only the fields that you wish to see.

The /**D**atabase **Q**uery **U**nique command operates just like the **E**xtract command, except it only copies unique records into the output block. By not specifying any query definitions in the criteria table, you can force Quattro Pro to copy only unique records into the output table. This is a good way of updating a database when you suspect that duplicate records exist.

What You've Learned

In this chapter, you learned the basics of data management using Quattro Pro's /**D**atabase menu. You should be familiar with the following concepts:

- Adding data to a database is easy when you use the /**D**atabase **R**estrict Input command.
- A database consists of a *field names row* and a *database area*. The field names row contains labels describing each *field* in a *record*. The database area stores all records.
- To sort a database, you define a *search block* and a *sort key*, and then select the /**D**atabase **S**ort **G**o command.
- You can search through a database and locate records that match very specific query definitions using the /**D**atabase **Q**uery **L**ocate command.
- You can use the /**D**atabase **Q**uery **D**elete command to search and delete records with specific criteria.
- Other **Q**uery menu commands enable you to extract records that meet specific requirements and delete duplicate records from a database.

Appendix A

Installation

Getting Started With Installation

Appendix A discusses how to install Quattro Pro. Even though Quattro Pro may already be installed on your PC, it helps to know how this process works in the event you need to reinstall the program at a later date.

After installing the program you can modify Quattro Pro's operating environment using the /**O**ptions menu commands. The commands on this menu enable you to fine-tune your copy of Quattro Pro until you create the most comfortable and productive operating environment. See Appendix B for complete coverage of the /**O**ptions menu commands.

This appendix provides step-by-step instructions for those of you who are using older versions of Quattro Pro (Version 1.0 or 2.0). There are a few extra steps to take if you are upgrading to Version 3.0 from a previous version of Quattro Pro, so be sure to read the material in this section.

> **Caution:** If you are upgrading from a previous version of Quattro Pro, skip ahead to the section titled "Upgrading to Version 3.0 from a Previous Version of Quattro Pro" before continuing.

This appendix also discusses how to augment your Quattro Pro screen font library once Quattro Pro is installed. Postinstallation font-building is possible using the INSTALL.WQ1 macro that arrives with your Quattro Pro package.

What You Need To Run Quattro Pro

To operate Quattro Pro, you must have at least the following hardware and operating system software available:

Hardware
IBM XT or AT compatible
512K (kilobytes) of RAM
4M (megabytes) of free space on your hard disk drive
A monochrome graphics display system Operating system
DOS 2.0 or later

If you have more advanced computer equipment than is listed above you are fortunate—Quattro Pro's operating performance improves noticeably with better equipment. Just answer the questions during installation to tell Quattro Pro about your computer equipment.

Installing the Program

Installing Quattro Pro is a three-part process. In Part I, Quattro Pro copies its program files to your hard disk drive. In Part II, you tell Quattro Pro about the type of computer equipment that you will be using with the program. In Part III, you install a library of screen fonts that Quattro Pro uses to display WYSIWYG spreadsheets and graphs.

Part I: Copying the Program Files

To begin installing Quattro Pro, do the following:

1. Place installation disk 1 into the A drive.

2. Type A:\INSTALL and press Enter.

After a moment or two, the screen shown in Figure A.1 appears.

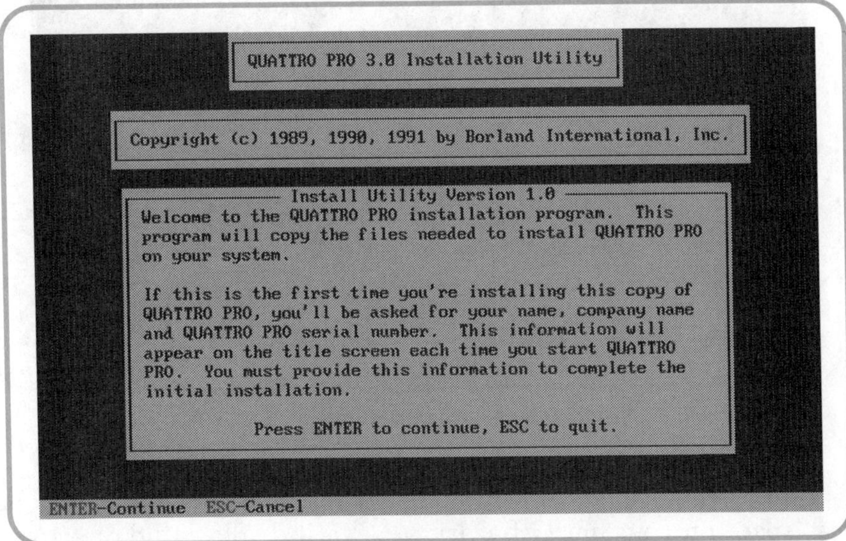

Figure A.1 The initial installation screen.

Tip: If the text of the Installation Utility is difficult to read, press Esc and exit INSTALL. Now type A:\INSTALL /B and press Enter, and Quattro Pro will display the Installation Utility in black-and-white.

This screen indicates that Quattro Pro needs certain information from you in order to complete installation. You can not complete the installation of Quattro Pro without the following information:

Your name
A company name
The serial number that is stamped at the top of install disk #1.

3. Press Enter to begin installing Quattro Pro.

Quattro Pro can install itself from any drive you specify. Usually drive A is the *source drive,* the drive from which you copy the Quattro Pro files (see Figure A.2). If you wish, you can install Quattro Pro from drive B. Press Enter to select A as the source drive.

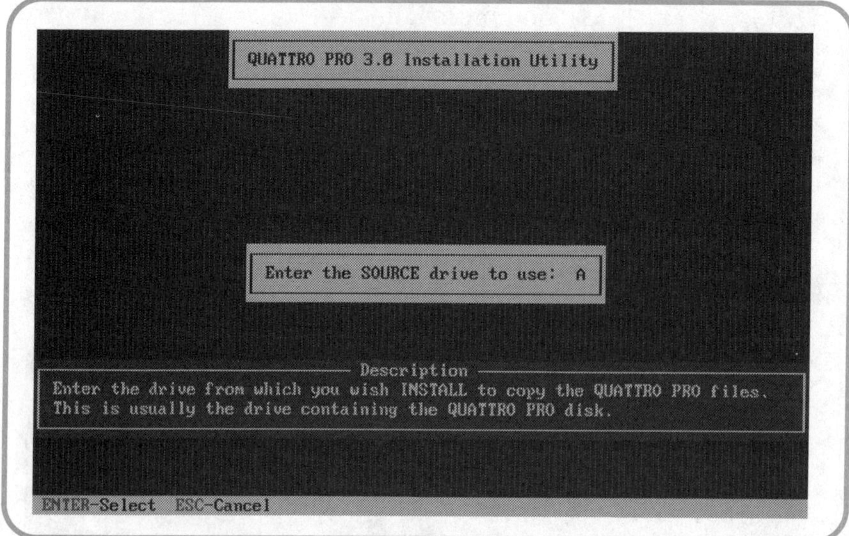

Figure A.2 Selecting the source drive.

First, the Installation Utility checks to see if you have enough free space on your hard disk drive. Next, it displays the directory where it will copy the files (see Figure A.3).

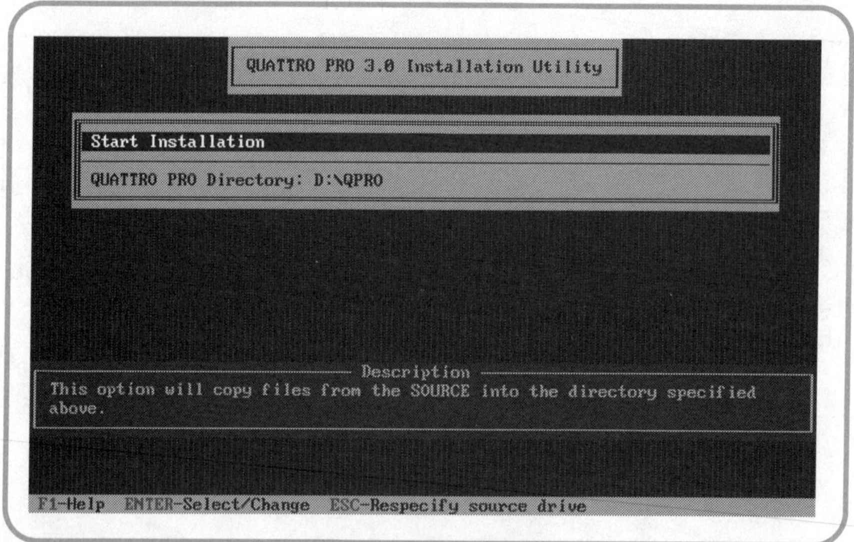

Figure A.3 Choosing the destination drive and the directory name.

If you wish to install Quattro Pro into a different path on your hard disk drive, press ↓ once, press Enter and type in a new path name. When you are finished, highlight Start Installation and press Enter to continue. To terminate the installation process at any time, just press Esc and Quattro Pro returns you to the DOS command prompt.

By default, the Installation Utility copies the Quattro Pro files to a path named \QPRO that it creates on your hard disk drive (unless you chose a different path name in the previous section). After copying all of the files on disk #1, Quattro Pro prompts you to place disk #2 into the source drive to continue installing (see Figure A.4).

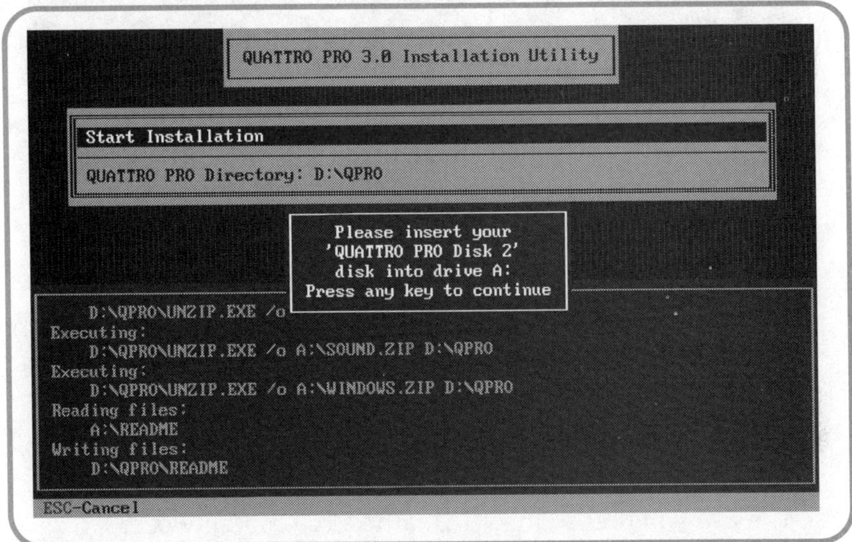
QUATTRO PRO 3.0 Installation Utility
Start Installation
QUATTRO PRO Directory: D:\QPRO
Please insert your
'QUATTRO PRO Disk 2'
disk into drive A:
Press any key to continue
D:\QPRO\UNZIP.EXE /o
Executing:
D:\QPRO\UNZIP.EXE /o A:\SOUND.ZIP D:\QPRO
Executing:
D:\QPRO\UNZIP.EXE /o A:\WINDOWS.ZIP D:\QPRO
Reading files:
A:\README
Writing files:
D:\QPRO\README
ESC-Cancel

Figure A.4 Copying the Quattro Pro files onto your hard disk.

> **Tip:** When you do not have at least 4M of free space on your hard disk, Quattro Pro displays an error message. If you see this error message, exit the installation program and delete files until you free up at least 4M of space on your hard disk drive.

When all the files are transferred, Quattro Pro displays the message shown in Figure A.5.

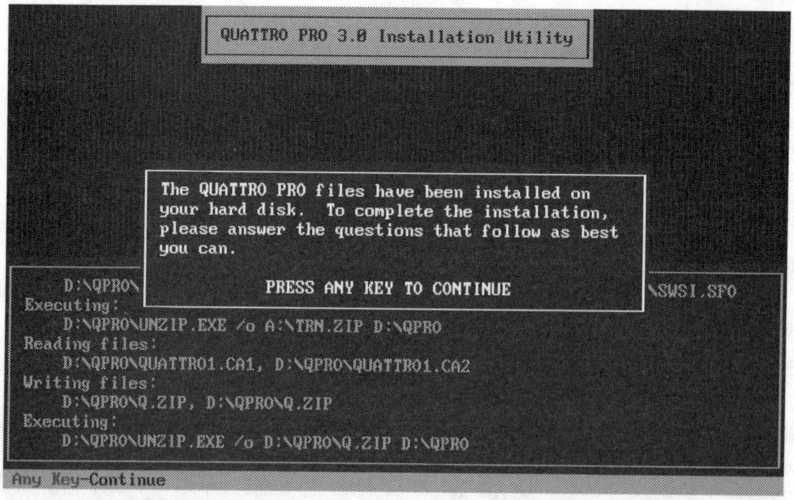

```
QUATTRO PRO 3.0 Installation Utility

The QUATTRO PRO files have been installed on
your hard disk.  To complete the installation,
please answer the questions that follow as best
you can.

PRESS ANY KEY TO CONTINUE

    D:\QPRO\                                            \SWSI.SFO
Executing:
    D:\QPRO\UNZIP.EXE /o A:\TRN.ZIP D:\QPRO
Reading files:
    D:\QPRO\QUATTRO1.CA1, D:\QPRO\QUATTRO1.CA2
Writing files:
    D:\QPRO\Q.ZIP, D:\QPRO\Q.ZIP
Executing:
    D:\QPRO\UNZIP.EXE /o D:\QPRO\Q.ZIP D:\QPRO
Any Key-Continue
```

Figure A.5 A successful file transfer.

Part II: Selecting Your Equipment

In Part II of the installation process you tell Quattro Pro about your computer equipment. Specifically, you do the following:

- Select a monitor type.
- Record your name and disk serial number.
- Choose whether to install Quattro Pro on a network.
- Modify your AUTOEXEC.BAT and CONFIG.SYS files.
- Choose a menu tree interface
- Select WYSIWYG as the startup display mode.

Selecting a Monitor Type

The Installation Utility detects whether you have a color graphics display card installed in your computer. You must, however, tell Quattro Pro whether your monitor is Color, Black & White, or Gray Scale (see Figure A.6).

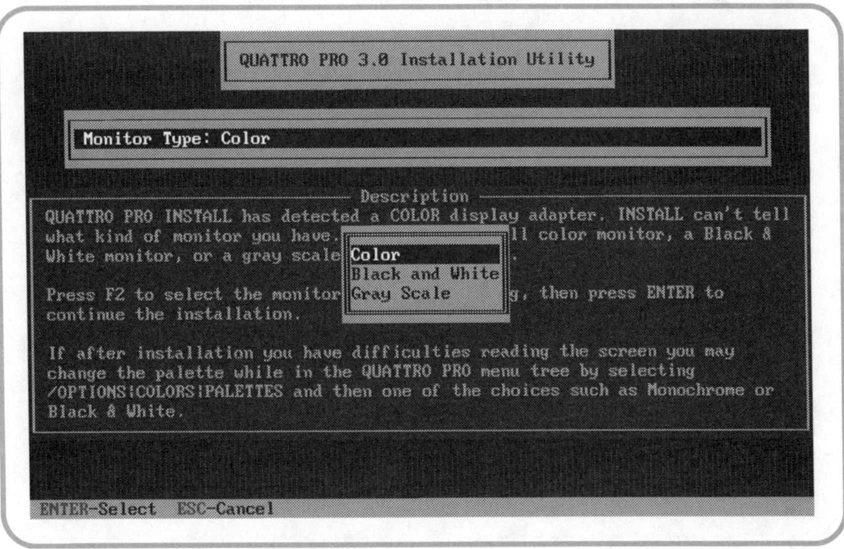

Figure A.6 Specifying a color or monochrome monitor.

To change the default selection, press F2, use the cursor-movement keys to move to your selection, and press Enter. When you are finished, press Enter to continue or press Esc to quit.

Recording Your Name and Disk Serial Number

Next, Quattro Pro prompts you to enter your name, company name, and the serial number that appears on Disk 1. You must supply this information to continue with the installation.

Installing Quattro Pro on a Network

Quattro Pro next asks if you wish to install Quattro Pro on a network server. The default setting is No (see Figure A.7).

To install Quattro Pro on a network server, press F2 and highlight Yes, then press Enter. If you are operating on a network, you should let your Network Administrator install Quattro Pro because Quattro Pro requires very specific information about your network before it can complete the installation.

If you are unsure about what to do, simply select the No option and press Enter to continue with the installation.

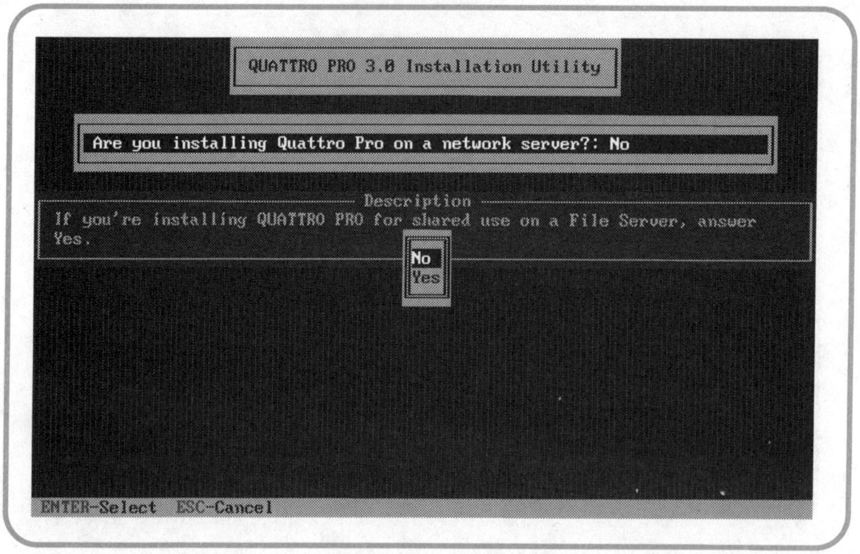

Figure A.7 Select the No option to install Quattro Pro on a single-station PC.

Modify your AUTOEXEC.BAT and CONFIG.SYS files

The Installation Utility next asks if you wish it to make changes to your CONFIG.SYS and AUTOEXEC.BAT files so that Quattro Pro can run properly on your computer. You should let it do this for you. When prompted, press F2, highlight the Yes option, and press Enter (see Figure A.8.)

To change these files yourself, use a word processing program in nondocument or DOS text file mode. The CONFIG.SYS file must contain the following statements:

```
BUFFERS=20
FILES=20
```

Then add QPRO to the PATH statement in your AUTOEXEC.BAT file so that you can load Quattro Pro from any directory on your hard disk drive.

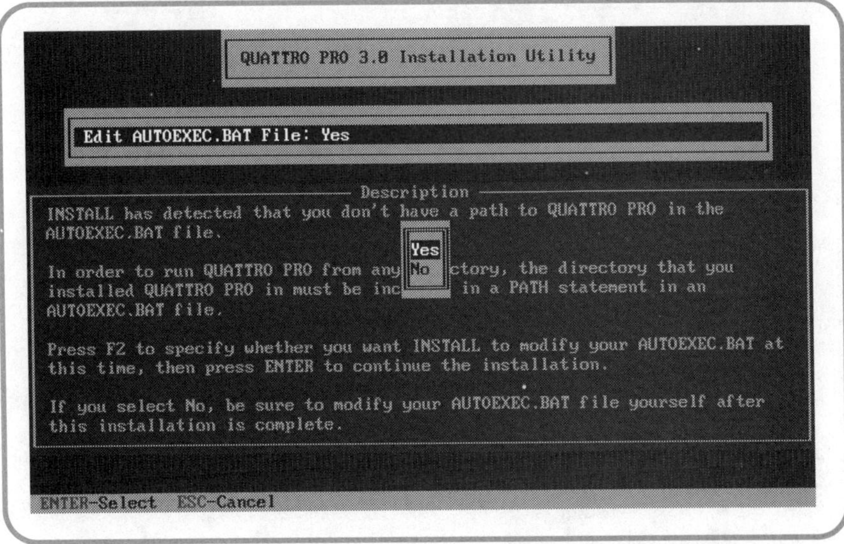

Figure A.8 Letting Quattro Pro make changes to your AUTOEXEC.BAT and CONFIG.SYS file.

Selecting the Menu Tree Interface

A user interface is a fancy way of saying menu tree. As you know, Quattro Pro can display one of three menu trees: Quattro Pro, Quattro, and Lotus 1-2-3. The user interface prompt allows you to choose one of the two Quattro menus as the default menu tree that displays each time you start a work session.

In the Installation Utility, the user interface default is QUATTRO—the menu tree for Quattro Pro (see Figure A.9.)

To accept this menu tree, press Enter. To change to a different menu tree, press F2, use the cursor-movement keys to highlight your selection, and press Enter twice.

> **Tip:** If you are a Lotus 1-2-3 convert, you may want Quattro Pro to load the 1-2-3 menu tree. To do this you first must complete program installation. Load Quattro Pro into your computer and select the /**O**ptions **S**tartup **M**enu Tree **1**23 command. Select /**O**ptions **U**pdate to save this as the default menu tree for future work sessions.

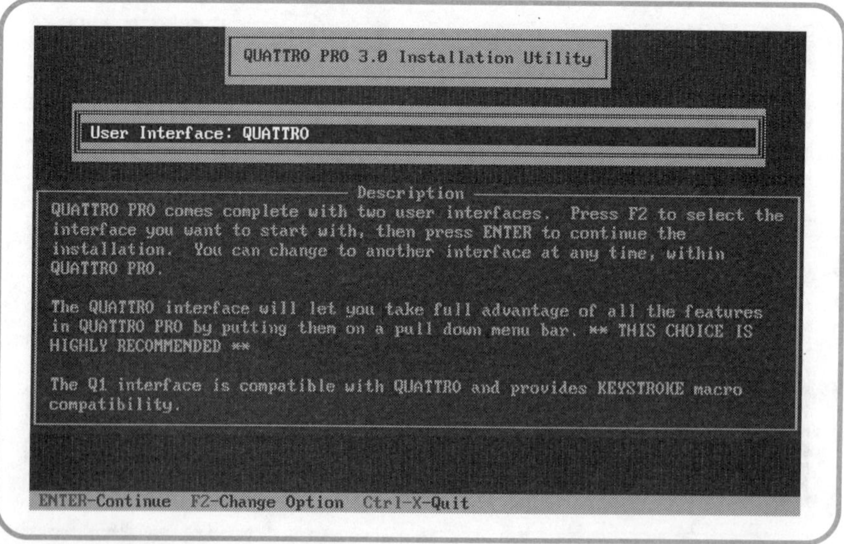

Figure A.9 Choosing the default, startup menu tree.

Selecting a Printer

Next, you must select a printer manufacturer and model from the Printer Manufacturer screen (see Figure A.10). Press F2, use the cursor-movement keys to highlight the appropriate manufacturer, and then press Enter.

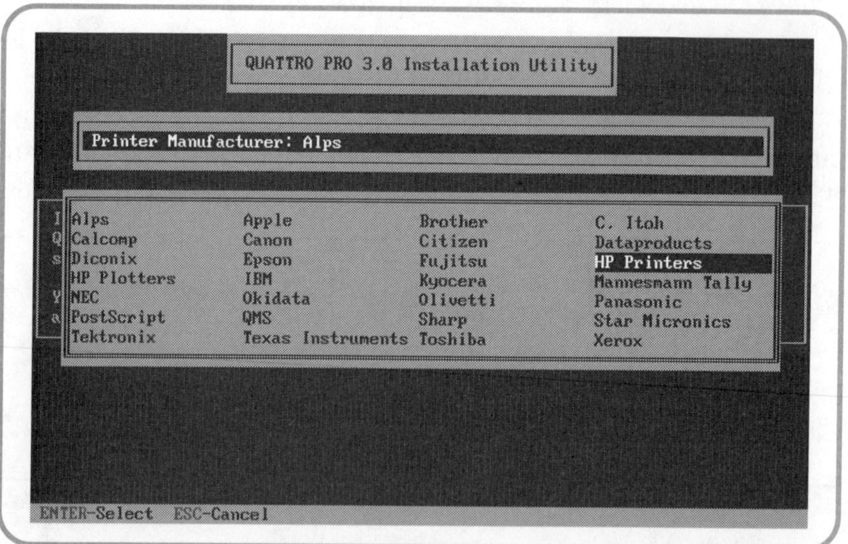

Figure A.10 Selecting HP Printers as a printer manufacturer.

If your printer manufacturer is not on this screen, check your printer manual for information on the types of printers your printer can emulate. Many printers emulate Epson, IBM and HP printers.

After you select a printer manufacturer, Quattro Pro displays the Printer Model screen (see Figure A.11). To choose a printer model, highlight the appropriate name on the list and press Enter.

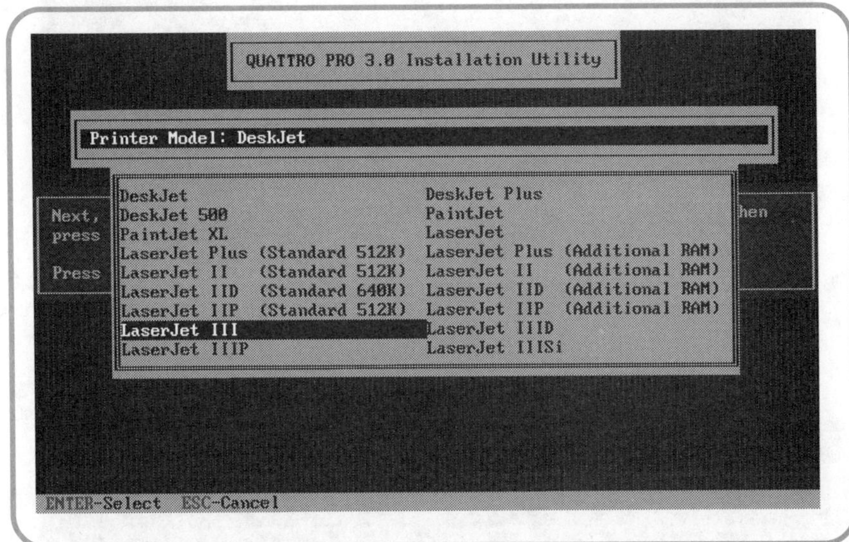

Figure A.11 Selecting LaserJet III as a printer model.

After you select a printer model, Quattro Pro asks you to choose an initial mode and resolution at which to print spreadsheets and graphs. Figure A.12 displays a selection that tells Quattro Pro to print on 8 1/2 x 11 inch paper in 300 x 300 dots per inch (dpi) mode. This setting permits high-resolution printing.

To select a medium resolution printing mode, press F2 and select a different mode. The actual dpi ratings available on this menu depend on the individual printer. If you select an Epson LQ-2500 printer, for example, the dpi rating in high mode is 360x180.

Selecting WYSIWYG as the Default Display Mode

Now you decide whether or not you wish to use WYSIWYG as the default display mode (see Figure A.13). The WYSIWYG display mode offers a crisp, high resolution display—it is the best of all available Quattro Pro display modes. To use this display mode you must have an EGA or VGA graphics display card installed in your PC.

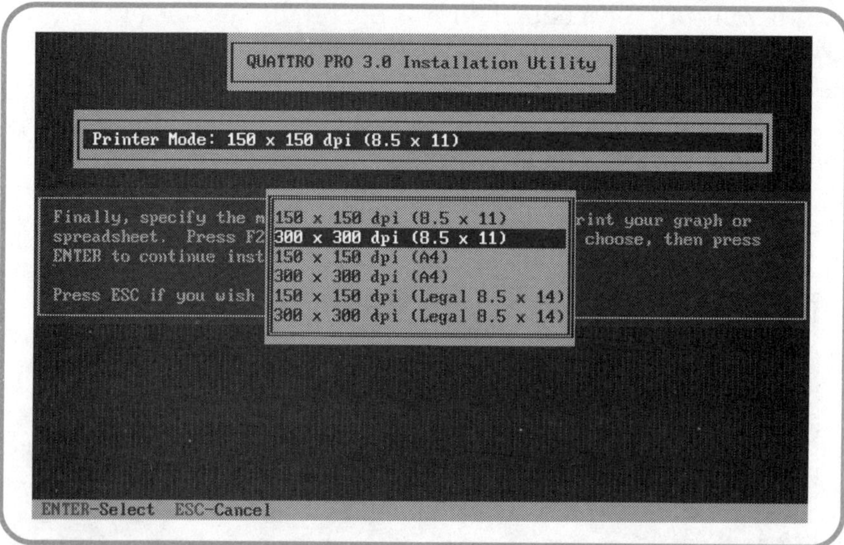

Figure A.12 Selecting a default printer mode and resolution.

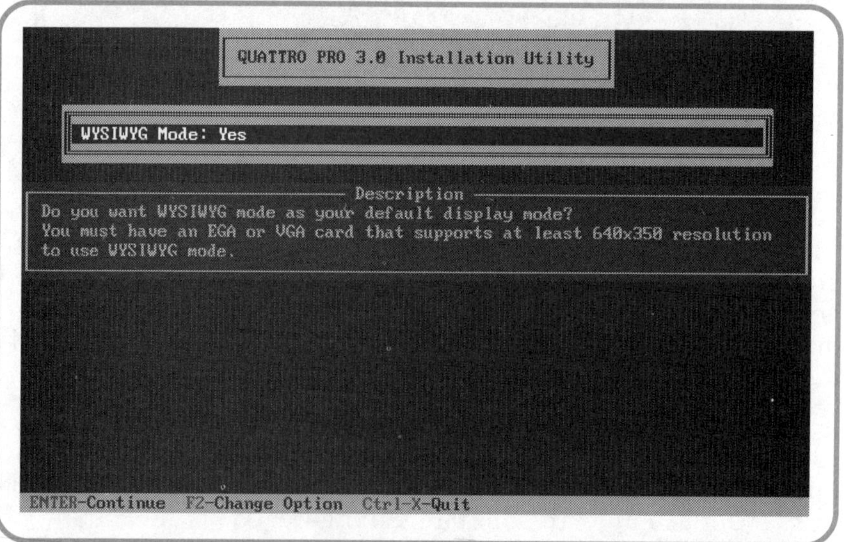

Figure A.13 Choosing WYSIWYG as the default display mode.

If you select Yes, Quattro Pro will use WYSIWYG as the default display mode each time you begin a new work session.

Installing Quattro Pro for use with Microsoft Windows 3.0

Quattro Pro next asks if you wish to install Quattro Pro to work with Microsoft Windows 3.0. If you own a copy of Windows 3.0, select Yes. Quattro Pro prompts you for two additional pieces of information: Is this a first-time Installation and What is Your Windows Path. After supplying this information, press Enter to continue.

The next time you load Windows, Windows installs a special Quattro Pro icon. To load Quattro Pro into your PC, double click on the Quattro Pro icon with your mouse.

Choosing A Character Set

The last prompt in Part II of the installation process asks you to choose the character set used by Quattro Pro. A character set tells Quattro Pro how to display special characters with its Bitstream fonts. The choices on this menu are Standard U.S. and Standard European. The default setting is Standard U.S.

If you want to display any special characters (mathematic symbols, graphics symbols) or diacritical marks (accent marks above letters) that are part of an international character set, press F2, choose Standard European, and press Enter. When you are finished, press Enter to continue.

Part III: Installing the Font Library

In Part III of the installation process you install the Quattro Pro screen font library. You can install up to 150 screen fonts during this part of the installation.

It normally takes Quattro Pro anywhere from 20 seconds to 1 minute to build a single screen font. If your machine has an 8086 processor chip (an IBM XT-class machine) Quattro Pro requires up to 2 hours to install the entire set. If your machine has an 80386 processor chip (a 386-class machine) this entire operation takes only 10 minutes!

Each installed font takes up from 2K to 6K of storage space on your hard disk drive. Larger font files require more space, from 6K to 12K. To install all 150 fonts (the Swiss/Dutch/Courier option) Quattro Pro requires about 825K.

You should install the entire font library. If you choose to install a partial set of fonts, however, be aware that Quattro Pro needs to build fonts during certain work session operations. During these times, you must wait as Quattro Pro builds (installs) the needed font. In an upcoming section you learn how to reinstall your font library so that you no longer have to wait during your work sessions.

Completing the Installation

When the installation utility successfully installs Quattro Pro, the screen shown in Figure A.14 is displayed. Press Enter to leave the Installation utility, or reboot your machine to place all installation settings into effect.

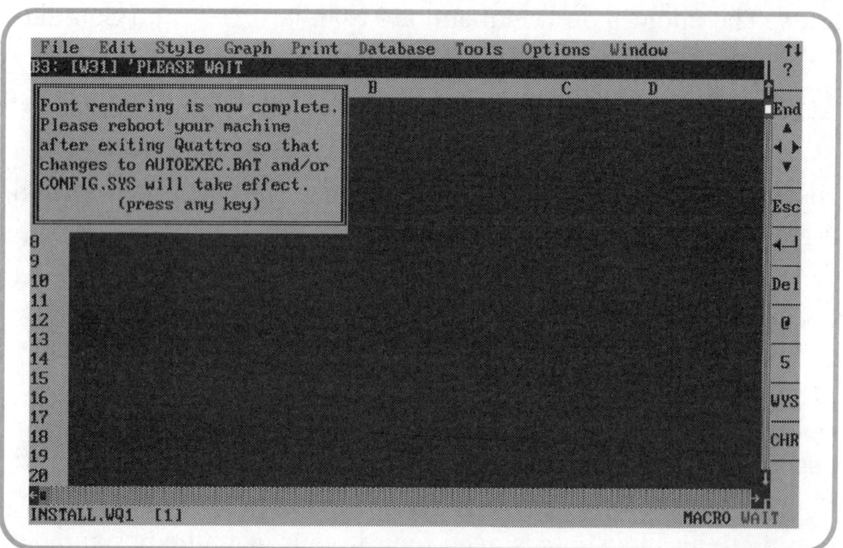

Figure A.14 The Font Rendering Is Now Complete screen.

If Quattro Pro fails to transfer all of its files, you must begin the process again. Program installation can fail for a number of reasons. The most common reason for failure is because your hard disk drive is full. Make sure that you have 4M of space on your hard disk before attempting to install Quattro Pro.

Upgrading to Version 3.0 from a Previous Version of Quattro Pro

Upgrading from Version 1.0 or 2.0 to Quattro Pro Version 3.0 is simple, but requires caution and forethought on your part.

The Version 3.0 Installation Facility does not automatically upgrade your Version 1.0 or Version 2.0 files. The only "old version" files that you may use with Version 3.0 are the spreadsheet files (.WK*), the workspace files (.WSP), the clip art files (.CLP), and the custom menu tree files (.MU). Copy these files to another directory (outside of the \QPRO directory) before you install Version 3.0.

The following step-by-step procedure shows you how to prepare a hard disk drive for Version 3.0 installation. It is assumed that you have two Quattro Pro directories: \QPRO, where the files from previous versions reside, and \QPRO\FONTS, the subdirectory where all previous versions of the font files reside.

> **Caution:** Be sure that you have copied all of the files you wish to keep before you perform the following steps. You will be deleting many Quattro Pro files from at least two directories on your hard disk drive.

1. At the DOS command prompt, type CD\QPRO\FONTS and press Enter to log onto the FONTS subdirectory.
2. Type DEL *.* and press Enter to delete all Version 1.0 or Version 2.0 font files from the FONTS subdirectory.
3. Type CD\QPRO and press Enter to log onto the QPRO directory.
4. Type DEL *.* and press Enter to delete all Version 1.0 or Version 2.0 program files from the QPRO directory.

You must remove all Version 1.0 or Version 2.0 program files and font files from your hard disk drive prior to installing Version 3.0. Don't mix program and font files from the versions, because you may get unpredictable results during your work sessions.

Adding Screen Fonts after Quattro Pro is Installed

Bitstream fonts do not come prebuilt when you purchase Quattro Pro. To use a font Quattro Pro must create a bit-map file for that font. A bit-map file stores data about a font's typeface, style, and point size for your screen or printer.

A bit-map font file can be built in three ways: during program installation, during a work session, and by using the INSTALL.WQ1 macro that arrives with your Quattro Pro package. This section of Appendix A contains information about adding fonts to your screen font library using the INSTALL.WQ1 macro.

When you install the program, Quattro Pro offers five choices for creating Bitstream fonts:

Choice	Fonts installed	Storage Required
None	None	None
Limited	6 Swiss	38K
Swiss	30 Swiss	162K
Swiss & Dutch	30 Swiss and 30 Dutch	325K
Swiss, Dutch Courier, Swiss and 30 Dutch, Dutch italics	30 Swiss, 30 Courier, 30 Swiss Italic, 30 Dutch Italic	825K

During installation, the decision you make about building the initial Bitstream font library has an impact on your Quattro Pro work sessions. Quattro Pro can display and print only fonts that have been built. If you select the Limited option, Quattro Pro installs only six Swiss fonts. The Limited option installs the smallest amount of fonts. This means that Quattro Pro will need to build others during a work session.

If you choose the fourth option, however, Quattro Pro builds bit-map files for all 150 screen fonts.

Building Bitstream Fonts With the INSTALL.WQ1 Spreadsheet

During program installation, Quattro Pro copies a spreadsheet file named INSTALL.WQ1 into the /QPRO directory. Once retrieved into Quattro Pro, the macro displays a startup menu. Press Enter once and Quattro Pro displays a second menu that lists all of the options.

To use INSTALL.WQ1, do the following:

1. Load Quattro Pro into your PC.
2. Select /**F**ile **R**etrieve (Quattro Pro displays the filename prompt box.)
3. Highlight INSTALL.WQ1 and press Enter to retrieve the spreadsheet. (Quattro Pro displays a brief message about postinstallation font-building.)
4. Press Enter to display the list of available font libraries (see Figure A.15).

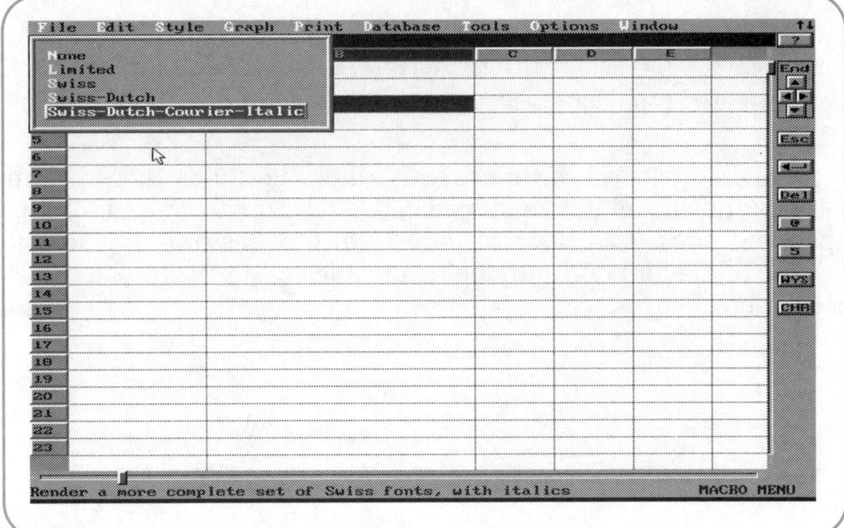

Figure A.15 Selecting a library choice on the font-building menu.

5. Highlight the name of the library you wish to install and press Enter.

Once Quattro Pro begins building the fonts, the program displays a status message at the top of your screen. This message describes information about the current font-building operation (see Figure A.16).

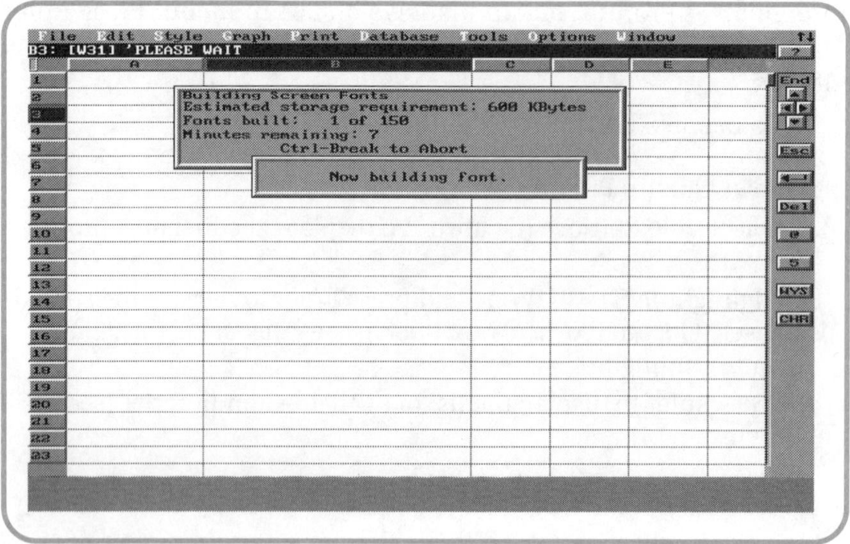

Figure A.16 The font-building status screen tells you how much time and disk space is needed to install the fonts you specified.

When Quattro Pro finishes installing the fonts, the program returns you to the active spreadsheet. To cancel a font-building operation, press Ctrl-Break. Quattro Pro finishes building a draft version of the font currently being installed and returns you to the active spreadsheet.

Appendix B

Setting Program Options

In This Appendix

- *Evaluating Quattro Pro's options*
- *Setting hardware, color, and international options*
- *Switching display modes*
- *Defining startup options*
- *Customizing the mouse palette*
- *Learning about other options*

What Are Your Options?

During program installation, Quattro Pro uses the data you supply to create a set of default settings that govern how the program works with your computer. There are two types of settings, *system* and *global*. Quattro Pro allows you to customize system and global settings (also called *options*) to suit your needs and preferences using the commands on the /**O**ptions menu.

When you turn your computer on at the start of each work session and load Quattro Pro, the *system options* exercise control over your screen, printer, RAM (random-access memory), and more. These options can be changed temporarily so they affect only the current work session, or they can be modified permanently so they're in effect every time you load Quattro Pro onto your system.

Global options determine the characteristics of the default spreadsheet that appears when you first load the program. In Quattro Pro, global options regulate such things as cell formats, spreadsheet protection, the recalculation mode, and more. You can override global options on an individual spreadsheet using the commands on the /**S**tyle menu.

After you make modifications to system or global options, select /**O**ptions **U**pdate to put these modifications into effect the next time you load Quattro Pro. The **U**pdate command saves *all* default option settings you can change, including those set on other menus (such as the /**P**rint **L**ayout and /**G**raph **C**ustomize Series menus).

Figure B.1 shows the /**O**ptions menu. Take some time and review the commands in the two sections of this menu. The commands in the top portion of the menu control system options, and the commands in the lower portion control global options. **U**pdate saves all updated options so they are in effect the next time you load Quattro Pro. This chapter reviews the options on the /**O**ptions submenus that you'll use most.

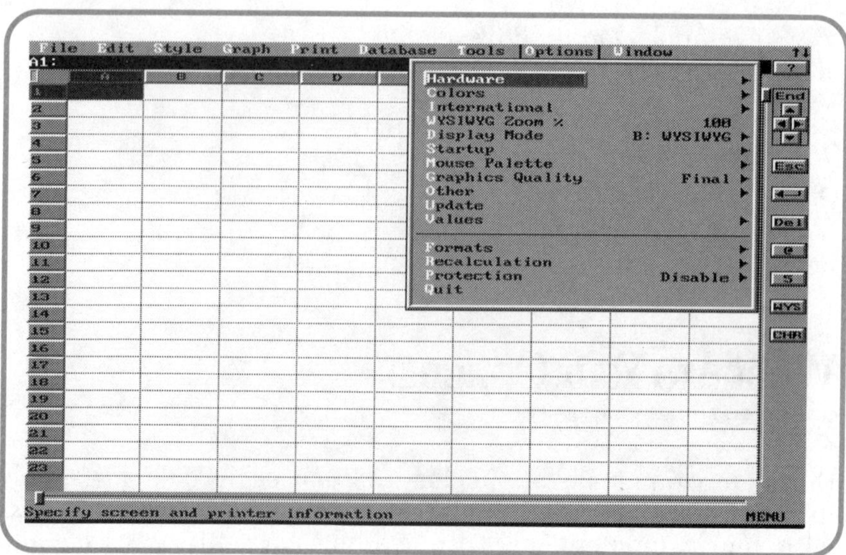

Figure B.1 Reviewing the commands located on the /Options menu.

Learning About Hardware Options

The /**O**ptions **H**ardware command controls the screen and printer definitions Quattro Pro uses to display and print your spreadsheet data. There are three commands and three informational fields on this menu, as follows:

Screen	Defines the screen display system.
Printers	Installs and reconfigures printers.
Mouse Button	Selects the mouse button you use to control click selection.
Normal Memory	Displays the number of available bytes in RAM. Also shows total bytes and the percent available.
EMS	Displays the number of available bytes in expanded memory. Also shows total bytes and the percent available.
Coprocessor	Indicates whether a math processor is installed.

The following two sections examine ways to modify the hardware options.

Modifying the Screen Display

When you install Quattro Pro, the program automatically detects your screen display type. To select a new screen display type, or to change the current display settings, select the /**O**ptions **H**ardware **S**creen command. There are four commands on the **S**creen menu, as shown in Figure B.2.

The ***S**creen Type* option allows you to select a specific screen display adapter to use with Quattro Pro. Autodetect, the default setting, forces Quattro Pro to evaluate your screen type on its own. It's usually a good idea to let Quattro Pro's default setting determine the screen type.

The ***R**esolution* option allows you to select different screen resolution settings. The higher the resolution setting, the sharper the picture. Again, it's a good idea to let Quattro Pro choose this feature for you, because it can automatically pick the highest resolution setting for your particular screen display system.

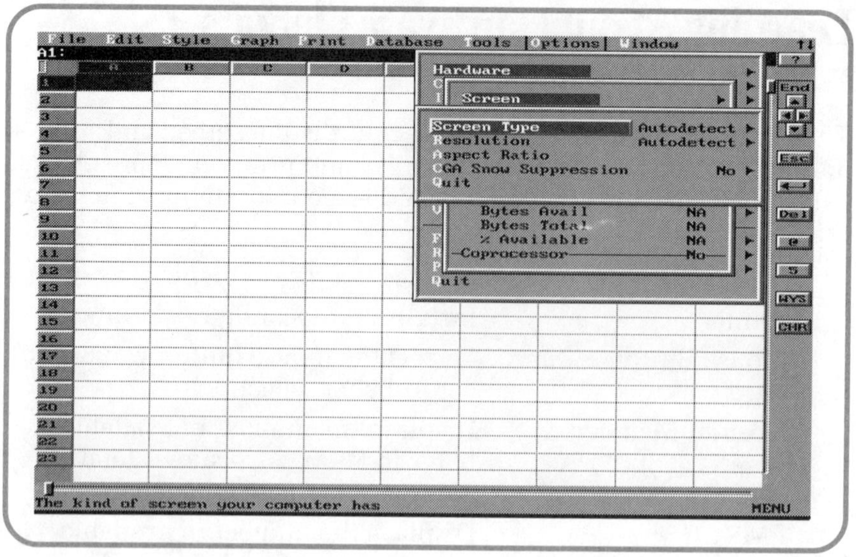

Figure B.2 Reviewing the commands located on the Screen menu.

> **Note:** You can't change the **S**creen Type or **R**esolution options when the /**O**ptions **D**isplay Mode command is set to **B**: WYSIWYG. Select a different display mode setting if supported by your system before attempting to modify either of these options.

The *Aspect Ratio* option sets the height-to-width display ratio for your screen, ensuring that your graphs are geometrically correct and do not look flat or oval. To adjust the aspect ratio, select /**O**ptions **H**ardware **S**creen Type **A**spect Ratio. Quattro Pro displays a circle; you can adjust its shape by pressing the ↑ and ↓ keys. Draw a circle that is round and then press Enter to accept that aspect ratio.

The *CGA Snow Suppression* option eliminates the screen flicker sometimes encountered with color graphics adapter (CGA) display systems. If this happens on your system, select /**O**ptions **H**ardware **S**creen Type **C**GA Snow Suppression **Y**es to eliminate the flicker.

Installing and Controlling Printers

When you install Quattro Pro, you supply information about your printer so that the program knows how to properly print spreadsheets and graphs. Select the /**O**ptions **H**ardware **P**rinters command if you need to change these printer settings, or if you want to add a second printer. There are seven commands on this menu, as shown in Figure B.3.

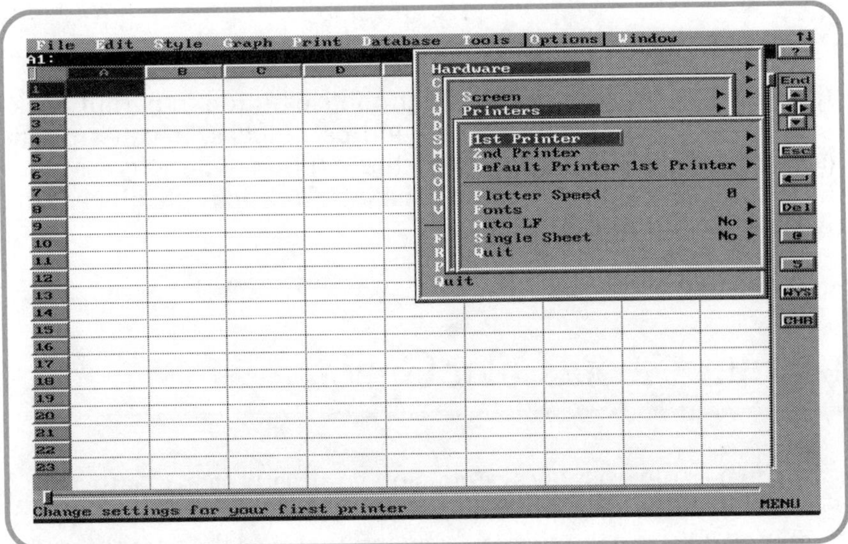

Figure B.3 Reviewing the commands located on the Printers menu.

The ***1****st Printer* and ***2****nd Printer* options enable you to install up to two printers to use with Quattro Pro. Chapter 4 has Quick Steps demonstrating the use of these two commands.

The ***D****efault Printer* option allows you to choose which of the two printers Quattro Pro will print to.

The ***P****lotter Speed* option allows you to choose the print speed for a color plotter. The fastest setting is 9, and the slowest is 1. The default setting, 0, tells Quattro Pro to print at the fastest speed supported by your plotter.

The ***F****onts* option allows you to tell Quattro Pro that your HP laser printer has font cartridges, and controls the scaling of all scaleable fonts.

The *Auto LF* option tells Quattro Pro whether or not to issue a carriage return at the end of each printed line. In most cases your printer controls this feature automatically.

The *Single Sheet* option allows you to feed individual sheets of paper into your printer, one at a time. By default, Quattro Pro assumes that you are using continuous feed paper. To change this default setting, select /**O**ptions **H**ardware **P**rinters **S**ingle Sheet **Y**es.

Switch Mouse Buttons

By default, Quattro Pro uses the left mouse button to permit click-selections of menus, commands, and cell blocks. If you are left-handed, you may wish to select the /**O**ptions **H**ardware **M**ouse Buttons **R**ight command and switch control of click-selections to the right mouse button.

Learning About Color Options

If you own a color display system, you've already seen Quattro Pro's wonderful color display. When you select the /**O**ptions **C**olors command, Quattro Pro displays a menu that lists the program areas where you can modify colors. There are seven commands on this menu, as shown in Figure B.4.

On the **C**olors menu, highlight the program area you wish to color, press Enter, and Quattro Pro displays a special coloring tool called the coloring palette (see Figure B.5). Notice the tiny rotating bar on the coloring palette. It sits atop the current color selection. To modify the current color selection, press the arrow keys and move the rotating bar until it is atop a different color combination. Press Enter once to select that color combination. Quattro Pro immediately redraws the screen display so that it shows the new color combinations.

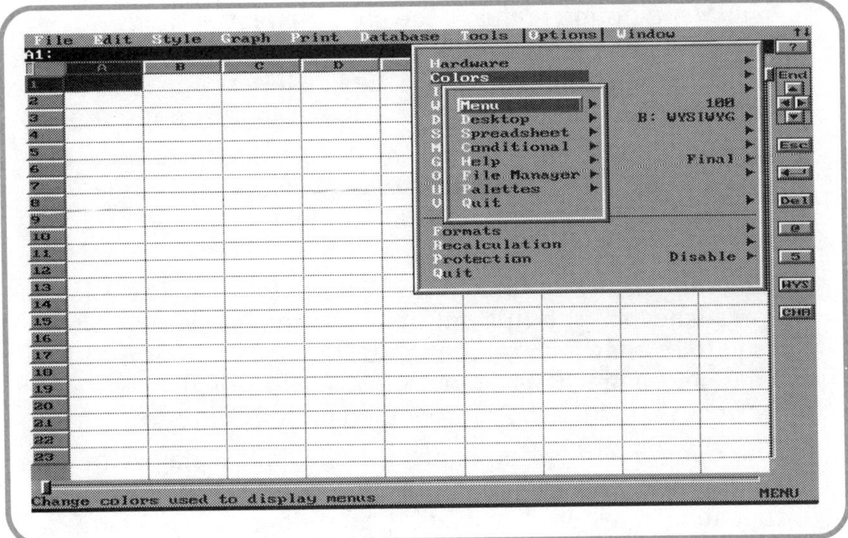

Figure B.4 Reviewing the commands located on the Colors menu.

313

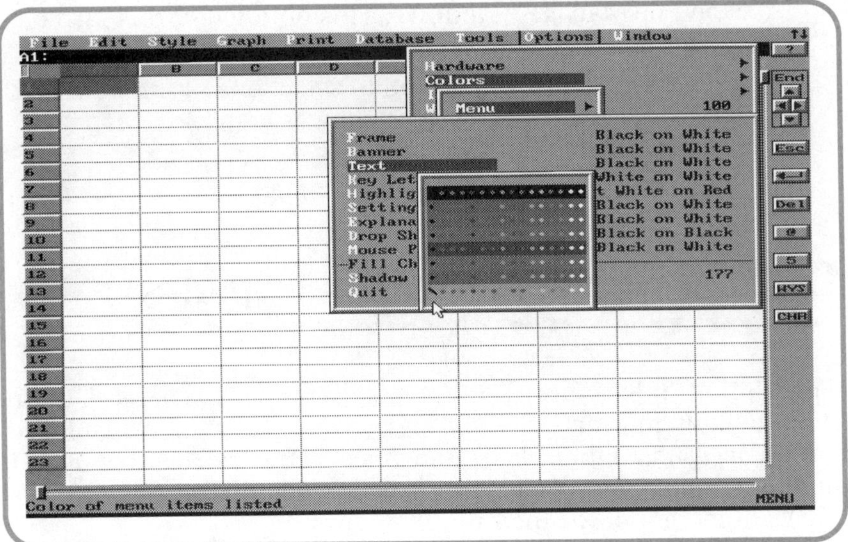

Figure B.5 You select color combinations using the coloring palette.

The ***Menu*** option controls the color display settings for Quattro Pro's pull-down menus. Use this option to change the colors of the menu frame, the key letters appearing in menu and command names, the menu text, and more.

The ***Desktop*** option controls the color display setting for the desktop area. Use this option to change the colors used to display error messages, the status line, the area behind a Quattro Pro spreadsheet, and so on.

The ***Spreadsheet*** option controls the color display setting for spreadsheets. With this option, you can change the color used to display data on the input line, labels, shading, drawn lines, and more. This command also controls the color settings that Quattro Pro uses to display WYSIWYG mode.

The ***Conditional*** option controls the color display setting for special numbers and formulas that you define on the menu that appears when you select the /**O**ptions **C**olors **C**onditional command.

The ***Help*** option controls the color display settings for the windows that appear when you press F1 for Quattro Pro help.

The ***File Manager*** option controls the color display setting for the File Manager windows. This option controls the color display of text, marked text, the inactive cursor, and more.

The ***Palettes*** option allows you to select one of three predefined coloring schemes. The choices are **C**olor, **M**onochrome, **B**lack & White, and **G**ray scale.

Learning About International Options

The /**O**ptions **I**nternational command allows you to change Quattro Pro's default international settings, which affect the display of currencies, punctuation, dates, and times. There are seven commands on this menu, as shown in Figure B.6. The default settings appear at the right margin of the menu in the figure.

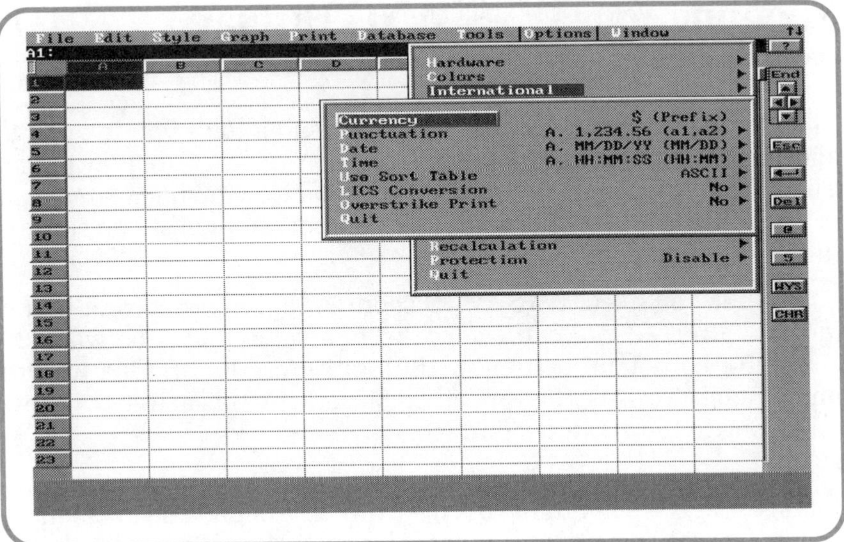

Figure B.6 Reviewing the commands located on the International menu.

The ***Currency*** option allows you to choose the symbol that Quattro Pro attaches to values formatted with the /**S**tyle **N**umeric Format **C**urrency command.

The ***Punctuation*** option allows you to select from among eight commonly accepted international punctuation formats.

The ***Date*** option sets the Long and Short international date formats Quattro Pro uses when you select the /**S**tyle **N**umeric Format **D**ate command.

The ***Time*** option sets the Long and Short international time formats Quattro Pro uses when you select the /**S**tyle **N**umeric Format **D**ate **T**ime command.

The ***Use Sort Table*** option determines how Quattro Pro sorts data with the /**D**atabase **S**ort command. The four options on this submenu are **A**SCII.SOR (the default), **I**NTL.SOR, **N**ORDAN.SOR, and **S**WEDFIN.SOR.

The ***LICS Conversion*** option converts Lotus International Character Set (LICS) characters into uppercase ASCII characters that can be used in Quattro Pro macros.

The ***Overstrike Print*** command allows you to print the accented characters used in languages such as French and German.

Zooming Your WYSIWYG Display

The /**O**ptions **W**YSIWYG Zoom % command allows you to enlarge and shrink a spreadsheet when you are in WYSIWYG display mode. The **W**YSIWYG Zoom % command is ideal for viewing a large area of a spreadsheet (one that normally can not be seen in one screen-full) in a single window.

When you select **W**YSIWYG Zoom % Quattro Pro prompts you for a *WYSIWYG Zoom percentage*. Enter a value that is between 25 and 200 (the default setting is 100) and press Enter. Quattro Pro immediately resizes the spreadsheet area in the active window according to the zoom percentage.

To enlarge the displayed spreadsheet area, enter a zoom percentage that is greater than 100; to shrink the displayed spreadsheet area enter a zoom percentage that is less than 100. Figure B.7 shows the appearance of a spreadsheet window when the zoom percentage is set to 200.

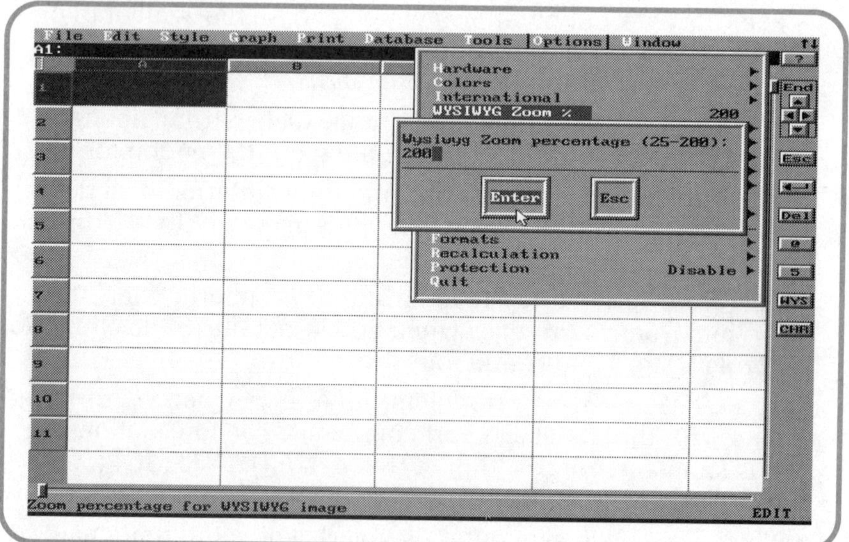

Figure B.7 Zooming a spreadsheet window to 200% enlarges column widths and row heights.

Learning About Display Mode Options

The /**O**ptions **D**isplay Mode command allows you to change the on-screen appearance of Quattro Pro. During program installation Quattro Pro asks if you wish to use WYSIWYG as the default display mode. If you choose No, Quattro Pro defaults to an 80x25 text mode display (the screen displays 80 characters from top to bottom, and 25 characters from left to right). Depending on your graphics card, you can also view Quattro Pro in one of several extended (condensed view) text modes.

If you choose Yes, Quattro Pro uses WYSIWYG as the default display mode. To use WYSIWYG you must have an EGA or VGA graphics display system. Of the two display modes, WYSIWYG is the preferable one because it displays all presentation-quality enhancements (such as shaded cells, custom fonts, and drawn lines) as you construct your spreadsheet applications. This is not possible from text or extended text mode.

When you select /**O**ptions **D**isplay Mode, Quattro Pro displays the menu shown in Figure B.8. The extended text modes are useful for showing more of a spreadsheet in one screenfull. The **F**: ATI VGA Wonder mode, for example, can show a screen that is 132 characters long by 44 characters wide.

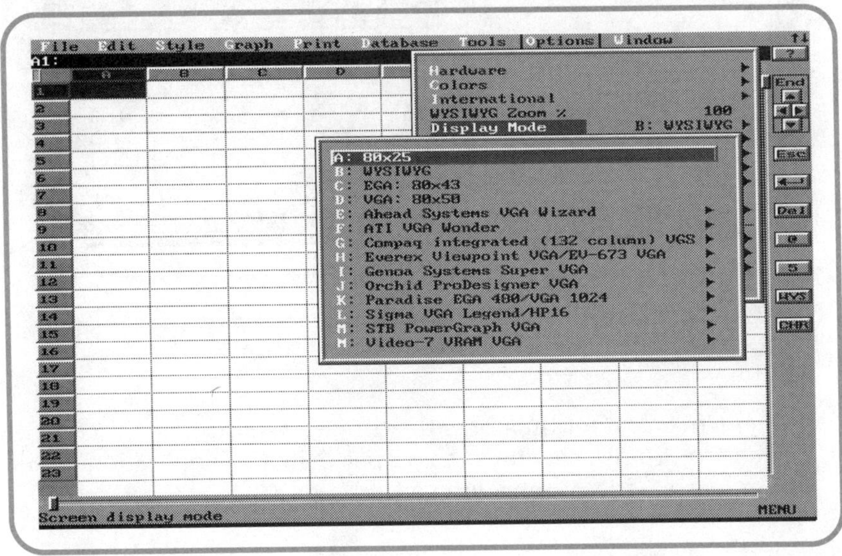

Figure B.8 Reviewing the options located on the Display Mode menu.

> **Tip:** Your screen will not appear like the one in Figure B.8 without the right graphics display card. For instance, if you own a Hercules monochrome card, you'll only see the **A**: 80x25 display mode option.

Learning About Startup Options

The **S**tartup command allows you to define the default startup settings Quattro Pro uses each time you load the program or open a new spreadsheet. Figure B.9 shows the six startup options that appear when you select the /**O**ptions **S**tartup command. The default settings appear at the right margin of the submenu.

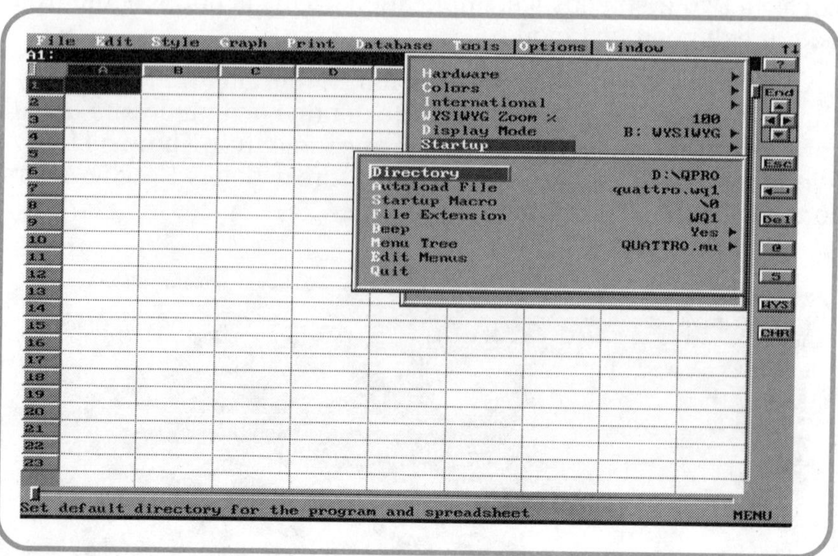

Figure B.9 Reviewing the commands located on the Startup menu.

The ***Directory*** option stores the directory path name that Quattro Pro uses each time you perform a file operation (such as saving or retrieving a file).

The *Autoload File* option tells Quattro Pro the name of a spreadsheet file to open each time you load the program onto your PC.

The ***S****tartup Macro* option tells Quattro Pro the name of a macro to execute each time you open a spreadsheet.

The ***F****ile Extension* option tells Quattro Pro the three-letter extension to add to spreadsheet file names.

The ***B****eep* option turns Quattro Pro's beep error tone on and off.

The ***M****enu Tree* option allows you to load one of Quattro Pro's three compatible menu trees. Your options are **Q**1, **Q**UATTRO (the default), and **1**23. For users with 1-2-3 experience, the quickest way to use Quattro Pro is to select the 1-2-3 menu tree.

Learning About Mouse Palette Options

The mouse palette is the vertical bar located at the right side of the Quattro Pro screen display. The icons on the mouse palette give mouse users the ability to perform many common spreadsheet tasks quickly with a mouse instead of the keyboard.

You can customize the functions of the lower seven buttons on the palette using the /**O**ptions **M**ouse Palette command. Once selected, a second menu appears (see Figure B.10). Select the **T**ext option to add up to three letters of text to a button. Select the **M**acro option to assign Quattro Pro macro commands like {ESC}, {BEEP}, {BREAK}, and {DEL} to the button. Once you click a button with a mouse, Quattro Pro performs the action defined by the macro you assigned to the button.

> **Tip:** By default, Quattro Pro assigns special macros to buttons 6 and 7 on the mouse palette. The WYS button invokes a macro that switches you to WYSIWYG display mode, and the CHR button invokes a macro that switches you to the 80x25 text display mode. Even though Quattro Pro preprograms mouse palette buttons 6 and 7 you can reassign their function at any time.

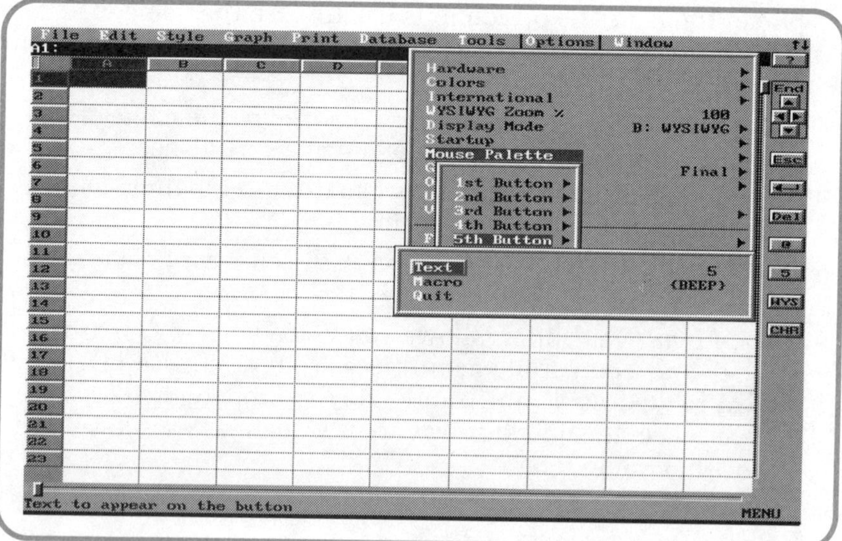

Figure B.10 Reviewing the Mouse Palette button menu options.

Learning About Other Options

The /**O**ptions **O**ther command gives you access to options which will become more important to you as you use Quattro Pro more. Figure B.11 shows the five options available on the **O**ther menu.

The *Undo* option turns Quattro Pro's Undo feature on and off. The Undo feature reverses many Quattro Pro operations, returning your spreadsheet to its appearance before the last command execution.

The *Macro* option enables you to specify the extent to which Quattro Pro redraws the screen display while executing a macro. By suppressing macro redraw, you speed up macro execution. The choices on this submenu are **B**oth, **P**anel, **W**indow, and **N**one.

The *Expanded Memory* option determines which Quattro Pro program elements reside in expanded memory when it is available. The options are **B**oth, **S**preadsheet Data, **F**ormat, and **N**one.

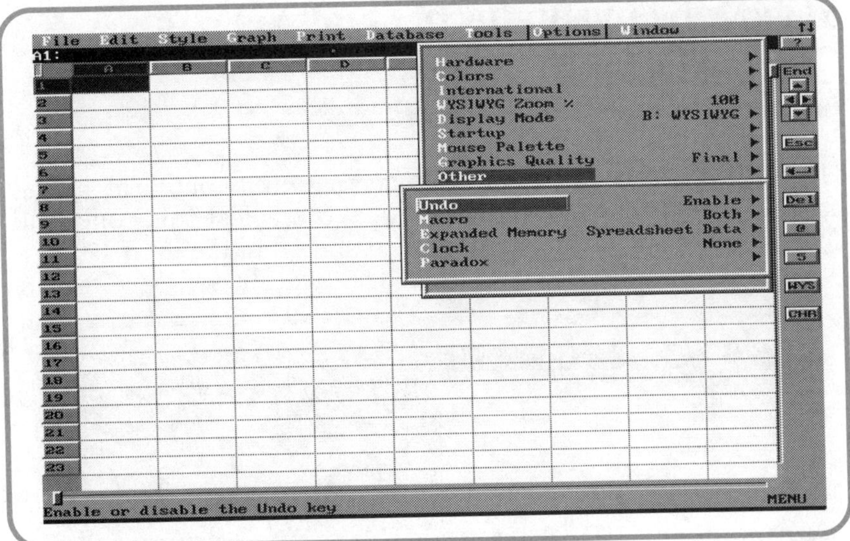

Figure B.11 Reviewing the options located on the Other menu.

The ***Clock Display*** option shows the current date and time on the status line in three formats: **S**tandard, **I**nternational, and **N**one.

The ***Paradox*** option allows you to set options for using Paradox files with a local area network (LAN).

Updating Option Settings

Always remember to save modified system settings as the new default settings for future work sessions. If you don't save your option selections, Quattro Pro reverts back to the old default settings. To update the option settings, select /**O**ptions **U**pdate.

Reviewing the Status of Quattro Pro's Current Default Settings

The /**O**ptions **V**alues command displays a noninteractive menu that lists all current default settings. When you select this command, Quattro Pro displays the status screen shown in Figure B.12.

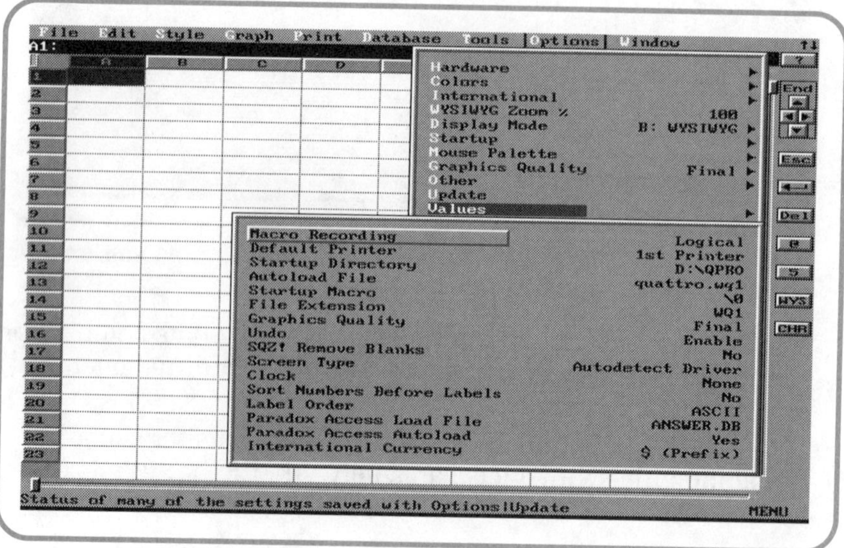

Figure B.12 Reviewing the status of a Quattro Pro work session.

Although you may not modify the settings on this menu, it remains a convenient tool for checking on the status of your Quattro Pro work environment. When you select the /**O**ptions **U**pdate command, Quattro Pro updates the information displayed on the **V**alues menu.

Learning About Global Options

The last three commands on the /**O**ptions menu control global spreadsheet options such as numeric formats, label alignment, and column width. You also control spreadsheet recalculation and protection with these commands. Refer to Chapter 7 for examples of how to use the following commands.

Use the ***F**ormats* option to choose the default numeric format for values, dates and times; to control global label alignment; to determine whether a spreadsheet displays zero values; and to set the default global column width.

Use the ***R**ecalculation* option to specify the recalculation mode, to control the order in which Quattro Pro calculates formulas, to specify the number of times that Quattro Pro evaluates formulas during recalculation, and to discover the location of formulas that contain circular references.

Use the ***P**rotection* option to enable global spreadsheet protection. In this mode, Quattro Pro prevents the user from changing or deleting the contents of cells that have not been unprotected with the /**S**tyle **P**rotection **U**nprotect command.

What You've Learned

- Quattro Pro gives you great latitude in determining how the program behaves during a work session. You can fine-tune the program's appearance and performance by modifying *system options* and *global options*.
- The **H**ardware option makes it simple to add a new printer or change the screen display definition, or switch mouse buttons.
- The **C**olors option allows you to create custom looks for your copy of Quattro Pro.
- The **I**nternational options come in handy if you wish to display a foreign currency, or use a different punctuation style in your spreadsheet applications.
- The WYSIWYG Zoom % command offers you complete flexibility for organizing the on-screen display of your spreadsheets.
- Quattro Pro displays spreadsheets in several different *display modes* that take full advantage of today's powerful graphics display systems.
- You always know the status of your Quattro Pro environment with the **V**alues command.

Index

3-D graphs, 185-187

A

Absolute (F4) function key, 123
absolute cell address references, 121-123
active spreadsheet, 241
active window, 241
  displaying number of spreadsheets, 258
aligning data in cells, 146-148
alphanumeric keypad, 13
Alt key, 13
Alt-F5 (Undo) key, 57
anchoring cells, 71
annotating graphs, 200-204
area graphs, 183
arguments, 110
arithmetic
  formulas, 110
  operators, 110-111, 115
ASCII rule, 279
AUTOEXEC.BAT file, 296

B

background recalculation, 116
bar graphs, 180-181
block names, 76-80
blocks of values, 151-152
borders, 12
bullets, 171-173

C

cancelling
  commands, 22
  menus, 22
cell address references, 123
  absolute, 121-123
  mixed, 121-123
  relative, 121-123
cell blocks, 63
  coordinates, 64-66
  copying, 72-74
  deleting, 76
    names, 81
  highlighting, 66-68

moving, 74-76
naming, 76-80
cell contents
copying, 51-54
erasing, 54, 76
moving, 51
Cell macro commands, 235
cell selector, 12
cells
aligning data, 146-148
anchoring, 71
editing, 57-58
entering
formulas, 40-45
labels, 34-36
values, 37-39
formatting data display, 148-150
protecting, 153
selector, 3
shading, 160, 165-166
unprotecting, 153-154
child menus, 21
Choices (F3) key, 80
CHR button, 19
circular references, 124-127
clicking, 18
clip art, 203-204
closing spreadsheet files, 247-248
Colors menu, 312-314
columns, 32, 241
deleting, 56-57
exposing when hidden, 159
graphs, 184-185
hiding, 159-160
in spreadsheets, 154
inserting into, 54-56
setting width, 154-155
single, 154-155
CONFIG.SYS file, 296
configuring Quattro Pro, 85
context-sensitive help, 28
Control Pane, 249-250
copying
cell blocks, 72-74
cell contents, 51-54
formulas, 121-123
@function commands, 119-121
program files, 290-293
criteria table, 281-282, 285
Ctrl key, 13
custom format settings, 84-85

D

data
aligning in cells, 146-148
entering into databases, 268-272
summarizing from several locations on spreadsheet, 253
data series, 177-178, 195-197
database area, 266
/Database Data Entry command, 265
/Database Query command, 265, 280-282
/Database Query Delete command, 286
/Database Query Extract command, 288
/Database Query Locate command, 285
/Database Query menu, 273
/Database Query Unique command, 288
/Database Restrict Input command, 265-269, 272
/Database Sort command, 285
/Database Sort Sort Rules command, 279
database statistical @function commands, 135-136
databases, 5-6, 263-265
automating data entry using macros, 272
copying records meeting specified criteria, 288

creating, 265
deleting records, 286-288
designing, 266-267
entering data into, 268-272
field names row, 266
querying, 280
returning to original order, 278
searching, 282-285
sorting, 273
modifying Quattro Pro's sort rules, 279
using sort keys, 274-276
/Database Sort Reset command, 279
date @function commands, 135
DATE mode shortcut key, 47
debugging macros, 232-234
default printer settings, 84-85
Del key, 54
deleting
cell blocks, 76
cell contents, 54, 76
columns, 56-57
graph names, 205
gridlines from spreadsheets, 164
hard page breaks, 171
lines in spreadsheets, 163
macros, 232
names, 81
records from databases, 272-273, 286-288
rows, 56-57
titles from graphs, 193
DESQview, 248
directories, 239
/QPRO, 239, 305
creating, 239
managing spreadsheet files, 239-241
root, 239
structure, 239
displaying graph names, 205
documenting macros, 223-224
DOS
DOS Shell, 25
returning to, 24-27
double-clicking, 18
dragging, 18
drawing lines, 160-163

E

/Edit Autosave Edits command, 205
/Edit Copy command, 51-54, 72-74
/Edit Delete Rows command, 272
/Edit Erase Block command, 54, 76, 272
/Edit menu
Autosave Edits command, 205
Copy command, 51-54, 72-74
Delete command, 56-57
Erase Block command, 54, 76
Insert command, 54-56
Move command, 51, 74-76
Name command, 76-80
Name Delete command, 81, 232
Name Label Right command, 214-215
Name Reset command, 81
EDIT mode, 284
/Edit Move command, 51-54, 74-76
/Edit Names command, 76-80
/Edit Names Create command, 281-282
/Edit Names Delete command, 81, 232
/Edit Names Label Right command, 214-215
/Edit Names Reset command, 81
editing
cells, 57-58
fonts , 167-171
formulas, 55-56
records, 284
End key, 68-71

entering dates into spreadsheets, 46-48
formulas into cells, 40-45
@function commands, 117-119
labels, 33-36
numbers into spreadsheets, 39
time, 46-47
values into cells, 37-39
ERR formula error, 124
error-trap, 132
executing macros, 220-223
exiting Quattro Pro, 24-25

F

field names row, 266
fields, 266, 278
/File Close command, 49
/File Close All command, 49
/File Destination command, 92-93
/File Directory command, 49, 248
/File Erase command, 49, 248
File macro commands, 235
file management, 48-49, 238-241, 248-252, 258
File Manager, 248-252
/File menu, 48, 237-238, 241-242
Close All command, 49
Close command, 49
Destination command, 92-93
Directory command, 49
Erase command, 49
New command, 48
Open command, 48
Retrieve command, 48
Save command, 48-49
Save All command, 49
Save As, 48
/File Cancel command, 242
/File Close All command, 49
/File Close command, 49, 247
/File New command, 48, 238
/File Open command, 48, 260, 244
/File Retrieve command, 48, 238, 244
/File Save All command, 49
/File Save As command, 48, 245
/File Save command, 48-49, 238
/File Utilities File Manager command, 248
/File Workspace Restore command, 259
/File Workspace Save command, 259
filenames, 32
files, 32, 237
AUTOEXEC.BAT, 296
CONFIG.SYS, 296
naming, 240
Paradox, 321
.PRN, 92-93
Q.EXE, 9
spreadsheet, 238-248
text, 92-93
workspace, 259
financial @function commands, 132-134
fonts, 166-171
footers, 96
formatting
blocks of values, 151-152
cell data display, 148-150
formulas, 37-40, 110
arithmetic, 110
building while in POINT mode, 71
calculating, 114-116
copying, 121-123
editing, 55-56
entering into cells, 40-45
@functions, 110
linking, 253-257
logical, 110-113
nesting parentheses, 115-116
solving in reverse, 136-138

spreadsheets, 123
string, 111-112
text, 110-112
@function commands, 117, 127
arguments, 117
command name, 117
copying, 119-121
database statistical, 135-136
date, 135
entering, 117-119
financial, 132-134
logical, 132
mathematical, 128
miscellaneous, 131
statistical, 128-129
string, 130
time, 135
function key-equivalent macros, 219
function keys, 15
Absolute (F4), 123
Choices (F3), 80
Pane (F6), 60
@functions, 110

G

global format settings, 142-143
global options, *see* global settings
global settings, 307
/Graph Annotate command, 200-204
/Graph Customize Series command, 177, 195-197
/Graph Customize Series Fill Pattern command, 196-197
/Graph Customize Series Reset Graph Quit Quit command, 191
/Graph Fast Graph command, 187-191
/Graph Group command, 191
/Graph Insert command, 207-208
/Graph Legends command, 193-195
/Graph Y-Axis command, 193
/Graph menu, 176
Annotate command, 200-204
Customize Series command, 177, 195-197
Customize Series Fill Pattern command, 196-197
Customize Series Reset Graph Quit Quit command, 191
Fast Graph command, 187-190
Group command, 191
Insert command, 207-208
Legends command, 193-195
Name Create command, 205
Name Display command, 205
Name Erase command, 205
Name Slide command, 206-207
Overall command, 177, 199-200
Series command, 176
Text 1st Line command, 193
Text 2nd Line command, 193
Text command, 193
Type command, 176
X-Axis command, 177, 197-198
X-Axis Title command, 193
Y-Axis command, 177, 191, 197-198
Y-Axis Title command, 193
graphs, 4, 176-179
3-D, 185, 187
adding
boxed text, 201
legends, 193
primary titles, 193
titles, 193
annotating, 200-204
area, 183
bar, 180-181
column, 184-185
creating, 187-192
names, 205
customizing, 199-200
axes, 197-198

data series, 177-197
displaying, 178-179
erasing
names, 205
titles, 193
high-low (open-close), 186
line, 179-180
names, 204-205
pie, 182
placing into spreadsheets, 207-208
printing, 209-211
rotated bar, 183-184
scaling axes, 198-199
secondary titles, 193
slide shows, 206-207
stacked bar, 180-182
text, 185-186
x-axis, 177-178
XY, 180-181
y-axis, 177-178
gridlines, 164

H

hard page breaks, 98, 171
hardware requirements, 178-179, 290, 309-310
headers, 96
help, 27-28
Hercules monochrome card, 318
hiding
columns in spreadsheets, 159-160
labels, 152
high-low (open-close) graphs, 186
highlighting cell blocks, 66-68
home position, 69
horizontal (landscape) orientation, 102-103

I

importing clip art, 203-204
input line, 12
INSTALL.WQ1 spreadsheet file, 305
Installation Utility, 9, 291-297, 302
installing
printers, 311-312
Quattro Pro, 289-302
instant macro name, 214-215
Interactive macro commands, 235
International menu, 315

K

keyboard macro commands, 215-218, 235
keys
Alt, 13
Alt-F5 (Undo), 57
Ctrl, 13
Del, 54
End, 68-71
slash (/), 13
sort, 274
Undo, 274
window keys in File Manager, 251
keywords, 27

L

labels, 32-33
entering into cells, 34-36
hiding, 152
prefixes, 35-37
landscape (horizontal) orientation, 102-103
legends, 193
line graphs, 179-180
lines, 160-163
Link options menu, 257-258
linking formulas, 253-257
literal strings, 111-112
loading spreadsheets linked by formulas, 257
local area network (LAN), 321
logical

@function commands, 132
formulas, 110-113
operators, 112-115

M

macro buttons, 19
macro command language, 234-235
macro library spreadsheets, 229-231
macros, 6-7, 213-216
automating data entry into databases, 272
creating, 217
debugging, 232-234
deleting, 232
documenting, 223-224
executing, 220-223
function key-equivalent, 219
keyboard equivalent, 215-218
menu-equivalent, 216
pasting, 225-228
recording programs, 224-228
replaying, 229
storing in libraries, 229
writing, 217-220
manual recalculation, 116
mathematical @function commands, 128
menu-equivalent macro, 216
menus, 19
cancelling, 22
child menu, 21
/Database, 265
/File, 237-238, 241-242
/Graph, 176
miscellaneous @function commands, 131
/Option, 142-143
/Options, 289-290, 307, 322-323
/Options Startup Directory, 248
/Print, 83
/Print Layout Update, 96
/Query, 282
/Screen commands, 309-310
/Sort, 275, 278
/Style, 143-146, 308
submenus, 21
/Window, 237, 258
mixed cell address references, 121-123
modes
EDIT, 284
POINT, 70
selecting WYSIWYG as default display mode, 299-300
modifying global format settings, 142-143
monitors, 294
mouse, 17-18
clicking, 18
double-clicking, 18
dragging, 18
palette, 18-19, 319-320
pointing, 18
releasing, 18
switching mouse button controls, 312
moving
annotated text, 202-204
cell blocks, 74-76
cell contents, 51
multiple sort keys, 275

N

naming cell blocks, 76-80
naming files, 240
nesting parentheses, 115-116
networks, 295
New command, 48
number (#) field, 278
numbers, entering into spreadsheets, 39
numeric keypad, 14

O

opening spreadsheet files, 246
operating system software, 290
operators, 110-115
/Options Align Labels command, 143
/Options Colors command, 312
/Options Display Mode command, 60, 310, 317-318
/Options Display Mode A: 80x25 command, 258
/Options Display Mode B: WYSIWYG command, 253
/Options Formats command, 142
/Options Global Width command, 143
/Options Hardware command, 309
/Options Hardware Mouse Buttons Right command, 312
/Options Hardware Printers command, 311-312
/Options Hardware Screen command., 309
/Options Hide Zeros command, 143
/Options International command, 314
/Options menu, 307, 322-323
/Options Mouse Palette command, 319
/Options Numeric Format command, 142
/Options Other command, 320
/Options Protection Enable command, 153
/Options Startup command, 318
/Options Startup Directory menu, 248
/Options Startup Menu Tree 123 command, 297
/Options Update command, 248, 279, 308, 321-322
/Options Values command, 322
/Options WYSIWYG Zoom % command, 254, 316
order of precedence, 114-115
orientation, 102-103
Other menu, 320-321
output block, 288

P

page breaks, 98
Pane (F6) function key, 60
Paradox files, 321
password protection, 243-245
pasting macros, 225-228
path names, 240
pie graphs, 182
POINT modes, 70
pointing, 18, 70-71
portrait (vertical) orientation, 102-103
prefixes, 35-37
primary spreadsheet, 253-254
primary titles, 193
/Print menu, 83
  Block command, 89, 208
  Copies command, 106
  Destination command, 90-92, 208
  Graph Print command, 209-211
  Graphics Printer, 106
  Graphics Printer command, 208
  Layout Dimensions command, 101-102
  Layout Margins command, 100-101
  Layout Page Break command, 98
  Layout Percent Scaling command, 98-99, 108
  Layout Reset command, 105
  Layout Values command, 105
  Print to Fit command, 108
  Spreadsheet command, 94
  Spreadsheet Print command, 99
/Print Print to Fit command, 99, 108
/Print Spreadsheet command, 94
/Print Spreadsheet Print command, 99

printers
  adding more than one, 86-88
  configuring Quattro Pro to your printer, 85
  defaults, 85
  installing, 311-312
  selecting, 298-299
  setup strings, 103-104
  text, 92
printing
  custom format settings, 84-85
  default printer settings, 84-85
  deleting hard page breaks, 171
  footers, 96
  graphs, 208-211
  headers, 96
  modifying, 100-101, 106
  print blocks, 88
  screen dumps, 84
  selecting destination, 90-93
  setting page layout, 96
  soft page breaks, 98
  spreadsheets, 83-98, 100-108, 171, 208
  to .PRN file, 98
  to screen, 94
  to text file, 92-93
  to text printer, 92
  using setup strings, 103-104
  viewing with Screen Preview tool, 94
.PRN file, 92-93
Program Flow macro commands, 235
protecting, 153
pull-down menus, 11, 21

Q

Q.EXE file, 9
/QPRO directory, 239, 305
/Query Block command, 282
/Query Criteria Table command, 283
Quattro Pro
  databases, 265-279
  exiting, 24-25
  File Manager, 248-251
  installing, 289-290
    choosing character set, 301
    completing, 302
    copying program files, 290-293
    for use with Microsoft Windows 3.0, 301
    on network, 295
    screen font library, 301-302
    selecting computer equipment, 294-299
  operating material, 290
  screen, 11
  starting, 9-10
  upgrading, 303
query operation, 280

R

random-access memory (RAM), 238
read-from-disk operation, 238
recalculating formulas, 116
recording macro programs, 224-228
records, 266
  copying, meeting specified criteria, 288
  deleting from databases, 272-273, 286-288
  searching, 282-285
  sorting, 273-276
relative cell address references, 121-123
relative reference, 121-123
removing titles from graphs, 193
replaying macros, 229
resize box button, 19
returning to DOS, 24-27
root directory, 239
rotated bar graphs, 183-184

rows, 32, 241
  deleting, 56-57
  inserting, 54-56
  inserting into spreadsheets, 54-56

S

saving
  files, 22-24, 242-243
  password protection, 243-245
  spreadsheets, 49-50
scaling
  graph axes, 198-199
  spreadsheets, 99
screen dumps, 84
screen fonts, 304
Screen menu, 309-310
/Screen Preview Color command, 95
/Screen Preview Guide command, 95
/Screen Preview Help command, 95
/Screen Preview menu, 94
  Color command, 95
  Help command, 95
  Next command, 95
  Previous command, 95
  Quit command, 95
  Ruler command, 95
  Unzoom command, 95
/Screen Preview Next command, 95
/Screen Preview Previous command, 95
/Screen Preview Quit command, 95
/Screen Preview Ruler command, 95
Screen Preview tool, 94
/Screen Preview Unzoom command, 95
screens
  changing display mode, 60-61
  input line, 12
  modifying display, 60-61, 309-310
  mouse palette, 13
  pull-down menu bar, 11
  Quattro Pro, 11
  split, 59-60
  spreadsheets, 12
  status line, 12
scroll bars, 12
searching
  databases, 282-285
  records, 282-285
secondary titles, 193
settings, 307
setup strings, 103-104
shading cells, 160, 165-166
shortcut keys
  DATE mode, 47
shortcut-key combinations, 21, 47
single columns, 154-155
slash (/) key, 13
slide shows, 206-207
soft page breaks, 98
sort key, 274
Sort menu, 275, 278-279
sorting
  databases, 273-279
split-screens, 59-60
spreadsheet files, 238-248
  INSTALL.WQ1, 305
spreadsheets, 32, 141-143, 241
  adding
    bullets, 171-173
    headers/footers, 97
  aligning data in cells, 146-148
  applications, 2-3
  borders, 12
  cell selectors, 3, 12
  cells, 2
    protecting, 153
    shading, 165-166
    unprotecting, 153-154
  circular references, 124-127
  column widths
  columns, 2, 32, 154
    deleting, 56-57

exposing when hidden, 159
inserting, 54-56
modifying widths, 156-157
deleting
columns, 56-57
hard page breaks, 171
lines, 163-164
rows, 56-57
drawing lines, 161-163
editing formulas, 55-56
entering
dates, 46-48
formulas into cells, 40-45
labels, 33-36
numbers, 39
time, 46-47
values into cells, 37-39
filenames, 32
files, 32
fonts, 166-171
formatting blocks of values, 151-152
formulas, 37-39, 40, 123
building while in POINT mode, 71
editing, 55-56
troubleshooting, 124
hard page breaks, 171
hiding columns, 159-160
home position, 69
inserting columns/rows, 54-56
labels, 32-36
lines, 161-163
linking, 253-257
loading spreadsheets linked by formulas, 257
macros, 225-228
managing applications relying on two or more spreadsheets, 259
modifying height and width, 156-159
navigating through, 16-17
pasting macros, 225-228
printing, 83-98, 100-108, 208
protecting cells, 153-154
recording macros, 225-228
removing gridlines, 164
rows, 2, 32, 54-57
saving, 49-50
to file, 22-24
scaling printouts, 98-99
scroll bars, 12
storing macros, 229-231
styles, 45-46
troubleshooting formulas, 124
values, 32, 33-39
viewing on split-screen, 58-60
windows, 32
stacked bar graphs, 180-182
starting Quattro Pro, 9-10
Startup menu, 318-319
statistical @function commands, 128-129
status line, 12
storing macros, 229
string @function commands, 130
string formulas, 111-112
/Style Alignment command, 147-148
/Style Block Size Auto Width command, 157
/Style Block Size command, 156-157
/Style Block Size Height command, 157-159
/Style Column Width command, 154-155
/Style Font command, 166-171
/Style Hide Column command, 159-160
/Style Insert Break command, 98, 171
/Style Line Drawing Bottom None command, 163
/Style Line Drawing command, 161-163

/Style Line Drawing Top None command, 163
/Style menu, 143-146
Alignment command, 147-148
Block Size Auto Width command, 157
Block Size Height, 157-159
Font command, 166-171
Hide Column command, 159-160
Line Drawing Bottom None command, 163
Line Drawing command, 161-163
Line Drawing Top None command, 163
Numeric Format command, 149-152
overriding global settings, 308
Protection Unprotect command, 153-154
Shading command, 165-166
/Style Numeric Format command, 149-152
/Style Numeric Format Currency command, 315
/Style Numeric Format Date command, 315
/Style Numeric Format Date Time command, 315
/Style Protection Unprotect command, 153-154, 323
/Style Shading command, 165-166
subdirectories, 239, 240
submenus, 21
system options, *see* system settings
system settings, 307

T

tables, 78-80
text
files, 92-93
formulas, 110-112
graphs, 185-186
printers, 92
time @function commands, 135
titles, 193
/Tools Macro Debugger Yes command, 232-234
/Tools Macro Instant Replay command, 229
/Tools Macro Name Delete command, 232
/Tools Macro Paste command, 226
/Tools menu
Macro Debugger Yes command, 232-234
Macro Instant Replay command, 229
Macro Name Delete command, 232
Macro Paste command, 226
Solve For command, 136-138
/Tools Solve For command, 136-138
/Tree Close command, 251
/Tree Open command, 251
Tree Pane, 251
troubleshooting spreadsheet formulas, 124

U-W

Undo key, 274
undoing errors, 57
values, 32-33
Values menu, 322
viewing
block names, 80
spreadsheets, 58-60
/Window menu, 237-258
Options Clear command, 59-60
Options Grid Lines Display, 164
Options Grid Lines Hide, 164
Options Grid Lines Hide command, 164
Options Horizontal command, 59-60

Options Vertical command, 59-60
/Window Options Clear command, 59-60
/Window Options Grid Lines Hide command, 164
/Window Options Horizontal command, 59-60
/Window Options Locked Titles Clear command, 271
/Window Options Row & Col Borders Display command, 259
/Window Options Row & Col Borders Hide command, 259
/Window Options Vertical command, 59-60
/Window Stack command, 259
/Window Tile command, 253-254
windows, 32, 241
split, 59-60
workspace, 241
workspace file, 259
write-to-disk operation, 238
writing macros, 217-220
WYSIWYG
button, 19
displaying, 19
drawing lines, 161
modifying row height, 157-159
selecting as default display mode, 299-300
WYSIWYG display, 316

X-Z

x-axis, 177-178
XTreePro, 248
XY graphs, 180-181
y-axis, 177-178
zoom button, 19

Sams—Covering The Latest In Computer And Technical Topics!

Audio

- Audio Production Techniques for Video $29.95
- Audio Systems Design and Installation $59.95
- Audio Technology Fundamentals $24.95
- Compact Disc Troubleshooting and Repair $24.95
- Handbook for Sound Engineers: The New Audio Cyclopedia $79.95
- Introduction to Professional Recording Techniques $29.95
- Modern Recording Techniques, 3rd Ed. $29.95
- Principles of Digital Audio, 2nd Ed. $29.95
- Sound Recording Handbook $49.95
- Sound System Engineering, 2nd Ed. $49.95

Electricity/Electronics

- Basic AC Circuits $29.95
- Electricity 1, Revised 2nd Ed. $14.95
- Electricity 1-7, Revised 2nd Ed. $49.95
- Electricity 2, Revised 2nd Ed. $14.95
- Electricity 3, Revised 2nd Ed. $14.95
- Electricity 4, Revised 2nd Ed. $14.95
- Electricity 5, Revised 2nd Ed. $14.95
- Electricity 6, Revised 2nd Ed. $14.95
- Electricity 7, Revised 2nd Ed. $14.95
- Electronics 1-7, Revised 2nd Ed. $49.95

Electronics Technical

- Active-Filter Cookbook $19.95
- Camcorder Survival Guide $ 9.95
- CMOS Cookbook, 2nd Ed. $24.95
- Design of OP-AMP Circuits with Experiments $19.95
- Design of Phase-Locked Loop Circuits with Experiments $19.95
- Electrical Test Equipment $19.95
- Electrical Wiring $19.95
- How to Read Schematics, 4th Ed. $19.95
- IC Op-Amp Cookbook, 3rd Ed. $24.95
- IC Timer Cookbook, 2nd Ed. $19.95
- IC User's Casebook $19.95
- Radio Handbook, 23rd Ed. $39.95
- Radio Operator's License Q&A Manual, 11th Ed. $24.95
- RF Circuit Design $24.95
- Transformers and Motors $24.95
- TTL Cookbook $19.95
- Undergrounding Electric Lines $14.95
- Understanding Telephone Electronics, 2nd Ed. $19.95
- VCR Troubleshooting & Repair Guide $19.95
- Video Scrambling & Descrambling for Satellite & Cable TV $19.95

Games

- Beyond the Nintendo Masters $ 9.95
- Mastering Nintendo Video Games II $ 9.95
- Tricks of the Nintendo Masters $ 9.95
- VideoGames & Computer Entertainment Complete Guide to Nintendo Video Games $ 9.50
- Winner's Guide to Nintendo Game Boy $ 9.95
- Winner's Guide to Sega Genesis $ 9.95

Hardware/Technical

- Hard Disk Power with the Jamsa Disk Utilities $39.95
- IBM PC Advanced Troubleshooting & Repair $24.95
- IBM Personal Computer Troubleshooting & Repair $24.95
- IBM Personal Computer Upgrade Guide $24.95
- Microcomputer Troubleshooting & Repair $24.95
- Understanding Communications Systems, 2nd Ed. $19.95
- Understanding Data Communications, 2nd Ed. $19.95
- Understanding FAX and Electronic Mail $19.95
- Understanding Fiber Optics $19.95

IBM: Business

- Best Book of Microsoft Works for the PC, 2nd Ed. $24.95
- Best Book of PFS: First Choice $24.95
- Best Book of Professional Write and File $22.95
- First Book of Fastback Plus $16.95
- First Book of Norton Utilities $16.95
- First Book of Personal Computing $16.95
- First Book of PROCOMM PLUS $16.95

IBM: Database

- Best Book of Paradox 3 $27.95
- dBASE III Plus Programmer's Reference Guide $24.95
- dBASE IV Programmer's Reference Guide $24.95
- First Book of Paradox 3 $16.95
- Mastering ORACLE Featuring ORACLE's SQL Standard $24.95

IBM: Graphics/Desktop Publishing

- Best Book of Autodesk Animator $29.95
- Best Book of Harvard Graphics $24.95
- First Book of DrawPerfect $16.95
- First Book of Harvard Graphics $16.95
- First Book of PC Paintbrush $16.95
- First Book of PFS: First Publisher $16.95

IBM: Spreadsheets/Financial

- Best Book of Lotus 1-2-3 Release 3.1 $27.95
- Best Book of Lotus 1-2-3, Release 2.2, 3rd Ed. $26.95
- Best Book of Peachtree Complete III $24.95
- First Book of Lotus 1-2-3, Release 2.2 $16.95
- First Book of Lotus 1-2-3/G $16.95
- First Book of Microsoft Excel for the PC $16.95
- Lotus 1-2-3: Step-by-Step $24.95

IBM: Word Processing

- Best Book of Microsoft Word 5 $24.95
- Best Book of Microsoft Word for Windows $24.95
- Best Book of WordPerfect 5.1 $26.95
- Best Book of WordPerfect Version 5.0 $24.95
- First Book of PC Write $16.95
- First Book of WordPerfect 5.1 $16.95
- WordPerfect 5.1: Step-by-Step $24.95

Macintosh/Apple

- Best Book of AppleWorks $24.95
- Best Book of MacWrite II $24.95
- Best Book of Microsoft Word for the Macintosh $24.95
- Macintosh Printer Secrets $34.95
- Macintosh Repair & Upgrade Secrets $34.95
- Macintosh Revealed, Expanding the Toolbox, Vol. 4 $29.95
- Macintosh Revealed, Mastering the Toolbox, Vol. 3 $29.95
- Macintosh Revealed, Programming with the Toolbox, Vol. 2, 2nd Ed. $29.95
- Macintosh Revealed, Unlocking the Toolbox, Vol. 1, 2nd Ed. $29.95
- Using ORACLE with HyperCard $24.95

Operating Systems/Networking

- Best Book of DESQview $24.95
- Best Book of DOS $24.95
- Best Book of Microsoft Windows 3 $24.95
- Business Guide to Local Area Networks $24.95
- Exploring the UNIX System, 2nd Ed. $29.95
- First Book of DeskMate $16.95
- First Book of Microsoft QuickPascal $16.95
- First Book of MS-DOS $16.95
- First Book of UNIX $16.95
- Interfacing to the IBM Personal Computer, 2nd Ed. $24.95
- Mastering NetWare $29.95
- The Waite Group's Discovering MS-DOS $19.95
- The Waite Group's Inside XENIX $29.95
- The Waite Group's MS-DOS Bible, 3rd Ed. $24.95
- The Waite Group's MS-DOS Developer's Guide, 2nd Ed. $29.95
- The Waite Group's Tricks of the MS-DOS Masters, 2nd Ed. $29.95
- The Waite Group's Tricks of the UNIX Masters $29.95
- The Waite Group's Understanding MS-DOS, 2nd Ed. $19.95
- The Waite Group's UNIX Primer Plus, 2nd Ed. $29.95
- The Waite Group's UNIX System V Bible $29.95
- The Waite Group's UNIX System V Primer, Revised Ed. $29.95
- Understanding Local Area Networks, 2nd Ed. $24.95
- Understanding NetWare $24.95
- UNIX Applications Programming: Mastering the Shell $29.95
- UNIX Networking $29.95
- UNIX Shell Programming, Revised Ed. $29.95
- UNIX System Administration $29.95
- UNIX System Security $34.95
- UNIX Text Processing $29.95
- UNIX: Step-by-Step $29.95

Professional/Reference

- Data Communications, Networks, and Systems $39.95
- Gallium Arsenide Technology, Volume II $69.95
- Handbook of Computer-Communications Standards, Vol. 1, 2nd Ed. $39.95
- Handbook of Computer-Communications Standards, Vol. 2, 2nd Ed. $39.95
- Handbook of Computer-Communications Standards, Vol. 3, 2nd Ed. $39.95
- Handbook of Electronics Tables and Formulas, 6th Ed. $24.95
- ISDN, DECnet, and SNA Communications $44.95
- Modern Dictionary of Electronics, 6th Ed. $39.95
- Programmable Logic Designer's Guide $29.95
- Reference Data for Engineers: Radio, Electronics, Computer, and Communications, 7th Ed. $99.95
- Surface-Mount Technology for PC Board Design $49.95
- World Satellite Almanac, 2nd Ed. $39.95

Programming

- Advanced C: Tips and Techniques $29.95
- C Programmer's Guide to NetBIOS $29.95
- C Programmer's Guide to Serial Communications $29.95
- Commodore 64 Programmer's Reference Guide $19.95
- DOS Batch File Power $39.95
- First Book of GW-BASIC $16.95
- How to Write Macintosh Software, 2nd Ed. $29.95
- Mastering Turbo Assembler $29.95
- Mastering Turbo Debugger $29.95
- Mastering Turbo Pascal 5.5, 3rd Ed. $29.95
- Microsoft QuickBASIC Programmer's Reference $29.95
- Programming in ANSI C $29.95
- Programming in C, Revised Ed. $29.95
- QuickC Programming $29.95
- The Waite Group's BASIC Programming Primer, 2nd Ed. $24.95
- The Waite Group's C Programming Using Turbo C++ $29.95
- The Waite Group's C++ Programming $24.95
- The Waite Group's C: Step-by-Step $29.95
- The Waite Group's GW-BASIC Primer Plus $24.95
- The Waite Group's Microsoft C Bible, 2nd Ed. $29.95
- The Waite Group's Microsoft C Programming for the PC, 2nd Ed. $29.95
- The Waite Group's Microsoft Macro Assembler Bible $29.95
- The Waite Group's New C Primer Plus $29.95
- The Waite Group's QuickC Bible $29.95
- The Waite Group's Turbo Assembler Bible $29.95
- The Waite Group's Turbo C Bible $29.95
- The Waite Group's Turbo C Programming for the PC, Revised Ed. $29.95
- The Waite Group's TWG Turbo C++Bible $29.95
- X Window System Programming $29.95

For More Information, Call Toll Free

1-800-257-5755

All prices are subject to change without notice. Non-U.S. prices may be higher. Printed in the U.S.A.

Reader Feedback Card

Thank you for purchasing this book from SAMS FIRST BOOK series. Our intent with this series is to bring you timely, authoritative information that you can reference quickly and easily. You can help us by taking a minute to complete and return this card. We appreciate your comments and will use the information to better serve your needs.

1. Where did you purchase this book?

- ☐ Chain bookstore (Walden, B. Dalton)
- ☐ Independent bookstore
- ☐ Computer/Software store
- ☐ Direct mail
- ☐ Book club
- ☐ School bookstore
- ☐ Other ____________________

____

2. Why did you choose this book? (Check as many as apply.)

- ☐ Price
- ☐ Author's reputation
- ☐ Quick and easy treatment of subject
- ☐ Appearance of book
- ☐ SAMS' reputation
- ☐ Only book available on subject

3. How do you use this book? (Check as many as apply.)

- ☐ As a supplement to the product manual
- ☐ In place of the product manual
- ☐ For self-instruction
- ☐ As a reference
- ☐ At home
- ☐ At work

4. Please rate this book in the categories below. G = Good; N = Needs improvement; U = Category is unimportant.

- ☐ Price
- ☐ Amount of information
- ☐ Examples
- ☐ Inside cover reference
- ☐ Table of contents
- ☐ Tips and cautions
- ☐ Length of book
- ☐ How can we improve this book? ____________________
- ☐ ____________________
- ☐ Appearance
- ☐ Accuracy
- ☐ Quick Steps
- ☐ Second color
- ☐ Index
- ☐ Illustrations

5. How many computer books do you normally buy in a year?

- ☐ 1–5
- ☐ 5–10
- ☐ More than 10
- ☐ I rarely purchase more than one book on a subject.
- ☐ I may purchase a beginning and an advanced book on the same subject.
- ☐ I may purchase several books on particular subjects.
- ☐ (such as ____________________)

6. Have your purchased other SAMS or Hayden books in the past year? ____________________

If yes, how many ____________________

7. Would you purchase another book in the FIRST BOOK series? ______

8. What are your primary areas of interest in business software? ______

- ☐ Word processing (particularly ______)
- ☐ Spreadsheet (particularly ______)
- ☐ Database (particularly ______)
- ☐ Graphics (particularly ______)
- ☐ Personal finance/accounting (particularly ______)
- ☐ Other (please specify ______)

Other comments on this book or the SAMS' book line: ______

Name ______
Company ______
Address ______
City ______ State ______ Zip ______
Daytime telephone number ______
Title of this book ______

Fold here

NO POSTAGE NECESSARY IF MAILED IN THE UNITED STATES

BUSINESS REPLY MAIL
FIRST CLASS PERMIT NO. 336 CARMEL, IN

POSTAGE WILL BE PAID BY ADDRESSEE

SAMS

11711 N. College Ave.
Suite 141
Carmel, IN 46032–9839

Extreme

Nature's Amazing Partners

By Katharine Kenah

Columbus, Ohio

Library of Congress Cataloging-in-Publication Data

Kenah, Katharine
Nature's amazing partners/ by Katharine Kenah.
p.cm.--(Extreme Readers)
ISBN 0-7696-3182-7 (pbk.)
1. Symbiosis--Juvenile literature. I. Title. II Series.

QH548.K46 2004
577.8'5--dc22

2004053604

Send all inquiries to:
School Specialty Publishing
8720 Orion Place
Columbus, OH 43240-2111

ISBN 0-7696-3182-7

5 6 7 8 9 PHX 09 08 07 06

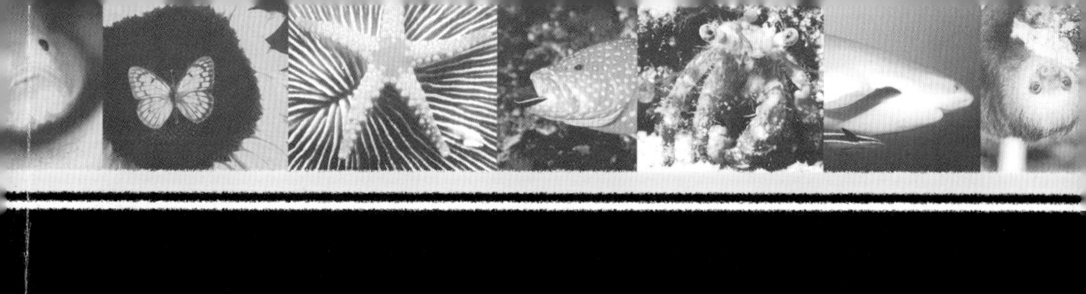

Some living things
work in pairs.
They help each other.
They are nature's
amazing partners.

Clown Fish and Sea Anemone

What do they do?
The clown fish cleans
the sea anemone.
The sea anemone keeps
the clown fish safe.

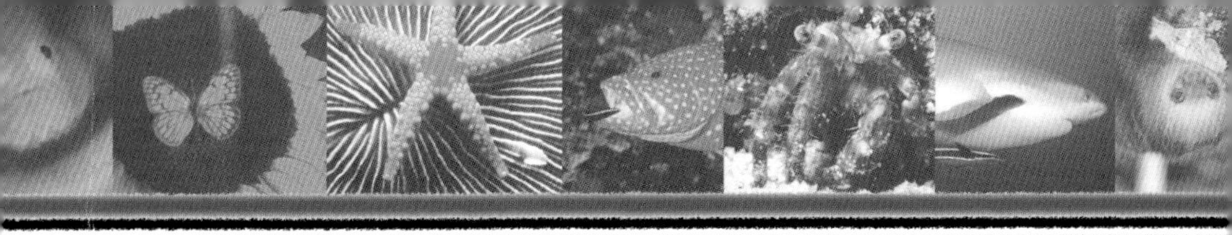

Tickbird and Rhinoceros

What do they do?
The tickbird keeps the rhinoceros free of bugs.
The rhinoceros keeps the tickbird full of food.

Elephant and Egret

What do they do?
The elephant kicks bugs into the air.
The egret eats the bugs.

Pitcher Plant and Tree Frog

What do they do?
The pitcher plant draws in bugs with its colors.
The tree frog eats the bugs.

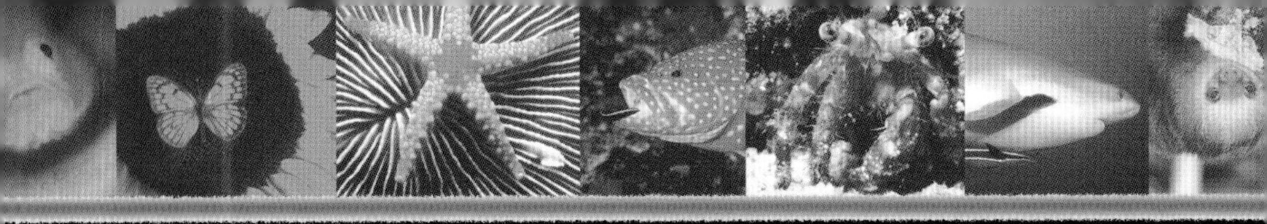

Plover and Crocodile

What do they do?
The plover cleans out food from the crocodile's teeth.
The crocodile gives the plover food to eat.

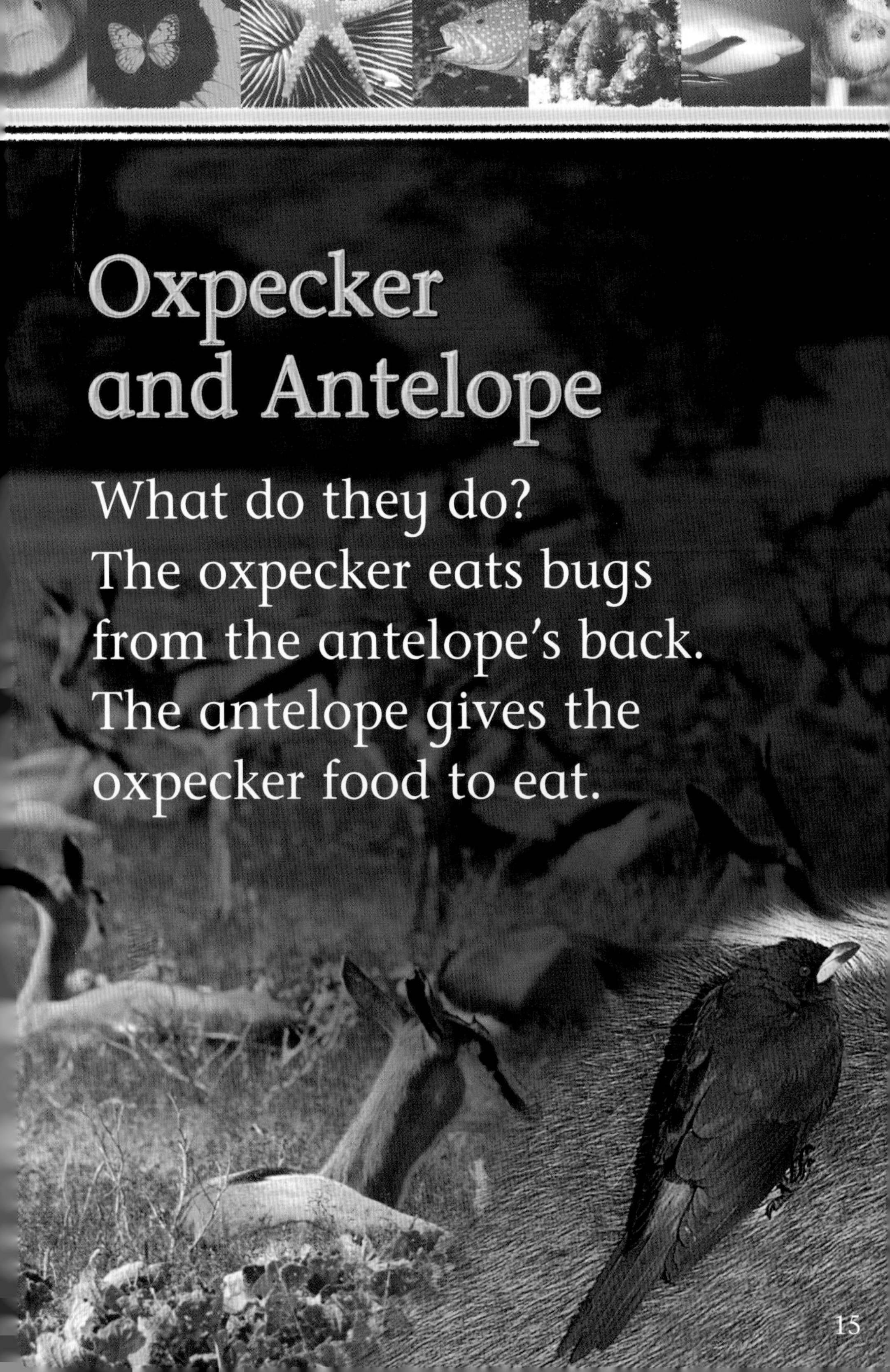

Oxpecker and Antelope

What do they do?
The oxpecker eats bugs from the antelope's back. The antelope gives the oxpecker food to eat.

Flower and Hummingbird

What do they do?
The flower has food
for the hummingbird.
The hummingbird helps
more flowers to grow.

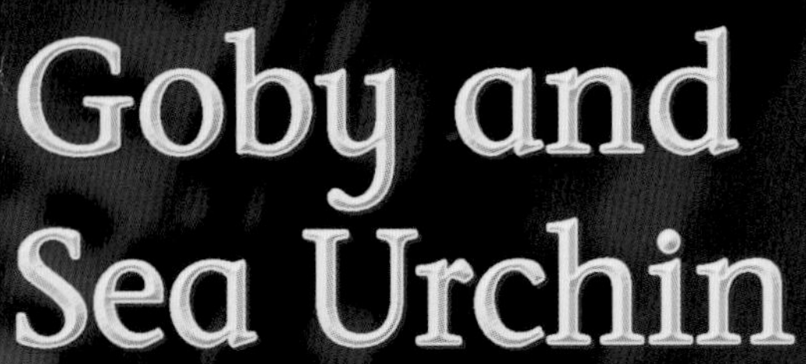

Goby and Sea Urchin

What do they do?
The goby helps the
sea urchin find food.
The sea urchin helps
the goby stay safe.

Sunflower and Butterfly

What do they do?
The sunflower has
food for the butterfly.
The butterfly helps more
sunflowers to grow.

Coral and Starfish

What do they do?
The coral houses
many small animals.
The starfish eats
these animals.

Wrasse and Grouper

What do they do?
The wrasse cleans bugs
from the grouper.
The grouper gives the
wrasse food to eat.

Hermit Crab and Sea Anemone

What do they do?
The hermit crab helps the sea anemone find food.
The sea anemone makes the hermit crab hard to see.

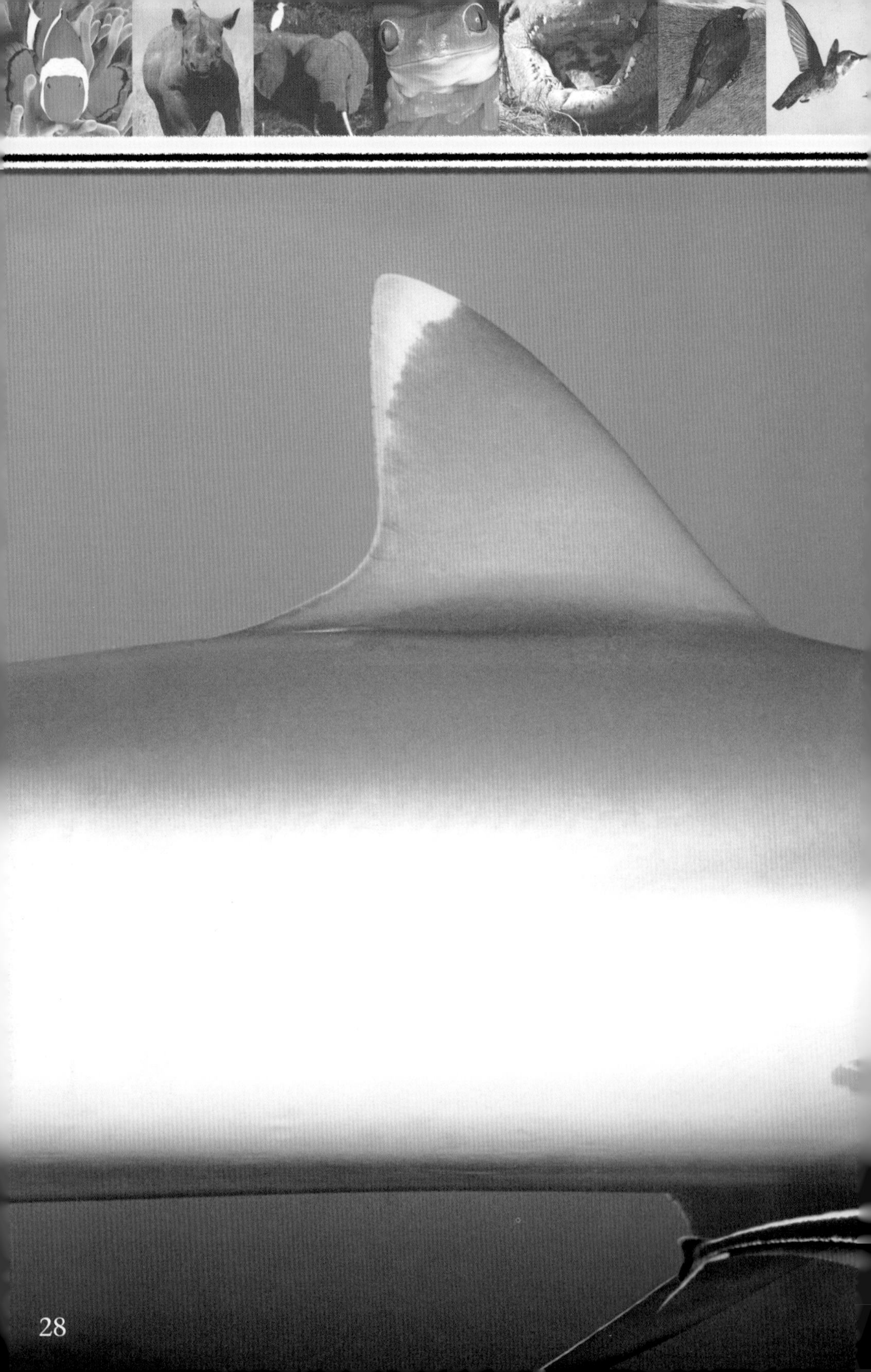

Shark and Remora

What do they do?
The shark gives the remora a free ride.
The remora eats the food that the shark does not.

Algae and Sloth

What do they do?
The sloth uses the green algae to hide in a tree.
The algae grows well in the sloth's fur.

EXTREME FACTS ABOUT NATURE'S AMAZING PARTNERS!

- Giant sea anemones grow more than three feet in diameter.
- Rhinoceroses can live for more than 50 years.
- Egret feathers used to be prized as decorations for women's hats.
- Pitcher plants have bristles on the tips of their leaves that point inward. Bugs slip down and cannot escape!
- Crocodiles' jaws are strong enough to break heavy boards into pieces.
- Oxpeckers act like alarm systems for other animals. They cry out a warning when they see danger coming.
- Hummingbirds' wings beat 60 to 70 times per second.
- Sea urchins do not have brains.
- Heads of sunflowers can hold more than 1,000 seeds.
- Starfish can have as many as 40 arms.
- To attract other fish, wrasse stand on their heads and wiggle their bodies.
- If hermit crabs cannot find empty shells to live in, they will pull snails right out of the ones they are using.
- The suckers on top of remoras' heads look like the soles of rubber boots.
- Sloths' curved claws allow them to hang upside-down in trees while they sleep.